WILD JUSTICE

WILD JUSTICE

The People of Geronimo vs. the United States

Michael Lieder and Jake Page

RANDOM HOUSE   NEW YORK

Library of Congress Cataloging-in-Publication Data

Lieder, Michael.
Wild justice: the people of Geronimo vs. the United States/
Michael Lieder and Jake Page.
p.   cm.
Includes bibliographical references and index.
ISBN 0-679-45183-8
1. United States. Indian Claims Commission—History.   2. Indians of North
America—Claims—History.   3. Chiricahua Indians—Legal status, laws, etc.—History.
I. Page, Jake.   II. Title.
KF8208.L54   1997   323.1'1972—dc21   96-29591

Random House website address: http://www.randomhouse.com/

Printed in the United States of America on acid-free paper

2   4   6   8   9   7   5   3

First Edition

Book design by Caroline Cunningham

PREFACE AND ACKNOWLEDGMENTS

In 1946, President Harry S. Truman signed into law an act of Congress that established a tribunal unique in history. The Indian Claims Commission remains the only judicial body ever created to award money to redress the wrongs done to a native population arising from the expansion of Europeans.

For three decades, the Commission decided claims brought by over 170 Indian tribes, until it was disbanded in 1978 and its few remaining cases were transferred to the United States Court of Claims. It heard evidence about life before the advent of white men and about much of the history of the relations between the United States government and the tribes it encountered. Despite the novelty of the Commission and the fascination of its subject, very little has been written about it. In this book, we explore whether the Indian Claims Commission Act was wisely conceived, how well the legal system was able to carry out the congressional purposes in passing the act, and, to the extent the purposes were frustrated, what that says about the capabilities of this country's legal system and about the relationships between the federal government and Indian tribes.

Although these issues require the analysis of legal decisions, we are not writing primarily for lawyers and presuppose no knowledge of legal jargon or doctrine. We hope that the book will appeal to readers who have never endured a first-year law school class, as well as to lawyers.

Our personal backgrounds reflect the diversity of our intended audience. Before Mike Lieder went to law school, he worked for four years for the two lawyers who figure most prominently in the book, Israel S. "Lefty" Weissbrodt and Abraham W. Weissbrodt, in their representation of tribes under the act, and has represented them in one dispute since graduation. Mike did not work on any of the cases discussed in this book. Jake Page is a professional writer, not a lawyer. He has ensured that the legal analyses in the book are understandable to nonlawyers and that the human dramas underlying each of the cases are not forgotten.

In order to focus the history, we concentrate on the story of one tribe, the Chiricahua Apaches, and its claims under the act. Many books have been written about the wars between the Chiricahuas and the United States, and several more about what happened to the Chiricahuas after the wars were over. In writing the chapters dealing with the tribe, we have drawn from both published works and primary sources. But little has been written about the legal proceedings, so we have tracked down judicial decisions, statutes, and other documents and tried to make sense of them. To facilitate any subsequent research, we have inserted note numbers at the end of many paragraphs.

The volunteered assistance of several persons deserves special mention. Abe and Lefty Weissbrodt consented to several interviews and made documents in their possession available for review. Jane Lang, a wonderful law partner, writer, and editor, spent many hours reviewing and suggesting revisions to a nearly final draft of the book. Mildred Lieder helped with the last-minute research. We thank all of them.

CONTENTS

INTRODUCTION

Like the miner's canary, the Indian marks the shift from fresh air
to poison gas in our political atmosphere; and our treatment of Indians,
even more than our treatment of other minorities, reflects
the rise and fall in our democratic faith.
—Felix Cohen, legal scholar

The Chiricahua Apaches produced leaders such as Mangas Coloradas, Cochise, and Geronimo in their bloody, centuries-long effort to defend their rugged desert home, located in parts of what is now Arizona, New Mexico, and northern Mexico, against the expansion of Spain, Mexico, and the United States. Few people would identify the Chiricahuas, or other American Indians, with the canary. A coyote or eagle seems a more appropriate analogy than a small songbird. Yet the comparison drawn by Felix Cohen, a prominent legal philosopher and the leading scholar of federal Indian law during the 1930s and 1940s, is apt in several ways. Like canaries, the Chiricahua Apaches were captured and imprisoned. To assure peace in the Southwest, the United States in 1886 made every Chiricahua man, woman, and child a prisoner of war, whether or not they had participated in warfare against the United States or were then capable of doing so. For the next twenty-seven years they were confined on army bases in Florida, Alabama, and Oklahoma. Although they didn't have to sing in captivity, the Chiricahuas had to learn to survive in the world of the white man—a world forced upon them, not chosen.

The Chiricahuas' imprisonment makes them unusual, if not unique. A few other tribes were imprisoned, but for much shorter periods. Probably the most well-known incarceration of a racial or national group in this country was the imprisonment of Japanese Americans during World War II, but when the war ended a few years after the initial roundups, the prisoners were freed. The Chiricahua imprisonment lasted many times longer. As the years of captivity dragged on and the formerly hostile warriors died off, the generation born into captivity became the majority. When they were finally released, few remained who remembered their people's homeland.

At one time or another in their lives, many Americans are harmed by governmental action. A state government may break a contract; a municipal employee may cause an automobile accident; a federal agency may exercise the right of eminent domain to build a new highway over private land. If the matter can't be resolved by negotiated agreement, the private citizen may sue the offending government. For most types of claims against the national government, the United States has established specialized courts and procedures to hear and resolve the disputes. One measure of the success of the American legal system is its ability to resolve such disputes fairly.

For scores of years, these courts and procedures were off-limits to Indian tribes. Unlike other Americans, they couldn't sue the United States for wrongs done to them, unless Congress specially agreed. In 1946, however, Congress created a tribunal called the Indian Claims Commission to hear and determine the Indians' claims. The Commission was unique in the world. Europeans who colonized other countries also committed many wrongs against their native populations, but had never given the natives the opportunity to sue the government for their injuries. Many members of Congress expressed the hope that the United States would finally make amends for the wrongs done to the tribes— wrongs, one might have supposed, that included imprisoning all of a tribe's members for twenty-seven years. The congressional action expressed this nation's highest ideals, at the same time that it contained the germ of its own subversion.

Virtually every tribe in the country, including the Chiricahua Apaches, took the opportunity presented by the Indian Claims Commission Act to sue the United States. This book tells the story of the Indian Claims Commission Act while focusing primarily on the claims of the Chiricahuas. It is a tale of warrior Apaches and twentieth-century Apaches, lawyers and judges, victory and defeat, hope and betrayal.

Like miners' canaries, carried into the shafts to detect the presence of noxious gases, American Indians generally, and the Chiricahua Apaches in particular, exposed limitations in the American judicial process through the claims they brought. Their litigation tested a system ill prepared to untangle claims unfamiliar to lawyers and judges and ill suited to resolve major issues of social policy. Instead of confronting the conceptual and evidentiary difficulties, the tribunals devised a set of principles designed to give every tribe the appearance of its day in court while actually protecting the public treasury against large recoveries. This sidestepping of the issues diminished the significance of the Commission, so that when Congress allowed it to expire in 1978, few people lamented, or even noticed, its passing.

WILD JUSTICE

ONE

WILD JUSTICE

Revenge is wild justice, which the more man's nature runs to,
the more ought law to weed it out.

—Sir Francis Bacon

On September 4, 1886, it rained in Skeleton Canyon, usually a good
omen for dwellers of an arid land. But it was not a good sign for Geronimo. A grim-faced man known throughout a vast area embracing northern Mexico and much of southern New Mexico and the American
Southwest, at the time he was probably the most feared man in the
United States, and many still consider him one of the best guerrilla
fighters in American history. He had insisted that Skeleton Canyon—
one of many gashes in the Peloncillo Mountains just north of Mexico
and lying along the border of Arizona and New Mexico—be the site of
his surrender to General Nelson Miles. He knew these mountains like
the skin of his palm and, if he changed his mind, he and his band of
about fifty, mostly women and children, could vanish like a puff of
smoke. They had managed for more than a year to outrun, outwit, and
outmaneuver five thousand U.S. troops—that is, one-fourth of the entire
U.S. Army. Geronimo remained proud of that feat until his death, often
speaking of the five-hundred-to-one odds he and his group had faced,
but he also continued to regret not having fought to the death, instead
of turning himself over to the mendacious General Miles. His surrender

in Skeleton Canyon brought an end to the Chiricahua Apache warpath, ending forever the violent resistance of free-ranging American Indians to the invasion of their land.

Not much more than a century ago, the word *Apache* was enough to make other residents of the Southwest shrink in fear, and the government was committed to eliminating the threat these "savages" presented to the orderly march of civilization, ranching, and mining into the area. (At the time, even academics of good intention called such hunter/gatherer Indians "savages." Next up the ladder were "barbarians," such as the sedentary Pueblo people who lived in villages and grew crops.) It took an embarrassingly long time to bring the last Apaches to heel, and ultimately lies and attrition, not military genius, were the weapons of choice.

The actual period of military attrition was short, almost abrupt, given the long history of the Apaches in the area. But early on, when they saw the ribbons of bluecoats coming from the east, many among them pronounced themselves *indeh*: dead. They knew that they could not win against these forces as they had before, but it was part of the Apache code of life, particularly among the loosely organized bands that came to be called the Chiricahua, to fight anyway.

·   ·   ·

If Hernán Cortés and his approximately one thousand Spanish soldiers had gone to, say, Venezuela or Florida instead of Mexico in 1519, he might have discarded the idea of conquest as a bad job. Most of the two continents in this hemisphere was inhabited by millions of people Cortés would not have found worth conquering since they did not possess what he wanted, chiefly gold. Instead, he stumbled upon the most magnificent of Indian civilizations—at least as he understood it. The Aztec emperor ruled over more than seven million people of many tribes and most of what is modern Mexico. The capital, Tenochtitlán, with three hundred thousand residents, was built on the shallow waters of Lake Texcoco, reached by well-engineered causeways. With its canals, its flat-topped pyramids, its clean plazas, its abundance of food grown on a clever form of raised beds, its elaborate zoological park, its ubiquitous aviaries, its richness of costume, feather, cotton, and *gold*, it struck Cortés as the most beautiful city in the world. The Aztec army's armored and helmeted soldiers had ruthlessly expanded the empire's borders and assured the flow of wealth back to the capital.[1]

Despite its grandeur and size, the Aztec empire fell to Cortés within two years, victim of the cannon, the horse, diseases brought by the Spaniards, and rebellious Aztec subjects whom Cortés had enlisted. Almost immediately the Spaniards began to extend their dominion, chiefly to the north. Their expeditions during the sixteenth century followed the river that would become known as the Rio Grande in search of the fabled cities of gold, the Seven Cities of Cíbola. They encountered more than sixty pueblos—dense clusters of adobe houses inhabited by farmers already knowledgeable in irrigation techniques. The Indians' souls were converted to the religion of Spain, Roman Catholicism, and the search for gold moved on.[2]

By the mid-1600s, the Spaniards had also established missions and built communities among the Indian tribes of northern Sonora and Chihuahua, not far from the present international boundary. The Spanish conquest was facilitated by staggering death rates among the Indian populations from diseases such as smallpox to which they had no previous exposure or immunity—in the sixteenth century alone, the first century of the Spanish presence, an estimated two-thirds of Mexico's native population perished—and later by large-scale intermarriage. It seemed inevitable that the Spanish would soon control all of what is now the American Southwest, for they had quickly vanquished every Indian population they had encountered. But, beginning in the early 1700s, Spanish expansion, not only along the Rio Grande but also in Sonora and Chihuahua, came to a halt. Only heavily armed wagon trains could still make the occasional and infrequent trip north up the Camino Real (the Royal Highway) through the badlands to replenish the supplies of the Spaniards in Nuevo México, by now a discouraged backwater of Spanish imperial ambition.[3]

The Spaniards had encountered a widespread population of nomadic Indians who farmed little and whose bows and arrows were no match for the Spanish cannons and harquebuses. But they could not be subdued. The Spaniards called them *Apache,* possibly from a pejorative Zuni Indian word meaning "enemy." In his early expedition, Coronado had made no note of them, probably because they saw him coming and hid in their mountain fastnesses. Later Spaniards did see groups of Indians living in *rancherías* (bands) near the Gila River. In 1598, when he set up the territorial capital of Nuevo México at the San Juan Pueblo, Juan de Oñate first used the word *Apache* in writing. By then, these "Apaches" seemed to roam widely throughout all the otherwise empty lands that surrounded the pueblo dwellers.[4]

They all spoke recognizable dialects of a single language, now called Athapascan, and they were relatively recent arrivals in the lands where the Pueblo people and their ancestors the Anasazi, who built the great ruins such as Mesa Verde and Chaco Canyon, had lived for hundreds of years. Like all the natives of this hemisphere before them, these Athapascans had crossed the Bering Strait from Asia, settling for the most part in southern Alaska and northwestern Canada, where many still remain. But for an unknown reason, and at an uncertain time, a large contingent of them began moving south, more than likely along one side or the other of the Rocky Mountain cordillera. They didn't bring much with them or leave much behind, so archeologists are unable to pin down their arrival in the Southwest, but an early Navajo hogan (house) has been dated to about 1500.[5]

They soon evolved into seven relatively distinct groups. The easternmost bands, the Kiowa Apaches and the Lipan Apaches, lived primarily in the southern plains of what are now Oklahoma and Texas. The Jicarilla Apaches occupied the northeastern region of New Mexico, the Navajos the northwest, and the Mescaleros east of the Rio Grande. The Western Apaches settled down in what are now the central highlands of Arizona. The Chiricahuas dwelled in an area stretching from the Rio Grande west into Arizona and south into Mexico.[6]

·   ·   ·

These designations do not mean that the members of an Apache group formed a single political unit. The people we now call the Chiricahuas never had a single political or religious leader. In aboriginal times, they did not even have a term to describe themselves collectively and distinguish themselves from other Apaches. Instead, they lived in relatively small groups that included a handful of extended families. Several of these groups made up loosely organized bands. Morris Opler, an anthropologist who worked with the Apaches in the 1930s, identified three bands: the *tcihene,* or the Red Paint people; the *tcokanen,* which may mean Tall Men; and the *ndendai,* or the Enemy people, named perhaps for their fierceness. He designated them geographically as, respectively, the Eastern, Central, and Southern bands. Other scholars and many Chiricahuas recognize another band, the *bedonkohe,* which was closely associated with the Central Band and from which Geronimo sprang.

In each band, one or more men would be called upon as leaders when joint action was needed, but typically, local groups made important decisions for themselves. It wasn't until the mid-nineteenth century, when conflict with the United States intensified, that leaders of entire bands emerged, such as Cochise, a man of such charisma that the Central Band was often thought of as the Cochise Band. Rather than any formal authority, leadership derived from character and persuasive powers—it also helped to be a medicine man—and the power of the chief was conferred upon him by the consent of the others in the group or band. In short, Chiricahua Apache society lacked centralized authority, making it radically diffuse compared to modern Western society, and whether the Chiricahuas actually constituted a single tribe would be a hotly contested legal issue in the second half of the twentieth century.[7]

Common language and customs, not centralized political authority, distinguished Apaches from other Indian groups, and gradations of language and customs differentiated each Apache tribe from the others. The Chiricahuas shared with their nearby Apache neighbors similar beliefs about their emergence into this world, two central male and female deities, various healing ceremonies, and masked dancers representing the protective Mountain Gods. The puberty ceremony for girls upon menarche was, and is, a major ceremony for all Apaches. Chastity was much prized: an unchaste girl could not have a puberty ceremony.

In the Apaches' matrilineal society, a man moved into his wife's group and thereafter owed allegiance and support to her family, even if the wife died. As a sign of respect, a husband could not speak to his in-laws, but did their bidding through messages from his wife. A man employed elaborately polite forms of discourse when in conversation with other members of his wife's family, and this kind of courtesy was most highly developed among the Chiricahua bands. Polygamy was permitted, although in most instances a man would marry his wife's sister, so as not to have two sets of in-laws to support.

Hunting and gathering were major components of the economy of all Apache tribes, especially the Chiricahua, who, unlike the other tribes, practiced virtually no cultivation. The fifteen million acres that the

Chiricahuas considered home consisted of classic basin and range country: mountain ranges, some reaching ten thousand feet, separated by
lower deserts. As elevation increased, so did annual precipitation, resulting in changes in vegetation and wildlife. Major sources of food included agave, nuts, game, and medicinal plants. Typically women did the
gathering and men the hunting, though men helped to gather the
crowns of the agave plant, which were then roasted in pits, becoming
mescal, a staple of the diet. Chiricahua groups had to be mobile to move
to the food as the seasons changed. The quest for food was wide-rang-
ing: the Chiricahua population never exceeded three thousand, or about
eight square miles per person. In a day, an Apache could walk from
desert through piñon and juniper forest, to parks of tall ponderosa pine,
to a dense forest of Canadian-type spruce and fir. In the autumn, in
these upper forests, stands of aspen made bright golden swatches among
the dark evergreens. The variety of life in such "sky islands" as the Chiricahua Mountains is still astonishing, and they supplied the Apaches
well. When it came time to fight for their home, the Apaches battled for
a beautiful land, one that had great and multiple meanings for them, as
well as spectacular beauty.[8]

It was the other part of the Apaches' economy that brought them
into conflict with neighbors: raiding. Opler called raiding and hunting
"rival industries" for the Apaches. "The man who has a deer ceremony
either does not go on raids or does not spend too much time on raids, so
he will not lose his luck with deer. . . . If you are too successful on raiding parties and bring back lots of booty, you become unlucky with deer;
you don't see the deer and become a poor hunter." The preraid ceremony was intended to promote concealment and prevent pursuit: the
point was to get in and out without being noticed, not to kill people.
Young boys were rigorously trained in the art of concealment—it was
said that an Apache could disappear behind a few strands of grass—and
endurance. They would be forced to run huge distances with a mouthful
of water to get the breathing right. Boys became men when they had
participated successfully in four raids.[9]

.   .   .

Without agriculture, the Chiricahuas relied on raiding more than other
Apaches, and their success made them the primary impediment to the
Spanish advance in Sonora and Chihuahua. Indeed, it was probably the

tempting presence of the Spanish settlers, with valuable prizes like horses, cattle, mules, weapons, and ammunition, that gradually led the Chiricahuas into such heavy reliance on raiding. The Spaniards also created a market for surplus booty: merchants in one community seldom inquired about the source of goods taken from another. Apache raids, largely by Chiricahuas, slowly forced the Spaniards to abandon their mines and ranches. Northern Sonora became depopulated and, as attractive targets disappeared, the Chiricahuas simply ranged deeper and deeper into Mexico. Meanwhile, the Spaniards raided back, frequently enslaving Indians, including Apaches, to provide cheap labor in mines and fields. Captive Apache women were often sold into prostitution. One Spanish governor boasted of having some ninety Apache slaves.[10]

Inevitably, people on both sides died in the raids, and the endless gyre of revenge swirled and grew, culminating in outright warfare. Spanish troops repeatedly campaigned in the territory of the Chiricahuas and other Apaches in retaliation for raids, and the Indians fought back. The family of a slain Chiricahua would agitate for revenge and, in a war dance, the warriors would act out the heroics they intended. If the enemy was slain, or the enemy camp deserted, the warriors would take booty, but under these circumstances, unlike raiding, the booty was subordinate to revenge.[11]

Pitched battles with the Spaniards were avoided because the Chiricahuas' inferior weapons put them at a severe disadvantage. Instead, they struck fixed, known targets with guerrilla mobility. If pursued, they would scatter throughout the countryside, gathering again at some prearranged place. They knew every water hole, every hiding place within their vast territory, traveled light, and could cover up to seventy miles in a day. With the horses and guns acquired through raiding, and hardened by the intermittent warfare with the Spaniards, all of the Apaches, but especially the Chiricahuas, became an extraordinary fighting force. After battling them for two years in the late nineteenth century, U.S. General George Crook called them the finest light cavalry in history.[12]

Mexico won its independence from Spain in 1821. The new nation hadn't the means for self-protection, and Apache raids intensified. Between 1820 and 1835, Apaches killed an estimated five thousand Mexicans and forced about four thousand more to evacuate the region. In desperation, the state of Sonora offered a bounty for any Apache scalp, and it is likely that many black-haired people, not necessarily Apaches, were killed. Twentieth-century Chiricahuas claim that scalping was not an aboriginal Apache practice, but one they acquired from the Mexicans.[13]

Such were the conditions in 1846 when war began between the United States and Mexico, the culmination of a series of mutual provocations beginning with the United States' annexation in 1844 of the Republic of Texas, which had tenuously won its independence from Mexico in the previous decade. Though outnumbered, United States troops won a string of victories, marching into Mexico City in September 1847. The next year the United States imposed the Treaty of Guadalupe Hidalgo by which, for a payment of $15 million, Mexico ceded to the United States all of the land now comprising California, Nevada, Utah, most of Arizona and New Mexico, and parts of Oklahoma, Colorado, Wyoming, and Texas. The United States acquired far more than the Southwest during the late 1840s. In the four years of President James K. Polk's administration, the United States added more land to its borders than in any other single term. In addition to annexing Texas and obtaining the land cession from Mexico, the United States acquired Oregon and Washington from Great Britain. In 1853, the Gadsden Purchase brought the southern strip of New Mexico and Arizona into American hands for another $10 million. The nation now stretched from the Atlantic to the Pacific. The government, however, would soon discover that problems beset the new land, including the presence of a formidable fighting force in the Southwest.[14]

·   ·   ·

Americans surged into their new domain. Gold was discovered in the Sierra Nevada of California in 1848, and miners and farmers arrived in such numbers that California had enough people to be admitted as a state in 1850. Oregon followed in 1859. Settlement began spreading from the West Coast toward the east as settlers continued to push westward from the midsection of the country. The growth rendered obsolete a policy for dealing with the Indians that had been adopted only a couple decades before. Since 1800, federal legislation had purportedly protected Indians against the intrusions of settlers. During the first decades of the nineteenth century, the law had not prevented adventurous miners and farmers from expanding into territories east of the Mississippi River guaranteed to tribes by treaties. Whenever conflicts had arisen, the government had fought recalcitrant tribes or purchased their lands for a pittance and moved them west rather than force its citizens to respect the boundaries of tribes' territories. Some tribes had been relocated westward several times as the frontier continually caught up to Indian policy. Instead of continuing to relocate tribes in a piecemeal fashion, the government in the 1830s had designated what is now Oklahoma, Kansas, and Nebraska as Indian Territory, inviolate against non-Indian acquisition. By mid-century this new policy was in a shambles as settlers exerted pressure to expand into Kansas and Nebraska. Once again, the government gave in. But it was clear that a western frontier for relocated tribes would soon disappear. Manifest Destiny left little room for the country's native occupants. Soon only pockets of unwanted land would remain.[15]

A new Indian policy was needed but, in the Civil War years, it was not forthcoming. Between 1850 and about 1870, federal policy toward all of the Apaches (federal officials knew nothing yet of distinctions between Chiricahuas and, say, Mescaleros) drifted aimlessly, making warfare all but inevitable. The non-Indians who wanted Apache land provided attractive new targets for raiding. As they depleted resources, such as game, they increased the Apaches' need to raid to survive.

In 1853, the governor of New Mexico Territory wrote to the commissioner of Indian Affairs: "Is it known that the Apaches are exclusively hunters . . . and that all other game and mescal is becoming scarcer and scarcer; and that they subsist chiefly upon the flesh of Horses, Mules and Asses, which they steal? To feed them, therefore, is an imperative duty if we do not intend to leave them no means to subsist but by robbing and stealing; and then have them shot for robbing and stealing." Four years later, an Indian agent wrote that, if the Chiricahuas were to survive on reservations, as had been suggested, they would have to be fed until they learned to farm, because if they "abandon their marauding expeditions . . . one half of their subsistence is cut off." [16]

Few people in the region were as perceptive as these public servants. Most whites, both public and private, thought the Apaches beneath contempt. The first Arizona newspaper called them "altogether different Indians from . . . any and all of the tribes with whom peace has been maintained by treaty. . . . In a word they do not, or will not, understand the advantages of peace and are destitute even of the selfish motive usual to the Indian character—the hope of reward. . . . They disdain to work, and had rather steal than hunt. Murder is their pastime and plunder their war-cry." An army lieutenant wrote that "the Apache cannot be tamed. Civilization is out of the question." In 1872, the commissioner of Indian Affairs characterized the Apaches as "treacherous and vindictive." [17]

That attitude facilitated what was to come: the taking of the Apaches' land by force and the extermination of any Indians who were foolish enough to oppose progress. Among the civilized nations of the Christian West, it becomes much less stressful to take an adversary's property or to kill him if he is deemed to be less than human.

·   ·   ·

When the first American troops arrived in Santa Fe after the end of the Mexican War, their stated goal was to protect the peaceful settlers and the Pueblo people from the raids of the Apaches and Navajos. Numerous forays into Apache country were made and resisted, and the mutual raiding continued. Meanwhile, in the south, the Chiricahuas, unlike the other Apache tribes, largely avoided hostilities with the United States—not because they had decided to forsake raiding, but because they had decided to focus their raiding more exclusively on the Mexicans and obtain peace dividends from the Americans. Two great Chiricahua leaders, Mangas Coloradas of the Eastern Band and Cochise of the Central Band, persuaded their people to try coexistence so long as the Americans didn't interfere with their forays into Mexico, the direction in which they had most often raided anyway.[18]

Mangas Coloradas (Red Sleeves) was over six feet tall, a superior military leader, with great powers of persuasion. He had every reason to distrust the Americans. His predecessor as charismatic leader of the Eastern Band, Juan Jose, had been lured into the camp of some "friendly" American trappers and killed for the one-hundred-peso bounty on his scalp. Then in 1852, Americans reopened some old copper mines in southwestern New Mexico, and almost immediately gold was discovered. While the White Eyes attempted to restrict Apache movement, they also depleted the game, adding to the Chiricahuas' need. The Apaches were affronted as well by the mining, for they considered it sacrilege to grovel and dig things out of Mother Earth. When Mangas went to discuss these things at a miners' camp, they tied him up and flogged him.[19]

Even so, Mangas agreed to a treaty that year calling for "perpetual peace and amity," and the Eastern Band also agreed to "abandon their wandering and predatory modes of life and to locate themselves, in permanent camps, and commence the cultivation of the Earth," in return for which the United States would feed, supply, and protect them. So the Eastern Band spent much of the 1850s near Ojo Caliente, or Warm Springs, near Mangas Coloradas' usual home, receiving rations, hunting, and attempting some farming. In 1859, a military observer wrote: "their crops . . . extended some 3 miles in length and are in fine condition. Mang[a]s . . . said this was his home and he could be found here at any future time, and that he wanted peace." [20]

Meanwhile, Cochise, who was Mangas Coloradas' son-in-law, had met Thomas Jeffords, one of the few white friends the Chiricahua would have for the remainder of the century. Jeffords had contracted to carry the mail between Tucson and Fort Bowie, which meant crossing Apache Pass north of the Chiricahua Mountains. After his riders had been repeatedly ambushed, he learned the Chiricahua language and traveled unarmed to Cochise's camp. Cochise admired Jeffords's bravery in coming alone among the Apaches and granted him his wish that his riders be able to pass through Chiricahua territory unharmed. People began streaming through the pass on their way to the gold fields of California. Cochise's band supplied the local stagecoach station with wood and once killed at least four hostile Apaches bent on attacking it. [21]

Despite numerous provocations, Cochise kept his word and kept the pass open until February 1861, when confusion and treachery changed the course of events for the Chiricahua for good. Members of another Apache tribe had abducted a child and some cattle from an American man named Ward and his Mexican wife, who erroneously blamed members of Cochise's band. In response to their complaint, an inexperienced and hotheaded young lieutenant, George Bascom, sent word that he wanted to talk with Cochise and Cochise unsuspectingly complied, taking with him his wife (Mangas Coloradas' daughter), his infant son Naiche, and three close male relatives. Cochise and his party were invited into Bascom's tent and, once seated, were accused of the abduction. Cochise denied the charge and was then accused of being a liar as well. No greater insult could be given; Apaches hate liars among their own people, and no man who once lied was allowed even to carry a message. Though deeply insulted, Cochise offered his help in finding the boy. Bascom responded by ordering the arrest of the Apaches until the

boy was found. Cochise drew his knife, slashed through the side of
the tent and escaped while sustaining a bayonet wound in his leg. The
others, not so quick, were taken prisoner. Cochise and some of his warriors promptly captured three Americans and twice offered these
hostages for those held by Bascom. The lieutenant refused to negotiate
and, instead, hanged the three male Apaches, letting Cochise's wife and
son leave. Infuriated, the Chiricahuas dragged one of their prisoners to
death and hanged the other two.[22]

. . .

Thus was unleashed possibly the most costly Indian war in the history of
the United States. For the next eleven years, the Chiricahuas spread terror and death in southern New Mexico, Arizona, and northern Mexico,
striking suddenly and in superior numbers at ranches, mines, and wagon
trains and even small contingents of troops and then vanishing into their
mountain retreats. The Chiricahua vengeance was made all the easier by
the virtual abandonment of the territory from 1861 to 1863 by the military, called to prosecute the Civil War.[23]

Even after soldiers returned in 1863, they had little success in impos-
ing order. Their numbers were limited, first by war needs and then, after
Appomattox, by the rapid demobilization of the army. The soldiers
could not guard every outpost and they could seldom catch the Apache
raiders. As one officer explained: "They carry almost nothing but arms
and ammunition; they can live on the cactus; they can go more than
forty-eight hours without water; they know every water-hole and every
foot of ground in this vast extent of country; they have incredible powers of endurance; they run in small bands, scattering at the first indica-
tions of pursuit. What can the United States soldier, mounted on his
heavy American horse, with the necessary forage, rations, and camp
equipment, do against this supple, untiring foe? Nothing, absolutely
nothing. It is no exaggeration to say that these fiends can travel, week in
and week out, at the rate of seventy miles a day, and this over the most
barren and desolate country imaginable. One week of such work will
kill the average soldier and his horse; the Apache thrives on it." [24]

It was a harsh war, viciously prosecuted by both sides. One traveler
wrote: "No white man's life was secure beyond Tucson; and even there
the few inhabitants lived in a state of terror. I saw on the road between
San Xavier and Tubac, a distance of 40 miles, almost as many graves of

the white men murdered by the Apaches within the last few years. . . . There is not now a single living soul to enliven the solitude. . . . Here were fields with torn down fences, houses burned or hacked to pieces by violence, the walls cast about in heaps over the once pleasant homes; everywhere ruin, grim and ghostly with association of sudden death." [25]

In 1863, General James H. Carleton led a regiment of California volunteers into the Territory of New Mexico. He intended to secure it for the North, which was easily done, and to solve the Indian problem—which is to say, the Navajo and Apache problem—which was not so easily done. Carleton planned to round them all up by force and stow them in a forty-square-mile reservation along the Pecos River in eastern New Mexico at a place called Fort Sumner. Under the command of Colonel Kit Carson, the famous mountain man, some five hundred Mescalero Apaches were sent there, followed by some eight thousand Navajos in what is still remembered as the tragic Long Walk. [26]

Carleton had less success with the Chiricahuas. They ambushed a large contingent of soldiers at Apache Pass. But in 1863, Mangas Coloradas received a message that the soldiers wanted peace talks, and when they raised a white flag, he entered their camp. In another betrayal of the trust Apache leaders put in such offers, the soldiers imprisoned Mangas, tortured him with heated bayonets and, when he protested, shot him dead. With the chief's followers watching from a distance, they buried his corpse in a shallow grave. The next day, according to a twentieth-century Chiricahua leader, Asa Daklugie, "they dug it up, cut his head off, and boiled it to remove the flesh. Then they sent the skull to the Smithsonian." [27]

The government's wrongheadedness went beyond such acts of brutality. Officials frittered away an opportunity for peace with the Eastern Band. After the murder of Mangas Coloradas, the band did not unite behind one leader: some followed an older man named Nana, the others rallied behind Victorio. In 1865, both leaders wanted to settle on a reservation at Warm Springs and make "lasting peace, one that will keep." With their followers, the two leaders waited near Warm Springs for a response, a wait of three months. Over the protestations of the Indian agent, General Carleton finally ordered the Apaches to move to Fort Sumner, adding "that they can have peace on no other basis; that we will continue the war until that result is produced, or the band is exterminated." The result was a resumption, indeed an intensification, of hostili-

ties. The Eastern Band was not about to leave their land for confinement
on land so poor and so crowded that the Mescaleros would soon sneak
out, and thousands of Navajos would die of disease and starvation before
the experiment was ended in 1868. Instead, Victorio and Nana left the
meeting and promptly resumed the war.[28]

The Chiricahuas' unwillingness to leave home should have been no
surprise. They had been fighting to protect their beloved homelands for
about a century and a half. The tie to the land was deep. If an Apache
"was born and grew up in a place, went away and was brought back, one
of the things he did was to roll at this place as a symbol of having come
home, of identification with the place. He would get down on the
ground and roll." [29]

.   .   .

In 1868, the United States elected Ulysses S. Grant president and soon it
had a new Indian policy. Seeking to end the conflicts in Arizona and
elsewhere, the administration of the former leader of the Northern
armies adopted a "peace policy," whereby reservations would be created
in areas not desired by non-Indians, and the Indians induced to move
there. Hostile tribes that stayed on reservations would be fed; the cost of
food, it was believed, would be far less than the costs of a war of extermination. Those who left the reservation would be hunted down and
punished. The policy bore immediate fruit with the Eastern Band. By
1869, they were "very destitute" and asked again that a reservation be
formed near Warm Springs. While no reservation was formally established, they were fed there. The federal agent enunciated for his superi-
ors the purpose of this generosity: "The demoralizing influence of free
gifts, if liberal, would cause these Indians in a few years to lose their discipline and confidence as warriors, and the large number of boys now
growing up . . . will not learn enough about war to make them danger-
ous." [30]

Though the Eastern Band was now at peace, Apache raids in northern Mexico and southern Arizona and New Mexico continued, and the
residents screamed for military action against the Chiricahuas, led by
Cochise, who was now nearing seventy. But President Grant was under
countervailing pressures. After Mangas Coloradas' death, and especially
with the Eastern Band and many other Apache groups peacefully accepting rations, Cochise had acquired a mantle of greatness in the east-

ern press. Humanitarians in the East took up his cause, particularly because of the bloodthirsty reputation of the Arizonans. In the most egregious incident, in 1871, a detail of infuriated vigilantes from Tucson swept down one night on unsuspecting Western Apache women and children being fed at an army post called Camp Grant, massacring about 140. A jury meted out frontier justice by refusing to bring convictions, causing howls of outrage from the East. Perhaps the Camp Grant massacre tipped the scales: President Grant decided to attempt a peaceful solution before unleashing a military campaign against Cochise and his band.[31]

The president selected General Oliver Otis Howard as his emissary. Howard was a deeply religious man, known as the Christian Soldier and the "praying general," who had lost an arm in the Civil War. In the fall of 1872, President Grant sent him to try talking with Cochise. Howard met with Tom Jeffords, Cochise's white friend. Jeffords knew that Cochise wanted peace. While the Chiricahuas had suffered far fewer casualties than their enemies, they had been decimated by a decade of war. The statistics are highly sketchy but they suggest that the combined population of the Central and Southern bands had been cut in half between 1850 and 1870—from about two thousand to less than one thousand. Jeffords told General Howard that he would take him to Cochise only if he went unarmed and without soldiers. Howard immediately agreed.[32]

Shortly afterward, Howard and Cochise met in the old chief's stronghold, an easily defended locale in a canyon deep in the Dragoon Mountains. Perhaps for the first time in United States history, representatives of the government and an Indian tribe negotiated from positions of rough equality, even if the two men could not have looked more different. Howard had a full dark beard and wore his empty sleeve pinned to the belt of his uniform. Cochise was about six feet tall, as he was later described by the governor of Arizona, with "shoulders slightly rounded by age, features quite regular, head large and well proportioned; countenance rather sad, hair long and black . . . face smooth, the beard having been pulled out with pincers, as is the custom of Indians." Howard intended to persuade Cochise to move to a reservation to be created near Warm Springs, but Cochise convinced him that the Chiricahuas should be located on a reservation in the Central Band's aboriginal home, on the border with Mexico and encompassing the Dragoon and Chiri-

cahua mountains. Howard also agreed that Tom Jeffords would be their
agent, the government's supervisor of affairs on a reservation, and that
no army troops would be stationed there. In return, Cochise promised
that his warriors would keep the peace and stay on the reservation.
Howard returned to Washington and President Grant accepted the
terms, creating the Chiricahua Reservation on December 14, 1872.[33]

.   .   .

Not everyone was pleased. General George Crook, who commanded
the army's forces in Arizona, wrote that the large, rugged reservation "set
apart for Cochise . . . affords great facilities for his outrages. In my opinion there will be constant trouble as long as he is allowed to occupy it."
Arizonans, predictably, were less restrained. A Tucson newspaper opined
that the reservation was created "in obedience to an unconquered, un-
punished and unrepentant thieving and murdering savage's demands.
. . . In permitting C[o]chise to dictate his own terms in so important a
matter . . . General Howard consented to a dishonor upon the nation
which that very act proved him unworthy to represent, and actually per-
verted an essential element to the President's excellent peace policy." [34]

But to the surprise of almost everyone in Arizona, Cochise and his
warriors kept their promise. They conducted no raids in the United
States, and in the summer of 1873, Jeffords could report wayfarers "traveling alone and unarmed," farmers and miners working unconcerned
about attack, and apparently universal "confidence in the good faith of
these Indians." Mexican authorities charged the Chiricahuas with the
same old raiding across the border, but investigations showed that most
of the raids were committed by other Indians, not the followers of
Cochise. The same newspaper that had howled about Howard's agreement acknowledged a year later that the Chiricahuas "have kept perfect
faith with the people of Arizona." [35]

In 1874, Cochise became ill. No medicine man's healing powers
helped. His people collected around him and waited, and on June 8 the
old chief died. "When it came," wrote an observer, "the howl that went
up from these people was fearful to listen to. They were scattered around
in the nooks and ravines in parties, and as the howling from one
rancheria would lag, it would be renewed with vigor in another. This
was kept up through the night and until daylight next morning." [36]

Neither of Cochise's sons, Taza and Naiche, could hold the allegiance of all the members of the Central and Southern bands who had chosen to live on the Chiricahua Reservation. The lack of a single source of tribal authority and a cut in the beef rations supplied to the reservation further weakened Jeffords's position. Nevertheless, the Chiricahuas avoided conflict with non-Indians until 1876. In the spring of that year a group of Chiricahuas was out hunting when an intratribal fight broke out. The dissident minority then killed three white men, arousing fears of a general uprising, and the governor of Arizona sent a telegram reporting "the blackest state of affairs" at the Chiricahua Reservation, which, if exposed, would "sicken and disgrace humanity." He urged that the Chiricahuas "be at once removed or placed under such police regulation as will protect our citizens and prevent raids and murders in Sonora." [37]

Subsequent reports were exaggerated even further, levering the old fears and alarms among the white populace, which had been looking with great longing at the Chiricahuas' land since the reservation had been founded in 1872. It contained "the best of Arizona," including valuable timber, arable land along the streams, and mountain ranges said to be "full of gold and silver leads." In response to the hue and cry, the commissioner of Indian affairs fired Jeffords for being too sympathetic to his charges, and on May 3, 1876, ordered a young man named John Clum, the agent at the San Carlos division of the White Mountain Reservation (east of present-day Phoenix), to move all the Indians on the Chiricahua Reservation to San Carlos. Only two years after Cochise's death, and on the pretext that three homicides in an extremely rowdy part of the world equaled an uprising, his bargain with the United States was dead by fiat. President Grant formally abolished the Chiricahua Reservation in October 1876, and until well into the twentieth century the Chiricahuas would not again see their aboriginal lands without an army in pursuit. The glowing forecasts of "gold and silver leads" soon proved understatements. In 1877, silver was discovered on the former reservation's western edge, and the town of Tombstone sprang up. While more famous for the smoking guns of Wyatt Earp and Doc Holliday, by 1886 it had produced almost $20 million of silver, enough to drop silver prices nationally and contribute to a brief depression.[38]

The Chiricahuas dreaded what awaited them at San Carlos—soldiers called the location "Hell's Forty Acres"—and when John Clum arrived, about 200 of them, mostly of the Southern Band, disappeared into Mexico, among them Geronimo and Cochise's younger son, Naiche. Reporting this, Clum made the first significant mention of Geronimo's name in government records. Cochise's other son, Taza, and about 325 Indians made the one-hundred-mile trek to the hot dry lands of San Carlos. Though aware that two-fifths of the Apaches on the Chiricahua Reservation had decamped for Mexico, Clum, whom the Chiricahuas later described as "an arrogant young man, hardly out of baby grass," pronounced the removal a success: "the terrible shade of that tribe's dreaded name has passed away."

The agency to which the nonfugitive Chiricahuas were taken was located within the aboriginal territory of the Western Apaches but was not a place where they, or any Indians, had lived. To the Chiricahuas, San Carlos "was the worst place in all the great territory stolen from the Apaches": grassless, gameless, its river sluggish and brackish, with pools that supported mosquitoes, bringing to the Apaches their first encounter with the "shaking sickness"—malaria. When Clum had been appointed agent in 1874 at the age of twenty-three, little had been done to improve the conditions. According to one soldier, everywhere there had been "the naked, hungry, dirty, frightened little Indian children, darting behind bush or into wickiup at sight of you; [e]verywhere the sullen, stolid, hopeless, suspicious faces of the older Indians challenging you." Within two years Clum had built an adequate physical plant and organized an Indian police force and a court over which an Indian judge presided to settle disputes between Apaches. He had convinced the Western Apaches to farm, won the confidence of the public officials of Arizona, and brought two other bands of Apaches to San Carlos. It was to this Apache dumping ground that the Chiricahuas were brought.[39]

·   ·   ·

Meanwhile, the members of the Eastern Band had been jerked back and forth for eight years. Their reservation near Warm Springs was relocated to the west in 1871 and then returned to the Warm Springs area in 1873, where it remained until 1877. In the eight years between 1869 and 1877, five different agents were in charge, all with a low opinion of their charges. They called the Apaches "probably the most troublesome and difficult Indians in the continent to control." They were "naturally indolent," "cruel," "a roving, thieving, war-loving tribe," and comparable to "very wild beasts of prey." [40]

Despite the instability and contempt, the Eastern Band, now often called the Warm Springs Apaches, remained at peace. One of the agents could boast that "Not one death has been laid to their charge of a white man or citizen within the past year; not a substantiated charge of plunder or robbery known to have been committed by them; . . . men, women, and children traveling with safety everywhere in their country, even without arms." [41]

It couldn't last. A number of Chiricahuas who had slipped away to Mexico before Clum removed them began to drift into the Warm Springs Reservation over the next two months, where they were permitted to stay. But then other escapees who had been raiding in Mexico, including Geronimo, brought their booty to Warm Springs with the idea of using it as a base of support. Clum was dispatched to the scene and in May 1877 surprised the renegades and put the hostile leaders in shackles. He hauled the prisoners the several hundred miles back to San Carlos, while some 450 other Chiricahuas, primarily the Warm Springs Apaches, were forced to trudge behind, even though Clum had no evidence that they had colluded with the raiders. The Warm Springs Apaches subsequently denied any involvement, saying that Geronimo and his people "were the Indians that committed the killings, stole live stock, and other crimes that our people were blamed with." At San Carlos, the raiders were thrown in jail and kept there until some other Apache leaders threatened Clum with a reservation-wide uprising if they weren't released.[42]

Believing himself underappreciated, Clum resigned in June 1877 and affairs at San Carlos deteriorated rapidly. A succession of incompetent, lethargic, and dishonest agents followed, abandoning Clum's efforts to give the Indians some control over their affairs via Indian police and courts. Instead, they decreed that all the Apaches become farmers on a land that could, at best, support livestock, and then failed to supply the training or equipment needed to permit even a chance of success. They permitted non-Indian miners and ranchers to encroach on the reservation, with the result that the government eventually severed several large pieces to accommodate the non-Indian demands. They also engaged in graft with the funds earmarked for buying rations and supplies for the

Apaches. In the early 1880s, a grand jury in Tucson (not a hotbed of Apache sympathizers), empaneled to look into another matter, was so outraged by the corruption it discovered at San Carlos that it indicted the agent. It expressed its "utter abhorrence of the conduct of Agent Tiffany and that class of reverend peculators who have cursed Arizona as Indian officials, and who have caused more misery and loss of life than all other causes combined. . . . In the meantime, the Indians are neglected, half-fed, discontented, and turbulent, until at last, with the vigilant eye peculiar to the savage, the Indians observe the manner in which the Government, through its agent, complies with its sacred obligations." [43]

.   .   .

Even had the "reverend peculators" been honorable men and discharged their duties properly, the Chiricahuas would still have been miserable. Like most Indians, they didn't conceive of land as a commodity to be bought and sold. They did not move their homes hundreds or thousands of miles from their birthplace to achieve some economic or other gain. They were extremely uncomfortable in these hot desert lands, and with the Western Apaches. The land was not theirs; neither, therefore, were their lives.

In September 1877, the Warm Springs Apaches made the first of three major breakouts over the next nine years. They "had no guns as all our weapons had been taken away from us, so we packed our few things and started back . . . on foot. The next day out our Indians were attacked by Indian scouts and United States soldiers. Many of our people being unarmed and unable to protect themselves were killed during this attack." Most of the band survived and made it back to Warm Springs. They were allowed to remain there until the fall of 1878 when the government decreed that they should return to San Carlos. One of the chiefs, Loco, reluctantly acquiesced, but not the other, Victorio. Decades later, he was remembered as saying: "I have tried to live a peaceable life, I have done no wrong, but you will not leave me and my people in our home land, so now I am going to these mountains. You can send troops after me, but I will fight for my . . . country. After I die or get killed, I have nothing more to say about my country here." [44]

Victorio and about eighty warriors went east, seeking to live with the Mescaleros across the Rio Grande, but that didn't work out. In September, his force swelled by Mescaleros, he began what came to be called the Victorio War, attacking a group of black cavalrymen, the famed Buffalo Soldiers. For a year, Victorio exacted an awesome price across the landscape of west Texas, New Mexico, and Chihuahua for the government's insistence that he live at San Carlos. American and Mexican troops combed the mountains but he repeatedly eluded them, striking at ranches, herds, and wagon trains. By July 1880, however, the Buffalo Soldiers out of Fort Davis, Texas, had cut him and his warriors off from water holes, and they were forced into Mexico. On October 15, Mexican troops surprised them in a mountain fastness called Tres Castillos, and the Apaches climbed higher into the mountains where a battle raged. At dawn Victorio's warriors began to sing the death chant, preparing for the hand-to-hand end. When it was over, seventy-eight warriors were dead, including Victorio, and another sixty-eight were herded off as prisoners. Some thirty escaped during the night and continued to struggle into 1881 against insuperable odds.[45]

.   .   .

That same year, in September, Geronimo engineered a breakout from San Carlos, or as it was then known, the White Mountain Reservation. Today, he is the best-known Chiricahua and one of the best-known Indian warriors in history, the implacable guerrilla fighter who was the last to give in. According to one United States general, Geronimo was "one of the brightest, most resolute, determined looking men that I have ever encountered. He had the clearest, sharpest, dark eye I think I have ever seen . . . every movement indicated power, energy and determination. In everything he did he had a purpose." But he was never a chief, and never commanded the allegiance of more than a small percentage of the Chiricahuas. Indeed, he was feared and resented by many members of the tribe. Timing partly explains his notoriety. The Chiricahuas were the last Indians to continue on the warpath in an organized way in the United States. All other Indian warfare against the white intruders had been squelched in 1881 with the end of Sitting Bull's resistance in the north.[46]

During the breakouts from the reservation, Geronimo always deferred to Cochise's younger son, Naiche, as chief. Geronimo sat at Naiche's left: he was the *segundo*. But he was a master strategist with an implacable hatred of the Mexicans, who had massacred his entire family;

and, to a lesser extent, of the Americans. Beyond that, he was a medicine man. The Chiricahuas believed that he had a vision, a power, that allowed him to know what the enemy would do, where he would come from and when.[47]

For nearly two and a half years after the breakout, from hideouts in the Sierra Madre in Mexico, Naiche, Geronimo, a Warm Springs Band leader named Chato, and some seventy other Chiricahuas eluded about four thousand Mexican troops and hundreds of United States soldiers, raiding on both sides of the border with vengeful fury. In April 1882, they made their most daring move (and perhaps most destructive for their fellow tribal members) when they sneaked back to the White Mountain Reservation to recruit the remaining Chiricahuas who were mostly of the Warm Springs Band. Unable to enlist their brethren voluntarily, the renegades compelled them to follow at gunpoint. About fifty of these unarmed captives were ambushed by Mexicans and killed; others suffered the same fate when they escaped their abductors.[48]

Indeh. Wild justice. The Chiricahuas were splintering, but their fighting spirit raged on.

Leaders in Washington considered the escape a major crisis and reassigned General George Crook to Arizona after seven years of fighting tribes in other areas. In his first tour of duty in Arizona, Crook had successfully bottled up the Western Apaches. He had a bushy beard and instead of wearing the blue uniform of the United States he sported a canvas suit and a weatherbeaten hat, thereby earning the name "Tan Fox" from the Apaches. Many Indians trusted him as a respectable adversary and a man of his word. Crook knew that traditional soldiering against the elusive tactics of the Apaches was useless, and enlisted Apaches as scouts to hunt down their hostile tribesmen. He was also aided by a new agreement between the United States and Mexico that troops from either country could cross the border in pursuit of hostile Apaches.[49]

In the spring of 1883, a Chiricahua raid into the United States gave Crook his chance. With 45 cavalrymen and 193 scouts, he tracked down some of the raiders and surprised them in their Sierra Madre stronghold. Most surrendered immediately. By February 1884, Geronimo and the other holdouts also had been returned to the White Mountain Reservation, near Fort Apache. Geronimo even tried his hand at farming for the next year.[50]

The last breakout occurred in May 1885. The prohibition on drink-ing—Apaches were enthusiastic users of a corn-based beer called *tiswin,* and also stronger spirits—and other restrictions became too much. Some 130 Chiricahuas, including Geronimo and 42 other warriors, took off again toward Mexico. They undoubtedly noticed the transfor-mation of their ancestral lands. Back in 1876 and 1877, when the reser-vations had been abolished, virtually no white people dared to live there. At the time of this last breakout, fewer than ten years later, twenty-six thousand people lived in the Chiricahuas' territory and the transcon-tinental Southern Pacific Railroad ran through it. About four hundred thousand head of cattle grazed there, and mines pockmarked the land. The old ways were over, and most of the Chiricahuas knew it. A few members of the Warm Springs Band went with Geronimo and Naiche, but the majority stayed behind on the reservation. The Chiricahuas were more riven than ever.[51]

The entire country was soon in an uproar over this latest escape. Crook called for Apache enlistees as scouts and fifty Chiricahuas, includ-ing Chato, a leader of the prior escape, joined up. They were "practically all the men of the [Warm Springs Band] old enough to fight . . . to-gether with many young boys who were really too young [to] carry the muskets." For ten months the trail was picked up and lost through Ari-zona, New Mexico, and Mexico. Ultimately the force swelled to about five thousand men. One-fourth of the entire standing army of the United States of America actively pursued a hostile force of about forty warriors or tried to defend the Southwest against their raids.[52] In the frontier army, desertion rates could run as high as a third in a year. The Apache scouts served virtually without any desertions in conditions as difficult as any Apache raider had ever experienced, and without respite. In the Indian wars of the West, only the two regiments of the Buffalo Soldiers could make a claim to such endurance and low desertion rates, but they were mounted. The Apache scouts preferred to go on foot. Their feet, one Chiricahua remembered, "were lacerated by the hot ground as well as cold and the sharp rocks . . . the gun and belts wore sores on their shoulders and hips . . . their day's work consisted of cover-ing a distance from 70 to 80 miles a day on a piece of bacon and a piece of bread." They also had to be careful that irregular Mexican troops did not pick them off to obtain the bounty on Apache scalps.[53]

Ten months after the breakout, in March 1886, the renegades approached Crook's force to ask for a parley. Under orders to obtain an unconditional surrender unless promises were "necessary to secure their surrender," Crook told the Chiricahua leaders that if they did not surrender, "hostilities should be commenced at once and [continue until] the last one of them [was] killed, if it took fifty years." The United States, he said, intended to imprison them in the East. The Chiricahua responded that they would surrender but only if they would be confined in the East "for not exceeding two years, taking with them such of the families as so desired," or if they were returned "to the reservation on their old status." Crook, believing his instructions gave him room to negotiate, accepted the former: two years in the East, with their families.[54]

That decided, Crook returned to Arizona, with the troops and scouts to follow with the renegade Chiricahuas. But bad news caught up with him. The commanding general of the army, Philip Sheridan, telegraphed him saying: "The President can not assent to the surrender of the hostiles" on the agreed terms of two years of imprisonment. Crook was told to obtain "their unconditional surrender, only sparing their lives." Unknown to Crook, President Grover Cleveland wanted the captives turned over to the civil authorities in Arizona for what would surely have been summary trials and execution. And there was more bad news. Almost simultaneous with Sheridan's telegram came word that thirty-eight of the Chiricahuas, about a third, including Geronimo, had bolted. They had encountered a liquor peddler who told them they would be murdered as soon as they crossed the line back into the United States.[55]

Crook wired Sheridan that to demand unconditional surrender by the remaining seventy-five captives would "result in their scattering to the mountains." The army remained silent, the Apaches continued to Arizona. In early April, they were loaded onto railroad cars and carried to Fort Marion, Florida, still believing that their stay would not exceed two years.[56]

· · ·

By now Crook had lost the confidence of President Cleveland and General Sheridan. He was relieved of command and replaced by General Nelson Miles, who had fought the Sioux and Cheyenne after the Little Bighorn. Over the next several months, Miles and his five thousand troops pursued the band of thirty-eight men, women, and children while correspondence flew back and forth between the Southwest and Washington over the question of what to do with the Chiricahua Apaches. Miles wrote a long letter to the assistant adjutant general, passed up the line to General Sheridan, dated July 7 urging that they all be moved away from the mountains of Arizona and New Mexico to eliminate "a disturbing element or a menace to the scattered settlements." Florida was not the right place because they "are a mountain race, accustomed to high altitudes, and would in a short time, most likely, die, if kept in the lowlands of Florida." Instead, they should be located on the Kiowa, Comanche, and Kiowa Apache Reservation in the Indian Territory (now Oklahoma) where "the clear water of the mountains, the climate, and the fertile soil would be congenial and beneficial to them." [57]

The governor of New Mexico disagreed, believing the farther away the better. As long "as they are in this region of the country, business must continue depressed, & immigration & development seriously retarded. . . . Previous to the recurrence of the raids of last year, the previous year having passed in peace, there was the beginning of active development & we were promised renewal of prosperous times. But these Apache raids stopped everything. . . ." [58]

The president and General Sheridan believed that for political reasons the Apaches couldn't be relocated anywhere west of the Mississippi, and ignoring Miles's warning about Florida, chose Fort Marion as the dumping ground for *all* the nonhostile Chiricahuas, even the scouts, until a "suitable place could be provided for them." As for Geronimo and the other renegade warriors, President Cleveland wanted them tried and executed. Queried as to whether sending the scouts, who had provided months of hard military service, to exile in Florida "might be considered an act of bad faith," Sheridan replied that "it was absurd to talk of keeping faith with those Indians." For more than a month, while the scouts still pursued the escapees, the government chose not to divulge the decision to ship them to Florida.[59]

By mid-August, the renegades remained unvanquished, but the toll of constant pursuit had exhausted them. On August 24, 1886, two Chiricahua scouts, Martine and Kayitah, along with less than ten soldiers under the command of Lieutenant Charles B. Gatewood, got within a few miles of the hostiles. Gatewood gave the scouts the risky task of ap-

proaching Naiche and Geronimo to arrange a conference. They succeeded, largely because they had relatives among the band, and on August 26, the Chiricahuas agreed to surrender to General Miles, provided
Gatewood would accompany them and they could keep their arms to
protect themselves against the Mexicans until their formal surrender in
Skeleton Canyon, just over the border.[60]

Miles first met with Geronimo on September 3. Ignoring President
Cleveland's instructions concerning the fate of the men, Miles told
Geronimo, via translations from English into Spanish and from Spanish
into Apache, that he, like all the Chiricahuas, would be reunited with
the others in Florida for an indefinite time, after which they would be
brought back to Arizona. Five days later, Geronimo, Naiche, and their
small party—along with Martine and Kayitah—were loaded on a train
for the East. A few weeks later, an even smaller band under the leadership of a son of Mangas Coloradas, hearing that Geronimo had given up,
surrendered to Captain Charles L. Cooper and some twenty men of the
Tenth Cavalry.[61]

·   ·   ·

The Indian wars in the United States were essentially over. The memory
of the Chiricahuas' long defiance against overwhelming forces arrayed
against them endured, even among the White Eyes. A judge would write
ten years later that "the history or traditions or myths of the human race
[probably do not contain] another instance of such prolonged resistance
against such tremendous odds." [62]

The government in 1886 was not satisfied with the removal of the
hostile Chiricahuas. With Geronimo's surrender, all the Chiricahua
scouts in the field were ordered back to Fort Apache and, in early September, disarmed. Chiricahuas recall that they then "were gathered together at Ft. Apache at the time of their weekly rationing and were
suddenly surrounded by armed soldiers and the able-bodied men were
taken aside and placed under armed guard in a stable; the women, children and old men were sent back to their camp." [63]

On September 7, about four hundred Chiricahuas, none of whom
had participated in the last outbreak and many of whom had scouted for
the United States Army, began a six-day trek of about a hundred miles
under heavy guard to the railroad station at Holbrook, Arizona. There
the terrified Indians were packed onto a special train with sealed win-

dows to prevent escape. During the seven-day trip, heat and lack of sanitary facilities produced a stench so overpowering that the soldiers were reluctant to enter the compartments. When the train entered a long tunnel, the Apaches, thinking that they were entering the earth, shrieked in terror and hid under the seats. On September 20, the survivors arrived at Fort Marion, Florida.[64]

Geronimo's train stopped for a few days in San Antonio, Texas, because the president still wanted the band turned over to Arizona to be executed as criminals. But when he learned that Miles had promised to ship them to Florida, he reluctantly decided that the sixteen men would be confined under "close custody" at Fort Pickens, on the opposite side of the state from Fort Marion where the women and children would be sent to join the other Chiricahuas. On their arrival on October 22, the men learned they were to be isolated from their families and protested that separation was a "violation of the terms of their surrender." It was to no avail.[65]

For a tribe whose population had dropped from about three thousand to five hundred in the space of one generation, twenty-seven years of captivity as prisoners of war had begun.

TWO

IMPRISONMENT

It is better that ten guilty persons escape than one innocent suffer.
—Sir William Blackstone

Most of the Chiricahuas transported to Florida in 1886 had not opposed the efforts of non-Indians to settle in their territory for many
years, if at all. They had refused to participate in the two breakouts from
the White Mountain Reservation led by Geronimo. Indeed, their service as scouts of the United States Army was critical to Geronimo's
eventual surrender. Not only had they served the army in 1885 and
1886, but some, during their imprisonment, were allowed to join the
army, and after their service they were *returned* to prisoner of war status.

Even if Geronimo and those who had joined him were guilty of violating laws of which they had no knowledge, the United States turned
Blackstone, the first great systematizer of Anglo-American law, on his
head. The government was willing to make ten or more innocents suffer
for the sins of each guilty Chiricahua.

. . .

Fort Marion, located in the middle of the sleepy provincial city of St.
Augustine on the Atlantic coast of Florida, was 180 feet square, a little
smaller than a football field. Offshore was a small island with a lighthouse. Five months before Geronimo's surrender in Skeleton Canyon,

the seventy Chiricahuas who had not fled after surrendering to General
Crook had been transported to this fort, with most of the men sent out
to the lighthouse island to live. Evidently the waves of this big body of
water fascinated them. They were provided with a few staples and told
how to turn the lighthouse lamp on at night and off at daybreak. When
they asked about meat for their diet, they were offered fishing tackle.
Apaches did not eat anything that lived in the water, nor did they eat
pork. This they would have to learn to do. After some period of time,
some of the men on the island were allowed to live within the confines
of Fort Marion, joining the women and children there.[1]

In August 1886, when asked about the fort's capacity to house the
rest of the Chiricahuas, Lieutenant Colonel Loomis E. Langdon, the
post commander, responded that it might be able to hold another seventy-five, but he recommended that no more be sent. The clothing that
was supposed to be issued for those already there had not been forthcoming—only a request for shoe sizes. Women and children, he wrote,
were "much in need of clothing; some women very scantily clad and
several children almost, if not naked." Some charitable ladies of the city,
he added, had offered to "raise money by subscription" and teach the
"squaws" to sew. He asked that the government pay the twenty dollars
needed for buying the material.[2]

Despite Langdon's advice, in September, about 400 more Chiricahuas were interned in Fort Marion: 380 who had been rounded up in
Fort Apache, including 100 children, and the handful of women and
children that had been separated from their men when Geronimo and
17 warriors were dropped off at Fort Pickens. Located on a barrier
island off Pensacola Bay on the western end of the Florida panhandle,
Fort Pickens was almost ten times larger than Fort Marion and so, in a
bizarre paradox, the warriors whom the United States most sought to
punish wound up in less straitened quarters than the innocents who had
refused to go with them.[3]

Some of Fort Marion's cells were in the basement, and the idea of
living underground horrified the Apaches. The army issued them tipis
that when pitched covered virtually all of the ground of the fort. They
even pitched them on the roof of the fort's building. It averaged out to
about sixty-five square feet per prisoner, or a space of eight feet by eight
feet. People used to living in small family groups scattered over millions
of acres, accustomed to the clear, dry air of the mountains, were now

huddled together cheek by jowl in the Florida humidity. Old warriors and relatives of the warriors at Fort Pickens lived within a few feet of the scouts who had betrayed them. During the day, women and children, and men under surveillance, were permitted to go outside the fort's walls and visit the town, but many were reluctant to take the opportunity, being, as the post commander pointed out, "apparently more afraid of the whites than the whites are afraid of them." A few made moccasins, lances, and beadwork for sale, but for the most part, these athletic and active people had nothing to do. In January, one observer wrote, "months have passed and no step taken to give employment to the minds of these wonderfully bright people." Some of the Apaches complained among themselves that the White Eyes would come and stare at them like animals on exhibit.[4]

To the exiles' lethargy, idleness, and fear, dismay soon arrived in the form of a small man named Captain Richard Pratt, commander of the boarding school established for Indian children in Carlisle, Pennsylvania.

·   ·   ·

President Grant's peace policy for Indians had included a notion of assimilation: Indians would be trained to act like other Americans. Using skillful public relations techniques, Pratt and other like-minded reformers convinced government officials that boarding schools provided an excellent sword to sever the intergenerational threads of tribal custom; they could instill both Anglo-American values and the manual skills necessary to survive in the white world. Although the use of boarding schools such as Carlisle to educate Indian children has declined during the twentieth century, until the last twenty years virtually all formal instruction of Indian children occurred in schools run by the federal or local governments or missionaries, not by Indians.[5]

Captain Pratt ran the Carlisle boarding school, famous today for the great Sac and Fox athlete Jim Thorpe, like a military camp. Upon arrival, boys had their hair cut short and were forced to put on trousers, thus stripping away their Indian identity. Males wore military-style uniforms; females simple dresses. Native languages were strictly forbidden.[6]

In response to early complaints that it was doing nothing to "civilize" the Apache exiles, the government twice sent Pratt to Fort Marion. In December 1886, he chose forty-four students between the ages of twelve and twenty-two. Four months later he chose another sixty-two.

Because married women did not have to go, some older men simply claimed some of the girls as wives. Parents tried hiding their children from Pratt and the soldiers. One family pleaded not to have all its children taken from them and had the difficult task of choosing which one to keep and which others to consign to whatever unknown fate awaited them in Carlisle. The Apaches protested to the post commander that "they were promised by the Government officers that they should not be separated from their children . . . separation—is what they constantly dread. Even a present of clothing to their more than half-naked children excites their mistrust and makes them very restless, because it looks to them like preparing them for a journey, a separation from their parents." [7]

Notwithstanding overcrowding, lack of activity, and forced schooling, sickness and death overrode all the other concerns. Many people had predicted that relocation to the humid Florida climate would decimate the Indians. One newspaper reported that experienced "army officers do not think there will be one of them alive in the next five years," as they will die off "like so many sheep." Another paper, reflecting the feeling of many White Eyes, decried this prospect: "If these Indians have committed crimes worthy of death, let the sentence of the law be executed and not in the refinement of cruelty, by inches or atoms." [8]

The predictions of high mortality proved accurate. In seven months at Fort Marion, eighteen prisoners died, an annual rate of more than 6 percent, almost three times the national rate at that time. [9]

.   .   .

At Fort Pickens, the Apaches fared a bit better. The city of Pensacola had actively lobbied for Geronimo. The long campaign to capture the last hostile Apaches had attracted a great deal of national attention, and boosters in Pensacola believed that "he [Geronimo] will draw as largely as Jumbo, for he has proven a bigger elephant to Uncle Sam." Newspapers compared Geronimo's island imprisonment to Napoleon's at Elba. [10]

The exiles were not crowded together at Fort Pickens and they had work: clearing the fort's grounds of debris that had accumulated during the twenty years in which the fort had not been used. The Apaches labored with neither insubordination nor apparent discontent. They were brought up not to complain, and believed to do so would simply make things worse. The influx of tourists, often over a hundred a day, provided diversion, and the Chiricahuas earned money peddling souvenirs. Souvenirs made by Geronimo sold the best, so he sold not only his own but also those made by the others.[11]

The Apaches did complain about one thing—their separation from wives and children. Geronimo maintained that it broke his agreement with General Miles at Skeleton Canyon, and the post commander at Fort Pickens recommended that the government grant the Chiricahuas' request, in part as a reward for their good behavior.[12]

That conduct probably assisted the campaign initiated by Philadelphian Herbert Welsh, the leader of the Indian Rights Association, after he visited Fort Marion in March 1887. Through letters to newspapers, private correspondence, speeches, and even a pamphlet, he called attention to the disgraceful conditions at Fort Marion and to the injustice done to those Chiricahuas who had not assisted the renegades, and especially to the scouts who had helped track them down. During their confinement in Florida, public opinion on behalf of the Apaches grew strong. President Cleveland, who had chosen Florida in the first place, felt compelled to find a more appropriate prison.[13]

In April, after several Cabinet meetings, the president decided to send to Fort Pickens the wives and children of the men there, and to move all the others at Fort Marion to Mount Vernon Barracks, an old arsenal thirty-one miles north of Mobile, Alabama. By the end of the month, the 448 remaining Chiricahuas left St. Augustine for good. Thirty women and children went to Fort Pickens, another 62 youths went to Carlisle, and the rest, 354, to Alabama. One year later, in May 1888, the prisoners at Fort Pickens were also shipped to Mount Vernon, reuniting all the adult members of the tribe for the first time in three years.[14]

. . .

Mount Vernon's 2,162 acres made it a vast improvement over Fort Marion. But virtually all the land that wasn't swampy was heavily forested, with sandy soil unsuitable for agriculture. The officers in charge never followed through with suggestions that the Apaches be taught forestry, so the Chiricahuas remained essentially idle and quickly grew to detest their new prison. Babies died from excessive insect bites, it rained much of the time, and the roofs of the old 1830s redbrick barracks buildings leaked. The humidity was worse than Florida's and their belongings

were always moldy. They built log cabins for themselves, minimally improving their housing conditions. They gambled and sold trinkets to the
few tourists. They tried to keep their spirits up by practicing the old traditions. Elders explained their history and traditions to children around
nighttime campfires. Puberty ceremonies were performed, and traditional weddings. But the Chiricahuas formerly had conducted these ceremonies high up in the mountains, not in a damp, dense lowland forest.
As one of them, Eugene Chihuahua, recalled, "There was no place to
climb to pray. If we wanted to see the sky we had to climb a tall pine." [15]

Their healing ceremonies were useless against the array of diseases
that attacked them—chiefly, malaria and tuberculosis. Nor were the
White Eyes' doctors' rites of use. The physician assigned to the base, Dr.
Walter Reed, who had not yet made his famous connection between
the anopheles mosquito and malaria, reported that the hot, rainy summer in southern Alabama increased the incidence of bronchial sickness
among the Chiricahuas. By the end of 1887, 21 tribal members had died
at Mount Vernon, about half from tuberculosis. And the children carried
their diseases with them to Carlisle. Despite the Chiricahuas' "uncom-
mon aptitude for learning," Pratt vowed to make no more recruiting
trips to the tribe because of the phenomenal death rates of their students. Of the 106 Chiricahuas taken to Carlisle in 1886 and 1887, 27
had died by May of 1889. Pratt blamed the decimation on more than
climate change. "While climate may to some extent have some influence
in aggravating and bringing a speedier termination, I think the deplorable and almost hopeless conditions surrounding them have a
greater influence. They have no home, no country, no future, and life has
become hardly worth living." It became a practice at Carlisle to send a
stricken youth back to Mount Vernon to die.[16]

Such death rates threatened the very existence of the tribe, and the
Chiricahuas had but one weapon. They fought back with birth rates
"higher than that of any other known people" during the years in Alabama. The years of warfare had created a large gender imbalance, with
many more women of child-bearing age than men, but the Apache tradition of polygamy stood them in good stead. Even so, their numbers
steadily dwindled. In late 1889, General Oliver Howard (he who had
parleyed with Cochise and was now commander of Headquarters Division of the Atlantic) sent his adjutant and son to inspect the situation at
Mount Vernon Barracks. The younger Howard reported that prompt ac-

tion was necessary "to avoid positive inhumanity." The death rate among the Chiricahuas was 6.8 percent, more than three times the "normal death rate of civilized people." Actually, Howard undercalculated the toll. Of 498 Apaches imprisoned beginning in April 1886, 129 were now dead. Forty-nine had perished in St. Augustine; 30 at Carlisle; and another 50 at Mount Vernon. One-fourth of those brought East had died in three and a half years. Howard's son echoed others in pinning this appalling record of deaths chiefly on "their location in the moist atmosphere of the sea-coast," and recommended prompt removal to some appropriate tract of land where they could build cabins and farm. "Another year's delay," he said, "would be criminal." If so, the government was four and a half times criminal, because it took until 1894 for officials to settle on a new location. By then, in spite of the extraordinary birth rate, the tribe would be reduced to about 300 members. The Chiricahuas dropped in numbers by *40 percent* in a mere eight years of imprisonment. By way of comparison, the Black Death carried off half the population of fourteenth-century Europe, but it took a hundred years to do so. Said Naiche, Cochise's son: "This is a bad place for my people; they are dying around me. The sun rises on my friends; they are here. The sun sets, and they are gone!" [17]

General George Crook came to check on his former scouts and was confronted by Chato, wearing the presidential medal he had received for good service in 1886, shortly before being imprisoned. He tore the medal off his chest and asked, "Why did they give me that, to wear in the guard house? I thought something good would come to me when they gave me that but I have been in confinement ever since I have had it." [18]

Crook joined the chorus: "The most ordinary justice would seem to demand a different course of procedure with men not only innocent of offense against the Government, but to whom the Government is largely indebted for services of the very greatest value, and which they alone could have rendered. . . ." He recommended "that immediate steps be taken to secure a reservation for them where they could be settled on farms of their own, to work for themselves, and to receive for themselves the full benefit of their labors." [19]

In 1890, Congress published Crook's and Howard's statements, along with other military reports. But the government found it difficult to agree on a solution. The undiminished hatred of the Chiricahuas in the

Southwest made a return to those territories (Arizona and New Mexico would not become states of the Union for another two decades) out of the question. Fort Sill, the military post in western Oklahoma originally suggested by General Miles in 1886, still appeared to be the best choice to officials, though removal to Carlisle, Pennsylvania, and to a tract in North Carolina also were enthusiastically championed. But an act of Congress passed in 1879 prohibited the removal of any Indians from Arizona or New Mexico to the Indian Territory, and therefore to Fort Sill, without prior congressional approval. The Arizona and New Mexico delegations firmly and loudly opposed waiving that barrier, evidently panicked that a band of three hundred babies and sickly adults would somehow manage another daring escape, make their way unarmed through utterly unknown territory to their old haunts, evading again the United States Army, and go back on the warpath, massacring the now much larger population of the Southwest. Western opposition led to such far-fetched schemes as locating them somewhere in the populous East. The Office of Indian Affairs was happy to be able to continue washing its hands of them, leaving them, as prisoners of war, to the War Department. Because the army itself had no other authority for housing them on an army base, in the eerie world often created by the "book," the Chiricahuas remained prisoners of war. And, while the executive and legislative branches of the United States pondered and deliberated, the Chiricahuas stayed on at Mount Vernon Barracks, performing their ceremonies and dying.[20]

Finally, in 1894, Congress responded. Overriding the renewed howls of the western delegations, it authorized the army to relocate the Chiricahuas to any military reservation in the country. The first idea was to cause their extinction as an ongoing tribe and the loss of their culture by scattering them among various forts. But finally the army decided to move them all to Fort Sill, Oklahoma. In October, the Chiricahuas were once again loaded on a train and hauled off to Fort Sill where the government, despite the growing lack of any justification, would confine them as prisoners of war for another nineteen years.[21]

·   ·   ·

Mount Vernon Barracks never became the popular tourist spot that Pensacola had been while Geronimo had been there. But a few people came to stare. Alabamians had not seen many Indians, after all, for a couple of

generations. They had begun to be moved out of the American South-
east in the first decades of the nineteenth century, and by 1840 most of
the region was devoid of Indians. In that period the United States procured, chiefly by a combination of force, bribery, and Indian discourage-
ment, the acquiescence of the leaders of the Cherokee, Creek, Choctaw,
Chickasaw, and Seminole tribes to a series of treaties. (Some of the
Seminoles ran off and simply disappeared into the Florida Everglades
and have been there ever since.) Most of the land now comprising
Florida, Alabama, western Georgia, western North Carolina, Tennessee,
Mississippi, and Louisiana was "ceded" by these tribes to the United
States in return for the grant of separate tracts that together comprised
all of what is Oklahoma with the exception of the thin panhandle above
that of Texas. This large piece of land, along with the lands to the north
comprising present-day Kansas and Nebraska (on which more northerly
tribes were resettled), was called Indian Territory. It was guaranteed at
the time to be territory in which non-Indians would *never* be allowed to
settle. In the words of the 1828 treaty with the Cherokees, the land
would be "a permanent home . . . which shall, under the most solemn
guarantee of the United States, be and remain theirs forever—a home
that shall never, in all future time, be embarrassed by having extended
around it the lines, or placed over it the jurisdiction, of a Territory or
State. . . ." [22]

The Five Civilized Tribes, as they came to be known after the collective agony of being uprooted and marched off to the Indian Territory,
had been for the most part village-dwelling agriculturalists and, even before their removal, had begun to acquire Anglo-American ideas about
such things as government. In their transplanted homes, these large
tribes (the Choctaw, Creek, and Cherokee tribes each consisted of some
twenty thousand people in the early nineteenth century) established
constitutional governments, schools, and economies capable of supporting all tribal members. The part-Cherokee Sequoia invented the first
written alphabet for an American Indian language. By the late nineteenth century the members of these five tribes shared many characteristics with the American middle class. But by then the United States had
broken its solemn guarantees.

Soon after the Civil War, the United States moved tribes from
Kansas, Nebraska, and elsewhere to the land promised forever to the
Five Civilized Tribes, who generally retained the eastern portions of

their territories. Cheyennes, Arapahoes, Osages, Poncas, and many others were moved into the western portions. And three southern Plains tribes—the Kiowas, Comanches, and Kiowa Apaches—which had roamed over much of what is now western Texas and Oklahoma prior to the Civil War, were settled in the southwestern portion of the Indian Territory, in the lands around Fort Sill.[23]

In addition to various "foreign" tribes, the government imposed the policy called "allotment" on what remained of the Indian Territory, the land now called Oklahoma, during the decade prior to 1894. The pressure for allotment had begun elsewhere even earlier, impelled by a powerful ideological belief called "individualism," a major concept in many fields of thought and endeavor. Even humanitarians enlisted in the Indian cause, having adopted individualistic beliefs, thought that the government should break up old-fashioned and outworn tribal allegiances and customs by conveying, or "allotting," plots of land to individual members of tribes so that they could become proper American farmers, with the same opportunity for success or failure as any other American farmer. As boarding schools would turn Indian children into non-Indians, allotment would transform adult Indians into non-Indians. Land-hungry whites added the clever twist that once an appropriate parcel had been allotted to each tribal member, the balance of its reservation, deemed "surplus," could be opened to non-Indians, with the tribe to receive payment for the loss of its surplus land. As a result of the process of allotting individual Indians and selling surplus land, Indian landholdings dropped from about 155 million acres in 1880 to about 65 million acres by 1930. This 60 percent reduction came about not as a result of war or disease, but through the actions of a Congress and a bureaucracy supposedly acting in the interests of the country's natives.[24]

And nowhere was this process more assiduously pressed than in the solemnly guaranteed Indian Territory. Between 1890 and 1893, more than ten *million* acres were opened to white settlers, who promptly organized the Oklahoma Territory. When the Chiricahuas arrived in 1894, the lands of the Kiowas, Comanches, and Kiowa Apaches remained intact, unallotted. But that fate was not far off.[25]

.   .   .

When the Chiricahuas disembarked from the train near Fort Sill, the Kiowas, Comanches, and Kiowa Apaches met them and took them to a place near a creek. Clear water ran down from the Wichita Mountains—nothing to equal the soaring craggy fortresses of the Chiricahuas, the Dragoons, or the Black Range, but mountains nonetheless. The air was dry, redolent with the smell of sage. There were mesquite beans ready to pick and the clear sign of deer. Unconcerned, probably altogether unaware of the uncertainties they faced with the inexorable opening of Oklahoma, the Chiricahuas rejoiced. One of them later explained, "When they brought me here to Fort Sill it was just like we had come out from a cloud and the cloud had gone away and the sun was shining again." They set to making wickiups, their traditional brush shelters, and slept under the stars. Their first night, for the first time in eight years, they heard the yip and howl of a coyote, like a distant relative welcoming them back to the West.[26]

Another welcoming ray of light was Captain Hugh L. Scott, selected by the army to be the Chiricahuas' agent. When he arrived at Fort Sill shortly before the Chiricahuas, he found that the post commander intended to treat them like animals. He "had announced his intention of building a palisaded pen somewhere away from the post, in which to corral the Apache prisoners of war, detailing a company of infantry out there as a guard over them for a month at a time." Scott countermanded that plan, and the commander was soon transferred. "He would have driven those Indians into running away had he remained in command," Scott wrote.[27]

Scott quickly won the confidence of the Apaches in his charge. Eugene Chihuahua would later recall that he "knew Indians and understood much of our needs." He promptly handed out food, blankets, and some clothing. He detailed a carpenter to help them build two-room houses but, most important, he let the important chiefs and scouts have their own villages far enough apart to afford each some privacy. In consultation with a white man named George Wratten, who had long been the interpreter for the tribe and had married an Apache woman, he gave each village headman a supervisory role.[28]

Scott told the Apaches that the army intended Fort Sill to be their permanent home. In 1894, the fort spread over almost 50,000 acres. Prior to the Chiricahuas' arrival, it had been scheduled for decommissioning. After the army abandoned the fort and gave the Chiricahuas adequate training and resources, Scott said, the government would allot the fort's primary tract to the tribal members (the other separate tract was woodlands considered unsuitable for allotment). But the primary tract was itself too small to allot each member of the tribe a parcel that the government considered adequate for self-support. Accordingly Captain Scott negotiated an agreement with the surrounding Kiowas, Comanches, and Kiowa Apaches under which they agreed to add about twenty-seven thousand acres to Fort Sill. He explained to these tribes that the government wanted the agreement in order "to provide a home" for the Chiricahuas, who would be located at Fort Sill "permanently." [29]

In 1895, Scott set out to establish a diversified agricultural economy. He bought nine hundred beef cattle, which, although nominally distributed to individual tribal members, served as the basis for a herd that was managed as a unit. He had about seven hundred acres of prairie sod broken so that each family would have about ten acres of tilled land, and issued them pigs, chickens, turkeys, and fruit trees.[30]

These efforts coincided with the return from Carlisle of the angry young Asa Daklugie, a nephew of Geronimo's who had been with Mangas in the last small group to surrender in 1886. Geronimo had insisted that Daklugie go to Carlisle to learn the wiles and ways of the White Eyes. In his eight years there, he had learned to read and speak English but chiefly had devoted himself to learning about cattle, as raising cattle seemed the least dishonorable way to earn a living. Daklugie had learned many of the ways of the White Eyes, but he didn't like them and, on his first meeting with Scott, an argument turned into an actual scuffle. But Scott put the young Daklugie in charge of the tribe's herd anyway. Within a few years, the Apaches had fenced the entire reservation. They grew great amounts of sorghum as fodder, and one year put up 350 tons of hay. Over the years the herd grew to about seven thousand head and was rated "the finest herd of Hereford cattle in the Southwest." [31]

Captain Scott left Fort Sill in 1897, and for the next ten years official reports were almost uniformly glowing. The commissioner of Indian affairs summed up the consensus: "under the wise and careful management and strict discipline enforced upon them by the military authorities, [they had] advanced in civilization far beyond reasonable expectations." [32]

But the Chiricahuas' opinions about their conditions differed from Washington's. They consistently asked to be freed of their prisoner of war status. James Kaywaykla said, "It is not right that the Government should hold our people as prisoners of war under the War Department. It don't look right to us and it is not right." Benedict Jozhe, whose son became a tribal leader almost half a century later, exclaimed, "Don't we have no rights in the United States or not? What is the trouble? Are we human beings in the United States? What are we? We are not Canadians or Africans and we are not from Europe but we are United States of America as we are born here." [33]

Officials replied disingenuously that the Chiricahuas were just "nominal" prisoners, a status imposed to allow them to live on an army base. Certainly, they did not live behind bars and did accumulate modest personal wealth through their cattle herd. But their status was distinctly different from that of other Indians, let alone other Americans. They could not leave the base for more than a few hours without the permission of the commanding officer. Whenever he gave them a job to do, they had to comply, without any compensation for their labor. They did not own the land on which they lived and had no possibility of acquiring it, as would become painfully obvious during the second decade of the twentieth century. Because of the restrictions, the opportunities of single Chiricahuas to meet potential spouses from off the reservation were limited, and even if a spark was lit, it almost never ignited: the Chiricahuas could not live off the reservation, and nobody wanted to marry into captivity. The Chiricahuas were denied the freedom to travel without permission, to labor for money, to acquire a permanent home, and to form a family outside the group.

The prisoner status was all the more ludicrous given that by 1912, only six male participants in the outbreak of 1885 and 1886 remained alive. Over half the Chiricahuas were born into captivity as prisoners of war, if, as one of the Chiricahuas' supervising officers, Captain Farrand Sayre, pointed out, "such a thing is possible." [34]

Ultimately the Chiricahuas would be freed, but not because their imprisonment violated the country's sense of justice.

·   ·   ·

Despite opposition from the Kiowas, Comanches, and Kiowa Apaches (their suit to block allotment is discussed in Chapter 7), the government allotted their lands surrounding Fort Sill and opened the surplus, more than two million acres, for settlement during the summer of 1901. Several towns sprang up, and the largest, Lawton, was only about ten miles from Fort Sill. As several officers had predicted, the exposure to white settlers harmed all the tribes in the area. Along with bankers, doctors, and smiths, towns offered gambling and liquor, and many Indians availed themselves of the opportunities. Within a year, the agent for the Chiricahuas wrote that the opening of the land to whites "has made whiskey easy of access to them and whiskey is the cause of nearly all the troubles and disorders that arise among them." [35]

Alcohol indirectly claimed the life of the most famous Chiricahua, Geronimo. At Fort Sill, he had initially engaged enthusiastically in farming, developing a love of watermelon. He joined the Dutch Reformed Church and taught Sunday school until he was expelled for gambling. He became a showman, often receiving consent from the army officials to leave the reservation to appear in fairs and other events, most notably Theodore Roosevelt's inaugural parade in 1905. According to some reports, the old warrior upstaged the president. Geronimo died four years later, in February 1909. According to Eugene Chihuahua, he and Geronimo obtained some whiskey, drank it, and fell asleep in the open. They awoke in a cold rain, and Geronimo had caught pneumonia. When he died, still regretting that he had not continued fighting, he was buried in the raiment of a chief and accompanied by his valuable possessions in a grave in Fort Sill, five hundred miles from his childhood home. His warriors stood guard over his grave for months, mindful of what had happened to Mangas Coloradas' remains. [36]

The opening of the lands of the Kiowa, Comanche, and Kiowa Apaches was one of the events resulting eventually in freedom for the Chiricahuas. The second was the Spanish-American War of 1898. The war revived the nation's willingness to invest in the military. In the first few years of the new century, the army shelved its plans to abandon Fort Sill and began expanding its military facilities. Captain Scott, remembering the promises that he had made in the 1890s, called this a "breach of faith" with the Chiricahuas, not to mention the other three tribes, who believed that the land they agreed to add to Fort Sill would be used by the Chiricahuas, not by soldiers. [37]

From 1902 to 1904, the army entertained a number of plans to remove the Indians from the fort, but they met with strong internal opposition. At one point, the agent in charge of the Chiricahuas wrote that he had persistently told them "that the Government would keep faith with them and that this reservation was their permanent home." Their removal, he went on, was "neither desirable, necessary, nor expedient and would constitute a crime against them." But the reprieve was short-lived.[38]

As long as Fort Sill was a cavalry base, the presence of the Indians had caused few complications. But by 1910, the army had selected the fort as an artillery training school. To use it as an artillery training base meant that nonsoldiers and livestock had to be removed. The white population in the area was enthusiastic; an expanded army post meant more business, and only the Apaches stood in the way. Suddenly the local congressional representative, Scott Ferris, became a great champion of the Chiricahuas, seeking their freedom and resettlement elsewhere, preferably in their old homelands in Arizona and New Mexico. He informed the Interior Department that he did "not want to be compelled to agree to have any part of those Indians al[l]otted on the Fort Sill reservation either now or in the future." [39]

The Apaches were not at all taken in. "All those Lawton people," one of them said, "are fighting for this land that we have got. . . . They think the Apaches are no good and say send them off to the Mountains." The Chiricahuas' fourth move in twenty-seven years nevertheless became virtually inevitable. There were only two obstacles: saying that another relocation would be in the Indians' interest was gainsaid by all the glowing reports since 1894 about how the Apaches were thriving; and a new location would have to be found.[40]

·   ·   ·

Government officials quickly set about removing the first obstacle. The newly appointed agent reported that the Chiricahuas "have gone backward, rather than forward in the way of progress" during the past decade. "Drinking is a common vice among them . . . They are not now willing laborers, as they used to be; and, excepting a small proportion of them, they could not make a living if thrown on their own resources, and deprived of the rations and the close supervision of some responsible head." Colonel (formerly Captain) Scott was sent to Fort Sill and found that his former charges had deteriorated in all respects since 1897: they no longer farmed their own fields; their pigs, turkeys, fruit trees, and other individual assets had disappeared; many were addicted to alcohol; their numbers had continued to decline. At this rate, Scott said, they would soon pass away entirely.[41]

These negative reports undoubtedly were exaggerated, just as the earlier positive ones had been. Asa Daklugie pointed out that it was government policy itself that had helped destroy incentive. "We do not have a foot of land," he said, "that does not belong to the government. The Apache cattle of which so much is said, do not belong to us. When an Apache secures money from the sale of cattle a portion of the sale goes to the Indian and the remainder is placed in an Apache fund at Washington, but during the time the Indian has this money, his rations are cut off, one month for each $35 received by him." [42]

Such reasoning was to no avail. In 1912, the secretary of the interior, who in 1909 had extolled the progress of the Chiricahuas to Congress, now reported that they "have retrograded mentally, morally, and physically. It is evident that some change should be made." [43]

.   .   .

Locating a permanent home for the Chiricahuas proved a more difficult problem than creating a disinformation campaign. While the Apaches unanimously desired their freedom, they divided over where they wanted to live. For the older tribal members especially, home lay five hundred miles away. The minority, especially younger adults with little if any memory of the old lands, wanted to remain at Fort Sill. Long afterward, Jason Betzinez wrote, "How could I be homesick when I had never had a home? Or pine for a country I never had—a country where I was only considered to be an enemy?" The younger adults were content with what they had, one of them explaining, "All of we young people want this land. . . . We don't think of anything outside of that. . . . We know that we can make a living here. . . ." [44]

Government officials began to look with interest at the Mescalero Apache Reservation in south-central New Mexico, approximately 475,000 acres of mountainous and heavily timbered land. The eastern aboriginal neighbors of the Chiricahuas, the Mescaleros were closest in language and culture, and members of the two groups had occasionally intermarried. Better yet, the Mescaleros were welcoming, voting in 1909 to let the Chiricahuas share equally in the reservation's resources. That same year, the Chiricahuas had their own vote (nonbinding on the government). Thirty-eight men voted to go to Mescalero, fourteen to stay at Fort Sill, and eighteen to return to their first reservation at Warm Springs. Colonel Scott then led a delegation of six men to Mescalero and Warm Springs. The delegation quickly eliminated Warm Springs as an option: "What a depressing sight it turned out to be! The whole country, once so fertile and green, was now entirely barren. Gravel had washed down, covering all the nice valleys and pastures, even filling up the Warm Springs, which had completely vanished." [45]

A choice between Mescalero and Fort Sill involved more than an expression of geographical preference; it meant a choice between lifestyles. The Mescalero Reservation was unallotted and the government had no plans to allot it. But for a handful of government employees and missionaries, no white people lived there. To move to Mescalero meant living among other Indians on tribally owned lands. To remain in Oklahoma meant breaking many tribal ties. The government contemplated allotting land on the boundaries of the reserve to those who remained, so long as there weren't too many of them. Representative Ferris opposed this scheme, fearing it would interfere with the army's use of the reserve, so in 1912 a new plan was devised. The government would purchase allotments of deceased members of the Kiowa, Comanche, and Kiowa Apache tribes north of the fort, and on these the Chiricahuas would, parcel by parcel, be resettled. [46]

That same year Congress began considering a proposed appropriation to pay for the relocation, which specified that Apaches who went to Mescalero would be freed from the status of prisoner of war. Those who remained in Oklahoma would continue as prisoners until allotments were found for them. [47]

Senator T. B. Catron of New Mexico expressed the attitude of the western congressional delegations: the Chiricahuas, he intoned, "belong to the savage lot or kind of Indians who were savages and who are still savages. It is true they are somewhat old, but not too old to advise and encourage others to go on the warpath, nor to lead them." Proponents of removal would not have "such a high opinion of the civilized condition of these Indians" if they "had seen or known of more men and women and children being murdered and slaughtered by these savages than these savages now number . . . had seen the times when you had to travel with an escort and go armed like an arsenal, when you parted with your friend that left on the stagecoach and said goodbye to him forever." Even if hostilities did not break out, the senator said, animosity would remain. "The descendants of those people who were murdered and killed and their relatives and friends still reside there. . . . These Indians will not meet friends anywhere." [48]

In response, advocates of the bill emphasized not the needs of the army nor the desires of Oklahomans (which clearly were the driving forces behind the plans to remove the Chiricahuas), but the injustice of further imprisonment. One representative pointed out that the Chiricahuas thirty years before had been "fighting for the same thing man has fought for ever since his creation. They were fighting in defense of their homes and trying to save their homes for their wives and children." Representative Ferris focused on those born in captivity. "It is too much to keep people more than 26 years in confinement for crimes which they never committed. It is too much to longer keep people as prisoners who were born into conditions for which they were in no manner responsible. We rail at Mexico and other countries that abuse their prisoners. I ask if we are not subjecting ourselves to just criticism to longer permit this to go on?" Eastern newspapers chipped in as well. One found a different analogy: "So in America in the twentieth century is to be found a case that is in every way comparable with those conditions which existed in England in the days when Charles Dickens as a boy was thrown into a London prison and there languished, because of debts that were owed by his father." [49]

Ultimately Congress settled the matter by punting to the executive branch: it appropriated $200,000 (later increased to $300,000) for the settlement of the Apaches on land to be selected by the secretaries of war and interior. They in turn appointed a two-person board, including Colonel Scott, which decided that only fourteen men were capable of supporting families in Oklahoma. Because this was too small a contingent to survive as a community, the board recommended in October that the entire tribe be removed to Mescalero. The Indian Rights Association immediately opposed the board's position, proclaiming that "The GREATEST FREEDOM OF CHOICE [should] be accorded all members of the tribe to determine whether they will remain on permanent homes to be selected for them in Oklahoma, or remove to Mescalero reservation, New Mexico." [50]

The secretaries rejected their own board's recommendation in favor of the Indian Rights Association's position. At a tribal council meeting in December 1912, each tribal member over age eighteen made the choice. One hundred and eighty-seven members (including minor children) would go to Mescalero, while seventy-eight would live on allotments in Oklahoma. Most older members, including all of the former chiefs and warriors, chose to go to the Southwest. Younger adults disproportionately chose to remain in Oklahoma. Of the sixty-nine members over forty-two years old (who would have been six or more when the Chiricahuas were removed to San Carlos and therefore had some memory of their ancestral homes), only seven chose to stay in Oklahoma.[51]

In April 1913, the majority of the tribe reached Mescalero and were free—as free as any reservation Indians (who as wards of the government were all still treated in many ways like minors). By March 1914, all the Oklahoma Chiricahuas had been placed on allotments, and a grim and unprecedented era in American history had ended. For twenty-seven years, every man, woman, and child of a distinct group of people had been imprisoned for the actions of a handful of their people in defending their ancestral homes. During that period, their numbers had been cut in half by disease, and those who remained were split into two groups separated by hundreds of miles. One group would live with another tribe; the other on scattered allotments with little organization to keep them together as a community. But they could all rejoice in at least two things: no longer were they prisoners of war, and never again would the Chiricahua Apaches be compelled to move.

THREE

A TRIBUNAL FOR INDIAN CLAIMS

Whatever your courts may decide and fix upon us as the amount justly
due us for the lands and rights taken from us will be as but a
leaf from the great tree of your wealth. . . .
—UNIDENTIFIED CHIEF OF THE COLVILLE AND OKANAGAN INDIANS [1]

Asa Daklugie detested the name Asa, which the people at Carlisle had
given him—he happened to be first in line when names were given out,
and as such received the first name alphabetically. Like the barbering of
his hair and the insistence that he wear trousers, he considered the re-
naming another barbarous act by the White Eyes, stripping him of his
Indian identity. Daklugie had protested vehemently in Pensacola that he
didn't want to go to Carlisle, but his uncle Geronimo had insisted. Daklugie had submitted unhappily, but as Geronimo had hoped, learned the
wiles and ways of the whites.[2]

In 1911, already acknowledged as a Chiricahua leader, Daklugie
spoke with a newspaper reporter and, proving he had learned some
things at Carlisle that his teachers might not have suspected, said he
thought his tribe should sue the United States for the value of the land
taken from the tribe in the nineteenth century. He estimated its worth at
$50 million.[3]

His estimate was not unreasonable. The United States had forcibly
removed his tribe from millions of acres, paying them nothing for it.

Now tens of thousands of settlers lived there. Vast mineral wealth had been taken out of the ground—by 1911 over $200 million of copper, gold, and silver from the boomtown of Bisbee, about $30 million of silver and other minerals from Tombstone, and millions of dollars more from districts such as Silver City, New Mexico—all once the realm of the Chiricahuas. Cattle grazed there, crops grew, timber was cut.[4]

Daklugie's idea of a lawsuit was an unfamiliar concept to his tribespeople. Before 1913, Chiricahuas had never owned parcels of land individually and at no time in their history had they ever had anything like a government with the powers to confiscate a tribal member's property. Band-wide leaders like Cochise and Mangas Coloradas had dealt primarily with external threats to their territory and way of life; most internal decisions were made by family or local groups. When disputes arose, they were resolved through mediation conducted by respected members of the community; the Chiricahua tradition did not include courts, judges, and lawyers. Geronimo had been wise to insist that his fiery young nephew go off to Carlisle.

.   .   .

Daklugie can be excused for not knowing what obstacles stood in the way of the kind of lawsuit he proposed. Most arose from an ancient doctrine inherited from English common law and shared throughout Europe—sovereign immunity, which says that a governmental body, the sovereign, cannot be sued without its consent. When the North American colonies declared their independence from England in 1776, they claimed the same immunity for their national government. Although sovereign immunity prevented citizens from going to court against the government, they had other avenues for obtaining relief. During the nation's first seventy-nine years, anyone with a claim against the government could submit it to Congress. In some instances, the Treasury Department investigated the claim, but ultimately Congress had to decide whether the claimant was entitled to payment and, if so, how much.[5]

Not surprisingly, Congress grew dissatisfied with this arrangement. Private claims consumed an inordinate amount of time, Congress lacked facilities to investigate such claims adequately, and the system encouraged bribery. As a solution, it enacted a law in 1855 creating the Court of Claims. Anyone who sought payment based on the government's supposed violation of any law or contract could sue in the new court. But the court was limited: unlike other courts, it had the power to recommend only one type of relief—the payment of money.[6]

The initial law also had a major defect. The Court of Claims didn't have outright power to award money judgments. Instead, it reported its findings to Congress and submitted a bill authorizing payment. Congress had to review the record and see if it agreed, so its workload was not substantially reduced. Before long Congress passed a new law that President Abraham Lincoln signed on March 3, 1863. This Civil War–era statute amended many aspects of the court's structure, procedures, and powers and, most important, provided that judgments of the Court of Claims were final, like the judgments of other courts.[7]

While opening the door to relief against the government more widely for most Americans, the 1863 act slammed it shut on Indians. Presumably angered that some tribes had supported the Confederacy, as well as by the raiding and warfare in which other tribes, including the Chiricahua Apaches, were engaged, Congress excluded from the new court's jurisdiction any Indian claim dependent on any treaty between a tribe and the United States. Theoretically this left open the possibility of a tribe bringing suit based on a law, regulation, or contract *other than* a treaty: only claims based on treaties were expressly precluded. But as a practical matter, the act barred judicial consideration of every Indian claim against the government, and this discriminatory bar remained in effect for eighty-three years. Until 1946, Indian tribes were in a position similar to that of all citizens before 1855—they had to ask Congress for special statutory dispensation to allow the court to hear their complaints.[8]

.   .   .

The first tribe to obtain such relief, called "special jurisdictional acts," was the Choctaw nation, one of the Five Civilized Tribes, in 1881. By 1946, numerous tribes had obtained one or more special jurisdictional acts, but most, including the Apache tribes, either did not try or were unsuccessful. The system ultimately proved unsatisfactory to both the government and the tribes. Many deficiencies plagued the system, including the same problems that had caused Congress to invent the Court of Claims in 1855 and problems unique to Indian claims.[9]

The problems began with the first step—getting the proposed special jurisdictional act before Congress. Someone had to investigate the tribe's history, assess which claims had probable merit, draft a bill that would allow the tribe to bring those claims, and find one or more legislators willing to introduce it. Most of the documents needed to buttress—or contradict—the collective memory of the tribe were located hundreds, if not thousands, of miles away in Washington, D.C. Even if a tribe could send some of its members there, few Indians were trained to read and analyze the documents, prepare a congressional bill, and make an effective presentation to Congress. They could hire lawyers to do all this, but almost no tribes had the money for attorneys' fees. And there was another catch. Although some tribes had substantial balances in the United States Treasury because, for example, the government had decided to lease portions of their reservations to white ranchers or to sell the surplus land of their reservations to white settlers, they could spend that money only for purposes that the United States deemed appropriate. Paying a lawyer to sue the government was something the government seldom deemed appropriate.

Some tribes represented themselves with the assistance—often of dubious quality—of the Office of Indian Affairs (later the Bureau of Indian Affairs). For example, in 1920 the Sioux tribe obtained a special jurisdictional act with the help of the Indian Office and then asked the prestigious law firm of Charles Evans Hughes, a former associate justice and future Chief Justice of the United States Supreme Court, to represent it on a contingent basis. That is, the firm would receive as its fee a percentage of any recovery if the tribe prevailed, but nothing if the tribe lost. After a thorough study, Hughes's firm informed the Sioux that unless their special jurisdictional act were amended in several important respects, the tribe would probably recover nothing. Unless the amendments were secured, the firm was not interested in representing the Sioux. Rather than returning to Congress as advised, the Sioux chose to hire local South Dakota attorneys who were either incapable of performing the same analysis as the New York firm had, or were blinded by the prospect of a large recovery and therefore a large fee. About twenty-five years later, when the litigation was finally concluded, Hughes's firm was vindicated: the Sioux didn't recover a penny, largely because of the objectionable statutory provisions.[10]

Other tribes tried to engage law attorneys to represent them on a contingent basis at the very beginning, to ensure a viable special jurisdictional act. But the magnitude of the task, and the risk that there would be no recovery, and thus no attorneys' fees, posed a serious obstacle. The undertaking was mammoth and the deck was stacked against the Indians. In one instance, two bands of Utes hired attorneys in August 1932 to investigate and formulate their claims on a contingent basis. Before drafting a jurisdictional bill, the Utes' lawyers had to research the facts to identify possible claims, analyze prior decisions of the courts along with prior jurisdictional acts to determine what provisions should be inserted in the bill, and line up congressional support. It took three and a half years merely for the bill to be introduced. Not many attorneys were willing or financially able to spend that much time preparing and steering legislation through Congress when they would be paid only if Congress ultimately adopted the bill, the president signed it, and the claims then were successfully litigated.[11]

Getting a bill through Congress and obtaining the president's signature was "perhaps the most disheartening of all the labors in pushing a claim." The executive branch was often responsible for the frustration. After being introduced, a jurisdictional bill, like almost any other kind of bill, was referred to Senate and House committees, which asked the executive branch for a report and recommendation on whether the bill should be passed. A negative report almost always doomed a jurisdictional bill. Issues other than the merits of the bill generally determined whether the recommendation was positive or negative. Within the space of six years, for example, the administration twice gave favorable and twice unfavorable recommendations to a virtually unchanged jurisdictional bill under which the Indians of California would present their claims collectively.[12]

Dealings with Congress could be even more frustrating. Both new and backlogged special jurisdictional bills—forty-nine in 1930, a phenomenal number considering that there were fewer than two hundred recognized tribes in the United States—always swamped the Indian affairs committees, which lacked the time and resources to consider the merits of each bill. The full Senate and House faced the same problems for those bills reported favorably by the committees. To minimize debate on bills that got committee approval, both houses began putting them on the consent calendar. This meant that the bill was passed if no member objected to it when it was called for consideration; if only one member objected, the bill was passed over until the next call of the consent calendar, but if three members objected, the bill was struck. During the 1930s and 1940s, one congressman, John Cochran of Missouri, objected to virtually every tribal bill. One attorney noticed that Cochran's "entire desk was filled with newspaper clippings, largely from Missouri newspapers, reporting that he had saved the government millions of dollars by objecting to Indian jurisdictional bills." Another claims attorney explained in 1945 that only one jurisdictional bill had passed "in the past five or six years," and that one got through only because "the watchdog [Cochran] did not happen to be on the job" when it was brought up.[13]

.   .   .

Even when the watchdog's absence permitted a tribe to negotiate the congressional gauntlet successfully and obtain a special jurisdictional act, the tribe's struggle had barely begun. On average, over twelve years elapsed between passage of the act and the final judgment from the Court of Claims. Worse, after 1920, the Indians almost always lost. Between 1886, the year of the first final judgment in an Indian claims case, and 1946, the courts decided 134 dockets involving Indian claims (many tribes divided their claims into several dockets). In only 28 did the tribes recover, and the percentage in which the tribes were successful declined over the years.[14]

A major cause of delay was also one of the primary reasons for the repeated Indian defeats. Starting in 1920, almost all the special jurisdictional acts provided that the United States could offset all sums expended for the benefit of the tribe, with a few exceptions, against the amount to which a tribe was entitled. To take advantage of the offset provisions, the government had to analyze all the expenditures it had made for a tribe over the decades. The government had retained records documenting thousands of purchases of goods and services but it had never compiled them. So, when a special jurisdictional act was passed, the General Accounting Office had to prepare one or more accounting reports reflecting all of the offsettable disbursements. Moreover, many a tribe, believing the government had mismanaged the tribe's own funds, asked the government to account for them, which required more time to prepare still more accounting reports. Litigation could not be concluded, and sometimes could not even start, until the reports were completed.[15]

To make matters even slower, until 1926 the General Accounting

TABLE 1

Recoveries by Decade in Cases
Decided Under Special Jurisdictional Acts

Decade	Number Decided	Number w/Net Recovery	Percent w/Net Recovery	Total Recovery	Average Recovery
1880–89	2	2	100	3,098,963	1,549,481
1890–99	6	6	100	2,914,042	485,674
1900–09	7	5	71	6,760,823	965,832
1910–19	7	3	43	4,345,794	620,828
1920–29	13	3	23	878,231	67,556
1930–39	60	7	12	12,963,642	216,060
1940–46	39	2	5	6,792,458	174,166
Totals	134	28	21	37,753,953	281,746

Office didn't have the funds to employ more than one person to work on such reports, and subsequently the department remained understaffed, resulting in long and damaging delays. The Choctaws obtained a special jurisdictional act in 1924 requiring them to file their claims within six years, but the GAO didn't finish its accounting until 1934. The tribe's attorneys couldn't file any claims until the reports were finished, but if they had filed after receiving the reports in 1934, the court would have dismissed the claims as untimely. The only recourse was to ask Congress for authorization to make a later filing. That was not granted until 1937, thirteen years after the original act.[16]

Offset provisions were inequitable as well as time-consuming. When disbursements were made, they were gratuitous: the tribes were not obliged to repay them. By unilaterally converting gifts to loans after the fact, the government gave new meaning to the term *Indian giver*. Many of the disbursements for the tribes were in fact for the benefit of the government itself or of non-Indians, like maintaining a government office on a reservation, or constructing a road across it. And many disbursements that directly and exclusively benefited Indian people, like purchases of food and clothing, were necessary because the government had prevented a tribe from supporting itself in its traditional manner. Finally, when a white man successfully sued the government in the Court of Claims, the government could not offset any money gratuitously spent to benefit him.[17]

The offset provisions played an important role in the string of Indian defeats, but more important were the extremely narrow interpretations that the Court of Claims and, on appeal, the Supreme Court, gave to special jurisdictional acts. The courts made a distinction between legal and moral claims. A tribe might contend, for example, that the amount the government had agreed to pay under a treaty for the cession of land was unconscionably low. This could have arisen from fraud or duress by the government's agents or from the Indians' lack of knowledge of the white man's ways. Too bad, said the courts; that gave rise only to a *moral* claim. On the other hand, a contention that the government had violated the terms of the same treaty—for example, by not paying all the treaty promised—gave rise to a *legal* claim. Very few of the jurisdictional acts, in the eyes of the courts, authorized them to consider moral claims. In fact, the Supreme Court suggested, without coming right out and saying it, that the Court of Claims might not have the power to consider moral claims, even if Congress purported to authorize it to do so. Consequently, throughout the first half of the twentieth century, the courts ducked all moral claims.[18]

As a result, claims such as that of the Creeks for loss of land by duress never saw the light of day. During the War of 1812, a Creek minority rebelled and Andrew Jackson, who over a decade later would become president, put down the rebellion with the help of the majority of Creeks. After the war, Jackson required the tribe, including those who had helped him put down the rebellion, to cede some twenty-three million acres to the United States as compensation for the uprising, for which the Creeks received no payment. Despite the obvious injustice, the courts decided that they had no jurisdiction to hear the Creek claim for compensation for the land lost. The practical impact of this and other decisions like it was to block tribes from recovering anything for many of the most egregious actions committed against them by the United States and its agents.[19]

It would be hard to imagine any more effective legislative and judicial ways to stack the deck.

.   .   .

After his inauguration as president in 1933, Franklin Roosevelt appointed Harold Ickes as secretary of the interior and John Collier as commissioner of Indian affairs. Collier, who during the 1920s had found the Pueblo Indians of New Mexico a healthy alternative to the excesses of Western culture, rejected the policies of the previous sixty years, which sought to destroy the tribal way of life by allotting tribal assets among the members of the tribe. Instead, he tried to protect, preserve, even expand tribal resources and revitalize what he perceived to be the important features of tribal cultures. Ickes and Roosevelt generally supported Collier's often controversial proposals, with the result that Roosevelt's twelve years as president were, according to Indian historian and political scientist Vine Deloria, "probably the best years in American history for Indians." [20]

An important component of Collier's plans was passage of an act that would permit Indian tribes to recover for past wrongs committed against them. In this, he had the concurrence of a growing number of government officials, legislators, and private attorneys who thought the special jurisdictional act system should be replaced. Claims awards, Collier thought, would add to the tribal assets and reflect the country's renewed commitment to treating Indians fairly. Ickes agreed; in 1935 he wrote that the "existing system is entirely too slow, cumbersome, and expensive, both to the Indians and to the Government. Practically everyone familiar with this situation earnestly advocates a more speedy, prompt, and effective method of settling those claims found to be just." The assistant solicitor of the Interior Department added that if "meritorious claims are to be almost automatically defeated, there is not much point in continuing the expensive farce of providing the claimants a day in court." [21]

Like many of Collier's programs, this one ran into trouble in Congress. The first bill to replace the special jurisdictional system with a specialized body to consider tribal claims was introduced in 1930, yet it took sixteen long years before both houses of Congress passed and the president signed the act creating the Indian Claims Commission. During those years, the function conceived for this proposed body changed dramatically. Early bills called for an "Indian Claims Court" that would attempt to mediate the negotiated settlement of all Indian claims. But this court would have been toothless, unable to force negotiation in good faith, and unable to decide any claims the two parties could not settle. These bills didn't come close to passage.[22]

Between 1934 and 1940, a series of bills was introduced, calling for an Indian Claims Commission with power to investigate all Indian claims, legal and moral, and to make recommendations to Congress about their resolution. These proceeded somewhat further toward enactment. The Senate twice passed this kind of bill, once in 1935 and again in 1937. The congressional session expired before the House of Representatives could consider the 1935 bill, and the House rejected the 1937 bill, opponents arguing that it would "open up the floodgates and siphon money out of the United States Treasury." One representative warned, "You can disregard millions and think of billions if the Indian claims ever get in the hands of this commission." Thus the efforts to create an investigatory and advisory commission also failed.[23]

At least one Indian claims attorney, Ernest Wilkinson, welcomed the defeat of these bills. He pointed out that Congress would still have to decide what action, if any, to take once the Commission made its recommendations. Such a commission, he feared, might simply add another hurdle for tribal claimants. President Roosevelt apparently shared this view. He opposed a bill in 1941 but commented that his attitude might be different if "Indian claims could be disposed of with finality through the establishment of an Indian Claims Commission." [24]

The outbreak of World War II largely stymied further consideration of Indian claims legislation until 1945. As the war wound down to a victorious conclusion, new Indian claims commission bills were introduced. Unlike the prewar bills, they proposed a tribunal that would hear and determine Indian claims. For this and other reasons, they posed a greater risk of opening the floodgates than the prewar bills. Nevertheless, one of the bills was amended, passed by both houses of Congress, and signed into law by President Harry Truman.[25]

·   ·   ·

Why the turnabout? To senators and representatives, one of the most, if not the most, important arguments in favor of the bills was the belief that passage would free them from the continual drain on their time and energy posed by Indians' repeated requests for special jurisdictional acts. But that argument had existed before the war, and was in itself insufficient to bring reform. Several factors tipped the balance.[26]

First, Indians had become widely publicized, decorated war heroes. A higher percentage of Indians than of any other ethnic minority joined the United States armed forces in World War II—about twenty-five thousand in all. A Pima was among those immortalized raising the flag at Iwo Jima, and a group of mostly Navajo "Code Talkers" transmitted radio messages in a code that the Japanese could never break. Newspaper and magazine articles trumpeted the heroic feats of the Indian warriors. A grateful Congress considered the new version of the bill. A House report proclaimed its desire to remove the barriers that kept from the courts a people who "have contributed voluntarily to the service of the Nation in a measure far out of proportion to their numbers in population, who have won an amazing number of decorations for military valor and sacrifice, and who have contributed to our war bond drives in a measure wholly disproportionate to their limited economic resources." On the floor of the House, Representative Francis Case of South Dakota said, "[N]o racial group in America showed greater loyalty to the Nation in her hour of trial during the late war than did the American Indian, and the Indian citizens of this country are entitled to an accounting, a settlement of their claims. . . . It is particularly due the Indians who have been wards of the Government, and who, when the testing time came, proved themselves staunch, true and courageous warriors for the cause of the United States." [27]

Besides such noble sentiments, proponents of the bill could (a bit ignobly) couch their appeals not only to those who believed in strengthening tribal organizations but also to those who sought to terminate federal responsibilities for Indians. Supporters of termination, like supporters of allotment before them, believed that individual Indians should assimilate into the dominant culture. Only ending special programs for Indians would free them, the terminators thought. Indeed, congressional advocates of termination had so grown in influence during the Roosevelt years that Collier, who made no secret of his opposing views, could no longer effectively represent the Bureau of Indian Affairs in Congress and resigned as commissioner in 1945. In appealing to the advocates of termination, proponents of the Indian claims bill could argue that once a tribe was paid damages for its claims, or learned that its claims were without merit, many of the more "progressive" members would dissolve their tribal relationships, leave the reservation, and seek their fortunes in the cities. This would in turn permit the Bureau of Indian Affairs budget to be slashed by at least 50 percent, and so the passage of the act would actually save the government money.[28]

A third new factor in the passage of the Indian Claims Commission Act was the cooperation of two men, Felix Cohen and Ernest Wilkinson. Both worked to fashion a bill as favorable to the Indians as possible without alienating congressional support, and then shepherded the bill through Congress. Though sharing the same dream, the men had dissimilar backgrounds.

Felix Cohen, the son of philosopher Morris R. Cohen, was a New York Jew who, by the age of twenty-six, had earned a law degree from Columbia and a doctorate in philosophy from Harvard and published a book, *Ethical Systems and Legal Ideas,* that established him as one of the leading legal philosophers of the twentieth century. He had worked in private law practice for only one year when, in 1933, he accepted a short-term position as associate solicitor of the Department of the Interior to draft the legislation that Collier introduced to overhaul federal Indian policy. The one-year appointment eventually stretched to fourteen. During his tenure, he became deeply interested in the rights of Indians, and he and his wife, both outdoors people, visited many reservations and became well known to Indians. Of more lasting impact, during this time he practically invented the field of federal Indian law with the publication of a *Handbook of Federal Indian Law.*[29]

Before the publication of the *Handbook* (in reality, a lengthy treatise), federal Indian law consisted of an unorganized and seemingly unorganizable collection of court decisions, treaties, federal statutes, administrative rulings, and unwritten practices. Cohen brought order to the chaos in a manner that served to further the rights and powers of Indians. The *Handbook* quickly acquired enormous influence: the Supreme Court cited it repeatedly in deciding Indian law cases, and Justice Felix Frankfurter wrote that it was "an acknowledged guide for the Supreme Court in Indian litigation." Based on his unrivaled scholarship, Cohen's testimony and opinions concerning the Indian Claims Commission carried great weight with Congress.[30]

Ernest Wilkinson, a Mormon from Utah, did not match Cohen's intellectual record, but quickly gained great influence in Congress with his thorough preparation and intelligent presentations. As he was winning over one originally hostile Senate committee with his testimony in 1940, a Wisconsin senator congratulated the Menominees of his state for "selecting a man of your ability to represent them." Another senator remarked that "The presentation he is making is one of the most able I have ever heard made to a committee of Congress." Unlike Cohen, Wilkinson was in private practice and in 1945 represented seven tribes.[31]

Individually and jointly, the two men shaped the bill at every stage of its progress through Congress. As originally introduced, it was largely Cohen's product, after a series of meetings between representatives of the Interior and Justice departments. Both Cohen and Wilkinson testified before the House Indian Affairs Committee. During the hearings, Cohen revised the bill once to incorporate some of Wilkinson's recommendations, and then, at the suggestion of members of the committee, the two men spent two days in conference working out a series of amendments. Wilkinson later recalled, "The redraft decided upon was somewhat of a compromise between our views. Generally, if either insisted that a provision remain in the bill, it was left in." The committee approved this compromise version unanimously, and Cohen, with contributions from Wilkinson, drafted the report from the committee to the entire House of Representatives that accompanied the bill. The two men had written and planned well. The House, deathbed of earlier Indian claims commission bills and of most special jurisdictional bills, passed the proposed legislation, without any dissent, on May 20, 1946.[32]

The bill went to the Senate Indian Affairs Committee where the Justice Department proposed a number of weakening amendments. The chairman of the committee conferred with Cohen, Wilkinson, and a representative from Justice, and Wilkinson consistently took the stronger position in opposition to the Justice Department amendments, while Cohen sought an intermediate ground. Through these efforts, they persuaded the chairman to moderate some of the amendments, but the bill that emerged from the Senate committee still would have considerably reduced the Indians' chances of significant success before the proposed tribunal. The Senate passed the bill without further amendment on July 17, 1946.[33]

It then went to a conference committee composed of members of both houses to resolve the differences between the two bills. Wilkinson wrote memoranda about many of the crucial differences and ultimately delivered to each conferee a booklet identifying each disagreement and his proposed resolutions, which he later was told became the "bible" of the conferees. Meanwhile Cohen backed up Wilkinson orally. In all but one instance, the conferees adopted Wilkinson's recommendations verbatim or nearly so. The version of the bill that emerged was as favorable as that the House had passed two months before. The Senate approved it on July 27, the House two days later.[34]

Victory was not yet assured, as President Truman placed budgetary concerns above justice for Indians. Cohen drafted a letter for the secretary of the interior's signature, pointing out that, except for the modest expense of the commission itself, the measure would have little budgetary impact until 1952–53 at the earliest, because it would be "practically impossible" to decide any claims in favor of a tribe until then. The letter apparently succeeded. Truman signed the bill into law on August 13, 1946, and his office released a statement, also drafted by Cohen: "I am glad to sign my name to a measure . . . which removes a lingering discrimination against our First Americans and gives them the same opportunities that our laws extend to all other American citizens to vindicate their property rights and contracts in the courts against violations by the Federal Government itself. . . . With this final settlement of all outstanding claims which this measure ensures, Indians can take their place without special handicap or special advantage in the economic life of our nation and share fully in its progress." [35]

Members of Congress had an even higher sense of the legislation's importance. One proclaimed it "the most constructive piece of Indian legislation . . . during the past quarter of a century." A second said it would give Indians "their day in the sun," and a third, the most optimistic of all, declared that it would "mean the dawn of a new era for the American Indian." [36]

·   ·   ·

Were these paeans realistic? The passage of the Indian Claims Commission Act certainly improved the conditions under which Indians brought claims against the government. It gave the Commission jurisdiction to "hear and determine claims of any Indian tribe, band, or other identifiable group of American Indians residing within the territorial limits of the United States or Alaska" that accrued on or before August 13, 1946. No more would a tribe have to struggle to investigate its claims and formulate a bill to lobby through Congress, or find someone else to do it. No more would a single legislator be able to block a tribe's right to present its claims before a court. No more would Congress allow one tribe to sue and not another, or impose more limited rights on one tribe than on another because the supporters of one tribe had greater influence in Congress. All tribes could now have their claims heard by a commission that, like a court, would have the power to decide. As for claims arising after August 13, 1946, the act gave the tribes the same access to the Court of Claims as other Americans enjoyed.[37]

On the other hand, the act did little by itself to address the old bugaboo: protracted delay. The act said claims had to be filed before the Commission within five years from the Commission's formation, or they would be forever barred. The act gave the Commission five years after that to decide all the claims. But it did not provide for more lawyers for the Justice Department to defend the claims or more accountants for the General Accounting Office. Nor did it provide for staffing the Commission: Congress would have to provide adequate resources each year if it wanted the Commission to have any chance of meeting its ten-year deadline.[38]

Given the failure to address the causes of delay, the timetable, unsurprisingly, proved totally unrealistic. The Commission's life would be extended five times, in 1957, 1962, 1967, 1972, and 1977. The first four extensions would be for five years apiece, and the last for about eighteen months. In total, the Commission would endure, not for ten years, but for over thirty-one, until September 30, 1978. And even then, its work was not complete. When the Commission expired, it transferred jurisdiction over about 65 undecided dockets (of some 610 it started with) to the Court of Claims.[39]

While the act's most important omissions concerned its failure to address the causes of delay, its most important provisions were those defining the types of claims the Commission could consider and the types of expenditures the United States could offset against the tribes' claims. It would do little good, after all, to create a special commission if it regularly threw out Indian claims as barred by the statute of limitations or, like the Court of Claims until 1946, as beyond its jurisdiction. It also would accomplish little if the Commission imposed offsets that obliterated any recovery. In sum, the sixteen years of effort to obtain a special tribunal for Indian claims would be wasted if more than 90 percent of the decisions were adverse to the tribes, as had happened between 1930 and 1946.

Normally a statute of limitations bars individuals from filing lawsuits unless they do so within a specified time after being injured. For example, claims against the government for the confiscation of property generally must be brought within six years of the taking. But Indian tribes had not been allowed to sue without a special jurisdictional act, and to limit them to wrongs committed within the past six years seemed unfair. Before the House Indian Affairs Committee, Cohen had quoted the words of an Indian leader: "We are told that you . . . have said that our claims are too old. Who made them old; who delayed the settlement? . . . We cannot bring suit against you in your courts. If settlement with us has been delayed, it has been due to your own fault. . . . Will you take advantage of your own fault? Will you say, I delayed a long time settling with my children; now because I delayed so long I will not settle with them at all? . . . We cannot believe that you . . . meant to take advantage of the poor Indian, and refuse to pay him because of your own delay." [40]

The argument proved irrefutable. The act waived any statute of limitations defense by the government. A tribe could sue for any wrong that had been committed by the United States since the creation of the country in 1776.

The act also gave the Commission broad jurisdiction over the types of claims it could hear and decide. It not only gave the Commission the power to resolve all claims based on established legal principles, but also contained two provisions resolving the moral claim/legal claim problem. First, the act expressly instructed the Commission to decide claims based on contentions that treaties, contracts, or agreements would not have been entered but for the government's fraud, duress, or unconscionable actions. Although courts generally did not assert the power to revise treaties on these grounds, treaties are similar to contracts, and by 1946, many courts regularly used these same doctrines to invalidate or revise contracts that would not have been entered into but for one party's wrongdoing or mistake. Thus, the provision for revision of treaties, contracts, and agreements seemed unexceptionable, merely ensuring that Indian tribes could recover for the same types of claims for which other Americans could recover, even though Indians' contracts with the United States frequently were denominated treaties. Under this provision of the act, a claim like the Creeks' arising from the treaty that Andrew Jackson had forced them to enter, which the Court of Claims had dismissed as outside its jurisdiction because it was moral rather than legal, was within the jurisdiction of the Commission. [41]

The other means of resolving the moral claim/legal claim dilemma, however, set off alarm bells in the Justice Department. It allowed the Commission to compensate Indian tribes for "claims based upon fair and honorable dealings that are not recognized by any existing rule of law or equity." Congress in effect said that the Commission could not duck any moral claim. The Commission had to impose liability against the government if it had harmed the tribes by acting unfairly or dishonorably. This special provision, proponents explained, was necessary because of the unique nature of the relationship between the United States and the tribes over the years. Indians depended on the United States to protect them, and the United States repeatedly claimed it was acting in the tribes' best interest. Any unfair behavior by the government violated the trust that the United States had forced the tribes to place in it.[42]

The act did not explain the standards by which the Commission should evaluate fairness and honor. But evaluate them it must. As the signing statement Cohen drafted for President Truman said: "This bill makes perfectly clear what many men and women, here and abroad, have failed to recognize, that in our transactions with the Indian tribes we have at least since the Northwest Ordinance of 1787 set for ourselves the standard of fair and honorable dealings, pledging respect for all Indian property rights. . . . It would be a miracle if in the course of these dealings—the largest real estate transaction in history—we had not made some mistakes and occasionally failed to live up to the precise terms of our treaties and agreements with some 200 tribes. But we stand ready to submit all such controversies to the judgment of impartial tribunals. We stand ready to correct any mistakes we have made." [43]

As for the pesky problem of offsets, the act in general allowed the Commission to deduct only those offsets that would be allowable in suits brought by non-Indians. If the entire course of dealings between the government and a tribe in good conscience warranted additional offsets, however, the Commission could deduct amounts spent gratuitously, except for certain types of expenditures, such as those made to run the government agency or for "other administrative, educational, health or highway purposes," which were barred as offsets in all cases. Granting the Commission the power to allow offsets against Indians that couldn't be offset against claims by non-Indians, if justified by the entire course of dealings, was the flip side of the provision letting tribes recover based on the government's failure to act fairly and honorably. Both provisions recognized the unique and complex nature of the relationship between the government and the tribes. Both, however, were ill defined. Presumably, under the entire course of dealings provision, if the Commission determined that the government's conduct toward a tribe as a whole was exemplary, even though in one or two instances it may have injured the tribe, the government would be entitled to assert offsets against the amount awarded to the tribe that the government could not claim against non-Indians. The Commission, or the Court of Claims or Supreme Court on appeal, would have to formulate the standards.[44]

·   ·   ·

If the goal of Congress and people like Cohen and Wilkinson was to give the tribes a fair chance to win money for past wrongs, they could take great pride in their accomplishment. Most of the major problems of the special jurisdictional act regime had been successfully addressed. But the debates over the Indian Claims Commission Act contained surprisingly little about the underlying wisdom of the goal. And the goal could have been questioned on several grounds:

Was it wise to create an entity that would use Anglo-American dispute resolution techniques to mete out justice instead of one that mediated claims as the Indians had done for disputes among tribal members?

Was it wise for this new entity to make awards based on past wrongs rather than present needs?

Was it wise to allow the Commission to award only money for wrongs done instead of restoring land or ordering that necessary services be provided?

Was it wise to ask the appointed commissioners to deal with the unique types of claims that the tribes would bring, including claims alleging that the government had acted unfairly or dishonorably, without requiring that they have any experience with Indian affairs or providing standards to guide their decision-making?

Only the proceedings of the Commission would provide the answers.

FOUR

PROMISED LANDS

There is no ghost so difficult to lay as the ghost of an injury.
—ALEXANDER SMITH[1]

All the superintendents of the Mescalero Reservation during the 1920s and 1930s agreed that Sam Kenoi was an agitator and troublemaker. Born in the early 1880s, Kenoi was orphaned when his parents succumbed to the diseases at the Mount Vernon Barracks in Alabama. He was raised by a prominent couple—a son of Mangas Coloradas and a daughter of Victorio. Like Asa Daklugie, who would become a political rival, Kenoi was sent to Carlisle, but he hated the regimented schooling and ultimately was allowed to return to Fort Sill. In 1913, he chose to go to Mescalero rather than stay in Oklahoma, and after serving in the American forces in World War I, his political activities began.[1]

To the consternation of the superintendents, he bypassed channels and contacted congressmen and White House officials directly about grievances great and small, often on behalf of self-appointed groups that had no standing in the tribal organization. In the late 1920s, shortly after he lobbied a congressman to distribute individually some of the moneys credited to the Mescalero tribe's account in the wake of a severe drought, Congress—lo and behold—enacted a law authorizing such a distribution. Deservedly or not, Kenoi claimed full credit.[2]

One of Kenoi's causes was close to an obsession. For over a decade,

he lobbied to have federal funds appropriated to compensate the Chiricahuas for their twenty-seven years of imprisonment. In the process, he
competed with scores of other tribes for the attention of a frequently
unsympathetic Congress.[3]

.   .   .

The Mescalero Reservation afforded fertile ground for the Chiricahuas
who had elected to live there. Here, in nearly half a million acres, were
mountains to pray from, rich grama grass as high as a cow's belly, and
clear streams. Deer were plentiful and, in the higher ground, elk. The
Mescaleros had already welcomed the remnants of the Lipan Apaches
and, briefly, the Jicarillas until a reservation was established for them in
the northern reaches of New Mexico.

The Mescalero Reservation also soon proved a fertile ground for
discontent. When the Chiricahuas from Fort Sill disembarked from the
railroad at Mescalero in April 1913, they discovered that the government
agents were not prepared to receive them. Instead, they were invited to
roam the reservation and find a place where they could establish their
own village, build houses, and run cattle. According to Asa Daklugie, the
Chiricahuas were aware that the Jicarillas had been a troublesome presence, outnumbering the Mescaleros. So the Chiricahuas hoped to live
away from their hosts, most of whom were clustered around the Indian
agency in the town of Mescalero. Daklugie had noted on an early trip
that the Mescaleros still dwelled in tepees and brush huts, living much as
most Apaches had some three decades before. And while the Chiricahuas still had plenty of bile and spite for the White Eyes, their long period of contact with them had brought changes. Many found houses
comfortable, and had adopted the White Eyes' standards of cleanliness.
They found such things lacking among their hosts, who also raised
sheep, which the Chiricahuas—by now, cattlemen—disdained. Other
small cultural differences separated them, like the elaborate, courteous
diction used by the Chiricahuas with their in-laws.

The Chiricahuas selected a location called Whitetail, in a narrow
canyon about eighteen rugged miles from the agency and forty miles
from the nearest off-reservation town. They spent their first winter there
in tents (except for Chato, the old scout, who, knowing he wasn't welcome, established a lonely camp some ten miles east of Mescalero). It

was the coldest winter the Chiricahuas had known, and they looked forward to the houses the government was supposed to build.

Most of them had a long wait. The delay was attributable in part to New Mexico's Senator Albert Fall, still a decade from disgrace in connection with the Teapot Dome scandal. Ever hostile to anything Apache, he sought to have the entire Mescalero Reservation abandoned and made into a national park that, conveniently, would abut his ranch, but even after Fall's campaign was defeated, the establishment of the Chiricahuas proceeded slowly and incompetently. The government constructed two-room homes for each family, "of lumber that went from the standing tree to the carpenters' hands in a month's time, so green that the sap oozed out with every nail driven into it." As the lumber dried out and shrank, "the snow in winter and the rain in summer bl[e]w and leak[ed] into [them]." Three wells were dug for a community spread along the canyon for six to seven miles, but during much of the first decade only one of the wells worked. Consequently, the Chiricahuas were forced "to haul water in barrels and tanks for domestic use and for stock a distance of from ¼ to five miles. . . ." [4]

Human effort could remedy housing and water deficiencies; it could not alter geographical constraints. The Chiricahuas had been trained in Oklahoma to be farmers and ranchers, and a few had also learned crafts. But they discovered that Whitetail, at seven thousand feet, had a growing season too short and undependable to sustain consistent yields in oats, their only cash crop. The agency started a cattle herd during their early years on the reservation, like the one at Fort Sill, but it was too small to produce the kind of income or jobs they had enjoyed in Oklahoma. The distance from towns and rugged topography also largely prevented them from selling their crafts or marketing whatever oats they were able to grow. [5]

Predictably, the Chiricahuas were soon destitute. When they arrived at Mescalero, their accounts totaled about $185,000, mostly from the sale of the Fort Sill cattle herd, which had been marketed rather than transported to Mescalero because of the fear of tick-borne Texas fever. By 1919, the Chiricahuas had invested about $26,000 in livestock, primarily sheep, and purchased about $13,000 in bonds. Only about $7,000 remained in their accounts. In 1918, a business committee composed of Asa Daklugie, Duncan Balatchu, and Eugene Chihuahua wrote that "some of our number are existing upon less food than white people feed to their dogs." The lack of work also meant idleness and boredom. The committee complained that there "are no means of employment or any regular work to be given to us. We just barely get along though we are trying our best to farm and find work in order to live." [6] To relieve the impoverished Indians the committee tried to obtain money to be distributed per capita.

Conditions improved somewhat during the 1920s. The account maintained in the United States Treasury for the benefit of all the Indians of the reservation, misleadingly named "Indian Moneys Proceeds of Labor" (IMPL), began to swell with revenues paid by a white timber company for the privilege of cutting trees on the reservation and by white ranchers to graze their stock on the Mescalero lands. Individuals for whom cattle or sheep had been purchased were credited with income from the sale of steers, lambs, and wool. Yet for most of the Chiricahuas and other Apaches, especially those who had not adopted the individualistic Anglo values of savings and investment and continued to share generously with kin and neighbors according to traditional Apache values, life remained precarious. And of course, conditions worsened again during the Great Depression.[7]

.   .   .

With empty hours and plenty of unhappiness, some of the Chiricahuas at Mescalero wrote petitions and organized to try to obtain better conditions. About eighteen months after arriving at Mescalero, nineteen adult males, who identified themselves as members of the Warm Springs Apaches, asked the commissioner of Indian affairs to be allowed to return to Warm Springs, where they "were born and raised." A year later, three of the signatories wrote to the commissioner again, this time asking to be returned to Oklahoma and allotted near the other Fort Sill Apaches.[8]

The efforts to relocate reflected the Chiricahuas' feelings that they were not fully welcome on the reservation. The Chiricahuas spoke a different dialect, dressed differently from the Mescaleros, and lived in a distinct district of the reservation; exiled from their traditional home, some Chiricahuas, called locally the "Fort Sills," felt they were treated like poor relations. At the same time, they noted, the Mescaleros saw Chiricahua houses and demanded houses for themselves; they saw Chiricahua cattle and the revenues from them and demanded cattle, too. Indeed, some of the Mescaleros complained that the Chiricahuas were "uppity." But such problems would soon abate in the most potent of cultural solvents. The combination of the old taboo against marrying relatives and the small size of the Chiricahua marriage pool made it difficult to find acceptable Chiricahua mates, so as the years passed intermarriages were welcomed. Socializing was inevitable at the agency trading post. Many Chiricahuas came to live among the Mescaleros near the agency, while others married Mescalero or Lipan Apaches who moved to Whitetail—Apache custom still dictating that males move into their wives' villages.

Along with the increasing geographical and biological integration came increasing political integration. In the late 1920s, the Mescaleros, Lipans, and Chiricahuas elected a ten-member tribal business committee that included Chiricahuas such as Daklugie as well as members of the other tribes. The reservation superintendent was largely responsible for the formation of the business committee, which he used to undermine the authority of Kenoi, who had organized a committee without the superintendent's blessing or a formal election.[9]

During the 1920s, a number of superintendents established Indian councils. To the northwest on the Navajo reservation, a tribal council was set up to rubber-stamp contracts permitting white firms to extract minerals from reservation lands. These groups had no real powers; no congressional statutes authorized their establishment and a superintendent could dissolve such a committee if it became troublesome. Superintendents hoped that the committees would facilitate reservation management by their subservient acquiescence to government policies or, as at Mescalero, by excluding from apparent authority anyone (like Kenoi) who was more difficult to control.[10]

The status of many of the councils changed in the 1930s. One of John Collier's most controversial proposals as commissioner of Indian affairs involved giving Indian tribes the right to organize by adopting a constitution and bylaws. Congress adopted the proposed legislation in modified form, which in 1934 came to be known as the Wheeler-Howard Act or the Indian Reorganization Act. Although prior approval of the secretary of the interior was required before a tribal government formed under the act could take any significant action, at least the superintendents no longer had the power to dissolve the government or modify its powers; only the tribal members, or Congress, could do that.[11]

Despite this legislative effort to empower tribes in a limited manner, the Anglo-American method of adopting a constitution and bylaws was utterly foreign to the tribes. Only a few, such as the Five Civilized Tribes, had adopted constitutions and formal political democracy after contact with Anglo-Americans. And although the Indian Reorganization Act did not prescribe the form that the constitutions should take, Collier's office provided sample drafts to the tribes establishing a tripartite form of government—executive, legislature, and judiciary—modeled on the federal and state constitutions, with little regard for tribal traditions and beliefs.

The Indians on the Mescalero Reservation quickly embraced the Indian Reorganization Act and adopted a constitution and bylaws, which were approved by the secretary of the interior in 1936. The documents established the Mescalero Tribe, composed of Mescaleros, Lipans, and Chiricahuas, to be ruled by a ten-person business committee. The Indians thus elected to subsume their separate tribal identities into one new legal entity, which bore the name of the largest tribe.

After two decades on the reservation, the Chiricahuas had voluntarily done what many decades of warfare, years of imprisonment and wayward government policy, along with the attrition brought about by disease, had not accomplished—the elimination of the Chiricahuas as a distinct tribal and cultural unit.

.   .   .

Accepting the denomination as Mescalero did not, however, mean that the Chiricahuas as a lineage had lost all influence. When the tribal business committee held its first meeting on April 1, 1936, Daklugie was elected its president. Neither did the merger mean the erasure of tribal memories. The Chiricahuas passed down stories of their prereservation years and of their imprisonment in Florida, Alabama, and Oklahoma. They also nurtured the dream of exorcising the ghosts of that imprisonment through compensation from the federal government. Sam Kenoi was at the center of efforts to make that dream a reality.

During the late 1920s and early 1930s, Kenoi worked with a Chippewa Indian from Minnesota named William Madison, who acted as a lobbyist for several tribes. Believing that the claims were not appropriate for a court determination, Madison instead told the Chiricahuas that he would work for passage of a bill that would compensate them for each day that they were imprisoned—he bandied the figure of two dollars per day, which, for the few who survived the whole twenty-seven years of imprisonment, would mean compensation of about $20,000. To pay for Madison's efforts, an unknown number of tribal members paid him five dollars per year out of their scarce funds—payments that were probably illegal because the secretary of the interior had not approved any contract between the Indians and Madison. The government, however, overlooked this, and in 1932, Madison and Kenoi cleared the first hurdle toward obtaining congressional relief: Senator Elmer Thomas of Oklahoma introduced a bill authorizing the secretary of the treasury to pay $25,000 to each of 171 named tribal members for damages caused by their years of confinement.[12]

The Hoover administration, however, issued an unfavorable report, which sidestepped the issue of whether the Apaches had been justly imprisoned and instead advanced the non sequitur argument that no appropriation should be made because of the amounts already spent in relocating the Chiricahuas in 1913. Congress adjourned in 1932 before the bill could be considered. During the next few years, a bill to compensate the Chiricahuas was not even introduced because Kenoi and Madison had a falling out in early 1933, when Madison and Daklugie worked on the prisoner-of-war bill. Kenoi considered that a betrayal: Daklugie was one of "Geronimo's bandits" who were justly punished for "the devilments which they did in [18]85 & 86." Kenoi believed that the Warm Springs Chiricahuas, and especially those who served as scouts, were the ones entitled to compensation.[13]

He nevertheless continued to work throughout the 1930s to obtain passage of a bill compensating the prisoners of war, and at his urging, Senator Thomas introduced yet another bill in 1939. Without a tribal advocate in Washington, however, the bill was dead. After 1939, the Mescalero Chiricahuas, like many other tribes, had no chance for relief. The United States financed and then entered World War II, and young Apache men enlisted in numbers disproportionate to their overall population.[14]

· · ·

In adjusting to the white world, the Chiricahuas who remained in Oklahoma faced somewhat different challenges. Their efforts were initially hampered by a similar bugaboo: the government's failure to live up to its obligations. Colonel Scott had promised in 1912 that they would receive food and clothing during their first year until they could raise their first crops. He also led them to believe that they would each receive an allotment of 160 acres of farmland.

During 1912 and 1913, Congress appropriated $300,000 to resolve the Chiricahuas' predicament, but it proved insufficient to move the majority to Mescalero and purchase allotments and rations for those remaining in Oklahoma. Faced with the monetary shortfall, the Indian Office decided to spend $3,000 for each head of family remaining in Oklahoma and $2,000 for others in purchasing allotments or constructing improvements on them. With a few exceptions, these sums bought tracts of only eighty acres and most of the parcels were only partly suitable for raising crops.

When possible, the government tried to mitigate the effects of the small allotments by purchasing two adjoining parcels for family members, creating a 160-acre homestead. Nevertheless, as many white farmers in the area discovered in the 1920s, a 160-acre farm was not sufficient to support a family. Further, while the government stretched out its $300,000 by cutting the expected farm sizes, there was still not enough to go around. For more than ten years, thirteen of the eighty-four Chiricahuas who decided to stay (twelve of them being minors) did not receive allotments. Given the reduced size of the allotments, and the delay in allotting 15 percent of the group, the government had placed serious obstacles on the very path the government itself had wanted the Indians to pursue: self-sufficiency through farming.[15]

Further imperiling the Chiricahuas' chances to succeed as farmers was the government's failure to provide the food, clothing, and other necessities during their first year, as promised. According to an Oklahoma congressman, this failure forced many to borrow during their first year, and some were unable to dig their way out of debt. Not until 1923 did Congress try to make amends by appropriating additional money for allotments for the thirteen neglected Chiricahuas and to pay $144 (the assumed cost of one year of rations at twelve dollars per month) to each of the eighty-four individuals (or their heirs) who had opted for allotments.[16]

The Chiricahuas' allotments, which covered a total of 6,400 acres or ten square miles, were scattered over an area exceeding 1,000 square miles—hardly conducive to maintaining contact with one another. The scattered allotments fell under the jurisdiction of the Kiowa Agency, which, in 1920, administered the affairs of some 4,500 Indians living on allotments distributed over about 7,000 square miles, an area about the size of Connecticut and Rhode Island combined. Unlike the Chiricahuas at Mescalero, the Oklahoma contingent inevitably received little administrative attention.[17]

·   ·   ·

From the standpoint of Indian cultural integrity, allotment, which was the dominant federal Indian policy between 1880 and 1920, was a disaster second only to the original onslaught of Europeans. In 1880 Indians held about 155 million acres of land; a half century later, their holdings had been reduced to about 65 million acres, or 40 percent.[18]

The disappearance of their land base was only the most obvious blow. The stated goal of the allotment policy was to transform Indians into self-sufficient farmers independent of their tribes. At least in theory, the government would own each parcel in trust until the allottee was judged competent to manage his or her own affairs, and not get swindled out of the landholding.

In practice, the policy was seriously flawed. It was premised on the erroneous assumption that essentially all Native Americans had the inclination and knowledge to be farmers; the assumption was not even true for white Americans. Even for those who did possess the necessary desire and skills, the policy often failed. Farmers typically borrow during the growing season and pay back their obligations at harvest time. As long as the government held Indians' land in trust, they could not mortgage it to obtain the money to carry on farming operations. Worse still, allotments frequently became virtually unusable because the estates of Indians who died intestate, as most did, were divided among all familial heirs. Within a generation or two, scores of individuals had interests in a single allotment, making it difficult if not impossible to decide which heir would live on the land or farm it. Indian agents, under pressure to reduce ration rolls and to produce statistics showing that tribal members were benefiting from their lands, frequently leased allotments to white farmers, ranchers, and miners and paid the proceeds to the owners' accounts—if they could determine the owners of the allotments with multiple heirs. Thus, in 1922 well over 90 percent of the allotted acreage in the Kiowa Reservation was leased to whites. And during Woodrow Wilson's administration, when the government declared large numbers of Native Americans competent to manage their own affairs, the allottees overwhelmingly sold their land, dissipated the proceeds, and ended up landless, often urban, paupers.[19]

But by and large, allotment worked well for the Chiricahuas who soon came to be known as the Fort Sill Apaches (further dissolution of the Chiricahua identity). As a group, they succeeded better in the white man's world than did most other Indians. In 1927, the superintendent of the Kiowa Agency said that they were "in the lead" in being able to support themselves. It was more than a matter of good work habits learned in the prisoner-of-war era. One Chiricahua remembers, "The Kiowas and Comanches and Kiowa-Apaches lived around us and we went to school with them. They were still very, very Indian in their ways. As far as we were concerned, they did a lot of things that were considered immoral, and they were dirty. They had scabies and lice. There were a few, but not many, who were clean and neat, so we really didn't associate with them." [20]

The Chiricahua allottees succeeded in the white man's world largely because of their self-selective nature. Those who chose to remain in Oklahoma and accept allotments were generally more willing to farm or otherwise engage in the Anglo economy, more Christianized, better educated, and less tied to the tribal group than those who chose to return to New Mexico. Exemplifying the attitude of many of the Fort Sill Apaches, Jason Betzinez wrote of those who returned to New Mexico:

> Eventually all these Indians, like other reservation Indians, will reach a higher state of culture. But my point is, they still are *reservation* Indians. As long as the Indian remains on the reservation he will develop only very slowly. He is, if anything, too well taken care of today. He doesn't learn to stand on his own feet, to earn his living entirely by his own efforts. The future of the Indian lies in getting out and settling down like any other American citizen, in supporting himself by agriculture, a trade, or a profession. All over the world, the tribal life is disappearing. It is archaic. As I have said many times, man must earn his bread and butter by the sweat of his brow. I have done it. So can the other Indians, and the sooner they start the quicker will they attain a more satisfying and useful life.[21]

The relatively successful acculturation of most of the Chiricahuas in Oklahoma did not mean that they dissolved their common heritage. As at Mescalero, the ties at first were largely informal. Families gathered on weekends, sometimes singing the Lonesome Songs, songs created or modified by those who, born into freedom, had lived twenty-seven years in captivity and were now trying to adapt to a new world. "They looked back to the time before the Apaches' imprisonment. They were sung to express the anguish of captivity, and to put into words the yearning for an earlier way of life." [22]

Common activities reached beyond weekend social events. Even before 1920, an informal three-man Apache business committee had formed, and it succeeded in its immediate goal, of obtaining funds to complete the allotment process and provide cash payments in lieu of the rations promised but not delivered during 1914.

The decision to seek fulfillment of promises and rights rather than special favors was typical of the thinking of Betzinez, one of the committee members. Against his will, he had been sent to Carlisle Indian School in 1887, where he learned blacksmithing skills and absorbed the self-reliant, individualistic ideas of its superintendent, Captain Pratt. After he returned to Fort Sill, he strenuously argued for allowing those Chiricahuas who wished to remain the right to select allotments near the fort. In 1913, he was unusual in several respects: he was a bachelor (he finally married, in 1919, a white woman who had been a missionary at Fort Sill before 1913); at fifty-three, he was the oldest person (other than parental dependents) who elected to stay; and he had a marketable skill in addition to knowledge of farming. Betzinez was adamantly opposed to accepting what he considered favors. As the Indian operations at Fort Sill were being discontinued, for example, the government officer offered him the blacksmith tools and forge that he had used for many years. Betzinez refused the gift; he bought the equipment instead. Through farming and blacksmithing, he was able to support himself until he retired in about 1940; thereafter he leased his farmland to a white farmer. And in 1958, at almost one hundred years of age, Betzinez supplemented that rental income by stumping the panelists on the television game show *What's My Line?* who were unable to guess that, as a young man, he'd been on the warpath with Geronimo.[23]

For Chiricahuas like Betzinez, imbued with individualistic ideals, joint lobbying was one thing, formal tribal organization another. The

Chiricahuas in Oklahoma, like the Mescaleros, were given the opportunity to organize and adopt a constitution and bylaws under the Oklahoma Indian Welfare Act of 1936 (the Indian Reorganization Act of 1934 had not applied to tribes in Oklahoma). During the late 1930s, the Fort Sill Chiricahuas rejected it. Betzinez, his wife, and four other by-then elderly tribal members led the opposition. They saw governmental attempts to persuade them to organize as part of a conspiracy to deprive them of their allotted lands and force them back to communal life. Acquiescence, they believed, would reduce the Fort Sill Apaches to the level of "reservation" Indians.[24]

.   .   .

One of the Chiricahuas who led the opposition with Betzinez was Sam Haozous. He had traveled a somewhat different route but had developed a similar outlook. He was born in 1868 near Warm Springs to a daughter of Mangas Coloradas and a father who was killed in a skirmish before his birth. Like Betzinez, he was taken into captivity; unlike Betzinez, he was not transported to school away from the tribe or given any formal education. Instead, at Mount Vernon he joined the army's Indian Company and learned to play the bugle. At Fort Sill, while a scout in the cavalry, he acquired stockraising and farming skills, taught himself how to read and write a little, and distinguished himself as an athlete who performed double somersaults for visiting dignitaries. And in 1910, at the age of forty-two, he married his third wife, Blossom Wratten, a seventeen-year-old daughter of a Chiricahua mother and the white man who had become the interpreter for the Chiricahuas in the early 1880s and accompanied them throughout captivity.[25]

The newly married couple decided to remain in Oklahoma, and settled on their allotments near the town of Apache. The closest Chiricahua families lived four or five miles away. The Haozous family raised cattle and hogs and grew cotton, corn, wheat, and oats. They were better off than many of the neighboring families and the other Fort Sill Apaches who tried farming. Nevertheless, life was not easy, and it got harder during the Depression. In the great Dust Bowl drought, Indians and non-Indians alike deserted the state in an exodus memorialized in John Steinbeck's novel *The Grapes of Wrath*. Yet Sam and Blossom were able to feed their family, and the Haozous family hung on. Throughout the years, the parents emphasized the importance of education, and several

children became scientists. Another, Allan Houser, was widely acknowledged as the leading Indian artist of the century; his powerful evocations
of the Apache—and the Indian—spirit are renowned worldwide.[26]

Sam, no less than his son, remained true to his tribal heritage while
succeeding in the white man's world. On many occasions when an
Apache needed help, Haozous would lend him money, or go to the
bank and take out a loan, knowing that the man might never be able to
repay it. Like many of the other Chiricahuas of his generation, both in
Oklahoma and in New Mexico, he sang Chiricahua songs, told traditional stories, and engaged in traditional crafts. It is no surprise that, despite his opposition to formal tribal organization, he became a leader in
the Oklahoma Chiricahuas' efforts to obtain reparations from the
United States for the wrongs committed against them.[27]

.   .   .

In this, Haozous and the Oklahoma Chiricahuas adopted a different approach from the Mescalero branch. Instead of seeking federal appropriations—which could be interpreted as a gratuity—for their internment,
they wanted a special jurisdictional act that would allow them to sue the
United States in the Court of Claims. In court they could prove that
their rights had been violated. And they believed they had the attorney
who could engineer such an act through Congress and win a victory in
court.

Grady Lewis was a Choctaw. He served as an army lieutenant during
World War I, graduated from the University of Oklahoma law school in
the 1920s, and was elected to the Oklahoma House of Representatives.
He was general counsel to the Choctaw nation for many years, and
served as a mediator and arbitrator with the National Mediation Board.
He also became the claims attorney for numerous Oklahoma tribes, including the Choctaws, the Absentee Shawnee, the Citizen Band of
Potawatomi Indians, and, in 1938, the Chiricahuas' neighbors, the
Kiowas, Comanches, and Kiowa Apaches. By 1939, he had developed a
"big reputation" among Oklahoma Indians for "fighting hard" for
them.[28]

After a meeting of the Oklahoma Chiricahuas, Haozous, Benedict
Jozhe, and Talbot Gooday, on behalf of an entity called the Fort Sill
Apache Tribe of Indians, entered into a five-year contract with Lewis on
December 1, 1939, to investigate and prosecute their claims against the

United States. Under its terms, which were approved by the Interior Department on February 15, 1940, Lewis agreed that his compensation would be totally contingent on a recovery for the tribe.[29]

Despite the difference in approach, the Oklahoma Chiricahuas fared no better than their New Mexico counterparts. World War II intervened before Lewis could make any progress, and the contract expired.

At the war's onset, then, what had formerly been the Chiricahua tribe had divided into two groups, each seeking redress from the government along different avenues. One was called the Fort Sill Apache Tribe, at best a loosely federated group of families with a shared heritage living on separate plots of land in the manner of the white culture around them. The other lived in the remote Southwest, among other Apache groups into which they were gradually assimilating. But despite being separated by approximately five hundred miles and by divergent attitudes concerning tribal relations, the groups were not completely distinct. Many of the Oklahoma Chiricahuas had friends and relatives at Mescalero, and vice versa. They also held in common the same ancient memories and grievances. With the passage of the Indian Claims Commission Act in 1946, however, they finally had a realistic opportunity to win compensation for those wrongs—the ghosts of the Lonesome Songs that haunted them still.

FIVE

THE COMMISSION BECOMES A COURT

Meet the first beginnings; look to the budding mischief before
it has time to ripen to maturity.
—WILLIAM SHAKESPEARE

When President Truman signed the Indian Claims Commission Act into law on August 13, 1946, the law, and the tribunal it called for, were without precedent. No other country colonized by Europeans had ever allowed its displaced natives to sue for wrongs done to them decades, even centuries, before. No other American law had instructed a tribunal to resolve disputes based not only on established legal principles but also on an undefined standard of fair and honorable dealings. Indeed, a great deal in the act was left open to interpretation, and the Indian claims commissioners, who would be primarily responsible for interpreting its ambiguities, had not been identified. Even the language that specified their qualifications left a great deal open to chance and politics.

The uncertainties did not end there. Nobody knew how many Indian groups would avail themselves of the opportunity to sue the United States. Perhaps by way of reassuring Congress that the law would not open a Pandora's box of claims that would strip the federal treasury, witnesses had testified during the hearings that most of the "better" Indian claims had already been presented to the U.S. Court of Claims—and by and large defeated by government attorneys. But no one knew

the history of all, or even a large percentage, of the tribes, so it was difficult to speculate about the number—or the nature—of possible claims.
Predictions of how successful any Indian claim might be before this tribunal were merely guesswork.

The act, in effect, created a tabula rasa awaiting the etcher's acid, and
this came in the form of a handful of early decisions by President Truman, the commissioners, and the attorneys for both the tribes (the plaintiffs) and the Justice Department, which represented the United States
(the defendant). Some of these decisions were thoughtfully considered,
but many were ingrained and unquestioned rejections of possible approaches to crucial issues, and all of them reduced the inherent uncertainties of the act and set the Commission on a largely irrevocable
course. The first of these decisions, President Truman's selection of the
initial commissioners, was one of the most important.

·   ·   ·

When it came to specifying the qualifications of the three commissioners, the Indian Claims Commission Act provided few constraints on the
president's discretion. It required only two things. First, two of the three
commissioners had to be members of the bar of the Supreme Court of
the United States. This sounds relatively august, even exclusive, but virtually any lawyer admitted to the bar of any state for at least three years
could, and still can, become a member of the bar of the Supreme Court
by applying and paying a small fee. In essence, the president could pick
two commissioners simply because they were lawyers. The second re-
striction was that not more than two of the three be members of the
same political party, assuring a degree of political bipartisanship.[1]

The early versions of the act had also required that at least one of the
three commissioners be an American Indian. The House committee
considering the bills deleted that requirement out of fear (however
disingenuous) that none of the relatively few lawyers with Indian blood
would be interested in serving. Instead, the committee expressed in its
report accompanying the bill the "hope that at least one member of the
Commission will be an Indian, if an Indian of suitable qualifications is
available. Such an appointment would help to instill confidence on the
part of Indian litigants in the impartial character of the Commission."[2]

The recommendation had merit, and not just in creating an appearance of fairness. To the extent that an Indian lawyer was steeped in a

tribe's oral traditions and history, he would probably be more aware of the understandings, or misunderstandings, under which tribes operated when they entered into transactions with the United States and of the pressures that brought them to the bargaining table. Without exposure to those traditions and histories, a white lawyer might be more likely to interpret a decades-old agreement for the conveyance of land from a tribe to the government in the same manner that he would regard an agreement between two white men. By appointing at least one Indian to the Commission, Truman would have increased the chances that it would weigh the understandings of both parties. Four Indians, three of whom were attorneys and two of whom were sitting judges, were recommended, but all were quickly rejected. The wishes of congressional committee members do not bind the president unless they are incorporated in a statute. More than twenty years would pass before Richard Nixon appointed the one and only Indian to serve on the Commission.[3]

If he wasn't going to select an Indian, Truman could have appointed someone with sensitivity to the Indian perspective, an unparalleled knowledge of Indian law, and the trust of many tribal leaders. Soon after the act was signed, the acting secretary of the interior urged the appointment of Felix Cohen, and several legislators along with representatives of various Indian rights organizations quickly added their support. Truman, however, rejected this choice as well.[4]

Apparently, Cohen's expertise and sympathy for Native Americans disqualified him. In March 1947, Truman selected three non-Indians who had no experience with Indian affairs or Indian law. According to Edgar Witt, whom Truman appointed as chief commissioner, the president said he wanted to name individuals without "bias or prejudice one way or the other." A laudable goal on the surface, it was impossible to achieve.[5]

It is at least theoretically possible to find a neutral decision maker or arbiter for two disputants who have similar understandings of the rules of the transaction that gave rise to their dispute, such as two drivers who have an automobile accident and disagree about who is at fault. A decision maker also may be deemed neutral when two disputants have divergent understandings of the rules, but a higher authority recognized by both of them, such as the government, has established a binding interpretation of them. But when the disputants diverge markedly in their understanding of the rules and neither acknowledges a higher authority, a decision maker would have to comprehend and equally weigh two radically different perspectives to be neutral. That is all but impossible. As a practical matter, in deciding whether the government had behaved fairly and honorably toward Indian tribes, each commissioner could give precedence either to Anglo-American principles or to the Indians' understanding of events. By nominating three non-Indians who had no understanding of the special relationship between the United States and the tribes, President Truman virtually ensured that the white man's perspective would prevail.

Making matters worse, the administration made little effort to ferret out the best non-Indian candidates from the twenty-seven men and one woman recommended to it. Instead, and hardly surprisingly, it selected the candidates with powerful and active political backing. Truman was an embattled president in early 1947, facing vociferous opposition from a Congress that had fallen into the hands of the Republicans. Given such contemporaneous postwar crises as the spread of communism, the future of atomic weaponry, and the economic and political disarray of Europe, it is little wonder that the appointment of Indian claims commissioners was left to politics-as-usual.[6]

. . .

The nominee for chief commissioner, Edgar Witt of Texas, was one of the "closest friends" of Senator Tom Connally. Connally, a Texas Democrat and one of the congressional leaders on foreign affairs, started lobbying for Witt in June 1946, two months before the act was signed into law, and called or wrote the president on his behalf virtually every month until Witt was nominated. Texan Sam Rayburn, the Speaker of the House until the Republicans won control of Congress in the 1946 elections, seconded Connally's recommendation. Witt's backers could point to a long and distinguished career. At the age of sixty-eight, Witt had already been a private attorney, a member of the Texas state senate for twelve years, lieutenant governor for four years, and the chairman of two federal commissions resolving private claims arising from relations between the United States and Mexico. Witt's record, and the support of his powerful friends in Congress, were more than enough to secure his nomination.[7]

The FBI background report on the second nominee, William Holt of Nebraska, cast doubt on his ability to be an effective commissioner.

While his associates praised his character and morals highly, his grades in law school had been "below average," the president of the insurance company that he served as general counsel for thirteen years considered him "probably a poor trial attorney," and a justice of the Nebraska Supreme Court rated him "steady" but "not a brilliant attorney." Given the unique powers and unprecedented mandate of the Indian Claims Commission, these reservations might well have disqualified him, except that Holt's chief advocate was Republican Senator Hugh Butler of Nebraska, chairman of the Senate Committee on Public Lands, which included Indian affairs within its jurisdiction. Holt's nomination as a Republican member of the Commission was all but assured.[8]

The appointment of the third commissioner, Louis O'Marr, owed as much to fortuitous timing as to political logrolling. When President Truman sent the names of his three nominees to the Senate on March 7, 1947, O'Marr, then the attorney general of Wyoming, was not included. The third nominee was Charles Brannan, assistant secretary of agriculture and, of course, a Democrat. When O'Marr's main supporter, Senator Joseph O'Mahoney of Wyoming, learned of his candidate's omission from the list, he made what were, according to a presidential aide, some "very caustic comments" about Truman's selections. Then, on March 11, Brannan asked the president to withdraw his name. Not wishing to further offend O'Mahoney, the second-ranking Democrat on the Public Lands Committee, the president nominated O'Marr the very next day, without waiting for the FBI to conduct a background check.[9]

The three nominees sailed easily through the Senate confirmation process. Witt, Holt, and O'Marr were approved on April 8, 1947, about a month after their nominations, and sworn into office two days later.[10]

The personalities of the commissioners, along with their biases, would help to determine how well they worked with one another, with the attorneys who appeared before them, and with the legislators who had to appropriate money for the Commission and fund the judgments it handed down against the United States. Chief Commissioner Witt set the tone. Congressmen referred to him as "our long-time and good friend" and "distinguished friend," and attorneys who practiced before the Commission had similar affection for him. Not surprisingly, these attorneys found the Witt-led Commission to be a friendly, relaxed forum and one very willing to grant extensions that made scheduling orders all but meaningless.[11]

For twelve years, Witt, O'Marr, and Holt worked together with re-markable unanimity. The Commission issued 169 opinions prior to O'Marr's departure. Of these, 157—over 90 percent—were decided unanimously. In the few dissenting opinions Witt was the most sympa-thetic toward the Indians. He dissented six times in favor of the Indians, once in favor of the government. O'Marr was the most predisposed to-ward the government. He dissented from the Commission's opinion five times, each time in favor of the United States. Both Witt and O'Marr occasionally also wrote concurring opinions, reaching the same result as the Commission for different reasons. Holt showed no signs of indepen-dent thinking. Over twelve years, he never dissented or concurred; he always agreed with one or both of his colleagues.

·   ·   ·

Before Witt, O'Marr, and Holt could write an opinion, they had to de-cide upon the procedures and structure of the Commission. They even had to determine what exactly was meant by the word *commission*.

Congress had debated the advantages of a court or a commission in resolving the Indians' claims, and it is important to understand some of the distinctions. Although many commissions now have the power to adjudicate disputes much like courts, during the 1930s and 1940s a commission was typically conceived as a fact-finding body that referred its recommendations to some other body, such as Congress, for decision or action. A court, on the other hand, hears adversarial arguments and renders a decision, subject only to appeal to a higher court.

Congress decided that the Commission, despite its name, would function largely like a court. It would hear factual evidence presented by the Indians and the government, decide which version of the facts it be-lieved, and make rulings of law subject to appeal to the Court of Claims. At Felix Cohen's urging, however, Congress provided that the Commis-sion would also have the power to investigate the facts itself. In deciding court cases, judges and juries may not conduct their own factual investi-gations, but must (with limited exceptions) consider only the evidence presented by the opposing parties. Congress required that the Commis-sion create an Investigation Division that would, at the Commission's request, uncover facts relating to claims and present them to the Com-mission, the Indians, and the government. This investigatory work appeared necessary for the fair resolution of decades-old, if not centuries-old, claims, where any documentary evidence was generated exclusively by, and generally was solely in the possession of, the government.[12]

To the commissioners, accustomed to traditional judicial procedures, the Investigation Division was an anomaly, an unfamiliar agency of dubious value. Attorneys for both the Indians and the government placed little if any value on such a division, preferring to perform their own research or to have it done by employees or experts under their direct control. The staffing and functions of the Investigation Division, inchoate at best, soon withered away.[13]

Did the Commission's failure to create an effective investigative arm seriously interfere with its ability to resolve Indian claims fairly and efficiently? During the hearings in 1946, Cohen had argued, "Unless an Investigation Division is available to do a thorough job of uncovering the facts in these cases, which the Indians' attorneys seldom do, there can be no assurance that the Commission will have completed the job for which it was established when it comes to the end of its term." Cohen may have correctly assessed the performance of many Indian claims attorneys prior to passage of the act. And in one appeal in the following decade, the United States Court of Claims rejected the Commission's conclusions because of huge gaps in the factual record, and criticized the Commission for failing to conduct additional investigations (see Chapter Seven). But as more and more claims were tried, lawyers learned the types of information required and where the documents could be found, which diminished the need for the Investigation Division.[14]

Thus, the failure to establish an Investigation Division wasn't significant because of the possible impact on the quality of the presentation of Indian claims, but because of what it indicated about how the Commission would function. It might be called a commission, but it would operate almost exclusively like a court.

·   ·   ·

The commissioners notified all 176 tribes then recognized by the federal government of the existence of the Commission and of their right to file the petitions that would start the judicial process by identifying their claims. The act gave tribes five years, until August 13, 1951, to file. Until just before the deadline, petitions trickled in slowly. But by the deadline, 370 had been filed on behalf of almost every one of the tribes.

Many described multiple grievances, which, when divided, grew to more than 600 dockets.[15]

The claims speak cogently about the attitudes that lawyers for the Indians brought to their jobs. So great a majority were land claims that many people misidentified the Commission as the Indian Land Claims Commission. These claims typically asserted that the United States had acquired tribal land without paying any, or adequate, compensation. The tribes generally asked to be paid an amount equal to the fair market value of the land at the time it was taken, together with interest from the date of the alleged wrongdoing to the date that the Commission issued its judgment. These claims differed little from those that white citizens bring when a government acquires their land or other property without fair compensation. As will be discussed in a later chapter, the Indian land claims gave rise to many unique and difficult jurisprudential and evidentiary issues, issues that lawyers and the Commission could not ignore despite their best efforts to fit the cases into patterns with which they were comfortable. One Department of Justice lawyer would state that "there is nothing as complex as these cases," yet the legal theories underlying the claims—for example, that the government must pay fair value when it acquires property without the consent of the landowner—were well established in Anglo-American law.[16]

The second-largest group of claims sought an accounting of the government's management of tribal funds and other assets. About one-third of all tribes filed accounting claims. The United States has acted like a private trustee—indeed, over the years the government repeatedly has referred to itself as the Indians' trustee—once tribes ceded their aboriginal lands and were confined to reservations. Under Anglo-American law, a private trustee owns the property (including money) comprising the trust, but is obliged to manage it in accordance with the purposes of the trust. Often, trusts are established for the benefit of a person, such as a minor child, who is deemed incapable of managing the property. Throughout the nineteenth century and most of the twentieth century, the United States has deemed Indian tribes incapable of managing reservation resources themselves. If the beneficiary demands it, a private trustee must disclose in court its management of the property and money comprising the trust. In demanding an accounting, therefore, attorneys for the tribes were asking for no more than any other beneficiaries of trusts routinely received. Like the land claims, the Indians' accounting claims raised a host of issues not faced in private litigation, but in theory they differed little from the accountings routinely required of private trustees.

In other words, in the vast proportion of the petitions, very few of the tribes' lawyers were willing to risk breaking uncharted legal ground. While the shelves of law books contained many decisions dealing with land and accounting disputes involving non-Indian parties, they had nothing to say about moral claims based on "fair and honorable dealings," a concept with little or no foundation in Anglo-American law. Almost all of the 370 petitions included only land and accounting claims, though many other types of claim could have been asserted. Indians had often been refused permission to practice their religion or to speak their own languages; they often were denied adequate education and deprived of the means of economic self-sufficiency. Adequate protection from the citizens of the United States had seldom been forthcoming. Animals, such as the bison, on which many tribes had depended for survival had been deliberately destroyed: General William T. Sherman, for one, had advocated the extermination of the bison as the most inexpensive way to terminate the culture and the resistance of the Plains Indians. Of course, a few attorneys did assert moral claims with no basis in Anglo-American law. One was made on behalf of the Chiricahua Apaches, who had been imprisoned for more than a quarter of a century.

The failure to assert claims based on fair and honorable dealings cannot be construed as either evidence of negligence by the tribes' attorneys or a conspiracy to deprive the Indians of their just awards. Rather, attorneys analyzed their clients' issues in light of contemporary legal concepts. Even if they recognized the possibility of asserting novel claims, they were unwilling to bear the risks of such lawsuits. The Indians, not as constrained by legal training or the costs of litigation, were more imaginative than their lawyers. Some, if not most, of their ideas would undoubtedly have been rejected out of hand by the Commission. For example, the Gros Ventres of Montana wanted remuneration because a member of the tribe (whom another tribe, the Shoshones, also claimed as one of their own) served without pay as a guide for the Lewis and Clark expedition during the first decade of the nineteenth century. The Commission might have found other claims not so easy to dismiss. The Mandans of North Dakota considered themselves entitled to compensation for the hides of all the buffalo slain on their lands by white hunters, but their attorney dissuaded them, presumably because of the legal doctrine that wild animals are not owned by anyone. Under a fair and honorable dealings standard, however, the claim does not seem so far-fetched: the government had encouraged the destruction of the bison precisely in order to starve and freeze the Plains Indians into sub-jugation—a policy that caused the Indians what is called, in the cool language of the law, "damage." Was the United States' policy any more honorable than the recent efforts of armed groups in Somalia and the former Yugoslavia to deprive entire populations of food and clothing, which the United States and the United Nations now justifiably con-demn? [17]

Obviously, there is no assurance that the Mandans' proposed claim, or many other of the claims without precedent in Anglo law, would have succeeded. Few such claims were brought and they generally fared poorly. But whatever the sources of their reluctance, by not filing such claims the Indians' attorneys assured that the tribes would not be com-pensated for them.

.   .   .

While claims attorneys struggled to determine the types of claims to file, the government's litigators from the Department of Justice served notice with their first motions that they would fight the claims as ag-gressively as they would any other lawsuits against the United States.[18] Legal ethics require lawyers to represent their clients zealously, and the government's attorneys, like any others, worked to win the best possible monetary result for their client, the United States government. The In-dian tribes, however, were not ordinary plaintiffs. The government had unilaterally assumed, and would continue to perform, the role of trustee or guardian, and as such, was obliged to act in the tribes' interests.

The government's dual position—defendant and trustee—could have, and perhaps should have, created a dilemma for its attorneys about the appropriate stance to take toward tribes' claims. It didn't. Even if the government attorneys recognized the existence of a conflict, they did not moderate their vigorous opposition to the claims. This surely saved the government money in the form of reduced damages, but the savings came at a significant cost. Like many plaintiffs, the tribes sought not only money damages but also vindication, some form of acknowledgment by the defendant or the court that they had been wronged. For the Indian tribes, whose collective memories of the wrongs done them decades before still burned bright, this goal was usually strong. When the government's attorneys succeeded in gaining the dismissal of a tribal claim on procedural grounds, they may have saved their client money but prevented a tribe from achieving any vindication—a feeling that would have strengthened the government's relationships with many tribes.

In many instances the government would have been better served by negotiated settlements. Instead, the government's attorneys not only asserted all available defenses to defeat tribes' claims, but throughout most of the Commission's history contested most cases to the bitter end. Not until 1958 did the government agree to a settlement. And in that case, the Coeur d'Alene tribe of the Pacific Northwest had been forced to prove the boundaries of its aboriginal territory and the value of that land at the time the government had taken it; all that remained to be adjudicated was the amount of offsets to which the government was entitled.

That pattern proved typical. In general, land claims were settled, if at all, only after tribal plaintiffs had survived a barrage of procedural motions from the Department of Justice and proved that the government was liable. The only outstanding issues resolved in negotiations were usually the number of dollars to be paid.

The Department's opposition to settling Indian cases even drew congressional criticism. In 1956, Representative Stewart Udall of Arizona complained that few Indian claims cases had been disposed of because "the Department has adopted a policy of refusing to compromise cases out of court." Whereas the Justice Department's antitrust division had adopted a settlement policy that resulted in relatively rapid resolution of disputes involving big businesses, "this other arm of Justice has adopted a flat policy of no out-of-court compromises or settlements. To me that is a harsh and unrealistic policy, and I do not think it reflects credit on the Government of the United States." [19]

The policy of filing myriad motions to dismiss and refusing to settle cases was primarily the product of one man, Ralph Barney. He headed the Department of Justice's Indian Claims Section from the 1940s into the 1970s, with a staff that grew from a handful of attorneys to forty-three in the late 1950s. Short and stocky, Barney exuded energy and cockiness, reminding one lawyer of the baseball shortstop and manager Leo Durocher, who coined the phrase "Nice guys finish last." Like other good litigators, Barney loved to win, but some claims attorneys for the tribes believed that he was driven by anti-Indian feelings that went well beyond the zest for combat. He repeatedly bragged of the long years it took for Indians to recover under the act. Anyone on his staff willing to discuss settlement with Indians' attorneys quickly fell into disfavor, and he vociferously urged that the department appeal virtually every adverse judgment it received. Only when Barney's supervising assistant attorney general disagreed with his "hard-ball litigation" tactics, and was strong enough to override his recommendations, were settlements made with any consistency. That did not happen during the Truman and Eisenhower administrations.[20]

·   ·   ·

One claim that the government's attorneys prudently did agree to settle, on the eve of trial in 1973, demonstrates the potential value of settlements achieved without the bitter taste of litigation. The United States purchased Alaska from Russia in 1867, and as traders and other American citizens filtered into the new territory, naval officers were appointed to protect American lives and property. Angoon, a fishing village located near present-day Juneau and populated by about 420 Tlingit Indians, was located within the naval protectorate. The Tlingits traded with white merchants, and by the 1880s some even were employed by traders.[21]

On October 22, 1882, the premature explosion of a harpoon bomb killed a shaman, or "medicine man," serving on a whaling boat operated by the Northwest Trading Company. The natives of Angoon forced the boat and its launches to shore, because under Tlingit custom all economic activities were taboo during the four-day mourning period, and demanded compensation of two hundred blankets from the company. If a member of one social unit (a clan) was killed or injured by a member of another clan, the offending clan had to pay compensation or the injured clan would exact justice—in the form of "an eye for an eye, a tooth for a tooth." For purposes of compensation, the Tlingits treated the Northwest Trading Company as a clan. Unlike in nineteenth-century Anglo law, fault was irrelevant—compensation was owed even if there had been neither intent to injure nor even negligence. The idea is hardly far-fetched. In the early twentieth century, every state adopted workers' compensation laws. If those laws had been in effect in 1882, the

Northwest Trading Company might well have owed compensation to the family of the dead shaman.[22]

The naval commander, E. C. Merriman, made no attempt to comprehend the "savages' " customs and resolved to punish the Tlingits. He assembled a force of over seventy officers, sailors, and marines and proceeded to Angoon with a heavily armed boat to demand a fine of four hundred blankets or he would destroy the village. It is unclear whether the two alternatives were communicated to the villagers, but on October 26, 1882, Merriman opened fire. The bombardment destroyed most of the village's houses, after which sailors and marines looted the existing structures, then deliberately set them on fire. They also systematically destroyed food stored for the winter and the Tlingits' canoes.[23]

Under the Indian Claims Commission Act, attorneys for the Tlingits filed a claim to recover the damages to the tribe caused by the bombardment—the only claim ever filed under the act for damages resulting from an attack on a tribe by government forces. In 1973, almost a century after the assault, attorneys agreed, subject to approval by the tribe, to settle the claim for $90,000, the estimated value of the tribal property destroyed during the assault. (Prior decisions of the Indian Claims Commission, discussed later in this book, had made clear that the Tlingits could not recover for the deaths or the destruction of property owned by individuals.) One of the tribe's attorneys traveled to Alaska to explain the proposed settlement to them. After he had done so, several old men who had arrived at the village hall carrying paper bags began to retell the story of the bombardment.

At the appropriate point the elders revealed the contents of their bags—the cannon balls that had destroyed the village. Nearly one hundred years before, the villagers had buried the evidence of the wrong done to them. Now that, in their view, the government was at least indirectly admitting its fault, the cannon balls could finally be unearthed. The amount of the settlement might have been a pittance, but the Tlingits felt partly vindicated. As the president of the village's central council said, "Basically all we want is for the U.S. Government to admit that they did a serious wrong to the Angoon people." [24]

The people of Angoon later sent a delegation to Washington, D.C., to request an official apology from the assistant secretary of the navy. The navy's only response was a letter stating, "The destruction of Angoon should never have happened, and it was an unfortunate event in our history." While the letter did not assuage any feelings of injury, it did not entirely erase the goodwill gained when the government showed itself willing to settle the score before the Indian Claims Commission. It was an opportunity missed in too many other cases.[25]

.   .   .

By August 1951, the deadline for filing petitions, the Indian Claims Commission became, for all intents and purposes, the Indian Claims Court. Whether such a body that looked, sounded, and acted like a court would meet the goals that Congress had intended—resolving all Indian claims, making amends for all past wrongs, and putting the Indians in a position to become self-supporting—remained to be seen.

SIX

THE FALL AND RISE OF THE IMPRISONMENT CLAIM

Territory is but the body of a nation. The people who inhabit its
hills and valleys are its soul, its spirit, its life.
—PRESIDENT JAMES A. GARFIELD

Under the Apache code of honor, an individual takes responsibility for
his or her own actions. It is easy to imagine, then, that Geronimo sometimes pondered the situation in which he and his handful of adherents
had placed the other Apaches who came to be known generically as the
Chiricahuas. But it *is* impossible to imagine that either he or any of the
other Chiricahuas distinguished between the pain they suffered from
war, exile, and imprisonment as individuals and that of the group as a
whole. Obviously, both Geronimo and Chato, the army scout he disdained, would have been aware during their time as prisoners of war
that both the Chiricahuas' way of life and members of the tribe themselves were dying. But to distinguish between one's own tribulations and
those of one's people would have been incomprehensible, without any
practical consequences. Yet upon passage of the Indian Claims Commission Act, this odd duality became a critical issue, as the Chiricahuas and
their attorneys soon discovered.

.   .   .

On January 29, 1947, even before the commissioners had been nominated by President Truman, Sam Haozous, James Kaywaykla, and Benedict Jozhe signed a new contract with their Choctaw attorney, Grady
Lewis, to replace the agreement with him that had expired during World
War II.

Although a capable writer and analyst, Lewis lacked the disposition
for the exhaustive research and the drafting of voluminous court documents necessary to prosecute an Indian claim. Those traits did not make
Lewis a poor choice, but they required him to find backroom assistance
to succeed. For example, he represented the Choctaws in a joint claim
filed with the Chickasaws that resulted in 1950 in the first judgment issued by the Indian Claims Commission in favor of Indians. According to
the Chickasaws' attorney, Paul Niebell, Lewis hired a journalist to write
the brief for him. Not surprisingly, it was long on facts and rhetoric and
short on legal analysis. Niebell was later told by one of the Indian claims
commissioners that they had "[thrown] Grady's brief out the window"
and had relied on Niebell's brief for both tribes.[1]

Whether the commissioners did indeed disregard Lewis's brief in
their deliberations, they certainly couldn't have called it dull. Early on, it
accused the "scheming emissaries of the United States" of robbing the
Indians of their land—"a fact which cannot, without juggling the truth,
be glossed in bouquets to the men who did it." Describing the negotiations that resulted in a treaty, the brief stated: "On the one hand was the
helpless ward; on the other, the unscrupulous representatives of the
powerful and faithless guardian. On the one hand, duress; on the other,
greed." A provision in another treaty was labeled "a cheap, surreptitious
device to lend legality to an act of banditry." [2]

Even today, such rhetoric is found more often in legal dramas on
television than in any courtroom, and the brief's heated descriptions of a
government rendering a once-powerful tribe dependent and then repeatedly cheating it ran on for over one hundred pages. The language
was all the more shocking at mid-century, when popular movies and
novels largely portrayed Indians as primitive savages who should be
mowed down to permit whites' heroic advance into the West, and who
allowed themselves to be corrupted into laziness and drunkenness, thus
proving their inferiority. Very few books described the perfidies committed by the white man that had contributed to the loss of Indians'
lives and cultures.[3]

In all probability, the commissioners shared the popular view that the white man had, by and large, treated the Indian fairly. Lewis's version of the Choctaws' plight flew in the face of these views and assumptions. To Ralph Barney, the head of the Justice Department's Indian Claims Section, it must have seemed the work of a madman. He, like Lewis, hailed from Oklahoma, but he was descended from the whites who settled there after the "surplus" lands were opened to settlement, not from one of the Five Civilized Tribes with whom the government had broken faith sixty years before. Barney promptly recommended that Lewis's brief be removed from the Commission's files because of its "scandalous, vituperative and impertinent matter." While agreeing that it contained "improper and unfit" language, the Commission declined. The brief apparently played little or no role in the Commission's ultimate decision about the Choctaws and Chickasaws, but it may have begun the slow process of reeducating the commissioners about the relations between the United States and Indian tribes.[4]

In 1947, as Lewis recommenced work on behalf of the Oklahoma Chiricahuas, the controversy over the ghostwritten Choctaw brief was still several years away. His first step was to enter into an agreement with Howard Shenkin, a young attorney in Washington, D.C., who agreed to do research and drafting work in return for 40 percent of any attorneys' fee received when and if the Chiricahuas prevailed.[5]

· · ·

A case before the Commission commenced with the filing of a petition. This document had to contain three elements. It first had to identify the "petitioner," then identify the acts that the United States had committed that had injured the Indians, and finally, it had to identify the provisions of the Indian Claims Commission Act that would allow them to recover for those wrongful acts.

Unlike many parties to lawsuits, the Fort Sill Apaches could not simply recount all of the government's misdeeds. Many of the significant events had occurred when the Apaches and the United States were at war. The Apaches then spoke a different language, and one that had no written component (their second language was Spanish, not English). They had a radically different culture, and even when U.S. decisions had been translated—often from English into Spanish and then into Apache—they were virtually incomprehensible to the Chiricahuas. The government documents were, for the most part, stored in Washington. To corroborate the events related by the Apaches amply enough to draft a petition, Shenkin had to track down published materials (generally accessible in the Library of Congress) or government documents (stored in the bowels of the Department of the Interior and in the National Archives).[6]

Almost immediately, he ran into difficulties. In a letter, he asked Lewis, "Who are our clients? Are they all the Apache Indians now known as the Fort Sill Apaches? Do they include just the Warm Springs band, or all of the Chiricahuas?" Few nineteenth-century government officials had understood the Apaches' social structure or language. (Indeed, anthropologists still argue over the number and names of the various bands in the Chiricahuas.) In any event, early documents contained a bewildering mishmash of references to tribes and bands, and after 1886, when it became convenient to treat all as members of one group, almost all references to separate bands disappeared. For Shenkin a most pressing question was: Had those who decided to stay in Oklahoma in 1913 been members of only one of the aboriginal bands? The documents explained little.

Lewis's initial answer may have sown even more confusion. Using the name "Chiricahua" as the name for the Central Band, as government agents tended to do during the 1860s and 1870s, rather than as the name for a tribe that included several bands, he responded, "Our clients are those known as the Fort Sill Apaches. They are the Warm Springs group rather than, and opposed to the Chiricahua Apaches." Lewis's response mirrored Haozous's opinion on this matter, but it reflected the erroneous belief that all members of the Eastern, or Warm Springs, Band had stayed at Fort Sill, while all members of the other aboriginal bands had elected to move to Mescalero. While those Apaches who chose to stay in Oklahoma in 1913 did come disproportionately from the Warm Springs Band, other members of that band returned to the Southwest. By May 26, 1948, when the lawyers filed their petition, they had revised their thinking, presumably as a result of further research. The petition identified the petitioner as the Fort Sill Apaches, whose predecessors "were formerly known as the Warm Spring and Chiricahua bands of Apache Indians." This formulation was accurate, but ignored the hundreds of Indians at Mescalero whose predecessors also "were formerly known as the Warm Spring and Chiricahua bands of Apache Indians" whom Lewis and Shenkin did not purport to represent. Such problems in identifying the *client* are virtually unknown in other types of cases.[7]

In describing the wrongs committed by the government, the attorneys stated two claims. The first was for the imprisonment of the tribe. In an early draft of the petition, the lawyers described the government's actions in terms even more condemnatory than those Grady Lewis employed in the Choctaw brief:

> This phase of the claim represents one of the most notorious, and disgraceful, chapters in the history of the relationship between the United States and the North American Indian. The unconscionable incarceration of these Apaches is well known to students of Indian affairs. . . . There has been no dissent from the proposition that the conduct of the [United States] was most reprehensible; no one has yet seen fit to defend the actions taken. What is more, the kind of things the [United States] did to these Apaches, as this Petition will show, are very comparable to the Nazi criminalities in Europe. It is ill-fitting that the United States take the high moral tone it did at Nuremberg [at the Nazi war crimes trials] and not at least recognize and remedy, insofar as that is now possible, the similar sins of our American predecessors.[8]

The rhetoric was eliminated from the final version of the petition, but the charge was still severe:

> In September and October of 1886, the [United States], wilfully and maliciously, falsely imprisoned and confined as prisoners of war at Fort Marion, Florida, 450 Warm Spring and Chiricahua Apache Indians. These people were guilty of no offense, and were imprisoned solely because they were members of the Warm Spring and Chiricahua bands.

For this false imprisonment, the petition asked for damages in the amount of $7,500,000.[9]

The second claim reflected Lewis's and Shenkin's continuing confusion about which aboriginal group they were representing. On behalf of the Fort Sill Apaches, they sought the value of the 750 square miles included in the Warm Springs Reservation as it had been created in 1872. Their theory was that the Indians had possessed this land "from time immemorial," and that the government had recognized this possession when it set aside the land and had then violated Apache property rights by terminating the reservation. They valued this claim at $560,000. The petition made no claim for the land included in the Chiricahua Reservation in southeastern Arizona, presumably because of the attorneys' understanding that most of those who chose to remain at Fort Sill were Warm Springs Apaches. It also contained no claim for the loss of the millions of acres of aboriginal land not included in either of the reservations.[10]

Shenkin filed the petition at the offices of the Indian Claims Commission in Washington, D.C., in May 1948. More than seventy years after the Apaches were removed from the Chiricahua and Warm Springs reservations, more than sixty years after they were first imprisoned, and thirty-five years after they were finally released, the claims of some of them finally were presented to a tribunal of the United States.

. . .

The Indian Claims Section of the Department of Justice was grossly understaffed, and, despite normal rules of procedure that require prompt answers to petitions, the government often took years to respond. But not in this case. The attorneys for the government, Ralph Barney and Leland Yost, one of the first staff attorneys, did their best to assure an early and negative consideration by the Commission. On September 27, 1948, only four months after the petition had been filed, the government filed a motion to dismiss all the claims of the Fort Sill Apaches.

A motion to dismiss is a device by which a defendant, in this case the United States, asks the court to reject a claim without a trial because, even if all of the facts alleged by the petitioner are true, the defendant should prevail under the applicable legal rules, making a trial pointless. The purpose of a trial is to decide factual issues, and if, as a matter of law, the defendant should prevail under the plaintiff's version of the facts, there are no factual issues to decide.

The United States based its motion on three grounds. First, it contended, the Fort Sill Apaches, the smaller of the two groups into which the Chiricahuas divided in 1913, were not the proper group to bring a lawsuit on behalf of all the tribal members (assuming that a tribe even existed). Second, neither aboriginal possession of land nor the creation of a reservation by executive order created any property rights against the government. The Indians could have no claim arising from an executive order terminating a reservation that had been created by an earlier order, even if it was within their aboriginal territory. The most important contention was the third, which said that even if the government had falsely imprisoned the Indians as alleged, the wrong had been committed against each *individual,* and the Indian Claims Commission Act permitted Indians to sue only for wrongs committed against tribes or groups.

Lewis and Shenkin had until October 10 to respond to the government's motion or to request an extension, not nearly enough time, especially because Lewis was in New Mexico campaigning for a friend and soliciting business, and Shenkin, who had recurrent health problems, was in the hospital. Three days before the deadline, Shenkin asked his acquaintance David Cobb to step in.

. . .

Cobb was a partner in a two-attorney office with Israel S. Weissbrodt. They were an unlikely team. Weissbrodt, the middle of three children born to two illiterate Jewish immigrants from Galicia (now part of Poland), was reared in the Bronx. His father, who had arrived in New York without a penny or a word of English, had learned the window-washing business by watching others, and soon started his own. The parents saw education and professional careers as the hope for their children. They were rewarded when Israel, who had acquired the street name "Lefty," was admitted to Columbia Law School. He struggled during his first year at Columbia but, by dint of voluminous note taking and studying twelve hours a day, eventually excelled and graduated in 1933.

After graduating, Weissbrodt was hired by William O. Douglas, who had left a position at Yale to join Franklin Roosevelt's New Deal administration as head of the Securities and Exchange Commission. Sensitive to charges that the administration's lawyers in general and the SEC's lawyers in particular were heavily Jewish, Douglas decreed that Lefty's name would be listed as I. S. Weissbrodt on the government's records, and from then on he has been known either as Lefty or I.S.

Weissbrodt worked for several different federal agencies in Washington until 1947. During the late 1930s, he moved into a group house, and lived for the first time with non-Jews. One of them was David Cobb.

In contrast to Weissbrodt, Cobb was a product of the Massachusetts aristocracy. His forebears arrived on the *Mayflower.* Unlike Weissbrodt at

Columbia, Cobb sailed through Harvard Law School. In one class taught by Felix Frankfurter, whom President Roosevelt later appointed to the Supreme Court, Cobb passed his time listing in his notebook some of the polysyllabic words Frankfurter used rather than taking notes, a practice that amused Frankfurter when Cobb lost his notebook and a prankster turned it in to the professor. After graduating, Cobb also came to Washington to work for the New Deal.[11]

Cobb and Weissbrodt quickly became close friends. At the end of World War II, they went to work for the National Housing Agency, which was created to facilitate the construction of housing so that, in the words of President Truman, returning veterans would not have to live with their mothers-in-law. In late 1946, however, the administration substantially cut back the low-cost housing program, and in December, the head of the agency and then the senior legal staff, including Cobb and Weissbrodt, resigned in protest.[12]

Neither man had ever worked as a lawyer outside the government; Weissbrodt had never even been in a courtroom. Nevertheless, they went into partnership in early 1947, renting a small office on the third floor of a District of Columbia town house and taking on any and all clients. Initially business was slow, and they believed that they would have time to learn whatever was necessary for any case.[13]

· · ·

By October 1948, Cobb was busy representing government employees in loyalty hearings under the Federal Employee Loyalty and Security Program, which had been established in 1947 even before Senator Joseph McCarthy rose to infamy. With Cobb preoccupied, Weissbrodt took over for Shenkin with a three-day deadline staring at him. He knew nothing about Indian claims law—he had never even met an Indian. Little did he know that he would represent the Chiricahua Apaches for the next thirty years and that Indian claims work would become the major component of his legal practice.[14]

Weissbrodt's efforts to locate the elusive Grady Lewis failed. Next, he contacted the Justice Department's Barney and Chief Commissioner Witt. Although Weissbrodt had no authority whatsoever to speak for the Fort Sill Apaches, let alone represent them in legal proceedings, he asked for a sixty-day continuance, and the government and the Commission agreed.[15]

Once he finally became aware of the situation, Lewis enlisted Weiss-brodt and Cobb to perform research and draft an answer to the government's dismissal motion. This called for a nearly instant education in an area of law in which there was only one textbook—Cohen's treatise on federal Indian law—and very few qualified teachers. Despite the constraints of time, health, and knowledge, the attorneys for the Fort Sill Apaches found a winning approach to the first two issues raised by the government's motion—whether the Fort Sill Apaches could file claims on behalf of all the Chiricahuas, and whether the Indians had a viable claim arising from the closing of the Warm Springs Reservation. They argued that, based on the controlling legal principles, they might be able to prove facts under which the Fort Sill Apaches would be entitled to bring claims on behalf of all the Chiricahuas and under which they would be entitled to recover for the aboriginal lands included in the Warm Springs Reservation. Accordingly, they contended, the Commission should not decide these issues at this preliminary state. On May 6, 1949, the Commission concluded that, without giving both sides an adequate opportunity to research the facts, it did not have an adequate basis to throw out the claim for the value of the 750 square miles of land.[16]

A more daunting challenge for Lewis, Cobb, and Weissbrodt was the government's contention that the imprisonment claim was individual, not tribal, in nature. The Indian Claims Commission Act permitted claims to be brought "on behalf of any Indian tribe, band, or other identifiable group of American Indians." During the entire sixteen-year period Congress considered bills allowing Indians to sue the United States, few legislators or witnesses ever addressed the meaning of this provision. Those who did agreed that it meant that such claims had to be tribal, not individual, for obvious reasons. If every individual Indian or his descendants could sue for every wrong committed against him, the Indian Claims Commission would never finish its business. But nobody suggested how the Commission was supposed to determine whether a claim was tribal or individual.[17]

The government's attorneys cited as precedent the Supreme Court decision *Blackfeather v. United States* of 1903. The Shawnee Indians, who between the mid-eighteenth century and the early nineteenth century had been forced to migrate from what are now Pennsylvania and Virginia to Kansas, with several stops in between, sought compensation for

loss of personal property when white settlers and soldiers flooded into
their treaty-guaranteed Kansas territory. They claimed that during the
Civil War years between three and four hundred Shawnees had lost livestock, farm crops, household goods, money, and other personal property
valued from $75 to $7,000—in all, about $530,000. The Supreme Court
decided that Congress had not authorized the Shawnees to bring these
claims. The special jurisdictional act that allowed the Shawnees to sue
permitted only claims by a band, not an individual. The Court did not
explain, however, what made these particular claims individual.[18]

A lawyer faced with a prior decision by a higher court that states a
rule of law adverse to his or her client often tries to "distinguish" the decision. He argues that his client's case differs in one or more crucial respects, and therefore that the decision sheds no light on his client's
dispute or, better yet, actually supports his client's position.

The facts in *Blackfeather* were very different from those in the Chiricahua imprisonment claim, but because the Supreme Court had not
stated which facts were significant, it was difficult to identify which facts
made the Chiricahua case distinguishable. The pivotal point in *Blackfeather* could have been that the identity of the property taken or destroyed, the date of the wrong, and the value of the property differed
from one Shawnee to the next, thus requiring more than three hundred
individual trials. But in the Chiricahua case, the important facts were the
same for all involved: a single trial should suffice. The Court may have
decided against the Shawnees because they were hurt by the actions of
hundreds of individual citizens rather than by a common government
policy. By contrast, the government acted alone in imprisoning all of the
Chiricahuas. Finally, the Supreme Court may have decided that the
Shawnees' claims were individual because individual Indians, not
the tribe, owned the personal property and therefore individual Indians,
not the tribe, were damaged. The Chiricahuas, however, were complain-
ing of loss of freedom, not loss of property. A tribe, like a Western government, has a more direct interest in its citizens' personal freedom than
in their personal property, especially when that freedom is ended because they are members of the tribe.

Despite these uncertainties about how to interpret *Blackfeather* and
what relevance any interpretation had to the Chiricahuas' claim, Commissioner Holt, in his May 6 opinion for the Commission, relied on
Blackfeather in concluding that the imprisonment claims were individual

in nature, and therefore that the Commission had no jurisdiction over them. Holt suggested two different bases for his ruling without clearly understanding the distinction. The first, narrow basis was that the petition drafted by Lewis and Shenkin sought damages only for injuries that were by their very nature individual. The petition sought compensation for "the harm, suffering and humiliation," including the many deaths, of tribal members. According to Holt, the tribe had not grown sick or died; individuals had. Under this interpretation, the problem was just poor draftsmanship. Redrafting the petition, however, would not suffice under the second, broader, and predominant basis. Holt stated this position succinctly:

> We consider arrest and imprisonment a violation of personal rights of individual Indians. It is a personal wrong committed against each individual Indian concerned and not against the tribe or band of which the individual is a member. Any right to a claim for resultant damage suffered by such wrongful act is individual in nature and remains in the individual Indian. . . .[19]

This was not an attempt to construe the language of the petition, but an opinion about the nature of any imprisonment claims. It incorporates the Anglo-American concept that a person who is falsely imprisoned or otherwise suffers injuries to his personal freedom may sue for those injuries. Nothing in Holt's opinion indicates that he even thought about whether that concept made sense when *all* of the members of a tribe were imprisoned, not by happenstance, but because they were members of the tribe. Nor did anything in his opinion indicate that he had considered the "fair and honorable dealings" clause of the Indian Claims Commission Act. Just because claims for false imprisonment might be individual as a legal matter did not necessarily mean that they were individual as a moral matter.

The commissioners disregarded all arguments other than those based, however shakily, on prior precedents. To have had any chance of prevailing, Lewis and his associates would have had to find a Supreme Court decision that allowed a group to bring a claim for personal injuries suffered by one or all of its members. The closest they could come was a Supreme Court decision from 1883, *Baltimore and Potomac Railroad Company* v. *Fifth Baptist Church,* which permitted the church to sue the railroad "for the annoyance and discomfort to its members in the use of its property" caused by the railroad's construction of an engine house and machine shop on a parcel of land adjoining the church.

Commissioner Holt distinguished the *Fifth Baptist Church* decision by stating that the religious corporation had a right to sue because the railroad's operations interfered with worshipers' use of the property that the church, not its individual members, owned. Thus, Holt could have said, *Fifth Baptist Church* was consistent with *Blackfeather:* a group whose members were hindered in their use of group-owned property could sue; if a group's property rights were not damaged, however, only the individual members could sue.[20]

The underlying problem was that *no* decision squarely addressed the issue before the Commission. As would frequently be the case, the Commission had the opportunity to make *new* law or enunciate moral principles apart from the law. But its written opinion contained no meaningful analysis. After briefly discussing the *Blackfeather* and *Fifth Baptist Church* decisions, the Commission simply chose, without explanation, the most familiar position, one that would not coincidentally limit the government's potential liability under the act. Given the commissioners' backgrounds, this choice was hardly surprising.

．　．　．

The decision initially appeared disastrous for the Fort Sill Apaches and many other tribes. As important as the land claim was, the period of captivity was paramount. Only two months before, Lewis had written, "It is known by everyone who has the slightest knowledge of the subject that the principal claim of the Fort Sill Apaches grows out of their imprisonment as prisoners of war." He had compared their treatment to the Holocaust. Now the claim had been dismissed without a fair fight.[21]

The government's motion to dismiss, however, did not prove to be cataclysmic. For one thing, it introduced Weissbrodt, and to a lesser extent Cobb, to Indian claims work. When he acquired a client with a problem he had not previously encountered, Weissbrodt typically read background material, then sought an expert for practical advice. Following this system, he found that a Washington lawyer named James Curry had filed a complaint with the Indian Claims Commission on behalf of all the other Apache tribes of Arizona and New Mexico—Jicarillas, Mescaleros, and Lipans—as well as the Northern Tonto and Yavapai.

When they met, however, Weissbrodt discovered that Curry knew no more about Indian claims work than he did.[22]

Curry had briefly been employed as a lawyer for the Indian Service during the mid-1930s but had not worked on any Indian claims cases. However, he was friendly with Felix Cohen, and shortly after passage of the act, he agreed to work with two New York attorneys, one of whom, Henry Cohen, was Felix's cousin. These relationships gave Curry instant credibility in the Indian community, which he enhanced by serving as counsel for a nascent support group, the National Congress of American Indians. He exploited these entrees to solicit claims contracts from more than thirty Indian groups, using means that the commissioner of Indian affairs and a Senate subcommittee later branded as unethical.[23]

The solicitations might not have excited the concern of the commissioner and the senators, except that Curry lacked the money and legal staff to perform the enormous responsibilities that he assumed. His associations with Cohen and other attorneys, which would have provided both money and legal help, repeatedly broke down in mutual recriminations. A liberal who tried to do good for humankind in the abstract, Curry had trouble dealing with individuals. He was repeatedly forced to seek out new associations in return for a share of the possible contingent fees. He farmed out the substantive legal work to these new associates whom the tribal leaders had never even met. All this, the Senate subcommittee believed, was unfair to the Indians in at least two respects. Work on their claims was delayed, and tribes that thought Curry would act as their claims attorney were in reality engaging him to act as a brokerage service.[24]

Unaware of Curry's history, Weissbrodt agreed to research the claims of some of Curry's clients. In 1950, Curry, having found a few attorneys he could work with, and under increasing pressure to begin to prosecute his many clients' claims, entered into a three-party agreement with Cobb and Weissbrodt, and two attorneys in Duluth, Minnesota, Jay Hoag and Clarence Lindquist. The law firm of Cobb and Weissbrodt agreed to perform research in Washington, and to prepare all legal papers in return for one-third of any fee eventually earned. Hoag and Lindquist agreed to perform any research outside of Washington, to handle the trial work, and to pay the expenses of the litigation, all in return for the second third of the fee. Curry would retain the last third, in consideration of the supposed work that he had already done and his continuing

contacts with the tribes. (As it turned out, Curry was forced by the Department of the Interior to withdraw from all Indian claims work in the
early 1950s, but retained a reduced interest in the fee. The firm of Cobb
and Weissbrodt did virtually all of the work, and Hoag and Lindquist became, in effect, investors who did very little research and trial work on
their joint cases.)[25]

One type of legal paper that Cobb and Weissbrodt were supposed to
draft was the petition for each of Curry's clients. Petitions must be specific enough to put the defendant on notice of the claims against it.
Given the deadlines, Weissbrodt never had enough time to investigate
fully the history of the relations between the various tribes and the
United States. He was not aware of, and certainly had not evaluated,
every possible claim. Thus he became adept at drafting petitions precise
enough to satisfy the notice requirement but broad enough to cover a
wide variety of claims, both known and unknown. The petitions typically described certain wrongs in moderate detail but also contained
paragraphs speaking more broadly of the taking and/or mismanagement
of funds, lands, and resources and demanding an accounting from the
United States, the trustee.[26]

Weissbrodt applied this technique to the claims of the Fort Sill
Apaches. In retrospect, the government had filed its motion to dismiss—
and the Commission had decided it—too quickly. On the date of the
decision, May 6, 1949, more than two years remained in which tribes
could file petitions. So before August 13, 1951, Lewis, Cobb, and Weissbrodt filed three more petitions. The first amended the allegations concerning the land claim to include a claim for the loss of all of the
Chiricahuas' aboriginal land, not just the 750 square miles included in
the Warm Springs Reservation. The second alleged that the government, in violation of its duties to the Chiricahua Apaches, had permitted
persons to trespass upon and use the Chiricahuas' aboriginal lands. The
petition also more broadly stated that the United States had "dealt with
respect to the trust lands and trust property [of the Chiricahuas] to its
own advantage for its own benefit," and asked that the government be
compelled to account, not only for the trespasses, but also for its own
use of the tribal assets. Based on this and related language, Weissbrodt
was able to argue successfully twenty years later that the petition en-
compassed matters of which he was completely unaware at the time it
was drafted, such as the misuse of tribal moneys.[27]

In the third petition the Fort Sill Apaches again asserted an imprisonment claim, but with an important new twist.

.   .   .

Under our system of law, no one can reassert in a new lawsuit any claim that was decided in a previous one, except under special circumstances. This doctrine, called *res judicata* (the matter adjudicated), is designed to prevent endless relitigation of claims by losing parties. Recognizing that if the Indians repeated their allegations concerning the imprisonment, their claims would be promptly dismissed under the *res judicata* doctrine, Lewis and Weissbrodt filed a new petition saying that the imprisonment "thwarted [the tribes] in the advancement of their common purposes of their formation." In other words, the Apaches no longer sought to recover for injuries suffered by individuals who had been falsely imprisoned, but for injuries preventing the tribe from functioning as a tribe. The lawyers did not attempt to spell out what those thwarted purposes were: Maintaining the common culture? Dealing with other tribes and governments? Protecting tribal members? Further definitions would have to await future proceedings in the case.[28]

Discounting any distinction between this petition and the one previously dismissed by the Commission, the government's attorneys promptly filed a motion to dismiss the new imprisonment claim under the *res judicata* doctrine. They argued that the Commission's prior opinion that wrongful arrest and imprisonment are "personal wrong[s] committed against each individual Indian concerned and not against the tribe or band of which the individual is a member" precluded any contention that the tribe had suffered damage apart from that of its individual members.

Not so, the tribe's attorneys responded. The Commission's prior decision was based on language in the petition that focused only on harm suffered by individual tribal members: that language had now been corrected. Moreover, the Commission had not considered the impact of the "fair and honorable dealings" clause of the act, language it had acknowledged elsewhere was "unique as a ground upon which Indian claims may be founded."[29]

Unable to reach a decision based on the new written briefs and an oral argument, the commissioners took the highly unusual step of convening a second oral argument. This gave Lewis, a superb oral advocate, another chance to convince the commissioners not to dismiss the imprisonment claim. Even though the facts were not in dispute, he insisted that the commissioners understand the importance of the claim. "First, [the Apaches] were thrown out of their homes; second, they are imprisoned because they did not like it when they were thrown out." These actions "resulted in the absolute killing off of that race of people . . . in the absolute ruination of the Chiricahua and Warm Spring Apache bands."

Lewis explained in several different ways his theory that the Commission had thrown out the first petition because "we had not pleaded it well." He agreed "that perhaps we did urge an individual claim" in the first petition, but the present petition was "directed to making a tribal complaint." Accordingly, the language in the Commission's earlier opinion that imprisonment claims were individual in nature "has not a thing on earth to do with [the new petition]. You might have said Santa Claus had a gray beard, and it would have the same effect." [30]

Lewis's oral argument apparently was decisive. On December 29, 1950, less than two months later, the Commission issued a one-page order denying the government's motion to dismiss. It gave no explanation for its ruling. Presumably, however, it decided, as Lewis urged, to ignore the broad language of its first opinion and to interpret it, at least for purposes of the Fort Sill Apache claims, as dealing only with the language of the original petition. [31]

This by no means meant that the commissioners agreed that the Chiricahuas had been wrongly treated as prisoners of war for twenty-seven years. The Commission still would not allow the tribe to sue for any injuries suffered by tribal members as a result of their confinement. Instead, it permitted the Fort Sill Apaches to try to show that their members had been wrongly imprisoned for twenty-seven years and that the imprisonment "thwarted [the tribes] in the advancement of their common purposes of their formation." The order merely left an Apache foot in the door, with the possibility that the Commission might one day need to settle a dollar figure on the value of what anthropologists call a "culture."

Despite the ruling's narrow impact, the government's attorneys characterized the arguments of Lewis and Weissbrodt as "insubstantial, transparent, and fictitious devices." Their reaction was understandable. The opinion of May 6, 1949, had contained a broad pronouncement that would have barred any contention that an imprisonment claim could be tribal. Yet the Commission by its December 29, 1950 order seemed to retreat from its prior opinion without offering any explanation.

.   .   .

Subsequent decisions indicated that the government's attorneys need not have been overly concerned. Although the government lost this one battle on the individual/tribal issue, it won the war. In other cases decided over the next thirty years, the Commission cited its May 6, 1949 opinion to assert that claims were individual and therefore beyond its jurisdiction—and conveniently never mentioned its December 29, 1950 order.

Many of the claims that the Commission decided were beyond its jurisdiction involved the making, management, and sale of allotments. As a result, the Commission considered one of the major causes of tribal land losses off limits. It didn't matter that a reservation was allotted pursuant to a congressional act affecting all the members of a tribe, or that all of the allotments on the reservation were managed by government officials following identical government policies. And of course, because the United States had not consented to be sued by individual Indians for wrongs committed before August 13, 1946, no allottee had a legal remedy for any damage to or loss of his allotment. Many years later, Indians tried to circumvent the Commission's jurisdictional limitations by bringing suits in federal courts against individual non-Indian landowners as well as the federal government to recover lands that the United States had allotted in the nineteenth and early twentieth centuries to individual Indians and then allegedly wrongly permitted them to sell. These suits also failed. The courts held that the Indians' claims were barred by the statute of limitations; the government had waived it as a defense only in the Indian Claims Commission Act. No matter what argument attorneys for Indians advanced, the Commission's interpretation meant that no tribunal would ever consider a large class of Indian claims. It was as if the December 29, 1950 order existed only for purposes of the claims of the Fort Sill Apaches.[32]

.   .   .

While the Fort Sill Apaches were fighting to preserve their claims from 1948 through 1951, the Chiricahuas who had settled on the Mescalero

Reservation were busy with their own. On March 5, 1948, the Chiricahuas selected a five-person claims committee headed by Eugene Chihuahua, a tribal leader who as a young man had accompanied Geronimo and Naiche during the final breakout from San Carlos in 1885 and 1886. The committee promptly entered into a contract with Roy Mobley, an attorney from nearby Alamogordo, New Mexico, who, like so many others, had a brief and unhappy association with James Curry.[33]

The committee members identified several claims they believed should be asserted. Like their tribesmen in Oklahoma, they thought that the imprisonment claim was the most important. But before Mobley could complete a petition, the Commission issued its decision of May 4, 1949, stating that the imprisonment claims of the Fort Sill Apaches were individual in nature. Deciding that discretion was the better part of valor, Mobley filed a petition on August 15, 1949, that omitted any mention of the imprisonment. The only claim was for the taking of the aboriginal lands. He and his cocounsel in Washington, Guy Martin, discussed the possibility of reverting to Sam Kenoi's strategy of the 1930s—drafting a bill by which Congress would grant relief for the imprisonment—but no legislation was ever introduced.[34]

Both groups of Chiricahua Apaches had filed claims by the statutory deadline, August 13, 1951. Their trials, however, were still many years away. The commissioners and, even more, the government's attorneys faced hundreds of tribal claims, and in the latter 1950s, the Apaches' attorneys tried unsuccessfully to push their land claims to the fore. As a result, the Commission didn't hear the first Chiricahua claims, for the taking of their aboriginal lands, until 1962. By then, it had ruled on the land claims of scores of tribes, which established the parameters for the Chiricahua claims.

SEVEN

LAND CLAIMS:
FICTION WITH A PURPOSE

We have never put any price on our lands, or on the rights you took
away from us without our consent. All we have asked, all we now ask is
that the matter be settled; that you permit your Court of Claims
to decide whatever it is just for you to pay us.
—Unidentified chief of the Colville and Okanagan Indians [1]

The creation of the Indian Claims Commission to make financial
amends for any wrongful acts on the part of the U.S. government evi-
denced a certain nobility of spirit and disregard for financial consequences. The Commission was, as mentioned earlier, unique in the
history of European colonization, and its noble origins were stated most
clearly in the House report, drafted by Felix Cohen, that accompanied
the bill creating it:

> [W]hatever the amount may be to which the Indian tribes are justly
> entitled, the sooner it is paid the better it will be for the Federal Gov-
> ernment, from a financial point of view as well as from the standpoint
> of national honor.
> . . . [E]ven if it were true that the sums required to meet existing
> obligations to Indian tribes should turn out to be somewhat larger than
> the rate of actual recoveries in the past would suggest, your committee
> believe that this is hardly a relevant consideration in determining the

propriety of the proposed legislation. If the Government could save millions of dollars by refusing to pay its just debts to its Indian citizens and by continuing to refuse them access to the courts for the enforcement of obligations that the Federal Government freely assumed, it could save even more by denying its white citizens access to the Court of Claims. But nobody has yet suggested that the Government of the United States should balance its budget by defaulting on its outstanding obligations to its white citizens and denying them access to the courts. Why should we do this to our Indian citizenry? [2]

For Indian land claims, such idealism soon ran into the twin grindstones of political and fiscal realities and the incongruity of Anglo-American legal concepts and Indian cultures. By 1955, Chief Commissioner Witt testified to a congressional committee that, as a matter of "justice" to the Indians and the taxpayers, "[w]e owe them [the Indians] a moral duty of *some* compensation for taking away from them the lands where we found them, from which they were then making their livelihood." [3]

In other words, Witt now equated justice with balancing the interests of the taxpayers against the rights of Indians. Fairness and honor had little role in the equation; placating the tribes by awarding *something*, while protecting the Treasury by not awarding too much, was paramount. Nowhere was this goal more evident than in decisions involving the loss of tribes' aboriginal lands. Land claims comprised the majority of Indian claims, and the Commission's effectiveness would be judged largely by its success in hacking a trail through this thicket.

.   .   .

Anglo-American law contains a legal theory that, on the surface, addressed tribal claims for compensation for aboriginal lands taken without agreement. This theory is the *power of eminent domain*. Local and state governments, as well as the national government, have the power to take private lands without the landowner's agreement. For example, a municipal government may negotiate with a local landowner over the price of land needed for a road, but if no agreement can be reached, the government does not have to reroute the road—it simply takes the land under its power of eminent domain. The Fifth Amendment, however, guarantees the landowner a recourse. He may ask a court to determine the value of his property as of the date of taking, together with an adjust-

ment, typically measured by an interest rate applied up to the date of the
award, which the government has to reimburse him.

Many tribes argued to the Indian Claims Commission that the
United States had exercised its powers of eminent domain in taking
their aboriginal lands, and like white landowners, they argued that the
Fifth Amendment entitled them to recover the fair market value of the
lands taken, together with interest. Although private landowners are typically asked to yield relatively small parcels of land, while Indian tribes
had relinquished territory the size of states, this theory of eminent domain seemed straightforward enough. But it masked four huge differences between Indian and non-Indian eminent domain claims.

First of all, the owner of a parcel of land needed by the government
can usually be identified through deeds conveying title to the property.
The identity of the Indians who used an area of land was often difficult
to determine.

Second, the Indians had no records defining the boundaries of their
aboriginal territory, frequently confounding efforts to determine just
how much acreage had been taken.

Third, few if any Indian tribes had a concept of land ownership
under which real estate could be bought and sold. The Commission and
courts therefore had to determine whether Indians' aboriginal interests
in land constituted property rights subject to Fifth Amendment protection, or rights entitled to lesser protection, or no rights at all.

Finally, the market value of a tract of land in the Anglo economy had
virtually no relationship to the values that that same land had to its Indian occupants. How much, for example, was a Chiricahua Apache
mountain god worth? And even if the Commission opted to ignore Indian values, the absence of a market for tracts of land as immense as
those the Indians were forced to surrender made normal Anglo valuation techniques all but irrelevant.

·   ·   ·

Anglo-American law also contains theories that seemed to apply to the
claims of tribes that entered into treaties or agreements to sell their
lands. In petition after petition, tribes claimed that they had agreed to
cede their lands for far less than they were worth, and in these instances,
instead of the law of eminent domain, the Commission and courts grav-
itated to contract law. A party to a contract generally cannot escape its

contractual duties by claiming that it entered into a bad bargain. If a landowner agrees to sell a piece of land for $10,000 but, after the sale, discovers that it actually was worth $15,000, the seller cannot usually recover the additional $5,000 in court. There are exceptions. If, for example, the landowner was induced to enter into the agreement by the buyer's misrepresentation of important facts, or the buyer compelled the landowner to enter into the contract through economic or physical duress, or the buyer took unfair advantage of the landowner's lack of sophistication to arrive at an unconscionably low price, courts can, and do, award relief.

Various tribes made claims based on all these contract law doctrines. Yet here again, the readily available doctrines of contract law masked important differences between transactions among Anglo-Americans and transactions between the federal government and an Indian tribe. Usually treaties identified the Indian groups who occupied lands and sometimes the boundaries of that land, making resolution of those two issues somewhat easier than in the taking cases. But the Commission and courts still had to determine whether the nature of the Indians' possession of the land entitled them to compensation, and if so, how to establish the amount, let alone deal with the problem that few if any tribes entered into the cession agreements voluntarily and with understanding of their implications.

Many tribes also contended that the United States had wrongly taken or purchased portions of the reservations that had been established for them. Under the rubric of their accounting petition, the Chiricahuas even asserted a claim for Fort Sill. The reservation land claims raised many of the same issues as the aboriginal land claims, though less starkly. Thus, the Commission's handling of aboriginal land claims provides the best measure of the Commission's performance and of the American legal system's ability to fairly decide claims arising in a unique cultural context.

In struggling with the aboriginal land claims, the tribunals and the lawyers who practiced before them eventually created solutions that partook as much of fiction as of fact. Like colonial administrators around the world, they engaged in what one anthropologist calls "working misunderstandings." Instead of inventing new law to address an unprecedented situation, they bent the facts to fit a familiar collection of concepts and precedents.[4]

. . .

The first major problem was, simply, who could bring a claim?

The language of the Indian Claims Commission Act that knocked out any claims by individuals also required that aboriginal land claims could be brought only on behalf of the "tribe, band, or identifiable group of Indians" that had owned or occupied a particular tract of land. That seems simple enough, but it had already been muddied by a Supreme Court decision dating back to 1901. The justices can be described—charitably—as having been burdened by the prejudices of the age. In *Montoya v. United States,* they said, "Owing to the natural infirmities of the Indian character, their fiery tempers, impatience of restraint, their mutual jealousies and animosities, their nomadic habits, and lack of mental training, they have as a rule shown a total want of that cohesive force necessary to the making up of a nation in the ordinary sense of the word." The justices overlooked the notion that a strong sense of community—presumably inconsistent with "fiery tempers" and "mutual jealousies and animosities"—permitted most native groups to live together peacefully without Western-style governmental structures. Thus armed with ignorance and blatant racism, the Supreme Court justices took it upon themselves to define the concepts of "tribe" and "band."

"By a 'tribe'," the Court said, "we understand a body of Indians of the same or a similar race, united in a community under one leadership or government, and inhabiting a particular though sometimes ill-defined territory; by a 'band', a company of Indians not necessarily, though often, of the same race or tribe, but united under the same leadership in a common design. . . . It may be doubtful whether it [a band] requires more than independence of action, continuity of existence, a common leadership, and concert of action." Crucial to both definitions was the European concept that a political unit, whether a state, a tribe, or a band, needs a recognized government or leadership that can command common action.[5]

Among Indians, only a handful of groups qualified as tribes or bands when they lost their aboriginal lands. One was the Creek Nation. Before they were removed to the Indian Territory in the West as one of the Five Civilized Tribes, the Creeks during the early nineteenth century had a national council composed of the head men of the tribal towns. This council met at least once a year, and its decisions were promulgated as the will of the nation. The Indian Claims Commission concluded, "the Creek National Council had exclusive control over all the lands of the Creek Nation, and alone had the power of the disposition of them." [6]

The great majority of the groups that the United States government treated as tribes, however, could not qualify under the *Montoya* definitions. According to a leading anthropologist, A. L. Kroeber, "It was we Caucasians who again and again rolled a number of related obscure bands or minute villages into the larger package of a 'tribe,' which we then putatively endowed with sovereign power and territorial ownership which the native nationality had mostly never even claimed." Among the Chiricahuas, for example, extended family groups made most land use decisions, and even such "governmental" decisions as whether to go on a raid. Band leaders exercised charismatic power only for enterprises too large for the family groups; indeed, the years of conflict and crisis gave the likes of Mangas Coloradas and Cochise a prominence among band members that they would not otherwise have achieved. And even with such "superstars," virtually no political decisions were made among the Chiricahuas at what could be imagined to be the tribal level.[7]

If rigidly adhered to, the *Montoya* definitions would almost certainly have prevented the Chiricahuas, and most other tribes, from even bringing suits. Only family groups might qualify, but in the middle of the twentieth century it would have been impossible for an attorney to prove the boundaries of the lands occupied and used by each separate family group a century before. No wonder Howard Shenkin plaintively asked Grady Lewis in 1947, "Who are our clients?"

For the Indian Claims Commission Act to have any impact, a solution had to be found.

.   .   .

In 1848, in the Treaty of Guadalupe Hidalgo that ended the Mexican War, Mexico conveyed to the United States the land that would become California as well as most of the Southwest. That same year, gold was discovered at Sutter's Mill, and within three years some 150,000 pilgrims of Mammon flocked to California. Within a decade they transformed the landscape, ignoring any native claims to the lands and—with the help of the military—eliminating any Indians who got in the way of their dreams of riches.[8]

Before 1848, probably 100,000 or more Indians lived in California in more than five hundred small groups, each with its own territory. The flood of non-Indians decimated the native population and scattered the remnants. Recognizing the genocidal consequences of the California gold rush on the Indians, the United States government sent representatives to negotiate treaties. In return for the sanctuary to be provided by eighteen small reservations, the natives agreed to surrender all other claims to California lands. But before the Senate could vote on whether to ratify the treaties, the California legislature successfully petitioned Congress to reject them on the ground that the land in the eighteen reservations had a value of $100 million—too valuable to waste on the natives. No reservations were established, and the California Indians remained "mostly homeless and vagrant." Seventy-five years later, in the 1920s, the United States Senate remorsefully concluded that "The California Indians were deprived of their property in a manner shockingly in disregard of every consideration of justice and humanity." [9]

The Indian Claims Commission Act expressly authorized the Commission to make monetary amends for unfair and dishonorable actions. Actions branded by Congress as unjust and inhumane seemed to qualify. Yet attorneys for the California Indians had to overcome two formidable obstacles before the Commission would even hear their land claims.

First, by 1946, many of the five hundred California "tribelets" were extinct as cultural or political entities, so they could not sue. Although a person descended from a member of a tribelet could possibly sue on its behalf, actually finding descendants would have been next to impossible. Second, even if descendants could be found, the attorneys couldn't prove the boundaries of the territory of any given tribelet. As one lawyer testified, "Most of the evidence had been emasculated and destroyed, and there was really no one who could help us in our presentation as far as the clients were concerned. None of them knew the facts." [10]

After passage of the act, two groups of California Indians contacted attorneys who filed two separate petitions seeking compensation from the United States for the appropriation of aboriginal lands. Ernest Wilkinson, who had played such an instrumental role in the adoption of the Indian Claims Commission Act, represented one of the groups. In 1950, he became president of Brigham Young University and, seemingly indefatigable, continued to work on his law firm's Indian claims. All of the initial partners of the Wilkinson firm were members of the Church of Jesus Christ of Latter-Day Saints. Church doctrine contributed to the prominence of Mormon attorneys in representing Indian tribes. According to the Book of Mormon, Indians were believed to be the Lost Tribe of Israel. Church leaders did not regard Indians as "savages," as did so many other Anglos, but instead as backslid Christians who, if they were sincerely converted to Mormonism, would even become lighter skinned. The Mormons encouraged missionary work among the Indians and approved of efforts to obtain reparations for them.[11]

To avoid the problems raised by tribal extinction and the nearly total lack of information about the boundaries of hundreds of tribelets' lands, Wilkinson brought action on behalf of the Indians of California as a whole. Immediately, *Montoya* raised its exclusionary head: the five hundred tribelets had had no common leadership or territory; consequently, they were not a tribe or a band. The government moved to dismiss the petitions of both sets of lawyers. Wilkinson and the others argued that the Indians of California, although not a tribe or a band, *were* an "identifiable group of American Indians." On December 15, 1950, however, an unconvinced Commission unanimously dismissed both petitions.[12]

The Indians appealed to the Court of Claims. On May 6, 1952, it "reversed" the Commission's decision, saying the Indians of California were indeed an "identifiable group of American Indians." Judge Benjamin Littleton wrote the opinion for the Court. A devout Methodist from Tennessee who was described upon his death in 1966 as "one of the most beloved judges who ever served on the United States Court of Claims," Littleton adopted an interpretation of the act that comported with what he believed was Congress's intent. "Congress intended," he wrote, "that all tribes, bands or groups of American Indians, should be given the right to have their day in court and have their claims adjudicated." In order to fulfill that intent when a tribe or band no longer exists, he reasoned, individual members of a modern group should be able to sue on behalf of the extinct group if those individuals could be identified as descendants of the extinct group. It shouldn't matter that the ancestors of the modern group lived in separate tribes.[13]

The government's attorneys screamed in outrage: the opinion was "pure and unadulterated judicial legislation." The act's language spoke of a tribe, band, or other identifiable group of Indians; it didn't mention a conglomeration of groups, mutually unintelligible languages, conflicting economies, and different cultures. Instead of merely interpreting the statute, as they avowed judges should, the Court of Claims had in effect inserted provisions that were not there.

The criticism, however, missed the mark. The phrase "other identifiable group" was broad enough to support Littleton's reading as well as the government's. Congress had failed to show how to resolve the concrete issue before the Court of Claims: whether the Indians of California were an identifiable group entitled to bring a land claim. Indeed, if legislators had been polled in 1946 about such a concrete issue, they almost surely would have expressed conflicting opinions about the right of the California Indians to sue. Given their silence on the issue, the Court of Claims had no choice but to make a decision that would elevate certain congressional purposes at the expense of others. The court risked the charge that it had appropriated a legislative function whether it chose a broad or narrow interpretation. In this sense, even the most strict constructionists in the judiciary routinely "legislate." [14]

·   ·   ·

When the case returned to the Indian Claims Commission to determine the boundaries of the land owned by this identifiable group, the Indian Claims Commission proved adept at reading between the lines of the Court of Claims' decision. It did not require the impossible—for the Indians to prove the boundaries of the land used by each tribelet— which would have blocked any recovery. Instead, on July 31, 1959, after thirty-nine days of trial and a record that entailed 3,838 pages of transcript testimony and 629 documentary exhibits, the Commission concluded that the ancestors of the Indians of California did have Indian title to most of what is now California. While the attorneys for the Indians readily acknowledged that they had not proven, nor had they attempted to prove, the boundaries of each tribelet's area of occupation, the Commission concluded that such proof was unnecessary when the government's role in scattering the tribelets had rendered it impossible. "All" they had to do, which they had done, was prove the exterior boundaries of the lands used by all the tribelets considered as a single group. The government, the tribunal was saying, should not now benefit from its past wrongdoing. [15]

In 1964, attorneys for the government and the Indians agreed to settle the land claims for $29,100,000. For the California Indians the amount of the settlement was most important, but for other tribes it paled next to the determination that aboriginal land claims could survive the government's "tribe, band or other identifiable group" defense.

Here was the first of the fictions required in this complex, cross-cultural process. Nineteenth-century governmental leaders repeatedly combined various related groups, treating them as a single political and landowning entity. The Supreme Court in *Montoya* elevated the same error into legal principle. The expert witnesses in Indian claims cases explained to the commissioners that most Indian "tribes," like the Chiricahuas, were not politically unified, yet the Commission, like its nineteenth-century governmental forebears, combined related family groups into tribes or bands. It did so not because it believed that tribes were politically unified, but because information was rarely available on the family group. Thus deliberate fiction tailored to the available evidence replaced the Supreme Court's error in *Montoya*. In the Indians of California case, the Court of Claims showed the Commission that the fiction should be carried as far as necessary to allow a claim to be prosecuted. If plaintiffs could not possibly be squeezed into a tribe or band, the court said, we will call them an "identifiable group."

·   ·   ·

Proving land ownership was at least as complex as establishing the identity of eligible claimants. Once again, court decisions predating the Indian Claims Commission Act established the criteria: a tribe had to show that it had (a) used and occupied (b) a tract of land with definite boundaries (c) exclusively of other tribes (d) from time immemorial.[16]

For most tribes, each of these four requirements presented a problem. Even tribes with permanent village sites tended to hunt, gather food, herd animals, and worship far beyond the borders of the villages. How could a tribe prove that it used (and occupied) every acre within the outer boundaries of the areas that in fact some of its members visited only periodically? Were areas used only in transit, or even bypassed but lying between village sites and hunting or food gathering sites, part of a tribe's aboriginal territory? Usually, the farther a hunting or gathering group got from its village, the more likely it was to encounter members of other tribes or bands. Did either amicable or contested use of traditional foraging grounds by other tribes destroy the exclusivity deemed necessary for aboriginal title? Of course, the European incursion invariably altered the boundaries of tribes' lands. If the lands that a tribe used and occupied at the time the United States acquired them differed from those it had used and occupied previously, which lands, if any, were used and occupied from "time immemorial"?

Initially, the Indian Claims Commission took a predictably strict view of all this. During 1950 and 1951, it dismissed the aboriginal land claims of five tribes on the grounds that none of them had proven title to the lands claimed. Each of the four requirements proved a stumbling block for at least one of those five tribes.[17]

Once again, however, the Court of Claims was determined not to allow most or all aboriginal land claims to be dismissed. This attitude contrasted sharply with that of the Court of Claims during the first half of the twentieth century, when it repeatedly denied claims brought under special jurisdictional acts. One explanation for the reversal was the near complete turnover in judges since the 1930s. Besides Judge Littleton, who had been the most pro-Indian pre-war judge, all of the judges on the court during the 1950s were Roosevelt and Truman appointees, and were generally more favorably disposed toward Indian claims than their predecessors.

Only two of the five tribes whose claims were dismissed bothered to appeal, and the court reversed the dismissals of both. Based on those rulings, the Commission vacated its dismissal of the claim of a third tribe. The Court of Claims did not determine that any of the tribes actually had aboriginal title to the lands claimed: it merely directed the Commission to give weight to evidence it had previously discounted or that, in some of the cases, the Indians' attorneys had ignored. Reading between the lines, however, the Commission understood that the Court of Claims believed that such evidence often should suffice to prove a tribe's aboriginal title.[18]

Not surprisingly, the Commission went on to determine that each of the three tribes exclusively owned and occupied aboriginal lands. The lands totaled about thirty-two million acres, an area about the size of Alabama. The Commission eventually awarded those tribes collectively about $10 million for the claims it had dismissed a few years before.[19]

.   .   .

The Pawnees were the first of the five tribes to have their land claims tried. During the early nineteenth century, they were probably the most numerous and powerful tribe of the central Plains, numbering about twenty thousand to twenty-five thousand Indians. They lived about five months of the year in permanent villages in what is now eastern Nebraska, where they farmed; during the other seven months they hunted in a vast territory that included most of Nebraska and northern Kansas—estimated by their attorney to encompass about forty million acres.[20]

In the early 1830s, as the Pawnees came into contact with the white man, a smallpox epidemic cut the population in half in one or two years. In their weakened state, they offered little resistance when in 1833 the United States, busy locating eastern tribes into Indian Territory, asked them to cede the southern part of their land for a pittance. Pawnee numbers had dropped to approximately four thousand when the government approached them for yet another cession in 1857. The government now intended to open the Indian Territory of Nebraska and Kansas to white settlement. By that time, the Pawnees were defenseless against white encroachments and raids by their traditional enemies, the Sioux. They had no choice but to agree to limit themselves to a small reservation within their traditional core territory along the Loup River. Where they had once patrolled an area equivalent to a good-sized western state, they were now reduced to less than a township. Increasingly beleaguered by white settlements, the Pawnees agreed in 1875 to cede this last tie to their aboriginal home and move to the Indian Territory in what is now Oklahoma. The Oklahoma land was promptly allotted and the "surplus" sold during the 1890s. During the mid-twentieth century, the remnants of this once-mighty Plains tribe, now scattered across over twenty states, sought compensation under the Indian Claims Commission Act.[21]

The parties paid little attention to locating the Pawnees' aboriginal villages; the disputes before the Commission were over the much larger area in which the Pawnees had hunted. For the tribe to prevail, it had to convince the Commission that it had exclusively occupied and used the hunting lands. The Pawnees' attorney, Arthur Honnold, who represented several tribes before the Commission with little success, adduced three types of evidence on this issue. He had a few elderly (eighty- to ninety-year-old) tribal members testify about hunting trips they had made as infants or had heard about from relatives, information that was too imprecise to permit any definition of boundaries. Second, he introduced about sixty exhibits, mostly excerpts from published works. While some discussed Pawnee hunts, none was precise enough to define the territory.

The third and perhaps the most important piece of testimony was from Dr. Waldo Wedel, an archeologist for the federal government, who had written a book on Pawnee archeological sites. It included a description of the boundaries of Pawnee territories, which Honnold had adopted in defining the tribe's aboriginal land.[22]

Honnold, however, had pinned the tribe's hopes on an uncommitted witness. Expert witnesses came to understand that they were expected to be strong advocates for the party that engaged them, but Wedel apparently lacked that understanding. The government attorneys easily elicited from him testimony that no Pawnee archeological sites had been found throughout most of the territory the tribe claimed, and that his own description of the boundaries was based primarily on the published literature. He agreed that the western boundary, in particular, was a "considerably tricky proposition" and that his description was an "approximation," as he "wasn't primarily interested in the exact location of the boundary." Wedel testified that "I doubt very much that you could say any tribe had exclusive possession, if by that you mean that no other surrounding tribe could venture into the [hunting] territory." Much of the claimed land was "common hunting ground among several tribes." He explained—correctly, no doubt—that the Pawnees and other Plains tribes had a core region, beyond which their influence or strength diminished. The boundaries of each of the tribes, therefore, were "indefinite."[23]

By the time he was finished, Wedel's testimony had effectively sunk any claim of definite boundaries or that the Pawnees exclusively owned and occupied any land except their immediate villages. Not surprisingly, the Commission concluded on July 14, 1950, that the boundaries proposed for the entire tract were arbitrary, and even if boundaries could be defined, the Pawnees would have had conflicts with other tribes over that land. The Commission did not even award the Pawnees anything for the land surrounding their villages because they had neither tried to define its boundaries nor put forward any evidence defining the area. All claims based on the aboriginal landholdings therefore were dismissed.[24]

The Pawnees appealed, and on February 3, 1953, the Court of Claims reversed the dismissal of the aboriginal land claims and re-

manded the case to the Commission for further consideration. The
court expressed dismay at the huge gaps in the factual record and chas-
tised the Commission for not using its Investigation Division to try to
fill the holes. (Apparently the court did not know that the Commission
had not established such a division.) The remand to permit the parties to
introduce new factual information came as something of a surprise.
Generally, an appellate court decides an appeal based entirely on the
record created in the trial court. If that record is inadequate, one party
must bear the consequences, unless the trial court's erroneous rulings
caused the information gap, which was not the case here. But the Court
of Claims took the unprecedented step of performing much of the work
that Honnold should have done prior to trial.

The Court of Claims permitted its clerk, Margaret Pierce, who
would be appointed as an Indian claims commissioner in 1968, to spend
about three months at the National Archives researching the Pawnees'
aboriginal landholdings. She discovered that Honnold had spent a grand
total of one hour at the Archives. She located numerous documents
written by government officials that substantiated the Pawnees' claims
and, together with the documents previously in the record, the court
was able to tell a coherent story of the Pawnees' use of their lands. The
court did not direct the Commission to find for the Indians based on
this fuller record or attempt to define the tribe's aboriginal boundaries,
but suggested forcefully that the Pawnees would be able to meet the requirements for proving aboriginal ownership of a tract of land.[25]

Even the court's expanded documentary record may have been insufficient to establish the boundaries of the Pawnees' lands and eliminate
all conflicts over its use. (According to Pierce, an early draft of the opinion defined the boundaries of the Pawnees' aboriginal lands, but the
court decided that it shouldn't take over the roles of the parties and the
Commission to that extent.) Instead of locating additional evidence or
engaging another expert witness, Honnold immediately entered into a
series of stipulations with the attorneys for adjoining tribes. They drew
lines between their claims, with each tribe agreeing to waive all claims
to the land on the other's side of the line. The Pawnees agreed to relinquish their claims to millions of acres, most notably large areas of Kansas
that were sites of hunting expeditions and that Wedel had testified contained Pawnee archeological sites. As a trade-off, Honnold hoped to

eliminate disputes about the location of the boundaries and intertribal conflicts over the land within the boundaries.[26]

Honnold died before he found out whether this end run would work. It did.

In 1957, the Commission determined that the Pawnees had aboriginal title to all of the land to which they had stipulated with the surrounding tribes, about twenty-three million acres. Again, the government attorneys protested, arguing that because the government was not a party to the stipulations, they were not binding on the United States and the Commission should give the stipulations no weight in the matter. Putting them aside, the government said, the evidence presented by the Pawnees' attorneys did not establish the boundaries of the land that the Pawnees occupied and used exclusively.[27]

Technically, the government's attorneys were right. Most tribes proved the boundaries of their aboriginal lands through a full documentary record and through anthropologists who could present the oral history of the Indians that was often absent from the documents. According to Commissioner Witt, the attorneys "had practically every prominent anthropologist in the United States employed on one side or the other." The Pawnees had made no such effort to prove the boundaries of their former lands.[28]

The government's attorneys, however, missed the point. If it was clear that a tribe exclusively occupied and used some land, difficulties of proof shouldn't obstruct their recovery. The quality of the proof might affect the number of acres for which a tribe might recover, but seldom, if ever, should weak proof result in a dismissal. In this case, the Pawnees' own stipulations drastically reduced the extent of their claims.

.   .   .

By 1953, the Court of Claims had overridden the Indian Claims Commission on two key issues: the nature of the group that could bring a claim for the loss of aboriginal territory and the proof necessary to establish aboriginal ownership of a tract of land. On each issue, the court had interpreted the founding act liberally in order to remove obstacles to recovery. The decisions didn't secure any tribe's recovery, however. Three closely related issues still had to be resolved. First, did the United States' acquisition of a tract of land that Indians had occupied and used obligate it to compensate them? Second, if so, what had the land been worth? And third, did the United States have to pay interest from the date of acquisition to the date the Indians finally were paid, as the Fifth Amendment required when the government took land from private citizens? It took a long time, and several false starts, for the Supreme Court and Court of Claims to answer these questions.

Any discussion of the rights conferred by aboriginal possession of land must, as with so many analyses of federal law, begin with perhaps the most influential justice ever to sit on the Supreme Court, Chief Justice John Marshall. In his thirty-four-year term, which began in 1801, Marshall wrote three important decisions concerning the rights of Indian tribes in their lands. He characterized as "extravagant and absurd" the European idea that by establishing "feeble settlements . . . on the sea-coast" they "acquired legitimate power . . . to govern [the natives] or occupy the lands from sea to sea." Marshall was a realist, however. By the early nineteenth century, he was the Chief Justice of a burgeoning nation that had pushed virtually all of the surviving natives west of the Mississippi. He wrote that the "discoverees," such as the Cherokees, "once numerous, powerful, and truly independent found by our ancestors in the quiet and uncontrolled possession of an ample domain, gradually sinking beneath our superior policy, our arts and our arms, have yielded their lands by successive treaties, each of which contains a solemn guarantee of the residue, until they retain" little if anything of that domain. The Supreme Court, he recognized, had to hold that some rights were conferred by European "discovery," because it was "indispensable to that system under which the country has been settled" and "the property of the great mass of the community originates in it." [29]

Discovery, Marshall concluded, gave two types of rights. First, as against all other European nations, the discoverer acquired "the sole right of acquiring the soil and of making settlements on it." Second, as against the native occupants, the discoverer acquired the legal title to the land, but the Indians remained "the rightful occupants of the soil, with a legal as well as just claim to retain possession of it, and to use it according to their own discretion." As the successor to the European discoverers, the United States had the sole right to purchase from the Indians their rights of occupancy and possession, but until it did, those rights remained with the Indians.[30]

Marshall in effect said that property rights to land possessed by Indians were divided. The Indians had legal rights to occupy and use the land, but they could sell those rights only to the government. The government held the title to the land (called the "fee" in Anglo-American law), which it could convey to others, but always subject to the Indian rights of occupancy and use unless the government acquired those rights from the Indians.

In the most famous of the three Marshall decisions, *Cherokee Nation* v. *Georgia,* he rejected the power of the state of Georgia to extend its laws onto Cherokee lands. President Andrew Jackson supported Georgia's efforts to rule the Cherokees as a means of forcing them to move to the Indian Territory west of the Mississippi. He is reported to have said upon hearing of the ruling, "John Marshall has made his decision—now let him enforce it." Ignoring his executive duty, Jackson refused to protect the Cherokees from Georgia's assertions of authority. A few years later, the Cherokees were forced to move west, with tremendous loss of life. For much of the next century, Jackson's views concerning Indian property rights, not Marshall's, prevailed. Yet Marshall's opinions remained in the law books, never overruled and waiting for jurists more sympathetic to the Indians to take them seriously.[31]

Indian land rights reached their nadir in the early twentieth century. In the *Montoya* decision of 1901, the Supreme Court had articulated its disparaging view of the Indian racial character; two years later, it decided in the case of *Lone Wolf* v. *Hitchcock* that the property rights of Indians were worthless when Congress wanted their land. This case was brought by members of the Kiowa, Comanche, and Kiowa Apache tribes to block the enforcement of a congressional act providing for the allotment of their reservation and the opening of the "surplus" land to white settlement—the same act that, as described in Chapter Two, brought white farmers to the Fort Sill area and increased pressure to remove the Chiricahuas. The reservation had been granted for the occupancy and use of the Kiowas, Comanches, and Apaches by a treaty ratified in 1867, declaring that the land would not be taken away unless three-quarters of the tribal members consented in writing. In 1892, a majority of the three tribes had signed an agreement calling for allotment and the opening of the surplus lands. The plaintiffs in *Lone Wolf* contended that those signatures had been obtained by fraud, but the undisputed main point was that the requisite supermajority had not signed the allotment agreement. If the treaty bound the United States, Congress could not open the lands.[32]

Lone Wolf, the principal chief of the Kiowas, had fought against United States troops during the 1860s and 1870s, and had threatened that the Kiowas would return to the warpath if allotment was forced on them. As a realist, he ultimately opted for the white man's method of doing battle, the judicial system. The Indians engaged former Illinois congressman and federal judge William Springer to represent them, but the legal battle proved no more successful than a military one would have been. The Supreme Court acknowledged that prior opinions—such as Marshall's—had said that Indian title was as "sacred" as the white man's fee title, but opined that Indian title was good only as against private citizens or states that tried to dispossess tribes. Congress, on the other hand, the Court said, has "plenary," or absolute, power over Indian affairs and can abrogate a treaty and convert Indian property from one form to another. This plenary "power has always been deemed a political one, not subject to be controlled by the judicial department of the government." In other words, Congress could do whatever it pleased and the Indians had no recourse, even in the courts.[33]

The decision in *Lone Wolf* was not easy to reconcile with Justice Marshall's decisions, which had recognized substantial property rights in the tribes until the United States purchased their lands. *Lone Wolf* suggested that Congress had plenary power over tribal lands even before they had been purchased. The Supreme Court had to confront this conflict in three decisions during the 1930s addressing whether Indians were entitled to compensation for the taking of their reservation lands. By then, however, Indian policy had changed. Congress had rejected the old allotment policy with its aim of destroying tribal cohesion and had passed the Indian Reorganization Act with its emphasis on tribal sovereignty. The Supreme Court, then under Chief Justice Charles Evans Hughes, also held different views of Indian rights. In three different cases (brought under special jurisdictional acts), the Court held that, although Congress had the power to manage Indians' reservations and even to abrogate Indians' treaties, that power was limited by the Indians' right to receive fair compensation under the Fifth Amendment. The plenary power "did not enable the United States to give the tribal lands to others, or to appropriate them to its own purposes, without rendering or assuming an obligation to render, just compensation for them; for that would not be guardianship, but an act of confiscation." That principle has not since been seriously challenged. In the words of Justice Benjamin Cardozo, "Spoilation is not management." [34]

Did the same principle apply to Indian land rights acquired through aboriginal possession? If so, the Chiricahua Apaches, whose aboriginal lands were taken without any compensation, also were protected under the Fifth Amendment. But because few special jurisdictional acts let tribes sue for the loss of their aboriginal territory, the Supreme Court did not consider the issue until 1946.

.   .   .

Before the arrival of white settlers, eleven "tribelets" lived along the Pacific Coast in what is now Oregon. In 1855, a representative of the United States negotiated a series of treaties under which these groups agreed to cede their aboriginal lands in return for a reservation and monetary payments. The Senate failed to ratify the treaties of four of the tribelets, and consequently the government refused to make the negotiated payments. The Indians were placed on a reservation, but the government took more than three-quarters of it within a few years in response to pressures from white settlers, and then gave small allotments to the Indians residing on the remainder. By the early twentieth century, many of the members of these four groups were landless, and as late as the 1920s their average annual income was only $27 per person.[35]

Moved by reports of their poverty, in 1935 Congress passed a special jurisdictional act permitting them to sue for the appropriation of their aboriginal lands. The act did not guarantee any recovery; it merely opened the doors to the Court, which in turn would determine if the United States was liable. The special jurisdictional act identified the proper parties to bring suit, and a map accompanying the unratified treaty showed the boundaries of the bands' aboriginal lands. The only real defense against liability the Department of Justice could mount was to assert that a tribe did not have a property right in its aboriginal land that would permit recovery.

The issue reached the Supreme Court in 1946, a few months after passage of the Indian Claims Commission Act, in *United States* v. *Alcea Band of Tillamooks*. Chief Justice Fred Vinson's opinion, joined by three other justices, rejected the Indians' position that the special jurisdictional act permitted them to recover on moral, rather than legal, grounds. Unlike plaintiffs under the Indian Claims Commission Act, the Oregon Indians could recover only if the seizure of their lands violated their legal rights. However, the Indians did have a legal right to recover. Hearkening back to Chief Justice Marshall's opinions concerning Indian title and the 1930s opinions on the taking of reservation lands, Vinson stated, "Admitting the undoubted power of Congress to extinguish original Indian title compels no conclusion that compensation need not be paid." The government's attorneys had argued that Indian title derived from aboriginal occupancy, unlike Indian title recognized by the likes of treaties, was not legally compensable. The Court rejected the government's argument, noting that prior decisions drew no distinction about compensability between the two types of lands.[36]

Alcea was not unanimous. Three justices dissented, stating that the Oregon Indians should not recover. Justice Hugo Black took a third position. He agreed that the Indians should recover, but because the special jurisdictional act *had* provided that the government would be liable, with the only issue being the amount of damages. Black's interpretation of the statute would come back to haunt Indian claimants.[37]

The Court remanded the case to the Court of Claims to determine the amount of damages, but five years later *Alcea* was back on appeal. The Court of Claims had determined that the value of the land on the date of appropriation was about $3 million, and that—thanks to the nearly hundred-year delay in payment—the Indians were also entitled under the Fifth Amendment to interest of about $14 million: a total award of about $17 million. To the surprise of many attorneys, the Supreme Court, in a brief, cryptic opinion, held that the Indians were *not* entitled to interest. Interest cannot be awarded in claims against the United States, it said, unless expressly authorized by statute or under the Fifth Amendment. None of the former opinions in the case "expressed the view that recovery was grounded on a taking under the Fifth Amendment," and the special jurisdictional act contained no provision authorizing interest. The Court offered no other explanation.[38]

The Court's opinion was not only cryptic, but ingenuous. While it had never mentioned the Fifth Amendment in its 1946 opinion, it had said that the Indians had a legal right to recover. That amendment provided the only legal basis for recovery for an uncompensated taking of property by the federal government. Furthermore, as even this second

Alcea decision acknowledged, the Fifth Amendment entitled landowners to interest when the government did not make payment when it took property.

Finally, in early 1955, the Supreme Court provided an explanation in a case brought by a small clan of Tlingit Indians in Alaska called the Tee-Hit-Tons. They claimed that the United States had taken timber from their lands without payment, entitling them to fair compensation under the Fifth Amendment. Because the alleged confiscation occurred after August 13, 1946, the Tee-Hit-Tons could not sue under the Indian Claims Commission Act's "fair and honorable dealings" provision.[39]

In denying the Tee-Hit-Tons' claim, the Supreme Court repudiated virtually every point in its first *Alcea* decision, without forthrightly acknowledging it was doing so. It stated that "recognized" title and aboriginal title gave vastly different rights. "Where the Congress by treaty or other agreement has declared that thereafter Indians were to hold the lands permanently [recognized title], compensation must be paid for subsequent taking." Without congressional recognition, however, Indian occupancy "is not a property right." The Court held that the government may choose to protect Indians' right of occupancy, which *it* grants to the Indians. Incredibly, the justices now deemed that aboriginal Indian title arose from the government's *post facto* beneficence, not from the Indians' actual occupation of lands for a long period. Even so, if the government does choose to protect the Indians' right of occupancy, it may terminate it at any time and dispose of the lands "without any legally enforceable obligation to compensate the Indians." The logic of *Lone Wolf* had returned. Realizing that this reasoning called into question not only the first *Alcea* decision, but also the second one insofar as it allowed the Indians to recover at all, the Supreme Court went on to explain that the Oregon Indians had been able to recover, not because they had any legal right, but because their special jurisdictional act directed payment for their aboriginal title. Thus, Justice Black's concurring opinion in the first *Alcea* decision was now put forward as the Court's holding. The Supreme Court had rewritten history.[40]

Of course, the Court may, and occasionally does, overturn its own prior decisions, but generally the repudiation process takes longer and is admitted by the justices. Why did the Court deviate from its normal practices here? The first *Alcea* decision contained no logical flaw, nor did it radically depart from prior decisions. The only plausible answer is money.

In their brief to the Supreme Court in the second *Alcea* case, the government attorneys began not with a discussion of the law, but by describing in stark terms the financial implications of the first *Alcea* decision, which went far beyond the $14 million of interest awarded in that one case:

> For there are now pending, under the Indian Claims Commission Act, cases in which the recoveries sought total, with interest, more than ten billion dollars, of which the principal claimed amounts to $1,920,625,057 and the interest $8,936,666,947. Inasmuch as more than 100 additional contracts between Indian tribes and attorneys for suits under that statute have been approved by the Department of the Interior, it is not inconceivable that cases still to be filed would raise the total claims to more than fourteen billion dollars, a major portion of which would arise out of claims of interest.

Given that the total federal budget for 1950 was only $42 billion, those numbers were mind-boggling.[41]

They also were grossly exaggerated. The government based its estimates on the damage figures stated in the Indian petitions. In the hundred-plus cases tried by the Court of Claims under special jurisdictional acts between 1880 and 1946, however, Indians had recovered on average only about 2 percent of the amounts stated in petitions.[42]

The government's blatant scare tactics worked. The Supreme Court explained in *Tee-Hit-Ton* that it opted to allow Congress to make "contributions for Indian lands rather than to subject the Government to an obligation to pay the value when taken with interest to the date of payment. Our conclusion does not uphold harshness as against tenderness toward the Indians, but it leaves with Congress, where it belongs, the policy of Indian gratuities for the termination of Indian occupancy of Government-owned land rather than making compensation for its value a rigid constitutional principle."[43]

By the decisions in the second *Alcea* and *Tee-Hit-Ton* cases, the Supreme Court assured that, even if Indians could recover for the taking of their aboriginal lands (which was by no means assured in view of the Court's revisionist history in *Tee-Hit-Ton*), those recoveries would have little relationship to the value of the lands when taken. With interest payments barred, Indians would be paid in late-twentieth-century dollars for nineteenth-century wrongs. The two decisions thus formed one prong of Commissioner Witt's formula, enunciated only several months after the *Tee-Hit-Ton* decision, that the purpose was to give some, but not excessive, compensation. Indians, if paid at all for the taking of their aboriginal lands, would be paid an amount deemed "fair" to the taxpayers.

.   .   .

The *Tee-Hit-Ton* decision also focused attention on the more fundamental issue of whether Indians could recover at all. If the Oregon Indians recovered in *Alcea* only because the special jurisdictional act authorized a recovery, Indians could recover under the Indian Claims Commission Act only if that act authorized it. As Commissioner Witt testified to Congress in April 1955, "The Indian attorneys, and the Court of Claims, I presume . . . and our own Commission somewhat, are at sea right now as to whether [aboriginal] title will be compensable under our jurisdictional act." [44]

The Court of Claims came to the rescue of the drifting Commission less than a month later, on May 3, 1955, in the case of *Otoe and Missouria Tribe* v. *United States*. These were two confederated tribes that lived next to the Pawnees in what is now northeastern Nebraska during the early nineteenth century. Like their considerably more numerous neighbors, the Otoes and Missourias farmed in their villages for part of the year and hunted and gathered food over a much larger territory during the balance. Also like the Pawnees, the Otoes and Missourias ceded their aboriginal lands through a series of treaties, and eventually were removed to what is now Oklahoma. The two tribes wanted to recover the difference between the value of the lands to which they had aboriginal title in Nebraska and what the government had paid for them. [45]

Their claim differed from the Pawnees' in two important respects. In the first place, their ownership of lands, and even the extent of those lands, was undisputed: at the time the treaties were negotiated, government officials had declared authoritatively that the Indians owned the lands that were ceded. Aboriginal title was not in issue. Second, the Supreme Court decided *Tee-Hit-Ton* and cast doubt on the compensability of aboriginal title after the Court of Claims had ruled on the

Pawnee claim but before it decided the Otoe and Missouria claim. The Commission in 1953 had concluded that the Otoes and Missourias were entitled to compensation, but that ruling likewise had preceded *Tee-Hit-Ton,* so whether a tribe could recover for the loss of its aboriginal lands had not been in serious dispute.[46]

The government appealed the *Otoe* decision to the Court of Claims, and decided to make it into a "test case." Realizing that an adverse ruling would imperil a host of Indian claims, the tribes' lawyers joined forces. Luther Bohanon, attorney for the Otoes and Missourias, enlisted Marvin Sonosky, who had recently left the Department of Justice with a reputation as a strong legal analyst and writer. The Wilkinson firm and Jay Hoag, the Duluth attorney who had worked on the Curry cases with Cobb and Weissbrodt, also submitted briefs.[47]

Because of the Supreme Court's decision in *Tee-Hit-Ton,* the Indians' attorneys argued that the Indian Claims Commission Act authorized payment. They pointed to two provisions that created a right to recover: the Commission could hear and determine claims for revision of treaties and other agreements; and it could hear and determine claims based upon fair and honorable dealings. Ever stalwart in their defense of the government, the Justice Department lawyers argued that the two provisions dealt only with treaty lands, and conferred no new rights on Indians' aboriginal lands. In addition, the government urged that because it had no legal obligation under *Tee-Hit-Ton* to pay a cent for a tribe's aboriginal lands, any payment at all was a gratuity. By definition, a gift cannot be unconscionably small, unfair, or dishonorable. Hence, the government concluded, it could not be liable under either provision.

Once again, the Court of Claims rejected the government's arguments, and as in so many critical cases Judge Littleton wrote the opinion. *Tee-Hit-Ton,* he pointed out, was not decided under the Indian Claims Commission Act. He concluded that a majority in Congress in 1946 wanted the Commission to resolve Indians' extralegal and moral claims, including claims based on their Indian title property. Therefore, the Commission *could* award damages arising from the loss of tribes' aboriginal lands.[48]

The Department of Justice was not about to give up. It asked the Supreme Court to review the decision. Before making their legal arguments to the Court, the government's attorneys resorted again to scare tactics, arguing that the decision in *Otoe* would cost hundreds of mil-

lions, if not billions, of dollars. Even in their worst-case scenarios, however, they could not project the vast totals of the *Alcea* case because of
their earlier success in getting interest payments ruled out. The Indian
rebuttals proved more effective and, on October 10, 1955, the Supreme
Court declined to review the *Otoe* decision.[49]

Frustrated by the courts, the Department of Justice tried politics,
lobbying Congress to overturn the *Otoe* decision. In 1956 it issued a
press release stating that the decision in *Otoe* could cost the government,
and ultimately the taxpayers, several billion dollars. Then, at hearings before the Indian affairs committees of the House and Senate, the department proposed an amendment to the Indian Claims Commission Act
that would have limited Indian title claims to those arising under unratified treaties—the very position the government's attorneys had argued,
and lost, before the Court of Claims. When those committees proved
unreceptive, the department tried an end run: they went after the appropriations committees. Under the cover of requesting more funds for
new attorneys and experts to try the aboriginal land cases, Assistant Attorney General Perry Morton advised the House and Senate appropriations committees that the taxpayers might have to shell out vast sums to
repurchase most of the United States from the Indians. He suggested
that an amendment to the act would be desirable.[50]

Members of the appropriations committees enthusiastically supported Morton's suggestions. The government strategists, however,
hadn't anticipated the backlash, especially from the members of the Indian affairs committees, to so blatant an effort to circumvent normal
channels. Arizona Democrat Stewart Udall complained that Morton
"did not come back to the committee that originally handled this legislation—the committee which was considering, and is now considering,
the extension of this act—but approached a committee which has never
considered this legislation before and could very readily be misled."
Other congressional opponents disputed the estimate of probable costs
and argued that the Court of Claims had correctly interpreted the congressional intent in 1946. To amend the act now, they warned, would be
an act of "bad faith" and "cut the heart out" of the legislation. Tribes
again would flood Congress with requests for special jurisdictional acts
if the act was eviscerated.[51]

By and large, liberal Democrats led the opposition to the proposed
amendment, but the most important opponents were two conservative

Republicans. Arizona's Senator Barry Goldwater's conservative credentials were impeccable, but he had an abiding fascination with Indians.
With his usual bluntness, he told Congress, "I am critical of the Justice
Department in this instance. It has played a game and has lost, and it is
now proposing to change the rules. I do not believe that that is the fair
or American way to do things." [52]

Even more important than Goldwater was Senator Arthur Watkins of
Utah. He was considered one of the Hill's experts on legal matters, the
highest ranking Republican on the Senate Indian Affairs Subcommittee,
a strong Eisenhower supporter, and, like Goldwater, had a "life interest"
in American Indians. The Senate minority leader, William Knowland of
California, and representatives of the Eisenhower administration informed Watkins that they would be guided largely by his recommendations about amending the act. On July 6, 1956, he informed the Senate
that he had concluded that the Court of Claims decision in *Otoe* was
correct. When enacting the Indian Claims Commission Act, he said,
Congress had intended that the Commission should have jurisdiction to
hear and determine all the types of claims that Indian tribes had previously successfully lobbied Congress to include in special jurisdictional
acts. A few Indian groups, such as the Oregon tribelets in *Alcea,* had obtained authorization to bring claims for loss of aboriginal lands. The
purpose of the Commission was to resolve all such claims once and for
all. Inescapably, the intent was to include them within the Commission's
jurisdiction.[53]

After Watkins's pronouncement, not another congressional word was
uttered on behalf of the Justice Department amendment.

·   ·   ·

What had all this legal and political wrangling accomplished? The Commission now knew that it should disregard Supreme Court precedent
and strive to identify aboriginal groups in a manner that would facilitate
suits. It also knew that evidence concerning the extent of an Indian
group's aboriginal lands was sufficient even if it didn't meet the Supreme
Court's definition of Indian title. Finally, the courts and Congress had
made clear that tribes could be recompensed for the loss of those aboriginal lands. Nevertheless, the Supreme Court's rulings ensured that the
Indians' recoveries would be small because the Commission could not

award interest payments to adjust for the difference in the value of money between the time of a wrong and the time of compensation.

With liability issues largely resolved, the Commission needed a method for assigning a value to the land acquired from Indian tribes. If it established values too low, many tribes that had already received something for the cession of their lands might not be able to recover at all. On the other hand, the Commission and courts knew that the higher the valuations, the greater the fiscal impact of the statute. For the Commission to fulfill Commissioner Witt's description of its goal—"some," but not excessive compensation—valuation of aboriginal lands was crucial.

.   .   .

When a government takes property from a private citizen, it must pay the fair market value of the property as of the time of the taking. Fair market value is defined as the amount to which a willing, knowledgeable buyer and a willing, knowledgeable seller, neither under compulsion to enter into the transaction, would have agreed. Similarly, when a court concludes that a contract price is unconscionable, it typically awards damages based on the property's fair market value at the time of the transaction.

Prior to passage of the Indian Claims Commission Act, the Supreme Court had ruled that the United States must pay fair market value to an Indian tribe when it took land from its reservation. Attorneys for the Indians now argued that the same principle should apply when the United States took lands to which a tribe had aboriginal title. Accordingly, the Commission should look at all of the assets that would contribute to the value of a tribe's land, including assets that had no value to the Indians, of which the government was aware when it acquired the land. In the Apache code, for example, grubbing in the earth for such metals as silver was demeaning, so the silver mining potential of their land was of no value to them; the white settlers who founded Tombstone had no such compunction.[54]

The Department of Justice disagreed. The Indians' should be paid only the value of the land *to them*.

Of course, mountains of documents described in poetic rhetoric just how deeply and variously Indians valued the land, but the Justice Department lawyers had in mind only economic values. In the Indians' aboriginal lifestyles, they saw no capital formation, no wages, no savings, no money. They saw subsistence only and proposed what was called the "nuts and berries" valuation. For example, in the *Otoe* case where the Court of Claims decided between the competing valuation theories, the government's expert said the ceded lands had been worth between two and fourteen cents per acre, judging by its subsistence value. This assessment made the price paid by the government for the aboriginal lands of the Otoe and Missouria tribes, about five cents per acre, appear fair. By contrast, the Indians' expert, using Anglo law's fair market approach, placed the value of the land at $1.50 per acre.[55]

Just as the Court of Claims rejected the government's position on liability in *Otoe,* it also rejected its position on valuation. Judge Littleton wrote that valuing the lands based on the economic factors that Anglo sellers and buyers would have considered important "more nearly accomplish[es] the fair settlement of these claims desired by Congress than the 'subsistence' approach advocated by the Government. Values cannot be determined on the basis of berries and wild fruits." In *Otoe,* the Commission arrived at a value of seventy-five cents per acre, which split the difference between the two appraisers (even though the government's appraiser had used the wrong valuation theory). This "compromise" value made the five-cent-per-acre price unconscionable, permitting the Indians to recover.[56]

Underlying the "nuts and berries" approach was a grossly faulty assumption, which the court not only did not criticize but probably shared. That assumption—like the fair-market-value approach used by the Indians' attorneys—measured only the economic value of land. The real value of land to a tribe included its role in maintaining group identity and continuity, its religious significance, its aesthetic qualities, and a host of other attributes. If dollar amounts could be assigned to these attributes in addition to a tract's subsistence value, the total value of their land to some, possibly all, tribes could have exceeded its Anglo-American market value. Of course, neither the Commission nor the legal system under which it operated had any viable means of placing dollar values on these attributes—and felt no need to invent them.

With this decision, the aboriginal cases were almost completely divorced from nineteenth-century Indian perspectives. The Commission employed Anglo definitions of tribes, bands, or other identifiable groups, used an idea of land ownership foreign to Indian tribes, created arbitrary boundaries for the aboriginal tracts of land, and used a method of valuation that had no relationship to Indian values. Dissenting from a valuation decision in which a fishing tribe was denied any compensation for fisheries lost as of the date of taking but was compensated for the value of gold deposits on its lands, a Court of Claims judge aptly described the paradox:

> In short, the Indians are being denied payment for the most valuable de facto [in fact] asset of which they were deprived and instead are being compensated for de jure [in law] assets they never could have reasonably supposed belonged to them. I am sure they will be greatly impressed with the wonders of the white man's justice.[57]

The fair market approach may have made valuations possible for the Commission, but only by employing major distorting assumptions. Appraisers generally value unimproved property by first identifying sales of comparable properties and then adjusting those sale prices to reflect differences between the sale properties and the one under valuation. In almost all aboriginal land claims there were no truly comparable sales. What Anglo had sold a prairie? The Commission could not properly use Indian conveyances to the government as benchmarks, because the tribes did not qualify as willing, knowledgeable sellers. Even when the appraisers found a large property—albeit many orders of magnitude smaller than tribes' aboriginal territories—sold by one white man to another around the valuation date, placing a value on the Indians' land remained very difficult. The appraisers had to determine whether improvements had enhanced the value of the supposedly comparable tract. An appraiser trying to adjust for the impact of a contemporaneous improvement can inspect the property visually and look at current cost and income records, but those sources of information did not exist when valuing properties from a century before. Moreover, any benchmark property usually was located near Anglo civilization: how much more valuable was such a site than a tract of prairie land in the middle of a roadless nowhere? Not surprisingly, considering the lack of a basis for an accurate accounting, the appraisals were usually so grossly divergent that they were all but useless.

Yet the chasm separating the parties' valuations gave the Commission tremendous flexibility. Typically the Commission identified deficiencies in each party's valuation and then chose a figure somewhere in between. The only control on its discretion was its prior valuation opinions. The Commission apparently tried to place consistent figures on tracts of land acquired at about the same time in the same geographic area. It was a minimal constraint at best, however, and almost invariably the Commission chose a figure closer to the government's appraisal than to the tribe's. As Witt assured Congress in 1956, "We have tried to be conserv-

TABLE 2

Valuations of Tribes' Aboriginal Lands in Cases Decided 1956–59

Tribe	Year of Valuation	Acres Valued	Plaintiffs' Valuation Per Acre	Defendants' Valuation Per Acre	Commission's Valuation Per Acre
Miami	1818	7,036,000	1.88	.20	.75
Coeur d'Alene	1887	2,389,924	14.74	1.40	1.95
Chippewa	1863	7,488,280	1.75	.05	.45
Nooksack	1859	80,590	2.29	.06	.65
Muckleshoot	1859	101,620	2.24	.09	.85
Omaha	1854	4,982,098	1.50	.55	.75
Snake, Piute	1879	1,449,305	2.07	.27	.40
Duwamish	1859	54,790	5.46	.40	1.35
Suquamish	1859	87,130	4.91	.10	.90
Snohomish	1859	164,265	3.70	.12	1.10
Nez Perce	1867	6,932,270	2.63	.06	.67
Averages			3.92	.30	.89
Weighted Averages			2.99	.28	.74

ative, however, in putting values on this land, because it is very difficult to determine what lands were worth in 1814 or in 1865 before they were ever really occupied by white citizens of the United States." [58]

With its wide discretion, however, the Commission could ensure that tribes recovered something. Unlike the Chiricahuas, most tribes had sold their aboriginal lands to the United States in one-sided agreements where the grounds for recovery included fraud and duress, as well as unconscionable consideration. And while the facts in many cases could well have supported revision of agreements on the basis of fraud or duress, the Commission relied almost exclusively on the unconscionable consideration provision, perhaps because repeated findings of fraud or duress would raise political hackles. Like courts handling Anglo contract actions, the Commission established no rules concerning the disparity between the sale price and the fair market value, but over the years few agreements were deemed unconscionable if the market value, as determined by the Commission, was not at least double the price. Between 1956 and 1959, the Commission decided eight cases, and it is probably no accident that in five the government's appraisers valued aboriginal lands at less than or about equal to the price the government had paid

TABLE 3

Valuations of Tribe's Aboriginal Lands
in Unconscionable Consideration Cases Decided 1956–59

Tribe	Amount Paid Per Acre	Defendants' Valuation Per Acre	Commission's Valuation Per Acre	Unconscionability?
Miami	.06	.20	.75	Yes
Coeur d'Alene	.10	1.40	1.95	Yes
Chippewa	.08	.05	.45	Yes
Omaha	.20	.55	.75	Yes
Duwamish	.44	.40	1.35	Yes
Suquamish	.42	.10	.90	Yes
Snohomish	.27	.12	1.10	Yes
Nez Perce	.05	.06	.67	Yes

for them. In all eight, however, the Commmission made sure it increased the government's appraisal enough to make it unconscionable, permitting the tribe to recover something.

The same pattern continued in later years. And when the Commission concluded that the value wasn't sufficiently high to support an unconscionability finding, the tribe appealed, and the Court of Claims almost uniformly reversed the Commission's decision and permitted a tribal recovery. In frustration, the chief commissioner in 1967 wrote:

> [M]uch confusion has been wrought and frustration experienced by all parties concerned each time this Court [of Claims] has reversed the Commission when we have ruled against the Indians on an unconscionable consideration claim. Because of the near perfect record of this Commission in being reversed each time it has dared to rule against the Indians, I am sure the Commission is not looking forward to any further success along this line.[59]

Undoubtedly, the courts and commissioners had a variety of reasons to arrange things so the tribes recovered *something,* but the most important goal was putting an end to Indian claims. Decisions denying any award for what Indians considered obvious injustices would, as the attorneys for the California Indians warned the Court of Claims, "send the Indians . . . back to Congress once again for corrective jurisdictional legislation." [60]

As a result of all the fictions devised to achieve this goal, judgments on aboriginal land claims wound up bearing little resemblance to our traditional notions of judicial proceedings. In the aboriginal land cases, Justice was not blind. Instead, the Commission took on the role of a social welfare agency, doling out limited compensation. But unlike an effective social agency, the Commission allocated welfare funds based not on present need, but on the consideration of events that had occurred decades, or even centuries, before.

It was in this eerie wonderland of rules and precedents, acceptable and unacceptable facts, that the Chiricahua Apache land claims would be heard.

EIGHT

AN ELEVEN-MILLION-DOLLAR MISTAKE

Suits at court are like Winter nights, long and wearisome.
—THOMAS DELONEY

Despite a snow and ice storm that took Washington, D.C., by surprise on December 11, 1962, five Chiricahua Apaches reached Room 4808 of the huge General Accounting Office building. More than seventy-five years after the Chiricahuas had been loaded into closed railroad cars and shipped to Florida, a tribunal would finally hear their claim for the taking of their aboriginal lands. At about 1:30 in the afternoon, the trial started as the plaintiffs' first witness, the world's leading anthropological authority on the Chiricahua Apaches, took the stand.[1]

In the decade since the Fort Sill and Mescalero Chiricahuas filed their petitions, they had seen major changes in the cast of characters working on the case and a government ambush that, if successful, would have ended all federal services to the Fort Sill Tribe. But if the Chiricahaus now thought their long wait was over, they were mistaken. Litigation of the Apaches' land claim would drag on for another sixteen years, until one federal judge was prompted to muse on the unpredictability of "fate."

. . .

In 1951, the firm of Cobb and Weissbrodt took on a third lawyer, Lefty Weissbrodt's brother Abraham. Abe's development as a lawyer had varied significantly from his brother's. As an undergraduate, Abe took over his father's window-washing business after his death. Basketball cut further into his studies. Abe played on the 1934 basketball team of the City College of New York under the tutelage of the legendary coach Nat Holman. His exploits that year eventually earned him election into CCNY's Hall of Fame. Weissbrodt then followed his brother to Columbia Law School, but window washing and basketball again interfered with his studies. Although he self-deprecatingly refers to himself as "the worst student in his class," he managed to graduate.[2]

Eventually Weissbrodt landed a position with the United States Treasury Department, but Pearl Harbor interrupted. He enlisted in time to participate in the invasion of North Africa in 1942, after which the army transferred him to legal work with Treasury Department representatives investigating businesses suspected of collaborating with the fascists. At war's end, the Justice Department hired him to help defend against a claim brought by a large Swiss corporation for alleged economic injuries inflicted by the Allies. In the examination of witnesses, Abe Weissbrodt found his calling as a trial lawyer.[3]

By 1951, he was an accomplished litigator for the Department of Justice, yet when his brother asked him to join Cobb and Weissbrodt he agreed. For both the Weissbrodt brothers, representing Indian tribes became not just a career, but a passion.[4]

In January 1953, less than two years after Abe Weissbrodt joined the firm, the Chiricahuas' original attorney, the Choctaw Grady Lewis, died of cancer. The Fort Sill Apaches had lost a passionate, silver-tongued advocate. In turning to Cobb and Weissbrodt, they gained superior strategists and tacticians in the increasingly complex labyrinths of Indian law. At a council meeting on January 25, 1953, six men, including Benedict Jozhe (who had assumed the leadership from the aging Sam Haozous), were authorized to sign a contract with the firm. Within weeks, the fate of the claims of the Fort Sill Apaches was in the hands of lawyers whose familiarity with their clients came only from what they had read in books and documents.[5]

For the next few years, the lawyers unearthed documents in the National Archives that would help establish the aboriginal territory of the Chiricahuas and detail the government's dealings with them. Meanwhile Lefty Weissbrodt counseled Jozhe to be patient. The Apaches' other claims (concerning imprisonment and trespass) depended at least in part on the lawyers' ability to prove the extent of the aboriginal lands and to recover for their taking. Whether they could do this remained in doubt because of the unfavorable decisions issued by the Commission during the early 1950s.[6]

Finally, in 1955, Lefty Weissbrodt gave Jozhe some provisionally good news. The Court of Claims had upheld, in *Otoe,* the Indians' right to recover for the loss of their aboriginal land under the act, and Weissbrodt hoped for a favorable result when the decision was appealed to the Supreme Court. Early in 1956, the Supreme Court declined to review the *Otoe* decision, and Congress, heeding the advice of Utah's Senator Arthur Watkins, firmly rejected the government's heavy-handed attempt to have the act amended. Later that year, it also extended the life of the Commission for another five years, until April 10, 1962. It was time to strike.[7]

.   .   .

Within a year, however, the Fort Sill Apaches' attention was diverted by a threat to their future as a tribal entity. This assault was made in the name of "termination," a new/old concept in the history of the ever-fluctuating federal policies toward the Indians, and a policy that is widely regarded today by Indians as little different from allotment—that is, a step toward their elimination as a people.

It must be remembered that, to gain sufficient votes for the Indian Claims Commission Act in the 1940s, its proponents needed the support of two opposite camps—those who wanted to strengthen tribal governments, and those who wanted to break them up and end all special federal services to Indians. As the 1940s drew to a close, the terminationists gained increasing strength in Congress and, after the appointment of Dillon Myer as commissioner of Indian affairs in March 1950, in the Truman administration as well. Myer, who had served during World War II as head of the agency in charge of confining Japanese Americans in relocation camps, sought to assimilate Indians forcibly into mainstream society. He had little success, as he lacked the muscle of terminationist legislation, and his heavy-handed tactics caused a backlash that scuttled most voluntary cooperation from the Indians.[8]

Only after a narrowly elected Republican Congress took office in 1953 could the terminationists begin to implement their program. House Concurrent Resolution 108, adopted by Congress as of August

1, 1953, declared it to be congressional policy, "as rapidly as possible, to make the Indians within the territorial limits of the United States subject to the same laws and entitled to the same privileges and responsibilities as are applicable to other citizens of the United States, to end their status as wards of the United States, and to grant them all of the rights and prerogatives pertaining to American citizenship." The resolution went on to state that Indians of California, Florida, New York, and Texas should be freed of federal supervision as soon as possible, along with five named tribes in other states.[9]

Unlike a law, a resolution creates no rights and imposes no duties, but Congress followed up Concurrent Resolution 108 with a series of acts calling for the termination of federal services to the Klamaths, Menominees, the Alabama and Coushatta tribes of Texas, the Grand Ronde and Siletz tribes of western Oregon, mixed-blood Utes, and Paiutes of Utah. This meant, among other things, that the Indians would be subject to state courts and state laws, including state property and income tax laws. These bills emerged in rapid succession from a joint subcommittee on Indian affairs formed to expedite termination, and were all enacted within three months in the summer of 1954. The Senate chairman of the subcommittee was none other than Arthur Watkins, the very same man who (two years later) led the Senate to support the decision in the *Otoe* case, a decision that proved most helpful to Indian claims.[10]

Termination advocates such as Watkins supported the Indian claims process because they saw the payoffs to the tribes as an appropriate step in gaining their willing acceptance of the termination policy. Termination, proponents believed, would liberate the Indians. In 1957, Watkins, probably the leading congressional exponent of termination, compared termination to the Emancipation Proclamation.[11]

Undoubtedly many adherents sincerely believed the Indians would flourish once termination was accomplished. What they did not understand was that a large percentage of people who had not chosen to be involved in a market economy, who had been denied any opportunity to make decisions for themselves for decades or, in the case of eastern tribes, for centuries, who had strong cultural and religious ties to a tribe and a tribal way of life, and who had not, for the most part, received an adequate Anglo education or skills training, could not immediately, or even with a few years' intensive tutelage (which few Indians facing termination received), survive by selling their labor in the white man's market. The believers also showed remarkable ignorance about the disastrous impact of the earlier allotment policy—notably the loss of millions of acres of Indian land. Meanwhile, some more realistic, not to say cynical, supporters of the termination policy welcomed termination because it permitted the transfer of valuable resources into the hands of whites who were "better" able to use them.

Termination had precisely that effect. The Menominees, for example, were selected for termination in 1954 largely because it was thought that the valuable commercial forest on their Wisconsin reservation would, if properly managed, provide the income and in many cases jobs for the Indians to survive without federal assistance. But it did not work that way once the reservation was abolished and the Menominees had essentially the same status as other Wisconsin citizens. Forest industries could not provide jobs for even a substantial percentage of tribal members, especially after new automated equipment was installed at the sawmill to increase efficiency. A quarter of the tribe's members were unemployed, and many lost utility services because they could not pay their bills. Social services also deteriorated. The hospital and school may have met the BIA's standards, but they did not meet the state's, so the state closed them down. Desperately trying to generate some income, the tribe began selling off its land. Waterfront lots went first. Congress finally repealed the Menominee termination act in 1973, but the damage to their tribal home may never be reversed.[12]

The true believers ignored not only the Menominees' lack of preparedness for the life being thrust upon them, but also the United States' legal and moral commitments. In the nineteenth century, during negotiations over the cession of their aboriginal lands, many tribes had asked to be placed under the jurisdiction of the Great Father in Washington rather than state and local authorities. They believed then (and still believe) that, no matter how unfair federal laws and federal courts have been, they generally treat Indians far more equitably than do state laws and state courts. Knowing that separation of Indians and settlers would reduce the likelihood of violence, the federal government had readily agreed to deny state and local governments any authority over the tribal members. Now that Indians no longer posed threats to the lives and property of non-Indians, the government reneged on its commitments.[13]

As the impact on the Menominees and other tribes became clear, Indian opposition crystallized. A member of the Sac and Fox tribe, Sadie Rhodes Tyner, plaintively wrote President Eisenhower in 1957:

> My heart is heavy. I am appealing to you in the cause of The American Indian. Why now are the restrictions removed it was agreed so long as there was an American Government The American Government would hold trust and be the Trustee for the remaining land that was left . . . of various Indian reservations and allotments. We The American Indians still have a very few older Indians living, and we also have some who are not as well educated. Where are now all those promises those promises are meaningless are of no meaning or value. Protections where is it now? [14]

Although many Democrats supported the policy, the torrent of termination legislation slowed to a trickle after the Republicans narrowly lost control of Congress in 1954. Nevertheless, the Eisenhower administration and Glenn Emmons, Eisenhower's chosen successor to Myers and an ardent if somewhat more diplomatic advocate of termination, still regarded Concurrent Resolution 108 as congressional policy. They continued to seek its implementation:

> The guiding philosophy of the Bureau is based on the premise that the provision of special Federal services to Indians as a class on an indefinite basis is contrary to the best interest of the Indian people. It follows, then, that there is but *one* reason for Bureau programs—to end the need for special Federal services. . . . [T]he objective is to promote economic and social conditions under which the Indians can prepare themselves for adjustment to unrestricted status.[15]

The Bureau actually had reported to Congress as early as 1954 that the Fort Sill Apaches were candidates for termination, but did nothing about it until 1957. Then, in September, two Bureau officials met with tribal leaders, including Jozhe and Sam Haozous, and informed them of plans "to end all federal relationships with the tribe, including trusteeship of tribal and individual property . . . and all federal services." The rationale was that the Apaches, then numbering about 130 persons in 25 families, were "well integrated into the communities . . . live in the same manner as a majority of their non-Indian neighbors," and have "always been somewhat aloof from Bureau services." One Bureau official reported on the meeting, "The great majority of the people present at the meeting thought that the type of program we had presented would be welcomed by the Fort Sill Tribe." [16]

Apparently the Bureau officials misread the Apache reaction. Benedict Jozhe was a soft-spoken man, but when the Bureau officials returned in January 1958, he led the opposition to the Bureau's proposal. The government's program contained some vague, unspecific assurances of educational and job training assistance, but the tribal leaders argued "that the Government has not lived up to its promises in the past and the readjustment program [the Bureau's euphemism for termination] would be no different from previous commitments made." Later, one official would acknowledge that Jozhe and others had been "rather eloquent" in their calls for tribal rejection of termination. Nevertheless, the Bureau officials responded, "The law for termination has already been passed, and there is nothing you can do about it. You may as well accept it now and get what you can, for you may get nothing later." The tribal members refused to be intimidated, voting 22–7 to discontinue discussions. About a month later, after Lefty Weissbrodt had obtained a promise of support from a leading Indian rights organization, the Fort Sill Apaches met again, this time without government officials, and unanimously adopted a resolution opposing termination.[17]

Stung by the Apaches' rejection, Bureau officials began preparing legislation terminating the federal relationship with the Fort Sill Apaches "without their consent" and without any further consultations with them, because the Indians, "even though in our opinion ready for complete termination, refused to take positive action toward the development of or consideration of such a program." The Bureau evidently saw no paradox in the notion of forcing people to accept a change of status in the name of freedom. Luckily for the Indians, the administration's policy shifted before the angered bureaucrats proceeded too far. In a radio address on September 18, 1958, Secretary of the Interior Fred Seaton said, "no Indian tribe or group should end its relationship with the Federal Government unless such tribe or group has clearly demonstrated—first, that it understands the plan under which such a program would go forward, and second, that the tribe or group affected concurs in and supports the plan proposed." The requirement of tribal consent brought to an abrupt halt virtually all further termination efforts.[18]

. . .

Among the Mescaleros, Lipans, and Chiricahuas on the Mescalero Reservation, termination was never a worry since not even the most ardent advocates of "readjustment" considered them ready for it. In 1953, unemployment among the approximately 1,200 tribal members was above 80 percent. "Only six Mescaleros had ever attended college. Living conditions were deplorable: most tribe members lived in tents or shacks without electricity or running water; infant mortality was high; and illness was rampant, especially respiratory infections, tuberculosis, and a persistent eye inflammation called trachoma." [19]

In these black times, the Business Council elected a new president in 1953, Wendell Chino. Half Mescalero and half Chiricahua, Chino was a descendant of Geronimo, but in his ability to deal with white men for the benefit of his tribe he more closely resembled Cochise. A short, squat man, he was still in his twenties when first elected and an ordained minister of the Reformed Church. He gave up preaching when he became president of the Business Council, and, after the tribal constitution was rewritten in 1964, president of the tribe. Except for several years during the late 1950s and early 1960s, Chino has served continuously in these positions and remains tribal president today.[20]

Chino knew that the economy the Bureau of Indian Affairs had imposed on the Mescalero Reservation, principally involving the sale of timber and grazing of livestock, could not support the tribe or its members. The reservation's isolation prevented most residents from finding off-reservation employment. Fueled by unwavering energy and ambition, and eloquent in both English and Apache, Chino began to turn the rugged beauty into an asset. The Mescaleros soon became one of the first tribes to foster tourism. By 1962, when the trial of the land claims began, Chino and the Mescaleros had taken only the first modest steps: a tourist center with a small motel opened in September 1956, and in 1962 the tribe borrowed $1.5 million from the United States to purchase a ski run built earlier by non-Indians.[21]

The Mescaleros under Chino were one of the first and most aggressive tribes to assert sovereign powers—an activist stance that many other tribes have adopted since the 1960s. Today, tribal governments, like state and local governments, impose and collect taxes, police their reservations, regulate commercial and social activities, prosecute numerous (but not all) crimes, adjudicate civil disputes, construct housing, and encourage business development. The extent to which tribal governments are willing to establish their own enterprises, such as the Mescalero motel and ski resort, probably exceeds most non-Indian governments.

What brought on this new activism? Certainly, World War II had exposed droves of young Indians to the worlds outside their reservations, and many returning Indian veterans insisted that they had earned for their people a better deal from Uncle Sam. Washington's termination policy provoked a unifying backlash as well; as has been said, there is nothing like a ready noose to focus the mind. By 1960, too, enough time had passed for the nascent governments formed under the Indian Reorganization Act to function reasonably smoothly. Nor were Indian tribes blind to the implications of the accelerative civil rights movement. Red would be beautiful, too. Tribal governments became increasingly aware of the potential of their combined strength. In sociological terms, American Indians were beginning to assert their identity as a single political ethnic group.

One essential precondition to a greater role for tribal governments was federal acceptance. When termination foundered in the late 1950s, the expansion of tribal governments became possible for the first time. The Kennedy administration and Interior Secretary Stewart Udall emphasized the strengthening of tribal institutions instead of their breakup. And the Supreme Court's 1959 decision in *Williams* v. *Lee* blessed the new federal and Indian attitudes.

In that case, an Indian trader—that is, a white merchant licensed by the federal government to operate on the Navajo Indian Reservation— sued a Navajo Indian in Arizona state court for failure to pay a debt. The attorney for the Indian, with help from the Navajo tribal government, argued that only the Navajos' own courts had jurisdiction to hear the claim. From about the turn of this century, the Bureau of Indian Affairs had run a rudimentary court system on the Navajo and other reservations, but the BIA system had handled only disputes between Indians, and precious few of them. The Navajo tribal government used funds from the lease of oil and other mineral rights to establish its own judicial system even as *Williams* v. *Lee* was wending its way through the state courts. The Navajos argued not only that their new courts had jurisdiction over the trader's lawsuit, but that they were the *only* courts with jurisdiction.

No doubt this idea, which clashed with the notion of termination and its goal of extending states' jurisdiction over Indians, startled the trader's attorney. Yet the Supreme Court agreed with the Navajos. It adopted the position enunciated by Chief Justice Marshall over a century before, and reiterated by Felix Cohen in his *Handbook of Indian Law,* that tribes retained their sovereign powers except to the extent expressly limited by Congress. The federal government hadn't barred tribes from establishing courts to rule on disputes affecting their members, so assertion of exclusive jurisdiction was within the Navajos' sovereign powers. In the three decades since *Williams* v. *Lee,* the Supreme Court has, with some notable exceptions, followed the same logic to permit tribal governments to expand their powers in new directions.[22]

Williams v. *Lee* marked a reversal of the direction of Indian law. Almost all of the Supreme Court cases involving Indian tribes during the first half of the twentieth century had been claims cases, ones in which the tribe contended that it had been wronged by the United States in the past. Since 1959, the Court's major focus has shifted to disputes about the powers and responsibilities of tribes in the present and the future. To be sure, claims cases have continued before specialized tribunals such as the Indian Claims Commission, but they have become a relatively quiet lagoon in the turbulent sea of Indian law.

. . .

While the Fort Sill Apaches were fighting off termination and the Mescalero Apaches were taking the first steps toward improving their economy and living conditions, attorneys were readying their land claims for trial. Cobb and Weissbrodt worked in Washington for the Fort Sill Apaches, while the lawyers for the Chiricahuas on the Mescalero Reservation—Guy Martin, William Sloane, and Roy Mobley—prepared for trial in New Mexico. Even though the Oklahoma and New Mexico Chiricahuas were descendants of the same aboriginal groups and therefore sought compensation for the taking of the same land, the two sets of attorneys prepared their cases separately, coordinating only the engagement of experts. Then, in March 1961, they agreed to consolidate the two claims under Cobb and Weissbrodt. The claims cases were very expensive and time-consuming to litigate, and the New Mexico attorneys were willing to defer in part because, as a member of the Mobley group acknowledged, Cobb and Weissbrodt had "emerged as one of the best Indian Claims firms in Washington." By 1961, the firm had already won judgments from the Commission totaling nearly $7 million ($1 million for the Confederated Tribes of the Colville Reservation in the state of Washington; $3 million for the Nez Perce Indians in Washington and Idaho; and $2.9 million for the Omaha tribe in Nebraska). On top of that, the firm had obtained favorable liability rulings for several other tribes in cases still awaiting final judgments.[23]

Eight months later, in November 1961, Lefty and David Cobb decided to dissolve the firm. Abe and Lefty promptly formed a partnership called Weissbrodt and Weissbrodt, which would continue into the late 1980s. Because Indian claims work had been a less important component of Cobb's legal practice than of the Weissbrodts', the divorcing partners agreed that the Weissbrodts would be responsible for all those cases, with Cobb receiving a percentage of any attorneys' fees subsequently awarded. Thus responsibility for representing Indian tribes, including the Chiricahua Apaches, that were scattered throughout the West came to rest on the shoulders of the two brothers from New York City.[24]

Their skills were complementary, though filial struggles frequently marred and eventually embittered their working relationship. Lefty, intense and attentive to every detail, managed the firm and wrote or directed the preparation of most of the legal documents. Short and wiry with a thick mane of hair, he worked obsessively, chewing on an unlit cigar as he paced back and forth or breaking pencil leads as he drafted documents in his unintelligible hieroglyphics. Abe did most of the firm's trial work and negotiating. He spent countless hours puffing on his pipe while carefully refining the questions he intended to ask witnesses or cutting through the clutter of details to identify the fundamental issues in a case. Far more relaxed than his brother, Abe also schmoozed tribal leaders, expert witnesses, Indian claims commissioners, and even the Department of Justice's lawyers.

After heavy turnover in the Justice Department, which led to numerous requests from the government for postponements (all of which the Commission granted), in the early 1960s the Apaches' case was assigned to Frank DeNunzio and Howard Campbell. According to Abe Weissbrodt, both men, by then approaching retirement age, gave every indication that they would be ending their legal careers as soon as possible. Campbell, who took the lead during the trial, wasn't skilled at examining witnesses. But their strategic error, rather than any questioning deficiencies, would prove to be the primary source of the government's undoing in this case.[25]

More than the configuration of the legal teams had changed by the time of the trial. As early as 1956, members of the White House staff had lost confidence in the Commission, in no small measure the result of the *Otoe* decision, which left the government exposed to hundreds of millions of dollars in possible liabilities. President Eisenhower's advisers focused, however, on the slow pace of decision-making, which, they believed, interfered with their termination policy. By the end of 1956, shortly before the Commission was originally expected to expire with all claims resolved, it had issued final judgments in only seventy-four of the over six hundred dockets. Of the seventy-four completed dockets, sixty-four had been dismissed without awards, most without time-consuming trials. The great majority of the remaining claims could not be so readily disposed of. At this pace, Indian claims would fester for decades.[26]

White House proponents of termination deluded themselves into believing that some tribes opposed "readjustment" because they feared they would lose their claims before the Commission if their federal relationship were ended, and some "advanced" individual Indians refused to break their tribal relations and move to the cities for fear of losing their share of any tribal recovery. If the claims could be resolved quickly, then that opposition would dissipate. The Eisenhower administration misunderstood the strong ties that bound tribes together, but its campaign changed the composition of the Commission.[27]

Not only did the president's men deceive themselves about the bases for Indian objections, but they also blamed the wrong people for the slow pace at which Indian claims were being resolved. One real culprit was the Department of Justice, both for its refusal to settle Indian claims cases and its failure until after the *Otoe* decision to ask Congress for money to hire enough attorneys and other staff to defend the claims. And Congress had failed to appropriate sufficient funds for the department even though Witt had told it, "The Department of Justice has never had . . . an adequate force of lawyers and researchers. . . . In the case of plaintiffs, 100 or 200 attorneys may be involved and yet the Government has a force of 12 or 15." By 1956 the Department of Justice had asked for more than five *thousand* extensions.[28]

The commissioners might have done more to pressure the Justice Department to keep up. More forceful judges might have imposed sanctions on the government for its delays. But such measures would have been inconsistent with Chief Commissioner Witt's nature. His rationalization was probably correct that, had the Commission resorted to the drastic remedy of granting default judgments to the tribes when the government failed to meet deadlines, the judgments would have been overturned by the Court of Claims or indirectly by Congress.[29]

Untroubled by such facts, administration officials finally pressured Commissioners Witt and O'Marr to depart. The Civil Service Retirement Act called for the automatic retirement of an employee who was seventy years old and had worked for the government for at least fifteen years. In 1956, both Witt and O'Marr were over seventy, Witt had served in the federal government for more than fifteen years, and O'Marr, just under that. Witt resisted, arguing that judges were excepted from the mandatory retirement provision of the Civil Service Retirement Act and that the Indian claims commissioners in reality were judges, but eventually both he and O'Marr gave in.[30]

O'Marr was the first to go, in July 1959. To succeed the man who had been the strongest opponent of the Indians' claims, President Eisenhower appointed none other than former Utah senator Arthur Watkins, who had both spearheaded the termination movement and blocked the Justice Department's efforts to have the Indian Claims Commission Act amended to abort virtually all aboriginal land claims. Then seventy-two years old, Watkins had just lost his 1958 bid for a third Senate term.

When Witt resigned the next year, Eisenhower redesignated Watkins chief commissioner. Over the next seven years, he brought important assets to the job, including great energy, integrity, congressional contacts, and legal acumen. Five years before he had chaired the Senate committee that recommended the censure of Senator Joseph McCarthy—probably the highlight of Watkins's political career. But his exemplary handling of the McCarthy investigation may also have been his political undoing: he attributed his 1958 defeat largely to conservative Utah voters angry over his role in the punishment of their hero.[31]

Despite his intellect, Watkins was domineering, arrogant, and inflexible. As shown by his efforts as a terminationist leader, he had little aware-

ness of or sympathy for the cultural differences between Indians and
white Americans. This blind spot was especially troublesome in someone who was supposed to rule impartially on claims. One leading anthropologist, who had testified on several occasions before the original
commissioners, refused any more claims work after testifying once before the doctrinaire Watkins. Not surprisingly, Watkins, although constrained by prior Court of Claims decisions to conclude that the United
States was liable in most cases, generally took as progovernment a position as precedents would allow. Near the end of his tenure he would
castigate the Court of Claims' "extremely liberal and favorable attitude
. . . toward Indian tribal claimants" in a written submission to Congress.[32]

Watkins and Holt, the holdover commissioner, were both Republicans, so President Eisenhower had to appoint a Democrat to take Witt's
seat. He had an ideal candidate in T. Harold Scott, an attorney for the
Federal Trade Commission. While appointment to the Commission was
a consolation prize for Watkins, to Scott the appointment to a federal
board or commission was a career goal. He bombarded the Eisenhower
administration throughout the 1950s with obsequious requests for appointment to a bipartisan commission and enlisted congressmen from
his home state of Colorado on his behalf.[33]

Watkins, Scott, and Holt served together for a little more than seven
years. During this time, they did not stray from the practices for resolving aboriginal land claims established by the courts and Commission
during the 1950s. Tribes almost always recovered on their aboriginal
land claims, but the Commission valued the lands conservatively (Scott
less so than the others), and there was no adjustment for the difference
between the value of a dollar at the time the lands were lost and at the
time of payment.

The congenial working atmosphere established by Witt changed,
however, as Watkins attempted to dominate the other two commissioners. Holt dared to disagree with Watkins only once in over 120 opinions,
but Watkins and Scott increasingly disagreed. In nine cases, Scott dissented from the decisions of Watkins and Holt to argue for the tribal
plaintiffs, and in several other instances he wrote concurring opinions
trying to limit the adverse implications of a decision for plaintiffs in future cases. Ideological differences mushroomed into such strong personal
animosities that Watkins informed White House staffers in 1967 that, if

Scott were nominated for reappointment, he would appear before Congress, presumably to oppose the nomination.[34]

.   .   .

As the trial of the Chiricahuas' land claim loomed, attorneys for both sides engaged experts to testify. Indians had testified in some of the early aboriginal land claim cases—the Pawnees', for example—but tribal attorneys had quickly learned that the Commission gave little weight to

TABLE 4

Terms of Indian Claims Commissioners

Name and Party Affiliation	Commencement	Termination
Edgar E. Witt (D) Appointed Chief Com'r Apr. 10, 1947	Apr. 10, 1947	June 30, 1960
William M. Holt (R)	Apr. 10, 1947	June 30, 1968
Louis J. O'Marr (D)	Apr. 10, 1947	July 31, 1959
Arthur V. Watkins (R) Appointed Chief Com'r July 1, 1960	Aug. 15, 1959	Sept. 30, 1967
T. Harold Scott (D)	July 1, 1960	June 30, 1968
John T. Vance (D) Appointed Chairman Mar. 19, 1968	Dec. 19, 1967	Sept. 30, 1978
Jerome K. Kuykendall (R) Appointed Chairman June 11, 1969	Dec. 19, 1967	Sept. 30, 1978
Richard W. Yarborough (D)	Dec. 19, 1967	Sept. 30, 1978
Margaret H. Pierce (R)	Oct. 16, 1968	Sept. 30, 1978
Theodore R. McKeldin (R) Interim Appointment	Nov. 21, 1968	May 1, 1969
Brantley Blue (R)	May 2, 1969	Sept. 30, 1978

stories by old men about the lands of their parents or grandparents. Indian oral history, the Commissioners decreed, was too "vague" and self-interested to be reliable. But the same information in the hands of an expert such as an anthropologist could carry considerable weight.[35]

An expert witness is supposed to be unbiased, no matter which side retains him. However, an attorney engages an expert only if the attorney believes that the witness will give testimony helpful to his case. Any potential expert who wishes to testify—whether for professional or financial reasons—and who knows how the system works accepts an engagement with the understanding that his view should support the client who retains him.

At the Chiricahuas' trial, the Weissbrodts called three expert witnesses and the government's attorneys called two. Two were crucial. Both sides recognized that the case pivoted around the testimony of Dr. Morris Opler for the Apaches and Albert Schroeder for the government.

In terms of the experts' credentials, the Indians outgunned the government. At the time of the trial, Opler was the president of the American Anthropological Association. He had done extensive field work on the Mescalero Reservation during the 1930s, and had written more than twenty books, chapters of composite works, and articles about the Chiricahuas. In short, he was the world's leading anthropological expert on the Apaches, and long before he was retained as an expert, he had published conclusions favorable to their claims.[36]

Schroeder, several years Opler's junior, had worked and written primarily in the field of archeology, which had relatively little significance in studying the Chiricahuas, who had traveled light, leaving few artifacts behind. He testified at trial as a "self-made ethno-historian," not as an archeologist. Moreover, his independence was subject to attack, because he worked for the government, primarily in the National Park Service, and had not studied the Chiricahuas before the government had engaged him as an expert witness.[37]

Schroeder's qualification deficiencies, however, weren't so severe to disqualify him as an expert. Accordingly, the Commission would weigh the logic of each expert's opinion, the evidence supporting his conclusions, and how well each expert could defend those conclusions on cross-examination.

·   ·   ·

Commissioners Witt, O'Marr, and Holt had developed a sensible, three-stage procedure for trying aboriginal land claims. The first stage concerned several of the issues of liability discussed in the previous chapter: Was the plaintiff a landowning group? If so, what were the boundaries of the land? And when was the land taken by or ceded to the United States? If the Commission ruled that the plaintiff group had aboriginal title to a tract of land, the second stage addressed the value of the land as of the date of taking or cession. In the third stage, the government sought to establish the value of the offsets to which it was entitled. Commissioners Watkins and Scott retained the three-stage approach. The Chiricahua trial in December 1962, which went on for eight days, didn't go beyond the first stage.

Relying on his 1930s field work, Opler testified that the Chiricahuas had constituted a single tribe divided into three bands and numerous family groups. Although they hadn't generally engaged in united political activity, they "had a linguistic unity, a unity in their economic and material endeavors, a unity in their social organization, and a unity in their conceptual life, a unity in their [a]esthetic life; a unity in every aspect of their life that made it inevitable that they be considered a tribe." [38]

Schroeder, by contrast, tried to bestow scientific dignity on the Supreme Court's sixty-year-old definition of a "tribe" by arguing that the main criterion for a tribe was "a political, a central, authority." Because the Indians whom Opler called the Chiricahuas hadn't possessed that type of authority, they couldn't have been a single tribe. Instead, Schroeder studied the names that officials of the Spanish, Mexican, and United States governments had assigned to Apaches within the area in dispute, and decided that there actually had been five distinct tribes. The government attorneys then argued that the plaintiffs couldn't recover because they hadn't brought the action in the name of the five tribes, nor had they tried to prove the territory occupied by each of them.[39]

Each Indian claims case was assigned to one commissioner, who supervised the preparation of the Commission's findings, which the other two commissioners then would review. Luckily for the Chiricahuas, their claim was assigned to Scott, increasing the likelihood of a favorable result, but it would not be issued promptly after the trial. The parties didn't complete their various posttrial written submissions until April 30, 1965. Then Scott ran into more delays. In early 1966 his staff lawyer resigned, followed by Watkins's resignation. In late 1967 three new commissioners were appointed. As a result, the Commission did not issue its findings until June 28, 1968.[40]

After the years of delay, at least the Chiricahuas were gratified with the result. Scott, writing for a unanimous Commission, completely rejected Schroeder's and the government's view that the Chiricahuas had consisted of five separate entities. Quoting extensively from Opler's testimony, he concluded that the Chiricahuas constituted a tribe, a single landowning entity. In view of the decision of the Court of Claims in *Indians of California,* and the many subsequent decisions that increasingly ignored *Montoya's* emphasis on political cohesion as the defining characteristic of a tribe or band (both decisions were discussed in Chapter Seven), the government probably could have prevailed on this theory only if it had made an effective presentation and the Indians a weak one. Opler, however, had been an exceptionally strong witness for the Chiricahuas. Abe Weissbrodt called him "one of the most brilliant men I have ever met," but perhaps more important was his fearlessness on cross-examination. Howard Campbell, the government attorney, never undermined his testimony. In fact, after the Commission overruled one of Weissbrodt's objections to a question, Opler responded so effectively that Weissbrodt jokingly apologized for trying to protect the witness.

In addition to Opler's unshakable anthropological evidence, the Weissbrodts presented compelling documentary counterevidence to Schroeder's position. Schroeder had relied primarily on the documents from the prereservation days, when government officials knew almost nothing about the Chiricahuas. The Commission found far more meaningful the reports of the agent who worked with Mangas Coloradas during the 1850s and who, after several years of close contact with the Apaches of southwestern New Mexico and southeastern Arizona, concluded that all of the Indians whom we since have called Chiricahuas were "identically the same people." [41]

The Commission then had to define the tribe's territory. During the trial, the Weissbrodts had claimed an area depicted on a map prepared by Opler and published in 1941. Again rejecting informant testimony in favor of Anglo documents, Schroeder had plotted on another map each site that white observers had described as being used or occupied by Chiricahuas. He had found that these sites were clustered in certain discrete areas that he denoted as "maximum habitat areas." If the Indians had aboriginal title to any land, the government attorneys argued, it was to these "maximum habitat areas," not the entire, far larger, tract they were claiming.

Schroeder's "maximum habitat area" testimony crumbled under Abe Weissbrodt's skillful questioning. He acknowledged that the historical documents did not reflect the extent of the Indians' hunting and gathering activities, that they had to hunt and gather over vast areas, and that these vast areas "very likely" included territory outside the maximum habitat areas. Schroeder also admitted there was no evidence of any occupancy or use of any part of the claimed area by Indians other than the Chiricahuas until after disruptions caused by the United States during the 1860s. Finally, he confessed that Chiricahuas had performed activities he had chosen not to consider "use and occupancy" throughout much of the claimed territory. Abe Weissbrodt subsequently wrote to Opler, who had returned to Cornell prior to Schroeder's testimony, that the government witness had become "most cooperative": "I wish you would have been there to observe the expressions on the faces of the government attorneys." In spite of Schroeder's concessions, the Commission managed to shave the area claimed by the Chiricahuas a little, but decided that the Chiricahuas had exclusively used and occupied about 15.6 million acres—an area only slightly smaller than the state of West Virginia—in southwestern New Mexico and southeastern Arizona.[42]

. . .

On the next issue, determining when the government extinguished the Chiricahuas' aboriginal title to their lands, the government lawyers made a critical mistake. As a rule of thumb, the later the valuation date, the higher the value—for two reasons. First, prices of most commodities, including land, have inflated throughout most of this country's history. More important, miners, ranchers, and settlers poured into newly opened territories, developing ways of using land previously considered unusable.

Determining the date of taking and therefore of valuation was generally clear for ceded lands: it was the date of the agreement between the United States and the tribe or the date that the agreement was approved by the Senate. Determining the date for *unceded* lands, however, was far more problematic. The Commission had to select one incident that constituted the act of taking.

The first choice was the date of a statute showing Congress's desire to terminate a tribe's right to use aboriginal land and occupy it. Since the *Lone Wolf* decision, courts had not questioned Congress's power to terminate a tribe's land rights. Congress, however, had not been involved with the Chiricahuas until after their imprisonment. The only conceivable congressional taking was an 1876 act stipulating that the Apaches of Arizona and New Mexico "shall not be allowed to leave their proper reservations." A lawyer would have argued that this order was not sufficient, applying as it did to all Apache tribes in the two territories.[43]

In the absence of a congressional taking, the Commission searched for a governmental action terminating a tribe's use and occupancy of its aboriginal lands. Knowing that, the Weissbrodts argued in their posttrial brief that the lands hadn't been taken until September 4, 1886, when Geronimo and Naiche surrendered to General Miles and the government began to ship the tribe to Florida. They had selected the latest defensible date, not only because they knew that in general a later date meant a higher value, but because a mineral appraiser had informed them that important deposits were discovered within the tract in the late 1870s and early 1880s. Because minerals discovered after the taking date would not contribute anything to the land's valuation, the 1886 date was critical for a large award.[44]

Surprisingly, the government did not argue for any taking date at all. This was not for lack of alternatives. In fact, under Commission precedents, 1877, when Agent John Clum removed the Chiricahuas from the Warm Springs Reservation, was more appropriate than 1886, and even earlier dates would have been defensible. For all practical purposes, the government attorneys, Campbell and DeNunzio, ignored the issue.

They may have believed that arguments for an early date would interfere with their contention that the Chiricahuas should not recover because of the immorality of their raiding activities. In their posttrial brief, they refined the argument marginally, contending that the Chiricahuas could not acquire Indian title because they had used the land "for no other purpose than as a staging area for the launching of raids, wars, and depredations and as a haven into which to retreat and hide."[45]

The raiding argument never had the slightest chance of success. When Campbell sprang the idea on Opler during cross-examination, the anthropologist first asked incredulously, "Am I supposed to criticize the morals of these people, and will this make their boundaries any different?" When Campbell pressed on, Opler pointed out that virtually all societies had a history of aggression and warfare, including the United States in starting the war with Mexico that ended with the conveyance of rights in what the Chiricahuas considered their home. The Weissbrodts and the Commission ignored the government's argument altogether, and it shriveled and died.[46]

The Commission then had before it only the Weissbrodts' position on the date of taking. Therefore, on June 28, 1968, it adopted the view that the 15.6 million acres of land had been taken, and should be valued, as of September 4, 1886, the day Geronimo surrendered in Skeleton Canyon.[47]

·   ·   ·

A decision on the value of those fifteen-odd million acres came quickly. Each party engaged a real estate appraiser and a mineral appraiser, and was ready for trial in January 1970.

The Weissbrodts had tried to avoid this trial altogether. After both sides had received preliminary reports from their experts, Abe met with Campbell and Ralph Barney (who remained in charge of the Indian Claims Section and opposed to settling the cases) several times during 1969, offering to settle the land claim for $16 million. But Barney refused to negotiate. Maybe he believed that since Scott and Holt had followed Watkins out the door in 1968, the new commissioners would look more favorably on the government's case. He was wrong. The new Commission, which turned out to be the most pro-Indian to date, valued the Chiricahuas' lands as of September 4, 1886, at approximately $16.5 million.[48]

During its tenure, the Commission placed higher values on the aboriginal lands of only six other tribes or groups: the Indians of California; the Kiowa, Comanches, and Kiowa Apaches; the Northern Paiutes; the Sac and Fox; the Sioux; and the Western Shoshone. Each of those six had possessed, according to the Commission, aboriginal title to millions more acres than the Chiricahuas. Thus, the Chiricahuas had done exceptionally well—by the Commission's standards.

Several factors contributed to the success, but the biggest was the late date of taking. According to the Commission, almost 40 percent of the $16.5 million represented the amount that a purchaser would have paid for the minerals in the tract as of September 4, 1886. The Commission had made clear in other cases that it would not issue awards based on speculative values. Boosters had trumpeted the mineral wealth of the Chiricahuas' tract during the 1860s and 1870s, but before the Indians' removal to San Carlos in 1876 and 1877, few Anglos felt safe enough to spend substantial sums on mineral exploration and development. A handful of courageous miners had removed as much as $10 million of precious metals by May 1877, but six months later the silver deposits of Tombstone and the copper deposits of Bisbee were discovered, and boomtowns sprang up overnight. By September 4, 1886, gold, silver, copper, and other minerals worth tens of millions of dollars had been extracted. Considering that Bisbee had yielded over $1.3 billion of copper through 1962, the Commission's mineral value of $6,375,000 as of September 1886 was conservative indeed. But it was many times greater than the value the Commission would have had to assign to minerals as of an earlier date.[49]

The rest of the territory in question was valued as cattle country, and again the late date for valuation helped the Apaches. In the decade before 1886, the transcontinental Southern Pacific Railroad was built through Chiricahua land, and the Atchison, Topeka & Santa Fe was built along the tract's eastern boundary. The excellent rail connections contributed greatly to the growth of the cattle industry in southern Arizona and New Mexico. The difference between taking dates of 1877 and 1886 added up to at least $6 million—a high price for the government to pay for its inept decision not to contest the date. But the Weissbrodt brothers had just begun to make the government atone for its mistake.[50]

·   ·   ·

Before the claims of the two groups of Chiricahuas had been amalgamated, Lefty Weissbrodt had filed three petitions on behalf of the Fort Sill Apache Tribe. One sought damages because the government had permitted people to trespass upon and use the Chiricahuas' aboriginal land. Preliminary proceedings on the trespass case began in May 1970. One look at the trespass petition and the government's Howard Campbell knew what was coming. Since the Commission had concluded that the land was not taken until September 1886, all twenty-six thousand non-Indians living on the tract on that date, the Weissbrodts would contend, were trespassers. They had grazed their stock on the Chiricahuas' grass, cut many of the Chiricahuas' trees for fuel and building materials, and, of course, removed millions of dollars of minerals from the land.[51]

Making matters worse, the Court of Claims in 1968, and the Indian Claims Commission in 1969, had established precedents. The Commission had made it clear that the government would be liable under the fair and honorable dealings clause if it assisted trespassers, by, for example, protecting them militarily or retroactively validating their illegal entries by granting them title to the land. The government had protected the miners and ranchers who moved onto Chiricahua land prior to September 4, 1886. Thus, as long as the Commission adhered to the 1886 date, liability for breach of the fair and honorable dealings clause seemed assured.[52]

The government began trying desperately, in the words of the Court of Claims, "to thrash itself out of the trap it had helped to dig for itself." On June 4, 1970, Campbell filed a motion asking the Commission to reconsider the 1886 date. That was denied in August, and he filed a new motion in March 1971, asking for essentially the same relief but with a slightly altered justification. The government, however, was stuck in its own quicksand. Normally, courts grant motions for reconsideration only when something like newly discovered evidence or a change in the controlling law makes adherence to the original decision grossly unfair. The government could point to no such event in this case; rather, it was seeking relief from its own strategic mistake. For this reason, it is unlikely that the Commission would have granted the government's motion even if it had been filed immediately after the liability trial. The government's delay, however, made it even more unlikely that the Commission would grant relief. A change in the date of taking would necessitate a new valuation trial, entailing substantial delays and thousands of dollars of extra costs.[53]

Rebuffed, the government's attorneys turned to an appeal of the aboriginal land case in the Court of Claims. However, like any party in a court case, the government had no right of appeal until a final judgment had come down. The Commission could not enter one until it had decided the third phase of the case—the amount of offsets to which the government was entitled.

The language of the Indian Claims Commission Act restricted the government's right to offsets, and to ensure that tribes recovered something, the Commission had strictly interpreted those rights. As a result, offsets were relatively small, and by the 1960s Ralph Barney was often willing to settle.

Perhaps realizing that no offsets would be allowed during the imprisonment period, or perhaps wanting a quick resolution in order to appeal the underlying judgment, the government readily agreed to settle with the Apaches—and for an especially small sum, $7,700. This let the Commission hand down on August 25, 1971, less than three months after it had issued its valuation decision, its final judgment in favor of the Chiricahua Apaches for the taking of their aboriginal land in the amount of $16,489,096.[54]

·   ·   ·

In early September, the Weissbrodts reported to Benedict Jozhe and Wendell Chino that the government attorneys were considering an appeal that, they regretted to say, "may take another 18 months or two years or perhaps longer." To avoid this additional delay, they made a daring proposal to Barney. If the government would agree not to appeal, the tribes would agree that the government could relitigate the date of taking in the trespass case. In other words, the Chiricahuas would retain the benefit of the 1886 date in the land claims case, but not in the trespass case unless the Weissbrodts could convince the Commission, against full government opposition, that the 1886 date had been correct. The risk was that if the Commission concluded that the appropriate date of taking was sometime in the 1870s, the recovery in the trespass case would be quite small. The Weissbrodts believed it was worth the risk in order to assure the bonanza on the land claims case, but they need not have exerted themselves because, characteristically, Barney would not play. The Weissbrodts then tried going over his head to the solicitor general, but that effort also failed and the government proceeded with its appeal.[55]

The government's lawyers had some reason for confidence. The Court of Claims had had a near-complete turnover of judges from those who had authored or supported the seminal decisions of the 1950s establishing tribes' rights to recover. As a group, their successors proved to be more progovernment, and became increasingly so in 1972 when President Nixon made three new appointments.

On appeal, the Justice Department attorneys gave up on the contention that the Chiricahuas had not constituted a single tribe and had not possessed Indian title to about 15.6 million acres. Instead they bore down on two issues—the date of taking, and the Commission's method of valuing the mineral resources.[56]

On June 20, 1973, they found out that they had once again made the wrong decision in refusing to negotiate. The Court of Claims narrowly "affirmed" the Commission's decision in both of these issues. Four judges indicated that if they could look at the issue anew they might conclude that the aboriginal land had been taken in 1876, not 1886. However, the government's failure to express a timely objection during the proceedings before the Commission "amounts to a waiver of the right to challenge the September 4, 1886 taking date." The three dissenters went further, arguing that the date of taking was clearly wrong. They acknowledged that the government attorneys had made a "tactical error" in not arguing for an earlier date at the appropriate stage in the proceedings, but urged that the case be returned to the Commission: "[i]t is a travesty of justice when the court admits that the date is probably wrong . . . and 16 million dollars is riding on such error." [57]

.   .   .

While the appeal of the land claim was before the Court of Claims, the parties tried the trespass claim before the Commission, on May 8–10, 1972. The same appraisers were summoned as expert witnesses, and they relied on much the same evidence as at the earlier trial. But this time, instead of estimating what a hypothetical purchaser would have paid for the Chiricahua tract on September 4, 1886, the experts estimated the amount that the Chiricahuas should have received for the use of their tract prior to that date.

In the Commission's decision on May 10, 1974, the Chiricahuas "won" on the liability issue as expected, but only partially on the damages calculations. The Commission rejected the Chiricahuas' efforts to recover for the use of all but the mineral resources. It concluded that, because of the absence of relevant information, their experts had speculated excessively about the amount of the nonmineral resources used. By contrast, lack of data concerning the value of the minerals removed prior to September 4, 1886, wasn't a problem. The mineral experts had been in remarkably close agreement: the Indians' expert had put the figure at about $55,200,000, the government's at $51,900,000. The Commission came up with $54,150,000. The major disagreement arose over the proper way to value what the Indians had lost from this mining. The Weissbrodts argued that damages should be measured by the profits earned by the miners—about $20.7 million. The government attorneys said that if the government was liable at all it should be at a royalty rate equal to 10 percent of the value of the minerals removed, or about $5 million. The Commission compromised in favor of the government, deciding on a 20 percent royalty rate, and awarded the Chiricahuas about $10,830,000.[58]

This was by far the largest award in a trespass case. Relatively few tribal attorneys even thought to include such a claim in their petitions, and the next largest award, to the Western Shoshones for minerals removed from their aboriginal lands in Nevada, was for only about $4.6 million.[59] Again, the government was hurt by the date of taking decision; the award would have been less than half as much if the date had been in 1877.

As certain as sunrise, the government appealed to the Court of Claims. By the time the court was ready to decide the appeal, on April 14, 1976, it had already let stand the decision in the land claim case and dismissed two premature procedural appeals in the trespass case. All this prompted Judge Philip Nichols, who wrote the opinion for the majority of the court, to describe the new appeal as "another phase of a litigation almost as full of dramatic contest, confrontation, and strange turns of fate, as is the history of the claimant tribe . . . in the period to which its claims relate, the nineteenth century." This time, Nichols gave the litigation its last important "turn of fate." [60]

.   .   .

Of the judges on the Court of Claims during the mid-1970s, Nichols held the most iconoclastic views. He thought Indian lands should be valued in terms of the resources important to the natives, such as fish, instead of the resources that Anglos valued, such as minerals. Nichols had been one of the three dissenters in the appeal of the Chiricahua land claim case. On the trespass claim, however, his hostility toward Indian recoveries for minerals extracted from their aboriginal lands placed him in the majority.[61]

It is unfair, Nichols said, to "mulct the United States for the sour and ignore the sweet." Miners may have removed minerals from the Chiricahua aboriginal lands before September 4, 1886, thereby subtracting from the value of the land, but miners and other non-Indians also constructed improvements and engaged in other value-enhancing activities. The court therefore was remanding the case to the Commission, Nichols explained, to determine the net amount, if any, by which non-Indian activities on the tract prior to September 4, 1886, diminished the value of the land on that date. That net amount would be the award.[62]

In theory, this seemed fair. In practice, it was impossible. The Commission already depended on fiction to value vast tracts of aboriginal land. Nichols's edict compounded the fiction by adding a time warp. The Commission would have to value the land as of September 4, 1886, in its physical condition before any non-Indian encroachment. The land would have to be treated as if it were in its 1860 condition, while technology, economic conditions, and the development of adjacent land would be weighed as they were in 1886. Something that never existed would have to be valued. For the next two years, the attorneys debated how to do this.

Finally, in early 1979, with Barney having retired from the Department of Justice, the government's attorneys and the Weissbrodts sidestepped the problem. They agreed, contingent on tribal approval, to settle the trespass claim, together with two other outstanding Chiricahua claims, for $6 million. The other claims—for the taking in 1913 of the Chiricahua interest in the Fort Sill Reservation and for the mismanagement of the funds of the Chiricahuas as disclosed by the government's accounting—were relatively small in value, probably less than a million dollars together. The settlement did not itemize the value of each claim, but the government knew that the Weissbrodts were willing to settle the trespass claim alone for about $5,400,000. Nichols's decision thus cut the value of the trespass claim approximately in half, from the $10,830,000 awarded by the Commission to the approximately $5,400,000 contribution that the claim made to the overall settlement.[63]

The Chiricahuas voted to accept the settlement, and the Court of Claims approved it on April 6, 1979. The land claims of the Chiricahuas were finally over, a bit more than three decades after Grady Lewis and Howard Shenkin had filed the original petition seeking $560,000 for the taking of the aboriginal land included in the Warm Springs Reservation. The incredible legal odyssey had resulted in total recoveries of about $22 million, about forty times more than originally sought.[64]

.   .   .

The Chiricahuas received the seventh-largest award issued by the Commission in an aboriginal land claim, and several million dollars more for trespassory damages. They were also awarded probably twice what they might have been if an 1876 taking date had been used. The brothers Weissbrodt exploited the government's error in not initially contesting the date. The result was an $11 million windfall for the Chiricahuas.

This does not mean that the Chiricahuas were adequately compensated, if the object was to put them in the financial position that they would have occupied if the wrong had not been done. Even if money alone could compensate the Indians for the loss of their homeland, fair compensation would demand the payment of interest from the date of taking until the date of payment. In compensating tribes, the Supreme Court has approved the use of a 5 percent *simple* interest rate to adjust for the delay in payment. If the Chiricahuas' land was worth $11 million in 1876 (any value is purely speculative), they should have been awarded over $56 million in 1979 using that same 5 percent simple interest rate. At a 5 percent *compounded* rate of interest, the Commission would have awarded them over one billion dollars for their aboriginal land! By either measure, the Chiricahua award should have been increased from the 1876 values by a factor of about ten, to over $100 million.[65]

NINE

THE RETURN OF THE NATIVES

Where today are the Pequot? Where are the Narragansett, the
Mohican, the Pokanoket, and many other once powerful tribes of our
people? They have vanished before the avarice and the oppression
of the White Man, as snow before a summer sun.

—TECUMSEH

A few legal scholars have stated that a major purpose of the Indian
Claims Commission Act was to eliminate the clouds that hung over
non-Indian titles by paying tribes money to relinquish any land rights
they had. About all these scholars have to back up this assertion is a single paragraph in a report from the House Indian Affairs Committee
backing the act's passage. It described a handful of Indian claims to land
that the United States had agreed to sell for the tribes' benefit, but chose
to convey without obtaining any payment for the tribes. "The status of
such lands," the committee wrote, "is often seriously clouded because
the Indian claim to these lands has never been finally adjudicated. This
situation, besides being unfair to the Indians, is a serious hindrance to
development in many parts of the country." [1]

In fact, in 1946, the tribes posed virtually no threat to the land titles
of non-Indians. The practical problem was, as usual, money. Attorneys
wouldn't have agreed to represent tribes seeking to reclaim land on a
contingency basis, because a successful suit would have yielded only

land, not a monetary award from which attorneys fees could be paid, and in 1946 few, if any, tribes had the financial resources to hire an attorney on a pay-as-you-go basis. And even if a tribe found an attorney to represent it, courts' interpretations of their jurisdictional limits created an almost insuperable barrier to success. State courts would have said simply that they had no jurisdiction over an Indian claim for the return of land—it was federal business. Federal courts would have ruled that their jurisdiction extended only to suits brought on behalf of the Indians by the United States Department of Justice, which was very unlikely to initiate a suit that might dispossess non-Indians. Yet it was to the federal government that the tribes had to look for vindication.

Not surprisingly, the United States, before 1946, had brought very few actions that even arguably clouded the title of non-Indians to lands outside an Indian reservation. Only one of these, *United States v. Santa Fe Pacific Railroad Co.,* had reached the Supreme Court, in 1941. In that case, the United States argued that land it had granted to the railroad in the nineteenth century was subject to the aboriginal rights of the Hualapai tribe of northern Arizona. The railroad eventually conceded the claim for lands *inside* the reservation, but defeated the claim for lands outside it, arguing that the Hualapais had voluntarily abandoned their rights to that land. This one claim, on which the railroad had largely prevailed, hardly posed a major threat to non-Indian landholders. Legislators before 1946 would not have attached much importance to eliminating such potential claims, especially as long as judicial doors were closed to land-recovery suits initiated by the tribes.[2]

Yet a close reading of *Santa Fe* suggested that, if tribes could initiate the suits, they could challenge the titles of non-Indians if they met two conditions. First, harking back to Chief Justice Marshall, the Court said only Congress has the power to terminate Indian title, and it will be deemed to have used that power only if it clearly indicates that intention. It followed that a tribe might have a claim if a state government or private individuals, instead of the federal government, had deprived the tribe of its lands, or if the federal executive branch acted without legislative direction. Second, the Court said the tribe must not have voluntarily abandoned its lands. Upholding the obvious, it said any tribe compelled to leave its lands did not do so voluntarily.

It would be more than two decades, however, before attorneys or tribes tried to test the waters charted by *Santa Fe*. The new explorers were outsiders. The members of the Indian claims bar were prejudiced by the paradigm in which they worked against the possibility of claiming that tribes still owned large areas of land that they hadn't possessed for decades or centuries. The claims lawyers were trained to think in terms of identifying the boundaries of a tribe's aboriginal territory, determining how much of that land (if any) was included in the tribe's reservation, and seeking damages for the entire difference. Continuing ownership of land outside a reservation never entered the equation. The new lawyers also often represented tribes that hadn't filed claims before the Indian Claims Commission—the eastern tribes that, according to Chief Tecumseh in the early nineteenth century, already had disappeared before the white man's oppression.

Although the new lawsuits were brought by new lawyers outside the bounds of the Indian Claims Commission Act, they cast troubling shadows over the claims brought under the act. Had the awards under the Indian Claims Commission Act cost tribes their right to reassert ownership over ancient lands?

·   ·   ·

The Oneidas started the exploration of the implications of *Santa Fe*. One of the six tribes of the mighty Iroquois Confederacy in what is now central and western New York State, the Oneidas by the 1770s had been converted to Protestantism, were clustered in large villages of wooden dwellings with glass windows, and raised bounteous crops of corn. As war between colonists and British became likely, most of the Iroquois tribes sided with the British, but the Oneidas supported the colonists and helped keep the then–northwestern frontier calm.[3]

As a reward, in a series of three treaties entered into between 1784 and 1794, the federal government guaranteed that the new nation would not interfere with the Oneidas' possession of their aboriginal lands, altogether about six million acres. New Yorkers, however, did not remain thankful for the wartime assistance or heed the federal treaties. As land hunger grew, the state negotiated transactions under which the hard-pressed Oneidas conveyed over five million of their acres in 1785 and 1788, and virtually all the rest by a series of treaties with the state negotiated between 1795 and 1842. New York ignored not only the federal treaties, but also one of the first acts of Congress—the Trade and Intercourse Act of 1790—and its successor, the Indian Nonintercourse

Act. Over the years, each version said that any transaction between a tribe and a state or private citizen that conveys Indian land is invalid and void unless a representative of the federal government participates in the negotiations.

When New York negotiated with the Oneidas in 1795, members of President Washington's cabinet notified New York governor John Jay of the Nonintercourse Act, a warning that he blithely disregarded. He certainly was capable of understanding the act's provisions; he had just resigned as the first Chief Justice to take what was then considered the more important position as a state governor. No doubt Jay correctly assumed that officials in Washington would not take concrete steps to protect mere Indians, no matter what wartime assistance or treaty promises had been given, but he did not figure on the Indians going to court two hundred years later.[4]

·   ·   ·

In 1951, the Oneida Indians filed claims for monetary relief before the Indian Claims Commission. The fact that the state, not the federal, government had deprived them of their lands forced the Indians' attorneys to break new legal ground. Instead of contending that the United States had acquired their lands unfairly, the Oneidas alleged that the United States had violated its duty to protect them from the state of New York. If the federal government was liable, damages would be measured in the usual way: by the differences between the values of the tracts of land at the times of the various cessions and whatever compensation had been paid for them.[5]

Not surprisingly, Justice Department attorneys sought to discredit the liability theory. Whatever the duty of the United States may have been to protect the Oneidas from New York State, they contended, it did not extend to liability for the payment of damages if the amounts New York State had paid were deemed unconscionably low. The Commission rejected the argument, ruling that the United States would indeed be liable if New York had paid less than fair value. The Oneidas' lawyer, Marvin Chapman of Chicago, won a string of preliminary victories on this issue in the 1970s. Perhaps the Commission's pro-Indian decisions merely manifested the general determination that every plaintiff tribe receive some award for the loss of its aboriginal lands, but, considering the legal obstacles, the victories were nevertheless impressive.[6]

Meanwhile a lawyer named George Shattuck was convinced that the state of New York had violated both the federal treaties with the Oneidas and the Nonintercourse Act when it had negotiated the treaties by which the Oneidas had ceded their lands. Indian law was not Shattuck's specialty—he was a young tax lawyer—but he convinced his prestigious law firm, Bond, Schoenek & King of Syracuse, to pursue relief for the Oneidas outside the Commission. Beginning in 1966, he tried to persuade the state of New York to settle with the Oneidas and, failing that, pressed the federal authorities to file suit on the tribe's behalf. For four years, the Interior Department steadfastly insisted that the Indian Claims Commission was the sole forum for such matters.[7]

Rebuffed on both sides, Shattuck reluctantly decided in 1970 to go to court to try to establish that the Oneidas still owned the lands that were the subjects of the treaties. Any litigation was risky, and this was especially so, because it was likely that no court would accept jurisdiction. Federal courts have jurisdiction over several classes of claims, but in the 1920s, an Indian in New York State had sought to recover a parcel of land from a non-Indian. The federal district court threw the case out, claiming that an Indian's possessory claim is no different from a non-Indian's: a landowner's right to possession, it held, is a product of state, not federal, law. Shattuck expected state courts to be no more receptive. Since the 1780s, New York's state government had contended that it, not the federal government, had jurisdiction over Indians located within its borders, but state law, as construed by the state courts, did not give those courts any power over the claims of Indian tribes.[8]

Trapped in this Catch-22, Shattuck chose to bring suit in federal district court against the counties of Oneida and Madison. He didn't ask that private individuals living on the contested lands be ejected. Nor did he ask the county governments to vacate their land. Instead, to test his legal theories, he sought only a ruling that the counties owed the Oneidas the fair rental value of the land for the two preceding years.

Shattuck's jurisdictional fears were soon borne out: the district court and then the appellate court ruled that they had no jurisdiction over the Oneidas' lawsuit. The next step was to ask the United States Supreme Court to hear the matter. That sole "protector" of the Indians, the

United States government, joined heartily with the state and the two counties in opposing the Oneidas' petition. Despite the overwhelming forces stacked against them, the Supreme Court on January 21, 1974, ruled unanimously in the Oneidas' favor.[9]

The Oneidas' claim, the Court said, arose from their aboriginal title, a product of federal, and not state, law. Furthermore, they had grounded their claims in alleged violations of federal treaties and the Nonintercourse Act, also both components of federal law. The claims thus arose under federal law and the district court had jurisdiction. The Oneidas finally had the forum they sought. But the Supreme Court went even further, stating that the Nonintercourse Act's provision that Indian title to land cannot be extinguished without federal consent applied "in all of the states, including the original 13." [10]

The justices of the Supreme Court almost certainly did not realize the forces that they had released. The *Oneida* case seemed to involve unique facts. Few non-Indians in 1974 realized that Indian tribes had occupied tracts of land throughout the Eastern Seaboard when the Constitution had been adopted. Probably the Court thought the case important primarily in establishing the primacy of federal law over state law in dealing with the tribes, as one more battle in the centuries-long struggle over the respective powers of the federal and state governments. But no matter what the intentions of the justices, large tracts of land in many of the original thirteen states were now fair game for the Eastern tribes that had long been out of sight and out of mind. By deciding that federal courts have jurisdiction over violations of the Nonintercourse Act, the Court opened a new era for Indian claims.[11]

.   .   .

The Oneida tribe was not the first to realize the fruits of its victory before the Supreme Court. The state of New York continued to oppose it vigorously, raising a multitude of defenses to its claims. One involved the Oneidas' pending claims under the Indian Claims Commission Act, and rather than risk the potentially far more valuable suit for the lands, the Oneidas dismissed their claim against the United States under the act.

While the Oneidas were bogged down in court, the Passamaquoddies of Maine adopted a different strategy that produced the first huge Indian success under the Nonintercourse Act. The Passamaquoddies had ranged over about a million acres in what is now northeastern Maine.

(Maine, originally a part of the Massachusetts Bay Colony, only became a state in 1820.) Before the American Revolution, the Passamaquoddies, like the Oneidas, were members of a large confederacy, the Great Council Fire or Seven Nations, whose member tribes occupied land north and east of the Iroquois tribes. The Passamaquoddies also fought on behalf of the colonists in return for promises from an agent for the Continental Congress that included protection for their hunting grounds. As with the Oneidas, these promises were forgotten as soon as the Indians were no longer needed. In 1794, finding themselves vastly reduced by disease and abandoned by the national government, the Passamaquoddies entered into a treaty with the Commonwealth of Massachusetts under which they ceded almost all of their land in return for a reservation of about twenty-three thousand acres along the Canadian border. By mid-twentieth century, they were still barred from voting in congressional elections and even from sitting in a white man's barber chair. Employment was virtually unknown; welfare payments were the primary source of income. And over the years, in a series of small transactions, they had lost about six thousand acres, about one-fourth of their already-small reservation.[12] Those six thousand acres—about ten square miles, or the equivalent of a small New England village—were the source of Maine's undoing.

Spurred by yet another threat to their remaining reservation lands, the Passamaquoddies sought legal help. They wanted to block the new intrusion and, if possible, to regain the six thousand acres. Bad luck proceeded on course: their first attorney was incapacitated by a drug charge. Then, in 1970, their luck changed when they turned to a young attorney, Tom Tureen, an Ivy Leaguer just out of law school. Like Shattuck, he brought a fresh perspective. He was convinced that the Passamaquoddies had a viable claim, not just for the six thousand acres but, under the Nonintercourse Act, for the million or so acres ceded by the treaty of 1794.

The young Tureen, employed by a nonprofit legal group called the Native American Rights Fund (NARF) beginning in the early 1970s, tried to enlist support from several of the corps of Indian claims lawyers in asserting continuing ownership of the aboriginal Passamaquoddy lands. These lawyers dismissed the idea: everyone *knew* Indians could not recover land. As far as the claims attorneys were concerned, it was money or nothing.[13]

As with Shattuck, Tureen had to overcome the jurisdictional barrier, and it was even higher than for the Oneidas, because the United States had never "recognized" the Passamaquoddies as a tribe. The federal government had entered into treaties with the Oneidas and, at least with respect to those who moved to Wisconsin, created a reservation for them. By contrast, Washington officials had virtually ignored the existence of the Passamaquoddies since the earliest days of the republic.[14]

The best way to overcome this and other potential weaknesses in his clients' claim, Tureen reasoned, was to have the United States sue on their behalf. Predictably, the government demurred. Tureen promptly sued the United States in federal district court, seeking an order compelling the government to prosecute a claim for monetary damages against the state of Maine on behalf of the Passamaquoddies. Although any violation of the Nonintercourse Act might affect the title to all of the former Passamaquoddy lands, Tureen, like Shattuck, decided initially to limit the scope of the claim—focusing only on lands owned by the state, and only on monetary, not possessory, relief.

The United States government could have defended itself by falling back on "prosecutorial discretion." This well-established principle holds that the judicial branch should not interfere with the decisions of executive-branch lawyers about whom to prosecute or sue. Had the government explained to the district court that it had declined to prosecute because it believed the tribe's case to be weak or because of lack of resources or even because of political considerations, the district court probably would have dismissed the Passamaquoddies' lawsuit. But the government raised a concrete legal issue instead. It argued, as Tureen had predicted, that the Passamaquoddies were never protected by the Nonintercourse Act because the federal government had not recognized them as a tribe. A court could get its teeth into that, and the federal district court soon did. On January 20, 1975, it ruled that the Nonintercourse Act did apply to the Passamaquoddies and that the government could not refuse to prosecute on that ground. Later that year, a federal appeals court upheld the decision.[15]

Faced with the court order, Department of Interior lawyers for the first time took the Indians' suit seriously. In January 1977, they recommended that the Department of Justice expand the case dramatically. They urged that ejectment actions be filed against all residents of the area claimed by the Passamaquoddies and their aboriginal neighbors, the Penobscots—in all, more than twelve million acres, or two-thirds of the state. If the Department of Justice agreed, the defendants would include not only the state, but also approximately 350,000 non-Indian residents, including the large timber companies that dominated the Maine economy.[16]

.   .   .

The Department of Justice never had to decide whether to adopt the Interior Department's recommendation. The cautious action of an established law firm with no role in the litigation of Indian claims, just in the issuance of municipal bonds, started a chain reaction that made further judicial proceedings unnecessary.

A municipality can raise money by issuing bonds, a form of debt in which the municipality agrees to repay the purchase price of the bonds together with interest at terms prescribed in the bonds. The Indian claims cast doubt on the validity of the land titles of the Maine municipalities located within the scope of the claims. The counsel to the bond issuers worried that if the municipalities' titles were declared invalid, they might have to default on their bonds. The bond counsel thus concluded in September 1976 that it could no longer give the bonds unqualified approval. Without it, the municipalities either could not have sold the bonds or would have had to offer substantially higher interest rates. The sale of more than $27 million in bonds was immediately delayed or canceled; doubts—even panic—arose about whether non-Indians throughout most of Maine would be able to sell or mortgage their lands. Legal arguments over events more than a century old suddenly gave way to the rhetoric of politicians and editorial writers facing a severe financial crisis.[17]

It took more than three years, but Maine politicians eventually reached an agreement with the federal government and Tureen's Indian clients. In return for the Indians' dismissing their claims, Congress appropriated $81.5 million to be placed into trust funds. Of that, $54.5 million could be used to purchase lands (based on prices previously negotiated with various landowners, it was estimated that each tribe would be able to purchase approximately 150,000 acres with the money). The remaining $27 million would be deposited into a permanent trust account. The Indians could spend the earnings of the trust account each year, but could not touch the principal. Federal and state legislation implementing the agreement also clarified for the first time the legal status of the tribes and the extent to which state laws would apply to them.[18]

When Tureen made his visit to Washington in the early 1970s to enlist support for his suit, one claims attorney told him that the recovery would be about thirty cents per acre, or under one million dollars. They received 80 times that, and five times more than the Chiricahuas were awarded for their much more extensive lands.[19]

The sheer size of the settlement transformed the lives of the Passamaquoddies in ways that no Indian Claims Commission judgment ever did for any tribe. Although some of the Indians' investments did not work out, the overall success of their strategy prompted the Harvard Business School to study it. They invested heavily in off-reservation enterprises, including a blueberry farm and a cement factory, designed to foster the employment of tribal members alongside non-Indians, and became a powerful economic force in the state. As the tribe's economic life improved, so did the well-being of its members.[20]

.   .   .

Buoyed by the outcome of the Oneida and the Passamaquoddy cases, more than ten eastern tribes have sought to recover land under the Nonintercourse Act. The Mashantucket (Western) Pequots of Connecticut are the most notable.

In the seventeenth century the Pequots were a tribe of about thirteen thousand, controlling an area of some two thousand square miles, primarily in what is now southern Connecticut. They quickly dominated trade between Indians and the Puritan settlers. But smallpox and other diseases soon cut their numbers by about 75 percent, and the Pequot War of 1637, the first war between Indian and non-Indian, followed. Fought by the Puritans with an unsurpassed barbarity, the war reduced Pequot numbers to under a thousand. The few who survived were forced in 1638 to sign a treaty declaring the tribe dissolved, and Puritan authorities banned the use of their name "to cut off the Remembrance of them from the Earth." [21]

Repenting slightly for its efforts to wipe out an entire people, Connecticut created a two-thousand-acre reservation in 1666 for the Western, or Mashantucket, Pequots. The colony's government reduced it to 989 acres in 1761. The number of permanent reservation inhabitants fell from between 150 to 200 during the eighteenth century to a grand total of 9 by 1858. The Connecticut General Assembly decided in 1855 to sell all but 180 acres, and throughout much of the twentieth century, *two* female residents, assisted by twenty-five to forty tribal members, clung tenaciously to this tiny base.[22]

The Pequots' fortunes began to turn when Tureen visited the reservation in the fall of 1974 as NARF's representative. They could not sue for the attempt to exterminate them prior to the creation of the United States, but Tureen concluded that they could sue under the Nonintercourse Act for the Connecticut legislators' sale of the bulk of the Pequot reservation as its resident population declined. In 1976, NARF filed a lawsuit on their behalf in the federal district court in Connecticut.[23]

Once again, the lawsuit put pressure on non-Indian landowners, and negotiations among the Pequots, Connecticut, and the United States ensued. They reached an agreement in the early 1980s, which was implemented by state and federal legislation. The state agreed to add twenty acres to the Pequot reservation. The federal government appropriated $900,000, up to $600,000 of which could be used to purchase additional lands for the Pequots, and extended federal recognition to the tribe, making it eligible for all the services and benefits furnished to federally recognized tribes. That $900,000 came to a staggering—by Indian Claims Commission standards—$1,000 an acre for the 809 acres for which the Pequots filed their claim.[24]

Like the Passamaquoddies, the Pequots invested their money successfully. They opened a large bingo parlor in 1986 and, despite the state's opposition, a casino in 1991. On their initial $58 million debt, they now realize an estimated one million dollars a day in profits! Their resort, which serves forty-five thousand meals a day, reportedly is the largest casino in the United States. The tribe has built homes, offices, and a fire station, lured back Pequots scattered across the country, added land to their reservation, and funded tribal research to strengthen their sense of community and revive traditional crafts. Three hundred and fifty years after virtually being wiped off the face of the earth, they have become a considerable, even feared, economic force in southern New England.[25]

. . .

The gross disparity between the settlements under the Nonintercourse Act and the Indian Claims Commission Act raises the question: Did the western tribes lose out by suing before the Commission?

Because of the nuances of federal Indian law, most tribes did not. No Supreme Court justice has questioned Congress's right to terminate a tribe's rights in land at any time and by any means. Granted, under certain circumstances, the United States may be legally obligated to pay fair value for the land, but the Supreme Court has made clear that if Congress chooses not to make any payment, the Indians are not entitled to the return of the property. Rather, if Congress subsequently elects to open a court's doors, the tribe then may sue for the money. The Nonintercourse Act claims are consistent with this doctrine. They have proceeded on the basis that eastern states purported to terminate Indians' rights without the involvement of the federal government, as Congress had required.

Thus tribes clearly have no claim to title to lands if their rights were terminated by an act of Congress or a ratified treaty. The United States acquired most tribal lands west of the Appalachians by one of these means.

Not all land, however. The government didn't enter into cession treaties with most of the tribes located in the huge expanse acquired from Mexico or dispossess them by acts of Congress. As with the Chiricahuas, the president created reservations by executive order and tribes were forced to move onto them.

In the proceedings under the Indian Claims Commission Act for most tribes that were dispossessed without direct congressional action, the issue almost invariably was not *whether* these tribes' aboriginal lands had been taken, but *when* they had been taken. The Weissbrodts never argued on behalf of the Chiricahuas, for example, that they still owned the vast aboriginal tract in Arizona and New Mexico; like almost all other claims attorneys, they assumed the land was gone and sought as much compensation as possible. By the time that the Chiricahua claims were decided, the Court of Claims and the Commission had established that when no congressional action could be specified for the date of taking, it would be deemed to have occurred when the United States "exercise[d] complete dominion adverse to the right of occupancy." In other words, when government agents prevented the members of a tribe from using their land or acted as if the Indians no longer had rights in the land, the Commission said the land had been taken: for the Chiricahuas, on September 4, 1886.

The doctrine that "complete dominion" constituted a taking was based, however tenuously, on the Supreme Court's decision in *United States* v. *Santa Fe Pacific Railroad Co.,* discussed earlier in this chapter. The Court of Claims and the Commission had seized upon two sentences in the opinion: " 'the exclusive right of the United States to extinguish' Indian title has never been doubted. And whether it be done by treaty, by the sword, by purchase, by the exercise of complete dominion adverse to the right of occupancy, or otherwise, its justness is not open to inquiry in the courts." This, the two tribunals concluded, meant that Congress need *not* be involved. Acts of dominion by federal agents were enough. But they ignored the lead sentence: "The power of Congress [to extinguish aboriginal title] is supreme." The Court of Claims and the Commission also ignored that, at one time, government officials without congressional authorization forcibly removed the Hualapais to a reservation created for other tribes outside the Hualapais' aboriginal territory. If the Supreme Court had believed that the exercise of complete dominion without congressional approval was sufficient to terminate aboriginal title, the Hualapais' title should have ended then. But it did not. The Supreme Court called this "a high-handed endeavor to wrest from these Indians lands which Congress had never declared forfeited. No forfeiture can be predicated on an unauthorized attempt to effect a forcible settlement on the reservation." Clearly, the Supreme Court then believed that aboriginal title couldn't be terminated without congressional action.[26]

The community of Indian claims judges, commissioners, and attorneys believed this pro-Indian decision out of date and ignored or creatively reinterpreted it, just as they did anti-Indian decisions such as *Montoya.* A strict reading of *Santa Fe* would have had too broad an impact for a country ruled by non-Indians. If *Santa Fe*'s requirement of congressional action had been seen as good law, Indian tribes would have owned much of the American Southwest.

Whether courts adjudicating claims for the restoration of land, rather than for money damages, would have similarly distorted the *Santa Fe* opinion is an unresolvable issue. However, even if they wouldn't have treated acts of dominion as a taking, they undoubtedly would have concluded that, in most instances, the lands had been taken because Congress had ratified the Executive Department's actions. Although the Chiricahuas weren't dispossessed by congressional action, Congress published several reports about their status as prisoners, passed the acts that allowed them to be relocated from Alabama, and provided for their eventual release. By these legislative actions, Congress accepted that the Chiricahuas had been dispossessed of their lands in New Mexico and Arizona. If the tribe had brought a lawsuit contending that they still owned part or all of their aboriginal territory, any court would have concluded that Congress had ratified the president's actions. Once congressionally ratified executive actions were taken into account, very few western tribes could have asserted viable claims for land restoration even if they had not sued under the Indian Claims Commission Act.

The conclusion that eastern tribes enjoyed a favored position in asserting claims for land restoration doesn't flow from the nature of what the Indians lost. A tribe was equally divested of its land whether a state or the federal government did the deed. Nor does the distinction arise from principles of fairness. The state of Connecticut treated the Pequots more fairly in 1855 when it sold 809 unnecessary acres than the United States treated the Chiricahuas in 1876 when it closed their reservation on trumped-up charges to allow Arizonans to start prospecting. Only the vagaries of the white man's law explain why tribes to which the United States abdicated their guardianship responsibilities have continuing claims on lands occupied by non-Indians, while other tribes, directly deprived of their lands by the federal government, do not.

·   ·   ·

Few western tribes nevertheless may have lost viable opportunities to claim present-day ownership by prosecuting their claims before the Commission. They fall into two groups: those that Congress apparently decided *not* to dispossess; and those that lost lands by means that Congress didn't sanction and of which Congress remained unaware and hence couldn't ratify after the fact.

The Western Shoshones may be the only tribe in the first group. On October 1, 1863, the federal government signed a treaty "of peace and friendship" with eleven "Chiefs, Principal Men, and Warriors of the Western Bands of the Shoshones Nation." The Treaty of Ruby Valley, which was subsequently ratified by Congress, specified that non-Indians could cross Shoshone land, build railroads on it, form mining and agricultural settlements, and establish ranches. In return, the federal government promised to pay goods worth $5,000 a year for twenty years to recompense any inconvenience the settlers' enterprise might cause. The treaty, however, contained no provision for the cession of land not included in the settlements or ranches.[27]

As was often the case, the agents of the federal government had very little idea of exactly whom they were dealing with. When intensive contact with Anglos began in the mid-nineteenth century, speakers of Shoshonean dialects inhabited a vast area in what is now western Utah, southwestern Wyoming, southeastern Idaho, and eastern Nevada. The westernmost of these bands, unimaginatively dubbed Western Shoshones by anthropologists and the Indian Claims Commission, primarily occupied the especially inhospitable lands of eastern Nevada, hunting and fishing to the extent possible but subsisting primarily on wild foods such as pine nuts, bunchgrass seeds, and roots. The Treaty of Ruby Valley was the only treaty signed with any of the Western Shoshone bands.[28]

Non-Indians who ventured into this desert found it no easier than the Shoshones did. Of the approximately twenty-two million acres in Nevada that, in 1962, the Watkins-led Commission found to have been aboriginal territory of the Western Shoshones, many millions of acres were never settled by non-Indians, and white men quickly abandoned much of the land they did try to subdue. Perhaps because so few non-Indians were present, the government saw little need to segregate the Indians: before the 1900s, it set aside only one small reservation for the Western Shoshones outside their aboriginal territory, to which few moved. Well into this century, many Shoshones combined some wage work with the traditional way of life, living in their ancestral areas and gathering food much as they always had. Few tribes in the continental United States have been as little disrupted by Anglo-Americans as the Western Shoshones.[29]

But the tribe never forgot the terms of the Treaty of Ruby Valley. During the 1920s, their most prominent traditional leader, Muchach Temoke, acknowledged that the old treaty permitted non-Indians to settle under the public land laws, but he contended that any land not settled upon remained Indian property. Indeed, that is the *only* interpretation that makes sense of all of the treaty's provisions.[30]

Temoke's efforts to have the Shoshone title acknowledged floundered for lack of a federally recognized political entity. The Indian Reorganization Act of 1934 provided an opportunity for organization, but, as happened in many tribes, traditional leaders resisted the white man's form of government. Eventually two related communities adopted a constitution. These called themselves the Te-Moak Bands Tribe, and contained only a tiny percentage of the whole Western Shoshone population. Many more communities sent representatives to the councils convened occasionally by Temoke and later his son Frank, but these councils had no federally recognized powers. Because the tribal council of the Te-Moak Bands had the government endorsement that accompanied organization under the Indian Reorganization Act, the newly formed Indian Claims Commission notified it, not the traditionalists, of the right to bring claims.[31]

The council engaged Ernest Wilkinson, who already represented several other tribes of the intermountain region, to represent all of the Western Shoshones. Some council members felt that the Western Shoshones still owned much of their aboriginal territory and told Wilkinson's firm they wanted their land returned, not "sold." The lawyers responded that the Commission did not acquire Indians' land; it merely compensated tribes for lands already taken. This assurance convinced the Shoshones to proceed—and it was true as far as it went. However, lawyers and judges operate on certain assumptions and preconceptions. The jurists who reinterpreted the Supreme Court's *Santa Fe* decision to permit rulings that Indian title had been taken without congressional involvement were unlikely to give much weight to a contention that a tribe's lands had *not* been taken. They readily would conclude that all of the Western Shoshone aboriginal lands had been taken; the idea that the tribe might still own millions of acres of land under aboriginal title would not cross their minds unless raised forcefully.[32]

In any event, Robert Barker, the attorney at Wilkinson, Cragun and Barker in charge of the case, argued that all of the Shoshones' lands had been taken. He didn't attempt to identify the dates of taking, an issue that, he believed, should be reserved for future proceedings. The government contented itself with arguing that the Shoshones had not met the requirements for proving aboriginal ownership and "the United States could not take from them what they did not have." Neither party introduced any evidence on the taking issue or analyzed the possibility that much of the land had never been taken. Apparently Associate Commissioner Holt, who in 1962 delivered the Commission's opinion in the liability stage of the case, did not consider that possibility either. Rather, the Commission determined the extent of the Western Shoshones' aboriginal territory and concluded that they were deprived of that land by the gradual encroachment of non-Indians and the gradual disposition of the land by the government. Identifying the crucial date when all these gradual encroachments and dispositions were magically transformed into a taking was left for future proceedings, which proved unnecessary.[33]

In 1966, the parties agreed that the Western Shoshones' aboriginal land in Nevada should be valued as of July 1, 1872. In October 1972, the Commission decided that the Indians were entitled to about $21.5 million for lands taken in Nevada and California and another $4.6 million for minerals removed from the Nevada lands before the taking date. By March 1974, the Commission had held a hearing on the offsets issue and all briefs had been filed. It was only then—before it could rule on offsets and issue a final judgment—that the Commission found out that some Western Shoshones did not agree that their lands had been taken.[34]

An ad hoc group composed primarily of traditionalists and calling itself the Western Shoshone Legal Defense and Education Association filed a petition asking that unsettled lands be excluded from the taking claim on the grounds that the Western Shoshones still owned them. The Te-Moak Bands, represented by Barker, opposed this, and in 1975 the Commission (and the Court of Claims on appeal the next year) agreed with Barker that the dissidents had waited too long to be allowed to disrupt the proceedings brought by the recognized tribal council, unless they could show that the organization's representation of the Western Shoshones was collusive or fraudulent. And the renegades had not presented any facts to buttress their allegations of improprieties against the tribal council and its lawyers.[35]

The dissidents did not give up easily. They gained control of the Te-Moak tribal council, and in November 1976 by a 3–2 vote fired Barker. Through new attorneys, the council asked the Commission to postpone further proceedings while it tried to obtain the return of land by other means. The Commission was unsympathetic. On the same day the Commission denied the Shoshones' motion for delay, it also decided the offsets issue and handed down its final judgment in the case. The Shoshones' only recourse was another appeal to the Court of Claims—where they lost again.[36]

In refusing to permit the Western Shoshones to reverse their position late in the litigation, the Court of Claims and Indian Claims Commission were, on the surface, following the same approach that they used when the government sought to change its position on the date of taking in the Chiricahua land case. There was, however, one important difference. The government selected its own representative in the litigation, the Department of Justice. The Western Shoshones didn't select the tribal council of the Te-Moak Bands as its representative. Instead, the defendant—the federal government—reached out to the tribal council, the governing body of only a small percentage of the Western Shoshones, to serve as the representative of the entire group. Given the tenuous relationship between the tribal council and most Western Shoshones, the Commission and court should have shown more care before issuing such a momentous ruling. Probably the jurists' beliefs that the Western Shoshones' new approach had no merit—that the government had taken all of the land—influenced their decision to reject the postponement of the litigation.

The Western Shoshones thus were stuck in 1979 with a final judgment for more than $26 million that they did not want, a judgment based on the Commission's conclusion in 1962 that all of their aboriginal lands had been taken. Since then, they have tried to minimize the impact of the judgment by refusing to accept payment. As of 1996, the $26 million sits untouched in the Treasury, growing interest. Despite the temptation of a big payoff, so far no Western Shoshone group has attempted to break ranks and take the money.[37]

Their forbearance, however, has not helped in court. In 1974, the government sued two Shoshone sisters, Mary and Carrie Dann, who were grazing stock on public land in numbers that, according to the Bureau of Land Management, exceeded their permit. The Danns, who were among the leaders of the Western Shoshone Legal Defense and Education Association and its successor groups, defended themselves on several grounds, including that the Shoshones retained aboriginal title to the land, making the permit unnecessary. The dispute eventually reached the Supreme Court in 1985 and in a unanimous opinion written by Justice William Brennan, the Court concluded that the deposit of the $26 million to the account of the Western Shoshones under the Commission's judgment precluded any assertion that the Indians still had aboriginal title to any land.[38]

. . .

The other group of western tribes that might have had viable claims to land ownership are those that lost lands by means that Congress didn't sanction and didn't know of until after the fact. Four of the tribes that have pursued ownership claims stand out. Two used Indian Claims Commission rulings that the lands in question had been part of their aboriginal territory to assist their lobbying efforts; a third tried unsuccessfully to obtain a favorable ruling from the Court of Claims; and the fourth successfully adopted a strategy similar to that of the Passamaquoddies and the Pequots.

The Pueblo of Taos was the first to seek the return of land. Taos is the easternmost of the Rio Grande pueblos of New Mexico. It dates back about a millennium, making it one of the oldest continuously inhabited communities in North America (the other two being the Pueblo of Acoma and the Hopi village of Oraibi), and it probably numbered about twenty thousand inhabitants when the Spanish arrived. By 1900, its population had declined a whopping 98 percent to some four to five hundred through disease and oppression. Given this catastrophic decline, the Taos Indians could control less and less land, and their aboriginal area accordingly plummeted from some three hundred thousand acres at the start of the Spanish period.[39]

Still part of Taos land as of 1900, however, was the bowl-shaped watershed surrounding Blue Lake, "the central symbol of the [Taos] Indians' religion as the cross is in Christianity." The souls of the dead, they believe, retreat to Blue Lake and from there give life to the people of today. Until the twentieth century, the people of the Taos Pueblo had preserved the sacred bowl and prevented its use by non-Indians, their rites there requiring absolute secrecy. In 1906, the approximately fifty-thousand-acre Blue Lake watershed was placed within the national forest system with the acquiescence of the Indians, based on assurances that they would have exclusive use of it. Institutional memories proved short. Soon the Forest Service treated the Blue Lake area much like any other part of the national forest, allowing multiple uses on a permit basis. During the 1920s, the Taos Indians were able to work out agreements with the government that prevented mining and logging operations and, in 1940, they won a fifty-year renewable permit from the Forest Service that somewhat enhanced the protections afforded their religious use of the land. Even so, non-Indian recreational uses continued to defile the hallowed ground, causing repeated conflicts.[40]

Dissatisfied, the leaders of the pueblo worked throughout much of the twentieth century for the return of their holy land. They filed claims under the Indian Claims Commission Act, and in 1965, the tribe won a complete victory on liability, the Commission concluding that the Taos Indians had exclusively occupied and used about 130,000 acres, including the Blue Lake watershed. The Commission described the lake as the Indians' "most sacred shrine" and "church." [41]

During the next five years, the Commission made no further rulings in the claims case in order to allow the Taos Indians to lobby for return of the Blue Lake area. Finally, in December 1970, Congress, led by the unlikely alliance of President Richard Nixon (one of the most sympathetic White House occupants that Indians have ever had) and two liberal senators, Edward Kennedy and Fred Harris, adopted legislation returning the entire area to the Indians.[42]

Because the Taos Indians astutely avoided a ruling that the lands had been taken, the Commission's decision (merely on title) did not hurt the tribe's congressional lobbying efforts. In fact, the decision *helped* the Indians by defusing a potential argument against passage. Without the Commission's decision, opponents of the bill could have challenged whether the Taos Indians had used the land from time immemorial, as they claimed. The decision eliminated aboriginal title as an issue, thus letting proponents of the legislation focus on their strongest arguments. They painted the bill as a fight for religious freedom, comparing Blue Lake to the sacred places of Christianity, Judaism, and Islam and speculating on the uproar that would occur if the government assumed administrative responsibility over one of those shrines and then permitted nonbelievers to camp on its grounds.

.   .   .

The circumstances surrounding the Forest Service's administrative treatment of Blue Lake were unique. A second type of administrative action that deprived tribes of land occurred with distressing regularity. As reservations were created during the nineteenth century, the government surveyed and marked the boundaries. Frequently, tribes and attorneys discovered during the twentieth century, the surveys were erroneous, depriving tribes of land. Surveyors seemingly operated under the unwritten rule, "When in doubt, construe the verbal description of the boundaries of a reservation against the Indians." Here was a golden chance for tribes to recover land: Congress hadn't authorized errors in surveys, and it would strain the ratification doctrine to argue that Congress had ratified an error of which it was unaware. Attorneys and tribes first had to realize that it was possible to claim that missurveyed lands hadn't been taken and then determine a strategy for recovering them.

The Confederated Salish and Kootenai Tribes were the first to try. They were composed of descendants of the Flathead, Upper Pend d'Oreille, and Kootenai tribes, all of whom had been placed on the Flathead Reservation in western Montana under the terms of a treaty with the United States signed in July 1855. On July 30, 1946, fifteen days before the Indian Claims Commission Act became law, Congress passed a special jurisdictional act authorizing the Confederated Salish and Kootenai Tribes to file their claims in the Court of Claims.[43]

One claim was for the taking of land excluded from the reservation by erroneous government surveys. In 1965, the Court of Claims ruled that some of the surveys were indeed incorrect and that, as a result, the United States had taken the missurveyed land. It then sent the case back to its trial commissioner to determine the value of the land as of the date of taking.[44]

Sometime after this ruling, lead counsel John Cragun of the Wilkinson firm altered the tribe's theory. Instead of seeking damages based on a taking theory, Cragun argued that the land (most of which had been placed within national forests) still belonged to the tribes.

Cragun had worked on Indian claims cases with Ernest Wilkinson before the creation of the Indian Claims Commission, and was a man of intelligence and wit. Yet in the case of the Salish and Kootenai, he made a losing decision. In 1968, the Court of Claims unanimously reaffirmed that the missurveyed land had been taken, meaning that the Indians no longer owned it. While acknowledging that only Congress could dispossess Indians of their "recognized title" land and that the surveyor's error was not congressional action, the court ruled that the treatment of the land as part of a national forest for seventy years constituted congressional ratification. This was peculiar ratification: the court could point to no legislation indicating that Congress was aware that the lands had been missurveyed, let alone manifesting an intent to divest the tribes of the missurveyed land, as required in *Santa Fe*.[45]

If Cragun had possessed a crystal ball and looked ahead to the Nonintercourse Act claims of the 1970s and 1980s, he might have devised a different strategy. No tribe yet has obtained a court order that it remains the owner of land that the government or non-Indians have possessed

for decades, if not centuries. The successful tribes have received one or
more favorable preliminary court rulings and then let the pressure of
those decisions work to their advantage in negotiating a settlement. The
Court of Claims, accustomed to thinking in terms of takings of Indian
lands, was especially unlikely to rule that the missurveyed land remained
under Indian ownership.

.   .   .

A peak called Mount Adams is sacred to the Yakimas of central Washington. Like the Confederated Salish and Kootenai Tribes, the Yakimas initially went to the Commission seeking compensation for the loss of a
large area of land, including their sacred mountain, that had been improperly excluded from their reservation by a government surveyor. The
Commission ruled in 1966 that an area comprising more than 120,000
acres, including Mount Adams, had indeed been missurveyed.[46]

Paul Niebell, the Yakimas' attorney who had worked with Grady
Lewis on the Chickasaw-Choctaw case, represented tribes in many
cases—by his own count thirty-eight—before the Indian Claims Commission. Only the Weissbrodts and a few others represented as many.
Born in 1901, Niebell had hoped to be a concert violinist and studied at
the Chicago Conservatory; when his money ran out, he decided to become a lawyer instead. His introduction to Indian claims cases came
during the early 1930s when he agreed to assist an Oklahoma attorney
working on a Seminole case. Like the Weissbrodts, once Niebell started
he was hooked.[47]

The Yakimas instructed Niebell that, instead of compensation for
Mount Adams, they wanted the land returned. The United States had
conveyed almost 100,000 of the 120,000 acres to non-Indians, and in
1968 Niebell negotiated a settlement that included compensation for
the taking of those lands. Most of the remaining acres, including Mount
Adams, were within a national forest. To get those lands back, Niebell
convinced the government and the Commission to defer any further
proceedings for two years (not indefinitely, like the Western Shoshones)
while the tribe sought the restoration to the Yakima Reservation of
Mount Adams by administrative or other means. It took slightly more
than two years, but the Yakimas eventually succeeded. The Interior Department supported the Yakimas, while the Agriculture Department
(which manages national forests) opposed restoration on the ground

that, under *Confederated Salish,* the lands had been taken. Ultimately, the administration sided with the Yakimas. By executive order of May 20, 1972, Richard Nixon restored about 21,000 acres of national forest land to the Yakima Indian Reservation.[48]

. . .

No story highlights what may have been lost by Indian groups that mechanically followed the prescribed Indian Claims Commission procedures more than that of the Puyallup tribe of Washington. It obtained a huge political settlement by avoiding a Commission ruling that its lands had been taken and adopting a strategy that emulated that of the eastern tribes.

The Puyallups were once a thriving fishing tribe on Puget Sound. European-carried diseases, however, ravaged the tribe during the first half of the nineteenth century, and by the time emissaries of the United States approached them for a land cession in mid-century, only about fifty remained, and they had little choice but to agree. The Puyallups consented in an 1855 treaty to settle on a reservation that, as defined by an 1857 executive order, included the mouth of the Puyallup River, the tidelands where the Puyallups traditionally gathered clams, and their harbors.[49]

Unfortunately for the Puyallups, the Northern Pacific Railroad chose the same area as its western terminus. A government survey conveniently excluded about five thousand acres that the Puyallups believed were part of their reservation, but developers were not satisfied. At their request, Congress passed legislation in 1887 allotting each of the Puyallups, selling the surplus lands, and (revealing the real aim of the legislation with a blatancy close to callousness) providing a mere ten-year trust period in which the allottees could not mortgage or sell their parcels, instead of the normal twenty-five-year period. The developers clearly were confident that in ten years they could lay their hands on the remaining Indian holdings. They were right. Virtually all of the allotments were sold, and Tacoma, the state's second-largest city, sprouted on Puyallup land.[50]

Like almost all other western tribes, the Puyallups hired claims attorneys and filed a claim under the Indian Claims Commission Act. In what turned out to be a blessing, the Puyallups chose poorly: two attorneys from Seattle who also represented many of the Puyallups' neigh-

bors. Based on the evidence presented, the Commission found that each
of the tribes had aboriginal title to only a small percentage of the land
claimed. In 1966, the Commission decided that the Puyallups had occupied and used merely fifty-eight thousand acres, less than one hundred
square miles.[51] As the attorneys, on contingent contracts, saw the
chances of big recoveries slipping away, they delayed filings for years on
end, needlessly prolonging proceedings.

Before the Commission moved to the valuation stage, the Puyallups
decided not to renew the attorneys' contract and demanded that their
case be dismissed. They acted on erroneous information, believing the
Commission had determined they had title to only eleven thousand
acres. They also misunderstood the Commission's powers, believing that
the United States, through the Commission, was terminating their title
to the balance of their lands in their reservation. The Commission, and
after the transfer of the case in 1978 the Court of Claims, recognized
that the Puyallups were operating under these misconceptions, and disregarded their distraught cries that the entire case was "fraudulent" and
"uncivilized and treacherous." [52]

The tribunals, however, should not have ignored the Puyallups' further contention that pursuit of the case after the Commission's liability
decision was also "foolish." When it was clear that the Puyallups had no
intention of going ahead with the case, the Commission ordered its staff
to come up with a land valuation based on evidence presented for the
neighboring tribes. The staff arrived at the figure of about $48,500.
Happily for the Puyallups, the Commission apparently realized the im-
propriety of issuing a binding decision on a tribe that wanted its case
dismissed. The Commission didn't issue its decision, but also didn't dismiss the case. The matter was transferred to the Court of Claims and, in
1979, eight years after the Indians insisted that the Commission "cease
and desist" with the case, the court respected their demand and dismissed their claims case.[53]

Having narrowly escaped that trap, the tribe filed a claim in district
court against the Port of Tacoma, seeking to establish its title to about
twelve and a half acres that had formerly lain in the bed of the Puyallup
River but became dry land when the Corps of Engineers straightened
the river channel in the late 1940s. Adjoining landowners promptly had
expanded onto this windfall with nary a thought about who might own
it. The Indians won. The district court in 1981, and then the Ninth Cir-

cuit on appeal in 1983, concluded that the tribe owned the land. Ownership of the bed, they reasoned, had been conveyed to the Puyallups when the reservation was created. And under the law applicable to all landowners in the state, a sudden change in a river's course, even one caused by engineers, did not alter the title to the exposed land. Nor had the riverbed been conveyed by any other means.[54]

Chaos threatened the polity of Tacoma. It was alarming enough that title to a twelve-and-a-half-acre parcel of prime real estate in the middle of the city's bustling port was threatened. But as many as a thousand landowners claimed other portions of the former riverbed. And the Indians' success gave credence to other yet-to-be-filed Puyallup claims to the tidelands where they had once clammed but that had been filled in to allow further development, as well as to uplands that had allegedly been missurveyed after the Northern Pacific announced its plans to make Tacoma its terminus. Title to real estate in the city worth between $750 million and $1 billion was suddenly under an ominous cloud. Virtually nobody was willing to buy the land or lend money on it. One study concluded that, if the dispute was not resolved, about $500 million in capital improvement projects for the port alone would come to a standstill, resulting in a loss of over six thousand permanent jobs and over eighteen thousand temporary jobs. Worse for city residents, the Puyallups were under no legal obligation to file their claims promptly or push them toward rapid conclusion.[55]

Finally, in 1988, all parties agreed to a settlement. The Puyallups, ably represented by Harry Sachse, agreed that, in return for ceding their claims, they would receive cash, land, and services from the federal, state, and local governments and private parties valued altogether at $162 million. The legislatures eventually agreed, and in 1990 the Puyallups obtained a settlement worth three thousand times as much as the Commission's proposed $48,500 award. The settlement was more than half again greater than the largest award ever granted under the Indian Claims Commission Act—an award the Sioux tribe won only after over a half-century of litigation over many millions of acres of land.[56]

The Puyallups had successfully ignored the strategy followed by the tribes that came before the Indian Claims Commission seeking damages from the United States for the actions of its legislature or agents. Instead, they won the same way the eastern tribes had with Nonintercourse Act claims: they challenged the titles of people whose only sins were buying land the federal government had failed to protect for the Indians. That the Puyallups could do so much better by suing "innocent" parties (the landowners), rather than the "guilty" party (the federal government), is just as illogical as the fact that eastern tribes obtained far better results than tribes that sued under the Indian Claims Commission Act, the measure enacted so Indians could finally obtain justice.

The mixed experiences of tribes with potentially viable claims to present ownership of nonreservation land show that preliminary rulings of the Indian Claims Commission Act could be used to further those claims, but that, for the unwary, it was a powerful trap. Felix Cohen once wrote that "to the cynic [federal Indian] legislation may frequently appear as a mechanism for the orderly plundering of the Indian." While this was not the intention of the Indian Claims Commission Act, authored in large part by Cohen himself, to an uncertain degree it became an orderly means of protecting historical plunder by thwarting Indians' ability to recover their former land.[57]

TEN

THE DEATH OF FAIRNESS AND HONOR

It is not desirable to cultivate a respect for the law, so much as
for the right.
—HENRY DAVID THOREAU

The language of the Indian Claims Commission Act seemingly compelled adjudicators to consider moral concepts outside the realm of legal
principles and attempt to distinguish between the law and the right. As
discussed in Chapter Three, it authorized the Commission to hear
"claims based upon fair and honorable dealings that are not recognized
by any existing rule of law or equity." Even if the government had complied with all legal requirements, the adjudicators would have to decide
whether the United States had acted fairly and honorably. But as to
what these ethical terms, *fairly* and *honorably,* meant, the act provided no
guidance. The commissioners and judges had to give them meaning.

For the most part, the Witt-O'Marr-Holt and Watkins-Scott-Holt
triumvirates that served the Commission for its first twenty years dealt
almost exclusively with land claims bearing strong doctrinal resem-
blances to the eminent domain and contract claims of non-Indians.
Some of their land-claim decisions in favor of the tribes purported to
rely on the fair and honorable dealings clause as well as established legal
principles: after all, the United States could be said to have treated a
tribe less than fairly and honorably whenever it acquired Indian land

without payment of fair (let alone any) compensation. Mention of the
fair and honorable dealings clause was largely an afterthought, however,
because the decisions could have rested solely on established legal principles.

The successors to Watkins, Scott, and Holt didn't get off so easily. In
1966, Congress began considering the Commission's third five-year extension. Frustrated by the slow pace of adjudications—less than half
(about 250 out of 600) of the claims had been resolved—some solons
advocated allowing the Commission to expire. Others blamed the current commissioners for the sluggishness, unwilling to recognize that
Congress had been, and continued to be, unrealistic in its expectations
about how long litigation of these complex cases would take. The Johnson administration argued for the Commission's continuation, pledging
to appoint commissioners more familiar with the Indian claims process.
Finally, on the act's expiration date of April 10, 1967, Congress extended
its term for another five years—but with several changes designed to
speed up the pace. It expanded the Commission from three to five
members, with at least two from each major political party; it mandated
that all cases be scheduled for trial to commence by the end of 1970;
and it said the current commissioners could continue beyond June 30,
1968, only if renominated by the president and reconfirmed by the
Senate.[1]

Shortly thereafter, Chief Commissioner Watkins decided to retire
before his tenure expired on June 30, 1968. President Johnson also decided not to reappoint Commissioners Holt and Scott.[2]

As a result, he could fill all five positions with new people. He named
three men in December 1967: John Vance, Jerome Kuykendall, and
Richard Yarborough. Vance, a Montana Democrat, had powerful congressional support: Senator Mike Mansfield, the Senate majority leader
from Montana and his former professor of law. Like too many of the
previous commissioners, and despite the president's pledge, Vance lacked
"any extensive experience in Indian claims." However, according to a
White House interviewer, whom Vance impressed, he had "a deep and
realistic interest in the American Indian—his problems and his future."
Johnson not only nominated him, but in early 1968 appointed him
chairman.[3]

Some of President Johnson's staff members advised against the appointment of the second nominee, Jerome Kuykendall. Hailing from the state of Washington, Kuykendall had come to Washington, D.C., in 1953 as President Eisenhower's nominee for chairman of the Federal Power Commission. When his first term on the FPC had expired, many Democratic senators, especially from the Pacific Northwest, had adamantly opposed his reappointment. Kuykendall favored big business over consumers and what they perceived as the public interest, and had accepted personal favors from private companies with frequent business before the FPC. Johnson's staffers believed that continuing hard feelings might make his confirmation difficult. They also had reason to doubt that he would make an effective Indian claims commissioner. One of his fellow commissioners on the FPC reported that, although Kuykendall was gracious and worked very hard, he tended "to get absorbed in individual cases and never developed a long view."

Counterbalancing these negatives, Kuykendall, a Republican, had been recommended by Senate minority leader Everett Dirksen, who informed the president that the Republicans on the Senate Interior Committee, as well as Senators Henry Jackson and Warren Magnuson of the state of Washington, supported Kuykendall. These considerations prevailed, and not only was he confirmed as a commissioner, but Richard Nixon later elevated him to the position of chairman and demoted Vance, an arrangement that would remain until the dissolution of the Commission.[4]

Johnson needed no help nominating Richard Yarborough, the third nominee; Yarborough was the son of longtime Texas Senator Ralph W. Yarborough. Despite severe rheumatoid arthritis that had deformed his feet, gnarled his hands, required operations on both hips, and rendered him dependent on painkillers, Richard Yarborough had managed to graduate from the University of Texas law school. By far the youngest nominee at thirty-six years old, he had only two years of private law practice, having spent the bulk of his time on his father's staff and on that of a Senate committee. His lack of legal experience did not faze Johnson, who wanted to find Yarborough a lifetime judicial appointment. (The timing of the appointment was fortuitous for Yarborough; the following year, his father broke with the president and supported Eugene McCarthy over Hubert Humphrey for the Democratic presidential nomination.)[5]

To fill the second Republican seat on the Commission in June 1968, the president broke new ground. Margaret Pierce, born in upstate New York in 1910, became the first woman nominee and the first to be familiar with the Indian claims process. A graduate of Mount Holyoke College, she had scrambled to overcome the discrimination that faced women in the workplace—especially intelligent and outspoken women—and to find work during the Depression. She had eventually landed a job as a secretary in the legal department of a New York City bank and had attended New York University law school at night. After graduating, she had moved to Washington and held a series of temporary legal positions with the federal government, one of the few employers then willing to hire female lawyers, although not to pay them as much as their male counterparts.

In 1947, the Court of Claims had hired her as its law clerk, and she had stayed for the next twenty-one years. In 1959 she became the court's chief clerk and reporter of decisions, evaluating briefs and the entire record before the court, recommending decisions to the judges, and preparing drafts of opinions.

Pierce was ambitious, but no woman had ever been appointed to the court, and the most conservative of the judges, Sam Whitaker, opposed her efforts to secure a post as a trial judge. A feminist long before it was politically popular, she wrote the president in 1967, and without any congressional sponsorship, asked to fill one of the vacancies on the Commission. She informed the White House that the Court of Claims had entrusted the examination and analysis of most of its Indian cases to her, and that her "work on the Indian claims cases has interested [her] the most." It was Pierce who had researched and drafted so many of the crucial Court of Claims opinions of the 1950s, including *Pawnee* and *Otoe*. Nothing came of her application for over a year, but apparently her experience and her status as a liberal Republican who had voted for Johnson in 1964 overcame her lack of congressional backers. She was nominated on October 8, 1968, and confirmed by the Senate two days later.[6]

Congress adjourned for the 1968 elections before President Johnson appointed the final commissioner. He temporarily filled the slot in November by the recess appointment of Theodore McKeldin, a former governor of Maryland and mayor of Baltimore, but Richard Nixon inherited the permanent responsibility of filling the slot.[7]

President Nixon's appointment of Brantley Blue in May 1969 as the fifth commissioner rivaled Johnson's appointment of Pierce in its break with the established pattern of appointing white males with little knowledge of Indian law or affairs. Blue, a "Lumbee" Indian, was born in Robeson County in southeastern North Carolina in 1925. The Lumbees, who comprised about a third of the county's population, were largely Cherokee but had formed a distinct identity after intermarriage with other tribes. Because many Lumbees speak with a trace of an Elizabethan accent, they are popularly believed to be descendants of Sir Walter Raleigh's "Lost Colony." From 1885 until 1970, Robeson County contained four segregated school systems—for whites, blacks, Indians, and mulattoes. Blue was the first graduate of the county's Indian school system to become an attorney, but in 1949 North Carolina refused to license a Lumbee to practice law or even, as Blue desired, to marry a white woman. He lived and practiced law in Kingsport, Tennessee, until the president, fulfilling a campaign pledge to appoint a qualified Indian, tapped him for the final permanent slot.[8]

The five new appointees served together for almost a decade until the Commission was dissolved September 30, 1978. This was the most productive and pro-Indian group of commissioners; however, they were divided by ideology. Yarborough and Pierce formed the center, but more dissenting opinions were issued from 1969 through 1978 than ever before. They came most often from Kuykendall, who, when dissenting, always sided with the government. When he joined other commissioners, Vance and Blue were most likely to dissent in favor of the Indians.

TABLE 5

Decisions by Commissioner Groupings

Years	Dockets Completed	Dockets Completed Per Year	Percent Completed with Award	Average per Docket Completed	Average per Award
1949–59	105	9.5	16.2%	$ 194,072	$1,198,680
1960–68	153	17.0	69.3%	$1,630,647	$2,353,670
1969–78	288	28.8	76.0%	$1,905,840	$2,503,682
Overall	546	18.2	62.6%	$1,496,653	$2,392,318

Prior to Blue's appointment, it fell to Vance, Kuykendall, Yarborough, Pierce, and McKeldin to confront the meaning and scope of the fair and honorable dealings clause. None of them had served more than eighteen months when the government moved to dismiss three claims brought by the Gila River Pima-Maricopa Indian Community.

The Pima and a smaller group of Maricopa Indians lived along the Gila River near what is now the sprawling metropolis of Phoenix, Arizona. They could hardly have differed more from their neighbors and enemies, the Apaches. While the Apaches as a whole engaged in minimal agriculture and the Chiricahuas none at all, the Pimas and Maricopas probably drew more of their subsistence from irrigated agriculture than any other native group in what became the United States. They built ditches along the lines of an earlier and even more agriculturally sophisticated Indian civilization, the Hohokam, and diverted the river's water through frail dams consisting of poles tied together with bark and rawhide and plugged with branches, reeds, and weeds. While Apaches tended to live in small family groups and roam over large areas, the Pimas and Maricopas lived in villages near their fields along the Gila. Whereas raiding served as an important component of the Apache, and especially the Chiricahua, economy, warfare was almost exclusively defensive for the Pimas and Maricopas. (They were nevertheless effective fighters. In 1857, ancient enemies of the Maricopas, the Yumas, sallied forth from the west. The Pimas and Maricopas annihilated the aggressors in the last significant battle between Indian tribes fought in the continental United States, leaving almost no survivors.) And while the Apaches resisted the encroachments of Spaniards, Mexicans, and Anglo-Americans, the Pimas and Maricopas by and large welcomed the arrival of the paleskins with their wheat and livestock. Such dramatic contrast with the Apaches prompted early Anglo-American adventurers to label them the "most civilized Indians in the United States."

After Mexico ceded its interests in the lands of the Pimas and Maricopas to the United States, the Indians did nothing to damage their "civilized" reputation. On their fifteen thousand irrigated acres, they grew enough corn, wheat, and other food crops to feed not only themselves but also the miners pouring through to California in 1849, and the travelers on the main stage line between El Paso and San Diego during the 1850s. They often traded crops for Anglo goods, but sometimes beneficently gave their food to the "needy" white man. During the 1860s and 1870s, the United States armed them and they fought and scouted alongside the Anglo soldiers in the wars to suppress the Apaches.[9]

Being "good Indians," however, did not help the Pimas and Maricopas when white men wanted their resources. Farmers and ranchers settled upstream along the Gila and began diverting the river's water to their own fields. Beginning around 1870, local agents of the United States reported to government authorities in Washington that, in many years, water was inadequate for the Indians' crops, and during some of those years, the river was completely dry in the growing season—depleted before the waters reached the Indians' fields. For about thirty-five years, while the economy of the Pimas and Maricopas was destroyed, the government took no steps to protect them. In 1905, Congress appropriated money to begin an irrigation project on their reservation, and over the next twenty-five years the government constructed a series of dams along the Gila River to store spring flood waters and to improve the diversion of water to Indian and non-Indian lands. Not until the 1920s, however, did it sue to establish the tribes' water rights.

In western states, water rights are prioritized by date, and when water is inadequate to meet demand, persons with prior dates receive their full water entitlement before those with later dates receive any. The Indians' rights were prior to any others on the river, whether those rights were seen as arising under the prior appropriation doctrine that has been adopted by most western states for non-Indians, or the reserved rights doctrine first recognized by the United States Supreme Court in 1908 as applicable to Indian reservations. The upstream settlers were infringing on the Pima-Maricopa rights, but that did the Indians no good until a court judicially established that priority. The government eventually prevailed, but by then it was too late. Through years of inadequate water supply, many of the Pimas and Maricopas had been transformed from industrious self-supporting farmers into paupers.[10]

By the mid-1920s, the government also had devastated their leadership structures. Before the Anglo period, the Pimas had recognized three levels of leadership. Two of the three levels—moral-religious leaders and an organization of adult males to manage the irrigation system—had operated at the village level, while villages had combined their resources under a war leader to deal with the Apaches and other hostile tribes. The war leader had become superfluous by 1880, and with water diminishing, so had the managers of the irrigation system. The government agent now planned and administered economic activities and represented the Indians to the outside world. Presbyterian missionaries had succeeded not only in converting most of the Pimas and Maricopas to Christianity, but also in replacing the final group of leaders, the moral teachers, with new Christian elders. For all intents and purposes, by the late nineteenth century traditional tribal leadership was no more.

In the early twentieth century, the government allotted two small parcels to each tribal member and encouraged the allottees to move onto their land, thereby contributing to the collapse of the villages. On the allotments, the agents induced the Indians to build adobe houses instead of the traditional brush roundhouses, and the resulting lack of ventilation probably contributed to the devastating spread of tuberculosis. The Indians also lost all voice concerning the education of their young. Most were sent to boarding schools, both on- and off-reservation, where at best they received an elementary-level education and instruction in a trade, and many had to seek jobs off-reservation. Whether intentionally or not, government policies had reduced the Pimas and Maricopas to complete dependency.[11]

·   ·   ·

At mid-century and for decades thereafter, Z. Simpson Cox served the Gila River Pima-Maricopa Indian Community as both general counsel and claims counsel. Cox was a dynamic figure who swept into a courtroom with his sons, who had followed their father into the law, trailing as part of his retinue.[12]

Cox showed far more imagination than most attorneys in framing claims. In addition to the normal land taking and accounting claims, he filed unusual property-related claims. For example, he reasoned, why should the government have taken money from the tribal coffers to pay operating and maintenance costs of irrigation systems that were necessary only because the government had failed to protect the water rights of the Pimas and Maricopas? More important to the history of the Indian Claims Commission, he also lodged three nonproperty claims for damages caused by (1) the government's failure to provide adequate educational services, (2) the government's failure to provide adequate medical facilities and personnel, and (3) the government's subjugation of "petitioner under wardship to a stagnation of self-expression . . . [which] bridled petitioner into cultural impotency." Translating this last claim, Cox sought damages for the destruction of the tribes' social structure and culture. Their economy, their government, their religion, and their ability to instill their beliefs in their children—all had been destroyed by the government's policies, and on behalf of the Pimas and Maricopas, Cox now demanded compensation.

The attorney for the government, David Marshall, filed a motion to dismiss. In a succinct argument, he gave three grounds for dismissal: the claims were individual rather than tribal in nature; because no treaty or contract obligated the government to provide educational, medical, or administrative services to the Pimas and Maricopas, it provided those services gratuitously and any shortcomings could not give rise to liability; and, if liability were found, the Commission could not compute damages. Of these, Marshall relied primarily on the argument that the claims were individual in nature. Not surprisingly, he never even mentioned the fair and honorable dealings clause: Marshall had no intention of breaking, or even entering, new metalegal ground with his dismissal motion.

The Indians' attorney, Cox, plunged into this thicket and challenged the government's assertion that no agreement meant no liability. As he told the commissioners during oral argument, "I believe the Indian Claims Commission Act means what it said. It doesn't say anything about having a contract or agreement and if you can't come in with a thumb print or a signature you can't recover. It says we have fair and honorable dealings among men, and this Commission will hear the evidence, and if it is fair, we lose, it is that simple." [13]

Simple it may have been, but Commissioners Vance, Kuykendall, Yarborough, Pierce, and McKeldin realized that the ramifications of Cox's reasoning would be anything but. They unanimously granted the government's motion for dismissal. Yarborough, writing for the Commission, acknowledged that the claims might "reflect a valid criticism of one-time governmental policies," but stated that the act was designed to provide monetary relief for specific acts of wrongdoing rather than an entire lengthy course of conduct. The government should not be a guarantor that its educational, medical, and administrative policies would work and should not risk monetary liability for policies that failed. He recognized that the Commission could enunciate a standard less stringent than a guaranty, such as the "due care" standard used in almost all negligence cases, under which persons are required to act with reasonable care so as not to injure others unintentionally. But how could that standard be applied in this case? In Yarborough's words, "Should schools have been provided as good as any others in the immediate area, or Arizona, or the Southwest, or the United States? Should they be tested by the educational standards of that year, or the decade past, or the decade to come? Should more 'Indian culture' as opposed to 'white culture' have been taught, and in day schools or boarding schools?" Rather than try to answer those questions, the Commission decided that the claims of the Pimas and Maricopas were beyond its jurisdiction.[14]

.   .   .

Cox, unswayed by the Commission's lack of willingness to face the unknown, appealed to the Court of Claims. This was no longer the court of Judge Littleton and his colleagues. Despite recognizing that "this precise type of claim has not, to our knowledge, been previously brought for adjudication" all seven judges agreed that the Indians' claims should be dismissed.[15]

In the majority opinion Judge James Durfee explained that the tribes' claims failed, despite the language of the fair and honorable dealings clause, because the United States had not entered into a "special relationship" with the Pimas and Maricopas to provide adequate education or health care or to foster their self-government. Relying on several prior decisions dealing with land or other property claims, he stated that the government has a duty, or a special relationship, to perform services for a tribe in only two situations. First, a special relationship arises if the government expressly obligates itself to perform those services by a treaty, agreement, executive order, statute, or the representations of its agents. No treaty, agreement, or statute gave rise to a special relationship with the Pimas and Maricopas. Second, if the government comprehensively "supervise[s] the affairs and transactions of the Indians," it undertakes a special relationship with the tribe under certain circumstances.

Durfee, however, made absolutely no attempt to explain why those circumstances did *not* exist in this case, where the government not only supervised, but was the provider of all the educational, medical, and governmental services the Pimas and Maricopas received, wholly supplanting the Indians' role. He simply wrote that the government's alleged affirmative acts of providing education, health services, and administration to these Indians did not give rise to a duty. Given his conclusion, it would be hard to imagine just what circumstances (if any) could exist in which supervision could give rise to a duty under the fair and honorable dealings clause.[16]

Judge Oscar Davis refused to join the majority's special relationship analysis, believing that it "could be misused in the future to deny recovery for claims for specific injuries truly redressable under the Claims Commission Act." He recommended a far more straightforward approach. Despite the broad language of the act, he said, Congress did not want "to grant compensation for all the detriment accruing to the Indians by our ongoing policy toward them." The fair and honorable dealings clause was not "a catch-all allowing monetary redress for the general harm—psychological, social, cultural, economic—done the Indians by the historical national policy of semi-apartheid." Instead, under the fair and honorable dealings clause, as under the rest of the act, Congress agreed to pay only "for specific deprivations of land or property or rights protected by treaty, statute, or then-existing law." The flaw in Cox's claims, Judge Davis believed, was not the lack of a special relationship, but the fact that the claims did not concern damage to *property*.[17]

He then frankly set out one of the considerations that probably underlay both Judge Durfee's and his own analysis. A claim that the federal government "has destroyed Indian peoplehood by failing to provide proper education, medical care, and self-government . . . could undoubtedly be brought by all Indian tribes and groups." In other words, if the Pimas and Maricopas could recover for the nonproperty injuries that they had suffered, so could many other native groups.[18]

The Court of Claims' concerns went beyond simply protecting the public fisc. It had in mind the Commission's doubts whether it could set a workable standard for determining whether the United States had met its obligations in its educational, medical, and administrative services. Judge Durfee, however, reached the opposite conclusion from Commissioner Yarborough.

In his opinion, Durfee stated that the legal system *was* capable of establishing standards for deciding if the government had breached its duty, if the Court of Claims had decided that a duty existed. He explained that in *Brown* v. *Board of Education* the Supreme Court had found that states' maintenance of separate school systems for black and white children was unconstitutional because the schools were unequal. If judges could do that, Judge Durfee said, they also could create standards for deciding if educational services provided by the United States to Indian children were adequate. Durfee's analogy betrayed his misreading of *Brown*. The Supreme Court had said that the stigma attached to the black schools made them inherently unequal, regardless of the quality of instruction and other educational services. It had avoided plunging into the quagmire of analyzing the adequacy of the educational services of a school system, an issue that would be especially messy for the Indian Claims Commission because the school system to be evaluated had to teach students coming from a radically different culture for whom English was, at best, a second language. Judge Durfee presumably also believed that the court could create standards to judge the adequacy of the government's medical services, but he did not attempt to explain how the court could articulate standards for rating the government's performance of any duty to foster, or at least not impede, Indian self-government and cultural continuity. Nor did he hint as to how damages were to be calculated. Commissioner Yarborough might have been new to Indian claims in 1968, but he showed far more appreciation than Judge Durfee of the limitations of the legal system.[19]

Judge Durfee's very words, however inadvertently, disclosed a more fundamental problem: his equation of law with fairness and honor. In asserting that the courts could create appropriate standards for measuring the government's performance, he fell back on the categories he knew—legal ones. To determine liability, legal analysis requires a court first to identify whether a duty exists, then to delineate a standard for measuring the party's conduct, and finally to compare the conduct to the standard. The Pimas and Maricopas, however, were not claiming that the government had violated any legal duty. They were claiming that the government had acted unfairly and dishonorably. Analyzing what is fair and honorable arguably involves the same steps as analyzing what is legal—a matter of duty, standards, and comparison of conduct to the standards—but the court never considered whether the same method of analysis should apply to a moral claim.

The judges avoided the unfamiliar terrain of ethical analysis and instead asserted that fairness and honor came into question only if the government had undertaken an obligation by agreement, law, or repre-

sentation, or if the government comprehensively supervised Indians' activities. In its dismissal of the Pima-Maricopa claims, the Court of
Claims payed only lip service to the idea that comprehensive supervision gave rise to a duty under the fair and honorable dealings clause, because the United States had comprehensively supervised educational,
medical, and governmental activities, but no duty was found. This left
only a duty arising from a specifically undertaken obligation. If the government specifically undertook an obligation, it was obligated to fulfill
that duty as a matter of law. Other provisions of the Indian Claims
Commission Act made the United States liable for violations of its legal
obligations. Judge Durfee's formulation in *Gila River* thus made the fair
and honorable dealings clause all but superfluous. Whatever Congress
had meant by including those words in the act, the Court of Claims had
now said that fairness and honor meant no more than compliance with
legal requirements. Nothing, in other words, transcended legal precedent.

Any tribe seeking recovery under the fair and honorable dealings
clause had only two avenues. It would have to convince the Commission or the Court of Claims that its claim differed from that of the Pimas
and Maricopas, or it would have to persuade the Court of Claims or the
Supreme Court to overturn *Gila River.*

The Chief Joseph Band of Nez Perce was the first to try.

·   ·   ·

Estimated by Lewis and Clark to have numbered eight thousand in the
early nineteenth century, the Nez Perce had controlled a vast area of
what is now central Idaho, northeastern Oregon, and southeastern
Washington. They subsisted primarily through hunting, gathering, and
fishing. The Nez Perce hunting territory had expanded considerably
during the late eighteenth and early nineteenth centuries after they acquired horses and developed their own distinct breed, the Appaloosa.
The relative freedom from diseases, the variety of food sources, and the
Appaloosas all increased the power of the Nez Perce so that, by the mid-
nineteenth century, they were, according to the Indian Claims Commission, "the largest, most powerful and influential nation of Indians in the
northwest area west of the Rocky Mountains." [20]

Their size and power, however, did not make the Nez Perce immune
to Manifest Destiny. In 1855, the Nez Perce agreed to a treaty under

which they ceded about half of their aboriginal lands, primarily in eastern Idaho, but the treaty still recognized their title to a reservation encompassing over 7.7 million acres, an area considerably larger than the
state of Maryland. Congress ratified the treaty in 1859, but the Indians
soon discovered that its words were all but worthless. Though the treaty
prohibited white men from living on the reservation without the tribe's
consent, miners started prospecting there in 1860, and the military declined to remove them. Then gold was discovered. Instead of punishing
the treaty violators, the government, embroiled in the Civil War, convened a council to obtain additional land concessions from the Indians,
and most of the Nez Perce realized that they had no choice. In June
1863, the chiefs representing the majority of the tribe's bands agreed to
a new treaty. The Nez Perce ceded about 90 percent of their reservation,
retaining only some 790,000 acres in present-day Idaho.[21]

A minority of Nez Perce, the members of four bands, refused to sign
the treaty, to regard themselves as bound by it, or to move to the Idaho
reservation. One band, which occupied the Wallowa Valley in the north-
east corner of Oregon and some adjoining areas in Washington, was
headed by Tuekakas, called Joseph by the white man. Gold hunger did
not swallow the Wallowa Valley, a place of verdant hillsides and crystalline
streams, and the Joseph Band, as it came to be known, lived there largely
undisturbed until the mid-1870s. In 1871, Tuekakas died and was succeeded by his son Heinmot Tooyalaket, or Thunder in High Mountains.
To Anglos, he also was known as Joseph.[22]

In the mid-1870s, white settlers began moving into the Wallowa Valley, and Chief Joseph attempted to defuse tensions on both sides. He and
several of the leaders of other antitreaty bands agreed in 1877 to meet
with General Howard, who had negotiated with Cochise five years before. The general was not as accommodating as he had been with the
Apache leader. Under threat of war, the Nez Perce bands abandoned
their homes and started to move to the reservation in Idaho. En route,
drunken young warriors killed several white settlers, and, believing
reprisals imminent, the Nez Perce reversed direction.[23]

Thus began one of the most justifiably famous campaigns in the history of the Indian wars. Joseph and other band leaders led a group of approximately seven hundred Nez Perce, most of them noncombatants, on
a roundabout 110-day trek of over 1,500 miles through Oregon, southern Idaho, and Montana, avoiding and when necessary defeating several

armies that together greatly outnumbered them. The flight ended only a few miles short of the Canadian border. After several days of skirmishes between the weary Nez Perce and surrounding soldiers, Joseph, like Geronimo nine years hence, surrendered to General Nelson Miles. Joseph's speech concluded with perhaps the most well-known sentence ever uttered by a Native American: "From where the sun now stands I will fight no more forever." In return, Miles promised Joseph that the Indians would be taken to the Nez Perce Reservation.[24]

Miles's superior, General William Tecumseh Sherman, overruled his field commander and ordered the Nez Perce imprisoned at Fort Leavenworth in Kansas. Just as the army would later imprison the Chiricahuas in the humid lowlands of Florida and Alabama, the Nez Perce were confined for about eight months in damp conditions between the Missouri River and a lagoon, where many contracted malaria. One writer compared the conditions to the infamous Confederate prison camp at Andersonville. Then in July 1878, the government shipped the Nez Perce to the Indian Territory, despite the warnings of the commissioner of Indian affairs that the southern climate would exacerbate the diseases to which they had already been subjected. As predicted, disease quickly exacted a heavy toll. When the government finally returned them to the Northwest after eight years of exile, their numbers had been reduced by about one third, and they were split into two groups. The government permitted 118 who had accepted Christianity to go to the reservation in Idaho, and consigned 150, including Joseph, who adhered to their native animist religion to the Colville Reservation in northeastern Washington, which served as a dumping ground for numerous tribes. Joseph's band found themselves among tribes with different languages and different customs and, for many years, they remained isolated.[25]

Overall, the government did not punish the Joseph Band quite as severely as the Chiricahuas for resisting removal to a reservation. Ironically, the government may have had slightly greater justification for reprisals against the entire Joseph Band, because all of them had fought against the government, whereas many of the Chiricahuas had helped the army hunt the hostiles. Nevertheless, the punishment was still severe for actions that most twentieth-century Americans would believe fully justified: defending their homeland against intrusions that the government had agreed to prevent, and resisting forced removal from that homeland.

· · ·

The descendants of the Joseph Band did not suffer for lack of adequate legal counsel before the Indian Claims Commission. The Nez Perce Tribe of Idaho, including the descendants of the "Christianized" members of the Joseph Band, engaged the firm of Wilkinson, Cragun & Barker. The Confederated Tribes of the Colville Reservation initially contracted with James Curry, and then the Weissbrodts.

As he researched the case in 1951 in order to draft the petition, the plight of the Nez Perce offended Lefty Weissbrodt's sense of justice and honor as deeply as had the story of the Chiricahuas. He decided to include a claim for the damage caused by their imprisonment and forced division between two reservations. The 1949 decision of the Indian Claims Commission dismissing the first Chiricahua claim for false imprisonment as individual in nature, however, alerted him to the risk of such a claim for the Nez Perce. Accordingly, he used much the same language as in the revised Chiricahua petition: "the Joseph Band suffered injuries in that it was thwarted in the advancement of its common purposes and was confined under conditions injurious to the health and well being of its individual members." [26]

Once filed, the unusual claim sat for more than eighteen years. It was tried on January 28, 1970, together with a Nez Perce land claim, with Abe Weissbrodt representing the Nez Perce.

The lawyer for the government, John Sullivan, put in no evidence at all concerning the claim for the damage to the Nez Perce as a tribe, and asked but two questions in cross-examination. In fact, he *admitted* that the government couldn't dispute the history, and "that there was some bad treatment there of the Joseph Band." But in papers submitted after the trial, he stated, "No grounds for recovery even approaching the ones asserted here have ever been considered to be valid even under the most liberal construction of the Act." That the government had treated the Nez Perce badly, he argued, did not mean that the government could be held liable under the act.[27]

· · ·

With Blue having succeeded McKeldin, the Nez Perce had a more favorable array of commissioners than that which had considered the claims of the Pimas and Maricopas. Even so, they lost.

Commissioner Yarborough, joined by Commissioner Pierce, wrote the opinion. He relied primarily on the *Gila River* doctrine that tribes could not recover under the fair and honorable dealings clause unless the government had violated a duty assumed under a treaty, agreement, order, or statute. Despite the Weissbrodts' efforts, Yarborough was correct that they could point to no document in which the United States had agreed not to imprison every member of the tribe for resisting removal and then trying to flee. Under the *Gila River* syllogism, no agreement meant no duty, and no duty meant no claim under the fair and honorable dealings clause.

Commissioners Blue and Kuykendall agreed with the result, but wrote separately to say that the Commission's hands were tied by *Gila River*. Blue had no doubt that "the government dealt neither fairly nor honorably with the [Joseph Band]. . . . [F]or all practical purposes the dealings resulted in the dislocation, dispersal, and ultimate destruction of the Joseph Band of the Nez Perce Tribe as a viable economic, social and political entity." By granting compensation for "the destruction of a viable way of life," he continued, "we would be striking at the real tragedy in American Indian history. In order to truly attempt to right the wrongs and rid our country of such outstanding grievances, perhaps wisdom would dictate that this Commission be empowered to act in such matters. However, I feel that legal precedents prohibit us from doing so." [28]

Was he correct that *Gila River* bound the Commission's hands? Not according to John Vance, the sole dissenter. In *Gila River* "the wrongs alleged were ones of omission. Here the wrongs alleged were blatant wrongs of commission." [29]

The other commissioners largely ignored his point, but Vance was drawing on a deep strain in Anglo-American jurisprudence. The law imposes a duty of reasonable care on anyone who chooses, or commits, to act in a wide variety of situations, from driving a car to constructing a house to attempting to save a drowning swimmer. In general, however, individuals aren't obligated to take any actions to help others. He was arguing that, in *Gila River,* the Pimas and Maricopas had sought to recover for what the United States did not do, namely, provide adequate education, health care, and a regime that would foster their self-government. By contrast, the Nez Perce claimed that the United States should be liable for deliberate actions: imprisoning them in the Midwest for eight years and then dividing them based on their religion.

Vance's argument had an obvious flaw. The United States *had* provided educational, health, and administrative services to the Pimas and
Maricopas, and the Indians had claimed those services were inadequate.
The government had escaped liability because the Court of Claims had
made the further distinction that the government's acts of commission
could not give rise to liability absent an agreement. Vance's simple characterization of the *Gila River* decision was off-base.

Yet there was also a strong thread of logic in his analysis. If it had cost
the United States five thousand dollars to provide the level of health, educational, and administrative services afforded to the Pimas and Maricopas, and it would have cost five *million* dollars to provide "adequate"
services, was it any business of the judiciary to say that the government
was obligated, absent an express agreement, to spend the larger sum, instead of devoting the money to other services? Viewed in this way, the
Pima and Maricopa claims did involve an act of omission—the failure to
spend more money.

By contrast, wrongly imprisoning a tribe and, in Justice Blue's terms,
causing its "dislocation, dispersal, and ultimate destruction," inescapably
constituted acts of commission. Under the Anglo-American system of
law, every individual has an obligation not to interfere with the freedom
of another, except in certain defined circumstances. No treaty, agreement, order, statute, or affirmative action is necessary to create that type
of legal obligation.

Vance's point was all the stronger because it was made in the context
of a fair and honorable dealings claim. Only a lawyer tangled up in legal
categories could seriously argue that imprisonment of all members of a
tribe for eight years in conditions that promoted extremely high death
rates couldn't be unfair and dishonorable unless the government had expressly agreed beforehand not to do such a thing.

The Weissbrodts never had a chance to appeal the Commission's decision to the Court of Claims. The Commission decided the liability issues connected with the land claim in favor of the Nez Perce,
necessitating a trial to determine the value of the land at the time of taking. The Commission, therefore, had not issued a final judgment, making
an appeal to the Court of Claims for the dismissal of the imprisonment
claim premature.

Before an appeal became timely, the Commission again addressed
whether it could hold the United States liable for thwarting tribal pur

poses by imprisoning tribal members. This time the plaintiff was the Chiricahua Apaches.

.   .   .

Lefty Weissbrodt reported to Benedict Jozhe and Wendell Chino in 1970 (before the decision on the Nez Perce claim) that the Chiricahua imprisonment case would "be one of the most challenging that has been presented in the history of the litigation of tribal claims." If any non-property claim could succeed, Lefty thought, it was the Chiricahuas'. He told the tribal leaders that the commissioners might conclude that the fair and honorable dealings clause provided a "basis for recovery." [30]

Justice Department attorneys disagreed. On May 17, 1971, two months after the Commission ruled against the claims of the Nez Perce, Richard Beal, for the government, filed a motion to dismiss the Chiricahuas' claim without trial, arguing that their claim was no different from that of the Joseph Band.[31]

Beal, who would become the head of the government's Indian Claims Section about nine years later, had appraised the legal setting correctly. The Court of Claims' *Gila River* decision bound the Indian Claims Commission, and four commissioners had already indicated in the Joseph Band case that they would not distinguish *Gila River* on the basis that it dealt with acts of omission rather than commission.

Lefty Weissbrodt, a man who measured the worth of an argument by its chance of success rather than its inherent merit, contemplated the same decisions. He concluded that the only viable argument the Chiricahuas could make was that the government had entered into a treaty or made a representation that created a special relationship and then violated it. If established, this would create liability under *Gila River.*

The only hope was the treaty on which Mangas Coloradas and five other Apache "chiefs" had placed their marks in July 1852. It did not involve the cession of any land. Instead, it provided for "perpetual peace and amity" between the Apache nation and the United States, the "free and safe passage" of American citizens through Apache territory, and the cessation of Apache raids into Mexico. The Indians acknowledged in the treaty that they were under the jurisdiction of the United States, and that the government could legislate and act "as to secure the permanent prosperity and happiness of said Indians." Of more meaning, a government representative present at the signing reported to Washington that

Mangas was told " 'that his people were under the protection of the Government of the United States,' 'that they would be protected,' and 'that they had the right to protect themselves. . . .' "The legal brief submitted by the Weissbrodts argued that this treaty created the special relationship that the United States then violated.[32]

It was a weak reed at best. The treaty did not serve as a guide for the future actions of either white men or Indians, and its provisions had often been violated by both sides by 1876, the date of the closing of the Chiricahua Reservation. Maybe more important, the treaty contained almost no promises from the United States restricting the scope of its powers in dealing with the Apaches.

Weak it may have been, but it nearly sufficed. The two pro-Indian commissioners, Vance and Blue, endorsed the argument in ringing terms in September 1971: "It is difficult to conceive of a situation wherein a strong, powerful and warlike group of Indians could more completely strip themselves or more completely and utterly depend upon the words, good faith and good intentions of the United States Government. If such does not constitute a special relationship, placing upon the Government a duty to protect, defend and preserve their safety, freedom and way of life, then it is hardly conceivable how any special relationship, placing a duty and responsibility upon the Government, could *ever* exist." The two commissioners overlooked the fact that after Mangas signed the treaty, the Chiricahuas continued raiding into Mexico and fought fiercely for their land, neither stripping themselves nor depending upon the words or good faith of the United States, especially after Cochise's disastrous 1861 encounter with Lieutenant Bascom. Based on their distorted view of history, Vance and Blue voted to deny the government's motion and to permit the tribe to present its claims at trial.

The strongly progovernment commissioner, Kuykendall, and one of the centrists, Pierce, relied on prior decisions concerning the impact of this particular treaty to conclude that the United States did not enter into a special relationship with the Chiricahuas. Pierce has described the case as "heartbreaking," but felt precedents bound her hands.

This gave Yarborough the pivotal vote. He commented that the events described in the tribe's allegations "demand the utmost compassion and sympathy from the Commission." But he adopted the central point made by Judge Davis in *Gila River:* the Indian Claims Commission had the power "to provide recompense for tribal property loss only." Because the Chiricahuas were not seeking damages for property loss in this case, Yarborough concluded, their claim should be dismissed without trial.[33]

.   .   .

The Weissbrodts appealed to the Court of Claims and called on their old friend and former partner, David Cobb, to help. The Chiricahuas' briefs to the court reversed the direction taken in the brief to the Commission. The 1852 treaty, the attorneys parenthetically noted, had created a special relationship under which the United States had the obligation to protect the Chiricahuas from wrongs committed by this country's citizens. The Apaches' claim, however, arose not from the government's failure to protect them from others, but from its own imprisonment and mistreatment of the tribe for twenty-seven years. The treaty, therefore, was virtually irrelevant to the claim.

Instead of focusing on it, Cobb and the Weissbrodts argued to the court that the government could be liable under the fair and honorable dealings clause even without a special relationship. Throughout the country's history, they pointed out, United States courts have held private individuals liable for wrongly imprisoning others. The government likewise had a "general" duty under "basic principles of law, equity and morality" not to wrongly imprison the tribe. No "special" duty was necessary. In effect, they adopted Vance's distinction between acts of omission and acts of commission, with somewhat different terminology and greater refinement. An express agreement creating a "special" duty might be necessary to hold the United States liable for an act of omission, such as a failure to protect a tribe from others, but was unnecessary to hold the United States liable for an act of commission for which any private citizen would be held liable.[34]

When the Court of Claims announced its decision on May 11, 1973, the judges had split three ways.[35]

Judge Nichols wrote the opinion for the three judges who thought that the Commission should grant the Chiricahuas a trial. The language of the act, he believed, did not expressly limit the Commission to claims involving property, and the history of the act indicated that the Commission's jurisdiction should extend beyond the types of claims typically brought under special jurisdictional acts. As the Weissbrodts and Cobb had urged, Nichols said that *Gila River* did not apply to the Chiricahuas' claims because it did not involve the "intentional infliction of harm by the directly employed agents of the United States." Granted, Nichols thought that, if the Commission heard the claim, the Indians might lose, because the government's actions should be judged against the code of war existing at that time. Nevertheless, he believed that the Chiricahuas should at least be given the opportunity to show that the United States had not lived up to that code. Thus, even the Weissbrodts' supporters shrank from opening the can of worms of fairness and honor; they merely substituted the code of war for the code of law.[36]

Three other judges gave the arguments of the Weissbrodts and Cobb short shrift. Although acknowledging with studied understatement "that the Apache Tribe did not prosper" from twenty-seven years of imprisonment, they adhered to the view that the United States could be liable only if an express provision created a special relationship, and the 1852 treaty did not suffice.

This gave Judge Oscar Davis the pivotal vote. Bowing to Judge Nichols's lengthy presentation of the legislative history of the Indian Claims Commission Act, Davis acknowledged that "the legislative history is not entirely clear." On balance, however, he had "no adequate reason" to change the position that he had expressed in *Gila River,* namely, that the Commission's jurisdiction was limited to claims "for specific deprivations of land or property or rights protected by treaty, statute, or then-existing law." [37]

Only one level of review was left: the Supreme Court.

.   .   .

Unlike lower courts of appeal, which have to consider any timely appeal, the Supreme Court can choose among the decisions it is asked to review. To increase the chances of the Supreme Court hearing their case, lawyers typically frame the issues so that they will apply in other cases. Cobb and the Weissbrodt firm chose to attack the doctrine that lay at the root of the two defeats. The Chiricahuas would challenge the "special relationship" doctrine enunciated in *Gila River* that virtually read the fair and honorable dealings clause out of the Indian Claims Commission Act. The Court of Claims' interpretation, they argued, "quite simply, nullifies the clause." The court "has seriously misconstrued an important jurisdictional provision of the Indian Claims Commission

Act. . . . Unless corrected by this Court, this misconstruction promises to permanently distort the application of the act and to frustrate substantially the purposes of its enactment." [38]

Briefs filed with the Supreme Court by two Indian rights organizations buttressed the Chiricahuas' position, but in the end only Lefty Weissbrodt's old boss, Justice William O. Douglas, voted in favor of hearing the case.[39]

The denial of review was not surprising. Of the fifty-five requests for review submitted to the Supreme Court between 1946 and 1978 in cases brought under the Indian Claims Commission Act, only three were granted. The Supreme Court considered lawsuits raising contemporary issues involving Indian tribes more important.

.   .   .

The Supreme Court's denial effectively ended almost all tribal hopes of recovering under the fair and honorable dealings clause for damage to their culture or social structure. The Weissbrodts and other Indian claims attorneys gave up the fight.

In the 1990s, looking back with continuing regret at the development of the special relationship doctrine, Lefty Weissbrodt theorized that timing may have been crucial. If the Court of Claims had considered the Chiricahua or Nez Perce claims before those of the Pimas and Maricopas, it might never have formulated the special relationship doctrine or, even if it did, it might have limited the doctrine to acts of omission. Cox's theory, he believes, was brilliant, but far too radical for the Indian claims commissioners and Court of Claims judges, who constructed a wall cordoning off virtually all fair and honorable dealings claims. If Weissbrodt is correct, Justice Department attorneys can take the credit for their decision, whether mapped out as part of a grand strategy or not, to challenge the Pima and Maricopa claims before attacking the Nez Perce and Chiricahua imprisonment claims.

The history of Indian claims does not support Weissbrodt's conjecture, however. The courts and the Commission repeatedly devised doctrines under which most tribes would recover *something,* but not too much. The claims of tribal destruction raised the specter of huge recoveries. That threat, combined with the uncomfortable moral terrain the claims would force the courts and Commission to explore, produced a retreat from the language of the Indian Claims Commission Act. It is difficult to imagine that the jurists would have been significantly more adventuresome if the Chiricahua claims had been considered first.

· · ·

The perversity of the "special relationship" analysis that defeated the Nez Perce and Chiricahua claims may be even more brightly highlighted by the solitary tribal success on a nonproperty claim under the fair and honorable dealings clause than by the various defeats. The Aleuts of St. Paul and St. George islands off Alaska ultimately recovered $8.5 million as compensation for a seventy-six-year period from 1870 through 1946 during which they were treated much like medieval serfs by the United States government. They recovered, however, not because the governmental actions offended the adjudicators' senses of fairness and honor, but because of provisions in two federal statutes that, according to the Court of Claims, created a "special relationship."

When Vitus Bering of Russia first sighted the Aleutian Islands in the mid-eighteenth century, about sixteen thousand Aleuts lived there, but their population was soon devastated by warfare and disease and the Aleuts submitted to Russian political control. In 1786, the Russians found the smaller chain of Pribilof Islands, including St. Paul and St. George, in the Bering Sea a couple hundred miles to the north of the Aleutians and about three hundred miles from the mainland of Alaska. The Pribilofs were remarkable for the fur seals that spend several months a year breeding in the thick fog of the islands, their only land home in the world.

The Russians decided to resettle several hundred Aleuts, who had subsisted primarily through communal sea hunts from their homes on the Aleutians, to the Pribilofs to kill and skin the bachelor seals (breeding animals and younger females were spared in order to maintain the production of sealskins). Humans had not previously inhabited the Pribilofs, for good reason—the islands were, in the words of the Commission, "cold, cloudy, windy, and wet." [40]

For the next eighty-one years, Aleuts lived on St. Paul and St. George under Russian control, until the United States purchased Alaska from Russia in 1867. Under principles of Western international law, the United States thereby acquired sovereignty over the approximately 370 Aleuts living on the Pribilof Islands. Three years later, Congress passed an act allowing the secretary of the treasury to enter into a twenty-year lease giving a company the exclusive right to take fur seals on the Pribilofs. The act required the secretary, in making the lease, to "have due regard to the . . . comfort, maintenance, education, and protection of the natives." Two twenty-year leases were entered, one in 1870 and the other in 1890, for the sole purpose of exploiting the skins of the seals and the labor of the Aleuts. During the forty years, the companies netted about $23.1 million in profits on less than $14.3 million of expenditures, an extraordinary profit margin of more than 150 percent. Over two-thirds of those expenditures were lease payments to the government, which realized a profit of about $8.7 million.

In 1910, with seal populations declining from open-sea hunting, Congress decided to forgo the middlemen. A new statute provided that the Aleuts should receive fair compensation for their labor and authorized the executive to provide the necessities of life and for the Aleuts' "comfort, maintenance, education, and protection." Between 1910 and 1946, the United States realized profits of about $14.6 million on expenses of just under $30 million.[41]

During this near-century in which the Aleuts were making millions for the government, Congress assigned jurisdiction over them not to the Indian Office (later the Bureau of Indian Affairs), but to the secretaries of the treasury and labor and commerce. These officials realized that continuing the flow of revenue required maintenance of an adequate workforce on the islands, and government agents adopted extraordinary measures to ensure its continuance. To discourage emigration, Aleuts needed permission to leave or reenter the islands. To guarantee a continuing supply of future laborers, agents threatened males with punishments if they did not marry. According to the Indian Claims Commission, the United States adopted a "policy of educational deprivation apparently aimed at keeping the Aleuts from so much knowledge of the outside world as would excite their aspirations for a better lot." The Russians, on the other hand, had devised a written language for the Aleuts, taught many to read both Aleut and Russian, and trained them in commercial skills in schools located both on the Alaskan mainland and in Russia.

The agent in charge was police, prosecutor, and judge, with unchecked power to fine Aleuts, put them in irons or imprison them, and check any type of internal dissent, even "crimes" such as sauciness.

The tribe had plenty of reasons to complain. A typical day's diet consisted of bread and coffee for breakfast, bread and tea for lunch, and potatoes and rice for dinner. Children would beg for food at the white mess hall and pick through the refuse; during World War II, a physician estimated that 75 percent would have no teeth by the age of twenty because of the lack of adequate nutrition. They also received inadequate housing, fuel, and clothing, making it virtually impossible for them to stay warm. Although sealing took only several months of the year, the agents compelled the people to work for the government during the balance of the year on tasks such as improving the agency compound. During the nineteenth century, the government paid nothing for this work; later it credited Aleuts' accounts, then charged the necessities it was obliged to supply against them.

When the Aleuts were evacuated from the islands during World War II, officials sought work for them "in units as large as possible in isolated areas" because the government could, in the words of one agent, "keep better control over the Natives if we had 15 men at one location rather than 3 men at each of 5 locations." A doctor reported that, while in Alaska, the Aleuts "were herded into quarters unfit for pigs, denied adequate medical attention; lack of healthful diet and even facilities to keep warm and are virtually prisoners of the Government though theoretically possessing the status of citizenship." [42]

The Indian Claims Commission ultimately determined that, while the operators and government were racking up $46 million in net profits, they paid their Indian laborers a grand total of about $4.1 million.[43]

It is difficult to imagine that the United States could treat any tribe more unfairly and dishonorably. Yet the Commission originally dismissed the Aleuts' claim. On March 24, 1972, about six months after dismissing the Chiricahua claim on a 3–2 vote, the Commission unanimously (Vance did not vote) threw out the Aleut claim without a trial. The claim, they said, was indistinguishable from that dismissed in *Gila River.*[44]

The Court of Claims, with only one dissenter, reinstated the claim on June 20, 1973. The judges did not suddenly abandon their "special relationship" analysis. They did not state that the government's behavior, if as bad as alleged, offended all bounds of fairness and honor. Rather, in this case, unlike the others, the United States *had* entered into a special relationship with the Aleuts. By the acts of 1870 and 1910, Congress had obligated the United States to afford the Indians fair compensation for their labor, to make sure that they received the necessities of life, and to provide for their "comfort, maintenance, education and protection." If the Aleuts could prove at trial that the government had violated those statutory obligations, the court said, they were entitled to recover under the fair and honorable dealings clause.[45]

The Aleuts' lawyers, Donald Green and Steve Truitt, did a magnificent job. Their experts located and synthesized masses of evidence from which the Commission could determine the net profits realized by governmental and corporate entities from the seal-skinning operations, the value of the compensation received by the Aleuts, and the cost of what they would have received if the United States had lived up to its obligations. The Commission concluded in 1978 that the government did not fairly compensate the Aleuts for their labor, afford them the necessities of life, or provide for their comfort, maintenance, education, and protection. To live up to those obligations would have cost the government about $15.3 million, an amount easily affordable in light of the profits. This was the total amount for which the Commission found the United States liable. Nothing was sought or awarded "for the consequences of malnourishment and disease which seemed for a time to have doomed the population to extinction," or for the "history of subjugation and exploitation." [46]

Both parties appealed the decision to the Court of Claims. To avoid delay and uncertainties, the tribe in 1979 agreed to settle for $8.5 million—a bit more than $100,000 for each of the seventy-five years of tribal serfdom. It may not seem like much in these days of huge awards arising out of single events, but the Aleuts were lucky. As Truitt told them when they were deciding whether to accept the settlement, "There has never been another Indian Claims Commission case which has allowed recovery under the Fair and Honorable Dealings clause without having some other clause of the Indian Claims Commission Act also involved. This case is unique. It's one of a kind." [47]

If Congress had remained silent, the Aleuts would not have been able to recover either, because the government's despicable conduct would not have been deemed unfair or dishonorable under the standards of *Gila River.*

. . .

As Commissioner Blue stated in the *Joseph Band* case, the dispossession of tribes was not "the real tragedy in American Indian history." Although the process could have, and should have, occurred far more humanely, the result—the loss of native lands—was probably inevitable. The decimation of native populations through diseases exposed vast areas that seemed largely depopulated to white men and to government officials, who simply took the land, shoving aside the remnants of the native population and invoking religious commandments to justify the result. Racism made the cruelties inflicted on the Indians seem unimportant.

The "real tragedy" was what happened after the Indians had been dispossessed of their lands. Sometimes deliberately, sometimes through ignorance, and often because of the low priority placed on the interests of the natives, the United States destroyed tribal ways of life without establishing anything viable to replace them. Yet in the *Gila River* and Chiricahua cases, the Court of Claims decided that, unless the government had expressly agreed not to destroy tribal existence or had expressly agreed to provide the foundation for a new life for the tribe, the Indians could not recover for these largely noneconomic injuries. With those decisions, the Court of Claims placed this tragedy largely outside the purview of the Indian Claims Commission and the remedies it could provide.

ELEVEN

ACCOUNTING FOR RESERVATION MANAGEMENT

Hegel remarks somewhere that all great world-historic facts and
personages appear, so to speak, twice. He forgot to add: the first time as
tragedy, the second time as farce.

—KARL MARX

Broadly speaking, the tragedies visited by white men upon the native
peoples came in three stages: the taking of their land; the destruction of
their cultures during the early reservation years; and finally the mismanagement of their reservations and financial resources. The Indian Claims
Commission revisited that history in roughly the same three stages. Land
claims generally were adjudicated first, then the few cases that established that tribes couldn't recover for destruction of their cultures absent
a special obligation, and finally the so-called accounting claims that dealt
with management of the tribal resources.

   This last group of cases arose because the conquest of the tribes and
the hundreds of treaties and agreements into which they were forced to
enter did not divest Native Americans of all of their lands. The
Mescalero Reservation was one of over one hundred Indian reservations
created during the nineteenth century. Even after the allotment policy
cut their landholdings by over half, Indians collectively had rights in
1930 to land about equal in size to the state of Nevada. Since then, land

loss has been arrested, largely thanks to provisions of the Indian Reorganization Act of 1934.[1]

The reservations generally had been located in places considered undesirable by white men, but as resources outside the reservations were increasingly used up or placed under private ownership, the agricultural, range, timber, and mineral resources on the reservations increased in market value. At least until the creation of tribal governments under the Indian Reorganization Act, and in many instances not even then, Indians had almost no say in the management of those resources. Congress passed the laws that determined whether non-Indians would be allowed to use the resources, and once such use was authorized, the Indian Office (renamed the Bureau of Indian Affairs) and its employees decided who would be granted the rights to use the resources and under what terms and conditions. The government then entered contracts with the non-Indians governing their use of the resources and supervised their operations to ensure compliance with the terms of their leases, permits, or other contracts. And at least until the 1930s, tribes also had almost no say over the use of the money generated by the sale or use of their assets.

In exercising management powers over tribal lands, resources, and money, top government officials consistently represented that they were acting as the Indians' guardian or trustee. The Anglo-American legal system long has imposed significant duties and strict standards of conduct on private trustees. Indian claims lawyers argued that the same duties and standards applied to the government as the largely self-appointed trustee for the Indians. A private trustee must not divert the assets of the trust to its own benefit or the benefit of third parties. Analogously, Indian claims lawyers contended that if the government elected to benefit the tribe by leasing its resources, for example, it had to charge a fair price and otherwise establish and enforce lease terms that adequately protected the tribe.

The law respecting private trusts not only imposes duties on trustees but also creates a procedure for enforcing those duties. The beneficiary of a private trust often doesn't know whether the trustee has faithfully executed its duties. The trust may have been created at a time when the beneficiary was considered incapable of managing its own affairs. Accordingly, the beneficiary may demand that a trustee "account" for its management of the trust assets, and the burden is on the trustee to show that it managed the assets appropriately. If the trustee has misappropriated or mismanaged any of those assets, a court typically orders the trustee to restore them.

.   .   .

Even before passage of the Indian Claims Commission Act, a few claims lawyers operating under special jurisdictional acts had challenged the government's management of tribal assets. The claims of two tribes—the Sioux and the Menominee—stand out.

The Sioux tribe obtained a special jurisdictional act in 1920 that resulted in twenty-four separate, and uniformly unsuccessful, claims. One claim sought an accounting for the government's management of Sioux funds. In response, the government prepared a report showing for what purposes it had been disbursing tribal moneys. The Sioux's attorneys challenged many of the payments as improper. Judge Littleton issued the opinion for the Court of Claims resolving the disputes in 1946, just a few months before passage of the Indian Claims Commission Act.[2]

The most important issue in the *Sioux* accounting case was whether the government's use of tribal trust funds to operate its agencies on various Sioux reservations and to pay the salaries of government employees was proper. The Justice Department attorneys argued that the payments were proper because the agencies and the government employees benefited the Indians.[3]

Judge Littleton disagreed. He concluded that the agent and those working under him had always been considered government employees. The federal government had always treated payment of their salaries and the expenses associated with their offices as its expense. Shifting the payment burden to the Indians once they acquired some money was inappropriate, because government employees had been and remained necessary to fulfill treaty and other governmental obligations. Littleton recognized that in the late nineteenth century the government had begun to institute programs such as agriculture and ranching for the direct benefit of Indians. Payment of the expenses of those programs, including the salaries of employees engaged specifically and entirely to run them, might properly have been payable from Indian funds. The government, however, had the burden of showing what portion the Indians properly should bear, and the government had not offered this kind of

proof. Accordingly, Littleton found the government liable for all payments from tribal trust funds shown in its own accounting report as
made for agency expenses.[4]

Judge Littleton then extended his analysis one step further. The accounting report characterized some expenses as for "agency and educational purposes," without showing the amount of money spent for
educational as opposed to agency purposes. Even if the payments for education had been proper, Judge Littleton said, the government could not
escape its burden of showing that money had been spent properly by
lumping these expenses together. And the judge then increased the
stakes associated with an inadequate accounting. If the government was
liable for disbursements from an account on which it had agreed to pay
interest, it would also be liable for interest from the date of the improper
disbursements until the date of judgment.[5]

Applying these principles, Judge Littleton ruled that the government
was liable for over $2.4 million on the accounting claims of the Sioux
on seven different reservations. The tribe, however, did not recover a
penny. The government was allowed to offset against its liability the
amount of expenditures that it had made gratuitously (without legal
obligation) for the Sioux from its own funds, and the amount of these
disbursements far exceeded $2.4 million.

·   ·   ·

The other important pre-Commission decisions involved the management of timber resources. The Menominees had lived in what is now
eastern Wisconsin long before French explorers encountered them in
the seventeenth century. They maintained a central village near the
mouth of the Menominee River and harvested wild rice—their neighbors referred to them as the Wild Rice Men—and berries, and hunted
and fished. Then came the land hunger of white settlers. In the words of
Oshkosh, the leader selected by the United States as the chief of the
Menominees, "The only time the Americans shook hands was when
they wanted another piece of Menominee land." Through a series of
treaties and orders between 1827 and 1856, the Menominees ceded to
the United States their rights to well over 90 percent of their land and
accepted a reservation embracing about 360 square miles, or about
217,000 acres, of heavily forested land in northeastern Wisconsin.[6]

On July 16, 1905, a tornado struck the Menominee Reservation, knocking down trees in a wide swath. Almost a year later, on June 28, 1906, Congress passed an act authorizing the logging of the downed timber. Government administrators, however, refused to take any action during the balance of the year, and fallen trees continued to rot. Work finally commenced during 1907, but due to a supervisor's incompetence, it took another year to complete. The value of the lumber plummeted and the Menominees paid excessive costs for shoddy work.[7]

The Menominees engaged Ernest Wilkinson to bring claims on their behalf. Proceeding under a special jurisdictional act that he had helped to obtain for the Menominees in 1935, he elicited a ruling from the Court of Claims in 1944 that the government had owed the duty of a trustee to the Menominees to manage their property prudently, that it had violated that duty and was therefore liable for the damages caused by that negligence. When the court calculated those damages seven years later, they came to $341,000.[8]

Next, Wilkinson embarked on the far more ambitious task of convincing the Court of Claims that the government had acted imprudently in the manner in which it had permitted standing trees to be harvested. Congress in 1908 had provided for the logging of standing trees on the Menominee forest consistent with protecting and preserving the forest, which was described in a congressional report as "the finest body of natural timber left standing in the State." Yet between 1908 and 1928, the government had permitted much of the "splendid" forest to be clear-cut, denuded to the extent that "reproduction will not develop into a forest fit for profitable cutting for more than 100 years."

Wilkinson succeeded. In a decision issued in 1950, the court ruled that this clear-cutting violated the congressional purpose and the duty of government officials to manage the Menominee forest, virtually the tribe's only income-producing asset, as prudently as they would have run their own business or personal affairs. With the United States' liability established, the parties were able to negotiate a settlement in 1951, saving the court from having to calculate the amount of damages suffered by the Indians as a result of this mismanagement.[9]

·   ·   ·

Although the *Sioux* and *Menominee* decisions were issued before the 1951 deadline for filing claims under the Indian Claims Commission Act, only about 50 tribes filed accounting and mismanagement claims under the act, less than a third of the 170 tribes that filed any claims. Undoubtedly the result in *Sioux* contributed to the reluctance of Indian claims lawyers to file accounting claims. The Court of Claims had dismissed the Sioux's petitions without award because of the offsets. The complexities of a fiscal accounting case hardly seemed worthwhile if dismissal would be the likely result. Claims lawyers may not have received much more comfort from the *Menominee* decisions. The reasoning of the court rested on specific congressional legislation, and very few statutes dealt with the management of a specific resource on a specific reservation. Unless the decisions were interpreted more broadly, they would offer little help to other tribes.

Despite the many open questions, lawyers who chose not to file accounting claims were shortsighted. The principles set forth in *Sioux* made claims arising from the mismanagement of tribal funds viable, even if the results in some cases might prove disappointing. *Menominee* did not ensure the viability of resource mismanagement claims for tribes without legislation specifically dealing with their resources, but the decisions also did not preclude such claims.

The Wilkinson and Weissbrodt firms were not discouraged. They filed claims on behalf of their clients, and went on to prosecute the cases that produced the seminal accounting and mismanagement decisions under the Indian Claims Commission Act.

Those decisions did not come quickly. All of the accounting petitions were filed by August 13, 1951, but no further proceedings could occur until the government prepared accounting reports of transactions involving Indian funds and resources that had occurred during the last half of the nineteenth and first half of the twentieth centuries. The work overwhelmed the accountants and bookkeepers of the General Accounting Office, and very few reports were completed before the late 1960s. In the meantime, land claims dominated Commission proceedings.

.   .   .

When the Indian Claims Commission finally began to address accounting cases in 1970, it issued a series of "interlocutory," or preliminary, decisions addressing the adequacy of the accounting reports that the government was preparing. Building upon the principles enunciated in *Sioux* and the two *Menominee* decisions, the Commission generally sided with the tribal plaintiffs.

From the Indians' perspective, these interlocutory decisions climaxed in 1973 with two decisions issued only two weeks apart. The first addressed whether the United States had been obligated to pay interest on or to invest tribal funds under the government's control, and if so, at what rates of return.

In 1883, Congress directed that any revenue attributable to a tribe that was "not the result of the labor of any member of such tribe" be paid into the United States Treasury for the benefit of the tribe. The Treasury promptly misnamed the account "Indian Moneys, Proceeds of Labor," or "IMPL." In the following two decades Congress authorized the Indian Office to allow non-Indians to use reservation lands for agricultural, grazing, lumbering, and mining purposes, in return for agreed-upon fees. Deposits to the IMPL account between 1883 and 1930 totaled hundreds of millions of dollars.[10]

The Treasury paid not one cent of interest on these prodigious deposits until 1930, when Congress directed the payment of interest at the rate of 4 percent per annum. Nor did the Interior Department invest any of the money to generate income for the tribes. Like a noninterest-bearing checking account, the money in the IMPL account benefited only the "bank," the Treasury of the United States, until it was expended.

In a number of different cases, the firms of Wilkinson, Cragun & Barker and Weissbrodt and Weissbrodt challenged the government's failure to pay interest or invest fallow funds until 1930. The Indian Claims Commission decided in 1970 that the issue merited intensive review, and consolidated the issue in a single proceeding. The two firms pooled their resources in researching and arguing the issue in the consolidated proceeding, which came to be known as *Mescalero–Te Moak,* after the Weissbrodts' client the Mescalero Apache tribe and the Wilkinson client the Te-Moak Bands of Western Shoshones.[11]

The firms knew they needed a statute or agreement that required the government to pay interest on the IMPL funds or to invest them. In this case they found what they were looking for: a largely forgotten act passed in 1841 in response to a general depression in the 1830s.[12]

Before 1841, the federal government usually had invested all its trust funds, Indian and non-Indian, in state bonds. During the late 1830s, however, several states defaulted and the federal government, which had been running a budget surplus, slipped into deficit financing, requiring it to issue its own bonds to balance its books. To minimize the risks associated with state bonds and to provide a source of money for the purchase of federal bonds, Congress provided in 1841 that all "funds held in trust by the United States, and the annual interest accruing thereon, when not otherwise required by treaty, shall . . . be invested in stocks of the United States, bearing . . . a rate of interest not less than five per centum per annum." [13]

To the Indians' attorneys, the law was manna from heaven. On its face, it seemed to apply not only to IMPL, but to all Indian trust funds. However, its sweeping impact ensured fierce resistance from the Department of Justice.

According to the government, the statute merely provided that, if the United States was required *by some other statute or agreement* to invest Indian trust moneys, it must invest in stocks or bonds issued by the federal government. The Department of Justice in effect argued that the proviso "when not otherwise required by treaty," really meant, "when required to be invested by treaty." This interpretation virtually stood the act's language on its head, and there was no evidence that Congress hadn't meant what it had said. The Wilkinson and Weissbrodt firms countered with a "plain words" argument that the act required government employees to invest the principal and interest in Indian trust accounts, and do so in stock (or bonds) issued by the United States paying at least 5 percent per annum, unless a treaty provided otherwise.

Unsurprisingly, given the clarity of the statutory language, when the Commission finally issued its opinion on October 4, 1973, all five commissioners sided with the Indians. They disagreed only over the proper measure of damages. Vance, Blue, and Pierce decided that under the 1841 act, tribes were entitled to a 5 percent return on both the principal balances and any accrued interest in the IMPL account, at least through 1930, when the 1930 law mandating the payment of 4 percent interest on the IMPL account took effect. In effect, tribes would receive 5 percent compound interest for any failure to make their funds productive. Yarborough and Kuykendall disagreed. They would have limited tribal recoveries to 5 percent simple interest, on the twin grounds that simple interest typically is awarded when a private trustee fails to make trust assets productive and that, if the United States had taken the money from the Indians instead of merely failing to make it productive, the government would have been liable under eminent domain law for damages measured by 5 percent simple interest.[14]

The dispute may seem minor, but the difference between compound and simple interest is staggering in Indian cases, because many years have passed between the wrongdoing and the judgment. If, for example, the United States became liable eighty years prior to judgment for $1 million, it would owe $5 million (the $1 million principal plus $4 million in interest) at 5 percent simple interest, but over $50 million at 5 percent compound interest. The balance in the IMPL account for all tribes exceeded $1 million during every year but one between 1902 and 1930, and reached a high of over $9 million in 1923. *Mescalero–Te Moak* raised the specter of astronomical judgments against the government.

. . .

Two weeks after its decision in *Mescalero–Te Moak,* the Indian Claims Commission issued its second major interlocutory decision in an accounting case. It involved the claims of the Blackfeet and Gros Ventre of the Blackfeet Reservation and the Gros Ventre and Assiniboine of the Fort Belknap Reservation, both in northern Montana, who had followed a long and tortuous path to dependency on reservation resources.

Anthropologists believe that, several centuries ago, a group of Indians concluded a lengthy migration from the Great Lakes through what is now southern Canada to the Rocky Mountains. There they gained possession of a vast territory east of the Rockies in what is now northern Montana and southern Saskatchewan and divided into three tribes closely related by blood, language, and tradition—in English, the Blackfeet, Blood, and Piegan. (Non-Indians called all of them the Blackfoot Nation or the Blackfeet—even though Piegans predominated in the United States—although they were no more unified politically than were most of the other Indian groups with which the United States purported to enter into transactions.)

The lives of the Blackfeet centered around the buffalo hunt, conducted on foot with spears, rocks, and arrows. In the eighteenth century the Blackfeet acquired horses, which they still call "elk-dogs," presumably because the first horses that they encountered were as large as elk and could carry baggage like dogs. As fur traders reached the northwestern plains, the Blackfeet acquired guns and a taste for Anglo-American material goods, which could be obtained through the sale of buffalo hides. By the mid-nineteenth century, the dependence of the three related tribes and the loosely affiliated Gros Ventre on the buffalo hunt was total. They were unprecedentedly prosperous, but so narrow an economic base ultimately facilitated their subjugation, as it did for other Plains Indian tribes.[15]

The members of the Blackfoot Nation made their first land cession, whether or not they understood the paper before them, in 1855. The Blackfeet relinquished their claims to land south of the Musselshell and Missouri rivers and agreed to permit non-Indians safe passage across their territory. In return, the United States agreed to spend $35,000 per year for the next ten years purchasing "useful goods and services" for the Blackfeet and promoting their "civilization and Christianization." Of the unceded land, still a huge area in what is now northern Montana from the Rocky Mountains to the eastern boundary of the state, the government negotiator stated, "This is your home. It will remain your home." [16]

When the appropriations under the treaty ended during the 1860s, the Blackfeet were no better off financially than they had been when the treaty was negotiated. The government agents had spent most of the money on food, clothing, and items previously obtainable through the buffalo-hide trade. The only long-term investment was in an incredibly foolish attempt to develop a demonstration farm in that dry northern climate among a people who had shown no inclination for farming.

The buffalo hunt again became virtually the sole means of support for the Blackfeet, but successful hunts became more and more difficult. Cattle increasingly consumed the buffaloes' range, while the United States encouraged non-Indian slaughter of the buffalo to hasten the pacification of the Plains Indians. The policy worked. The buffalo, which had numbered in the millions during the 1870s, essentially disappeared during the early 1880s. The Blackfeet broke into small bands, scrambling from hunting site to hunting site, searching in vain for buffalo. An estimated six hundred, over 20 percent of the tribe, died during the winter of 1883–84 of starvation and diseases.[17]

With the Indians reduced to complete dependency, the government approached the Blackfeet, Gros Ventre, and two other tribes that had settled in the eastern part of the Blackfeet Reservation, the Assiniboine and the Yanktonai Band of Sioux, for new land cessions. The government negotiators proposed to carve out three reservations for the Indians totaling about 3.5 million acres: Fort Peck in northeastern Montana for Assiniboine and Sioux, Fort Belknap, and Blackfeet. The Indians would cede approximately 17.5 million acres that comprised the balance of the Blackfeet Reservation. In return, the government would pay the tribes a total of $4.3 million over ten years, or about twenty-five cents per acre. The United States, as the Indians' trustee, would use the money to help the Indians become self-supporting, primarily by buying cattle and training the Indians to become ranchers. The negotiators reported that "the promise of stock cattle was the principal inducement which led to the cession of the vast territory relinquished to the government," ignoring that the alternative to agreement for the Indians was continued starvation. In 1888 Congress passed the acts ratifying the three separate agreements with the tribes.[18]

When the money from the sale of the land ran out in the 1890s, the Indians were no closer to self-sufficiency. The government permitted non-Indians to exploit the lands and resources of the Blackfeet and Fort Belknap reservations, and used the income withdrawn from the IMPL account to fund the government programs on the reservation.

.   .   .

About 115 years after the government began to manage funds and reservations resources for the benefit of the Blackfeet, the law firm of Wilkinson, Cragun & Barker, which represented the Blackfeet and Gros Ventre tribes residing on the Blackfeet and Fort Belknap reservations, received the government's reports accounting for that management. At a hearing in 1971, the attorneys tried to convince the Commission that the accounting reports showed on their face that the United States had expended hundreds of thousands of dollars improperly based on the principles enunciated in *Sioux*. They also asked the Commission to order the government to supplement its report with information about its management of the reservations' resources.[19]

Already staggered by the decision in *Mescalero–Te Moak,* the government's attorneys were struck again by the October 1973 decision in *Blackfeet:* on all of the important issues, the Commission sided with the Indians. First, the Commission ruled that the tribes would recover without need for trial the large sums spent, according to the accounting reports, on various forms of agency expenses. For example, of the

$350,000 that the government was obligated to expend for the benefit of the Blackfeet and Gros Ventre tribes under the 1855 treaty, a total of $64,000, almost 20 percent, was used improperly to pay various expenses of running the government agency. The Commission decided that the accounting reports showed on their face that $316,000 was disbursed improperly from all the accounts.

Second, the Commission extended *Mescalero–Te Moak* by ruling that the tribes were entitled to interest on the amount of the improper disbursements under the 5 percent compounded formula. This meant, for example, that if one of the tribes had $300,000 in its IMPL account at the start of the year and the government spent $50,000 properly, $150,000 improperly, and did not disburse the remaining $100,000, the tribe would be entitled to compound interest, not only on the $100,000 remaining in the account, but also on the $150,000 improperly expended.[20]

Finally, the Commission ordered the government to account for its management of the resources of the reservations and other tribal property. The accounting reports hadn't covered the government's management of the reservations' resources, even though the tribes' petitions demanded such an accounting. This was typical: the GAO had omitted information about resource management in all of its reports. Without knowing the terms under which non-Indians had been permitted to graze stock, cut timber, or extract minerals from the reservations, and whether the permittees had complied with those terms, the tribes' attorneys couldn't hope to evaluate the government's management. If the Commission hadn't ruled in the tribes' favor on this point, they possibly could have engaged accountants to pore through the voluminous records to extract the relevant information, but the GAO was better situated to perform the accounting work.

The Commission started its analysis of resource management with the proposition that, unlike private trustees managing commercial real estate, the government was not required to administer Indian reservations for profit. Reservations "are not like apartment houses which a trustee is expected to keep filled with paying tenants at all times." Because the government wasn't liable for making every acre productive, the Commission ruled, the government didn't have to account for lands and resources not used. On the other hand, the government would be required to account for its management or use of the resources and would be liable for any mismanagement when it had permitted a third party to use tribal rangeland, timber, or other resources, or had used those resources itself for nontrust purposes (such as using stone from the reservations to construct a public road). *Menominee* had established that the government could be liable for management of tribal resources in violation of express congressional strictures; the *Blackfeet* decision extended that potential to tribal resources on every reservation whether or not Congress had passed specific legislation, and placed the onus on the United States to come forward with information about its management of those resources. If the government failed to account adequately, the Indians were likely to prevail.[21]

. . .

The 1973 *Blackfeet* decision did not mean that the government was liable to the Indians for mismanaging any resources or funds other than the $316,000 that the accounting reports had shown were improperly expended. Trial would be required to determine the government's liability on all other issues. Nonetheless, Indian claims attorneys who had filed accounting and mismanagement claims prior to August 13, 1951, now could congratulate themselves for their foresight. Their clients apparently would reap a bonanza. They could seek damages for the mismanagement of both funds and resources. They could recover compound interest, not only on unproductive funds but also on the amount of improper disbursements. Under the logic of *Mescalero–Te Moak* and *Blackfeet,* it also seemed likely that the Commission would award interest on funds that should have been collected but were not, because, for example, the United States had undercharged a third party for the privilege of grazing stock on a reservation.

Moreover, the decisions seemed well grounded legally. *Mescalero–Te Moak* was based on clear statutory language, while the three major rulings in *Blackfeet* flowed directly from *Sioux, Mescalero–Te Moak,* and *Menominee.*

The realities of Indian claims litigation soon set in.

. . .

The most obvious turn of fortune occurred in 1975. To no one's surprise, the Department of Justice decided to appeal the decision in *Mescalero–Te Moak* to the Court of Claims. The government found a sympathetic tribunal. While all five commissioners had ruled that Indians were entitled to interest for the United States' failure to invest their trust funds and had disagreed only on whether that interest would be simple or compound, the Court of Claims ruled virtually unanimously against the Indians on the right to interest at all; only Judge Oscar Davis dissented.[22]

Judge Byron Skelton's opinion for the majority adopted the Department of Justice's argument in toto. Skelton, a Texas Democrat appointed by President Johnson, was a collector of Indian lore and artifacts, but in general an opponent of Indian claims. Through much of his opinion he excoriated the Commission for supposedly violating the principle that the United States is not liable for the payment of interest unless it expressly agrees to pay it, without even mentioning that the Commission believed that the 1841 act constituted such a commitment. When he finally did acknowledge the existence of the act, he stated that it "was merely a directive to the appropriate officers of the Government holding trust funds that were *required* by treaty, contract, or statute to be invested, to invest them *only* in stocks of the United States." He continued, "The sole purpose of the Act was to prohibit future investment of trust funds, that were required to be invested, in state bonds." [23]

The opinion is striking for its analytical gaps. In adopting the government's arguments, Skelton completely ignored the language of the act, the normal starting point for any statutory analysis. He did not attempt to explain how the statutory phrase "when not otherwise required by treaty" really meant "when required by treaty, contract, or statute." He also did not attempt to explain the error in the Commission's conclusion that one of Congress's purposes in adopting the 1841 act was to ensure that the moneys would be invested in debt instruments of the federal government to alleviate the strain on the federal budget. Instead he emphasized that at no time after passage of the act did the government behave as if it required all Indian trust funds to be invested in United States stocks. In other words, the government's consistent flouting of the mandate of the law was construed as evidence that the law didn't mean what it said.[24]

Here he misapplied the doctrine that significant weight should be given to the interpretation of an ambiguous statute by the agency charged with its administration. Skelton hadn't shown that the statute was ambiguous, the prerequisite for application of the doctrine. Even if he had, the government continued to invest Indian trust funds in state as well as federal bonds after passage of the act, behavior that on its face did not support Judge Skelton's view that the act prohibited investment in state bonds. If anything, the actions indicated that the statute was meaningless, a proposition for which nobody was arguing and which is anathema to courts. More fundamentally, permitting the executive department to vitiate a statute by ignoring any provision it does not like would confer a passive veto power on the executive branch that would be unconstitutional.

In his dissenting opinion, Judge Davis demonstrated the strength of the Indians' arguments that the 1841 act required the investment of trust funds in federal "stocks" at a return of at least 5 percent per annum. The government, however, had something stronger than logic: the impact of a pro-Indian decision on the public treasury. Davis reminded his colleagues, "If the [statute] so provides, we cannot refuse interest because the amount is relatively large." The reminder fell on deaf ears.[25]

The decision underscored the courts' propensity for manufacturing arguments, however specious, to prevent the tribes from realizing substantial recoveries. A private trustee generally is liable for lost interest or lost investment income if it fails to make trust assets productive, especially when the trustee uses those assets instead for its own benefit. The United States had failed to make the IMPL funds productive and instead had allowed the Treasury to use the money interest-free until disbursed. If the same rules applied to the government as to a private trustee, it clearly would be liable for interest. The United States' only legal shield was the rule that it was not liable for interest in the absence of a statute or agreement. To hide behind the legal doctrine when the United States did not permit the Indians to choose a private trustee (which would have had to pay interest) was unfair. But the Court of Claims had already established in *Gila River* that the United States could be liable for acting unfairly or dishonorably only if it violated a statute or agreement. Now the Indians had pointed to the 1841 statute that, according to its plain words, the government had violated. Even under the restrictive *Gila River* standard, the Indians should have prevailed. They did not. The court blatantly rewrote the statute to avoid the result it feared.

The rollback of potential interest awards did not stop with *Mescalero–Te Moak*. In a subsequent case, the Court of Claims decided that no statute required the government to invest or pay interest on accounts originally created during the 1930s and misnamed—again—Individual Indian Moneys (IIM). On many reservations, IIM accounts replaced the IMPL account as the primary depository and disbursement accounts. It followed that tribes also could not recover interest on any improper disbursements from those IIM accounts. The Commission got the message, ruling against awards of interest in other cases "in the context of the Court of Claims' seeming reluctance to find circumstances justifying awarding interest to Indian tribes." The government thus wasn't held liable for interest on money that it failed to collect, even if it would have deposited the money into an interest-bearing trust fund. This ruling effectively blocked any interest on damages arising from resource mismanagement.[26]

·   ·   ·

The repercussions of a second decision rendered during the early 1970s weren't as immediately obvious as the decision in *Mescalero–Te Moak,* but were almost as powerful. The decision resolved another claim brought by Z. Simpson Cox on behalf of the Gila River Pima-Maricopa Tribe.

During World War II, the United States removed from their homes and confined thousands of persons of Japanese ancestry—the only ethnic group other than Native Americans to be confined en masse by the United States government for noncriminal acts (African Americans were enslaved privately with the support of the government). Ironically, the United States decided to locate many of the internment camps on Indian reservations, and one was the Gila River Pima-Maricopa Reservation. The Indians had no choice in the matter; two agencies of the government negotiated the terms and only then informed the tribal council of the decision and the compensation to be paid.[27]

The government leased four tracts of land on the Gila River Reservation between 1942 and 1947. Two, amounting to about 1,300 acres for which the government paid the tribe one dollar per acre per year, were used as campsites where up to fourteen thousand people were impounded. The War Relocation Authority built barracks, warehouses, administration buildings, and utilities. At the end of the lease, the Authority removed salable improvements and destroyed others, leaving behind a mass of concrete and rubble estimated to cost $120,000 to remove: eighteen times more than the $6,500 rent paid and far more than the value of the land.[28]

In his petition, Cox included claims for unconscionable consideration and lack of fair and honorable dealings on the lease of all four tracts. Both the Indian Claims Commission in 1971 and the Court of Claims in 1972 unanimously ruled that the United States was liable for failure to restore the two campsite tracts. Damages were small, however. The established legal principle governing disputes between non-Indians is that "[w]here the expense of restoration exceeds the diminution in the market value of the property caused by the lessee's nonperformance, the diminution in fair market value is the proper measure of damages." Both tribunals embraced the rule in the *Gila River* case despite Cox's arguments. The Pimas and Maricopas could not recover more than the diminution in the fair market value of the land caused by the rubble, only a small percentage of the cost of restoration.[29]

Neither the Commission nor the court gave any indication that they understood the importance of this outcome. Claims attorneys, however, soon discovered that on reservation after reservation, the government's management had resulted in damage to timber and range resources.

If tribes could establish the United States' liability for permitting overgrazing and clear-cutting, two approaches to establishing the damages would have existed, but for the *Gila River* concentration camp decision. One would have focused on the diminution in value of the timber or range, the other on the cost of restoring the land. As with the restoration of the campsites, the cost of restoration generally would have dwarfed the loss of market value. The *Gila River* decision, however, eliminated that option; the smaller market-value figure became the sole measure of damages.[30]

The legal principle that damages from injury to land are limited to the lesser cost—restoration or the diminution in market value—makes sense when the land is privately owned, especially when it is commercial land. If land suffers damage that reduces its market value by $10,000 but that would cost $100,000 to restore, the owner theoretically is made whole by receiving $10,000. An owner who does not want to own the land in its damaged condition may sell it, presumably for $10,000 less than would otherwise have been paid, and buy equivalent, undamaged land elsewhere. The principle, however, was strained to its breaking point in Indian claims cases. To begin with, a tribe cannot sell its reservation. Diminution in market value means nothing. Moreover, many of the geographical features of reservations (especially those established within a tribe's aboriginal territory) have a spiritual significance that transcends the economic value of the resources.

As in so many other aspects of Indian claims cases, judges overlooked or ignored the Indians' perspective in applying legal rules. And the rules themselves deprived them of damages for actual losses.

·   ·   ·

These various decisions, all issued between 1972 and 1975, virtually ensured that tribes would recover something in every accounting case. If nothing else, accounting reports invariably showed that the government had expended some tribal funds to run the agency. Trials would determine whether the government would be liable for more than the amounts shown on the face of the accounting reports. As the attorneys began to prepare for accounting trials, however, the grim truth that the cases were virtually untriable became unavoidable.

Only one accounting case, that of the tribes on the Blackfeet and Fort Belknap reservations, was tried before the Indian Claims Commission. The Indians asserted six types of claims for mismanagement of: their funds; the sale of small parcels of lands from their reservations; and their range, timber, water, and mineral resources. In the initial phase of the case, which began in September 1976, fourteen expert witnesses testified and over four thousand exhibits were introduced. The plaintiffs' proposed findings of fact alone consumed over nine hundred pages.[31]

The parties devoted much of their efforts to the funds mismanagement claims.[32] Based on the historical documents, the Indians' attorneys argued that many disbursements that might appear from the accounting reports to have been made for the Indians' benefit were made at least partly for the benefit of the agency. For example, sawmills were constructed and maintained on both reservations, in large part through tribal funds. The mills cut logs for both the agency and tribal members. But when a tribal member desired lumber, a 10 percent toll was charged and he had to provide free labor in exchange for the millwork. The agency did not pay for its lumber. Other mills and shops such as the blacksmith and harnessmaker operated similarly. Because Indians had to pay to use the mills and shops but the government did not, the tribes' attorneys contended that they were run as governmental activities and the tribes should not have had to support them with their funds at all. In another instance, the accounting report classified a particular purchase in the category of "Indian dwellings," which category, the Indians' attorneys conceded, was proper. However, the voucher underlying the purchase identified the purchase as doors and windows "for repair of agency buildings and issue to Indians." This, the attorneys contended, lumped together improper expenditures with those that might have been proper in some unknown amount; under *Sioux,* the government had not accounted adequately.[33]

By using the principles enunciated in *Sioux,* but by examining the historical records and underlying financial documents that the Sioux attorney had ignored three decades before, the attorneys for the Blackfeet and Belknap Indians increased exponentially the number of disbursements that they could challenge as made for agency purposes. This strategy, however, also magnified the complexity of the case for both parties and the court, and raised issues of fairness. Was it reasonable to expect the government to account for individual disbursements on far-flung reservations decades after the expenditures were made, and to make distinctions between expenditures for agency benefit and for Indian benefit that were not made contemporaneously?

·   ·   ·

Magnifying the difficulties, the Indians' attorneys asserted two novel types of fiscal mismanagement claim. One grew out of dishonest agents. From 1893 through 1895, Major J. M. Kelley served as the agent at Fort Belknap, but he was removed after being charged with immoral conduct, misappropriation of property, and defrauding Indians. He was followed by Luke Hays, who in turn was succeeded in 1900 by Morris Bridgeman. During 1902, two inspectors, Charles McNichols and James Jenkins, discovered that Bridgeman had issued fraudulent vouchers, falsified payrolls, and made bogus purchases, all with tribal moneys. Bridgeman quickly caved in, stating in his defense that he was such a "hard and heavy drinker . . . that he could not have any knowledge of the falsity of [the vouchers]." McNichols described Bridgeman as "a poor, alc[o]holic, stupid fool, utterly dazed by recent events. . . . He has been a thief from boyhood but imagined that he was playing a safe game this time as he was only following the path of his predecessor." Hays, of whose guilt

McNichols was also convinced, committed suicide before Bridgeman's trial, but Bridgeman did not escape the judicial process. He was convicted and sentenced to three years in prison.[34]

Based on the evidence put together by the inspectors and contradictions between the accounting records and the historical documents, the Belknap tribes argued that fraud infected far more transactions than those for which Bridgeman was tried and convicted. As their attorneys acknowledged, however, "[t]he results of the Hays-Bridgeman fraud cannot be fully determined by the documents which have filtered into the 20th Century." The government's historian, Edward Barry, put the proof available to the plaintiffs in the 1970s in a harsher light:

> There is no evidence that everything that Luke C. Hays did was fraudulent or illegal. As a matter of fact there is no hard evidence that anything he did was fraudulent or illegal. Bridgeman's guilt should not be confused with the possibility that Hays is also suspect. You can't color all of the agents at Fort Belknap with the brush wielded by one man.

Both sides were correct. It *was* impossible to prove in 1975 how much of the tribes' funds had been fraudulently disbursed seventy-five years before. Whether the tribes would prevail on their fraudulent expenditure claim would depend primarily on the Commission's ruling on a single issue: Was the burden of persuasion on the Indians or the government? [35]

The second novel type of challenge was to negligent or improvident disbursements. Governmental policies changed directions in fits and starts, as agents came and went in Montana and administrations turned over in Washington. A project commenced with great fanfare and large expenditures in one year often was abandoned a few years later.

Schooling at Fort Belknap provides an example. In 1890, at a cost of about $19,000 in Indian moneys, the government constructed two large brick buildings as a boarding school so that, as at Carlisle, children could be removed from their families, forbidden to speak their native language, and weaned from traditional life. In 1897 an inspector described the school as a "disgrace to our civilization": overcrowded, improperly ventilated, badly lit, and without adequate water, sewers, toilets, bathing facilities, dormitories, and laundry. Conditions were little changed in 1901, when it was reported as having "a general air of neglect." [36]

Two years later, a new superintendent arrived. (Agents were redesignated "superintendents" when reservation employees became civil servants instead of political appointees.) Superintendent William Logan recommended that the boarding school be closed and replaced with four community day schools. He believed those would be cheaper to operate, provide better education, and be preferred by the Indians. Moreover, the cost of bringing the boarding school to a sanitary condition was prohibitive. It took five more years, but in 1908 day schools were constructed.[37]

The boarding school facilities remained inadequate, and a new superintendent declared in 1915 that an examination of the plant "made [him] sick." The next year Cato Sells, the commissioner of Indian affairs, visited "nearly all of the non-reservation and reservation schools," and proclaimed that "I do not recall seeing one anywhere where taken as a whole conditions seemed so unsatisfactory." In 1920 an inspector recommended that the boarding school be closed or improved to such a condition that "it will not disgrace the service." A new superintendent who arrived that same year promptly ignored that advice, making determined efforts to increase boarding school enrollment and using student labor to maintain the physical plant. The result was that the understaffed school could offer education through only the sixth grade, but during the 1920s it often took the overcrowded students twelve years to reach that level, because they spent so much of their time in unpaid labor. The decrepit boarding school was finally closed in 1934, and new schools constructed with Public Works Administration funds.[38]

According to the government's accounting reports, about $120,000 of the funds of the Fort Belknap Indians were used to construct, maintain, and operate the schools from 1896 through 1934. Had the Indians' money been spent wisely during those thirty-eight years? If not, should the government be liable for the amount of the improvident disbursements? And was it relevant that the government actually spent more of its own funds than tribal funds on education over the years?[39]

The issue of unwise disbursements was not limited to education. During the 1880s, when government agents procured the tribes' agreement to sell most of northern Montana, they informed the starving Indians that cattle-raising was their best hope for economic self-sufficiency. Despite these representations, only a small percentage of the funds of the Blackfeet and Belknap Indians was used to buy breeding stock or otherwise to develop a ranching industry. The few head of stock purchased with treaty money quickly disappeared. The Indians' attorneys charged that Superintendent Logan, who administered the reservation from 1902 to 1910 and who sought to foster widescale market agriculture at Fort Belknap, "deliberately destroyed the livestock industry." Without going that far, Barry, the government's historian, acknowledged that most of the agents until the 1930s concentrated on converting Indians into yeoman farmers rather than ranchers, and spent far more of the Indians' funds to further crop agriculture than ranching. These efforts, Barry summarized, were doomed from the beginning:

> Federal Indian policy required assimilation of the Indian people to the image of the small, independent farmer, an idea formed in the humid east and unsuited to the semi-arid Milk River Valley. The concept of the Indian as yeoman farmer on a small tract of land could not succeed. Equally unsuited to the area were seeds, irrigation techniques, and machines employed in the Valley by the Indian Service.[40]

Despite Barry's assessment that the agricultural efforts were futile, the United States, its attorneys stated, is not an insurer. "We are dealing with frontier times in an inhospitable part of northern Montana where nature itself could bring the wheels of progress to a grinding halt." Even if the government's management did not result in "absolute successes," as long as an ordinarily prudent person of that time period managing his own affairs reasonably could have made the same decisions, the United States had met its obligations, and should not be held liable.[41]

The tribes' attorneys hoped that the Commission would find the United States liable for whole classes of disbursements, such as all moneys spent on education and agriculture, based on the historical proof. The alternative was virtually inconceivable. The Commission would have to analyze each of the thousands of disbursements made over more than half a century to determine which ones were fraudulent, wasteful, benefited the government, or were otherwise improper under the applicable burdens of proof. And anyone reviewing the tens of thousands of pages of evidence knew that sufficient proof no longer existed.

. . .

The fiscal claims alone made the tribes' claims almost impossibly complex. However, they were only one of the six types of claims that the Indians sought to prove at trial. The grazing claims also raised novel legal and virtually insoluble evidentiary problems.

The tribes maintained that the government had mismanaged the reservations' range resources in three fundamental ways. Throughout the reservations' history, the government had allowed thousands of head of cattle owned by non-Indian ranchers to be driven across or graze upon the reservations without collecting any penalties, despite a statutory provision permitting a fine of one dollar per head for trespassing stock. Although some level of trespass was essentially undisputed by the government's attorneys, how could the parties estimate the extent of or place a value on trespasses occurring almost one hundred years before without adequate records? [42]

Second, after the government required non-Indian ranchers to obtain permits for the privilege of grazing stock on reservations, its agents allegedly had charged insufficient fees for them. However, proving what the government should have charged was not easy. Just as no comparable parcels existed with which to determine the value of aboriginal land purchased by the United States, no truly comparable parcels existed to evaluate the permit prices. Contiguous landholdings of state governments, railroads, and private citizens generally were much smaller than Indian reservations. National forests and national parks were comparable in size to Indian reservations, but stock grazing was prohibited in the parks, and the Department of Agriculture leased national forests at prices far below market value because of political pressures, just as it does today.

Finally and potentially most important, the government had allowed the ranges to be damaged through overgrazing, thereby reducing the number of head of stock that could be grazed upon them. The threshold, technical issue of whether the range had been depleted and, if so, how severely, was complex enough. On top of that, the government contended that range management was in its infancy during the early twentieth century. Researchers in the Forest Service were still developing range management principles while the supposed overgrazing was occurring. It was unfair, said the U.S. attorneys, to hold the government liable when its management accorded with contemporaneous private grazing practices. But repeated observations by the government's own inspectors that the range was being overgrazed undermined this argument.[43]

The government's point raised a legal conundrum. A detailed study of western range conditions conducted during the 1930s concluded that, overall, the carrying capacity of Indian reservations had been reduced by about the same percentage as the carrying capacity of private lands, indicating that the government did no worse job than the average private landowner. On the other hand, the national forests managed by the Forest Service were in far better condition, on average, than Indian reservations. Should the government's management be measured against its own expertise or the practices of typical private ranchers? And what if the overgrazing resulted from the large herds of wild horses the Indians maintained as status symbols despite repeated government programs to get rid of them, since they ate the same grasses as the officially sanctioned cattle? Was the government obligated to exterminate the horses over Indian opposition, or to accept the presence of horses and reduce the number of cattle?

Aside from these conceptual issues, evidentiary difficulties were staggering. The attorneys and expert witnesses in the Blackfeet-Belknap case could not analyze data that either had never been created or no longer existed. It was all very well for the tribes to say that the carrying capacity of the range had declined, but under the American legal system, a plaintiff normally has to identify what the defendant has done wrong. Should a range fence have been built in one place instead of another? Should water basins have been built so that the stock could use the range better? Was stock permitted to graze certain ranges in winter that were better suited to summer grazing? Did permittees graze more stock than allowed under their permits, thereby putting the range at risk? [44]

·   ·   ·

The Commission rushed to complete its business by September 30, 1978, but as the witching hour arrived, almost three years after the trial of the accounting claims, it still hadn't issued any decision in the Belknap-Blackfeet case. A partial draft was completed, but the Commission ultimately focused its energies on cases easier to resolve.

Uncompleted Indian Claims Commission cases were transferred to the Court of Claims. The consolidated Belknap and Blackfeet claims were assigned to Trial Judge John Wiese, and like the Commission, he faced a daunting task: he had to wade through volumes of proposed findings, briefs and trial transcripts and exhibits, and fabricate new legal principles to cover all the novel issues raised by the parties. And unlike the Commission, he had no experience with Indian claims to inform his work.[45]

After studying the record for over a year, Judge Wiese knew how he wanted the case resolved. At a conference held in early 1980, he encouraged the parties to resume settlement negotiations, which had been started several times before and aborted. This time, however, a change in the attitude of the Department of Justice toward the settlement of Indian claims assisted the judge's efforts. After three decades Ralph Barney had retired as head of the Indian Claims Section. He was succeeded by Donald Mileur, who shared Barney's hostility toward settling Indian claims. But Mileur quickly was replaced by Richard Beal, the attorney who had opposed the Weissbrodts in the Chiricahua imprisonment case. Beal and his superior, Anthony Liotta, were anxious to settle Indian claims in general, and accounting claims in particular. Within a year the parties had agreed to a settlement. In total, they agreed that the United States would pay the Assiniboine tribe about $2,170,000, the Gros Ventre tribe about $2,095,000, and the Blackfeet tribe $10,000,000.[46]

Settlement of accounting and mismanagement claims became the rule. Attorneys blanched at the prospect of litigating these all but impossible cases, and the trial judges of the Court of Claims (now called the Court of Federal Claims) strongly encouraged settlement. Most of the accounting cases were settled by 1982. Only in several cases since 1980 has a judge issued even an interlocutory decision.

Like other tribes, the two groups of Chiricahuas negotiated settlements of their accounting claims, without any trials or briefs except in the *Mescalero–Te Moak* case. The Oklahoma Chiricahuas had only minimal claims, making settlement easy. After their eviction from Fort Sill in 1913, they didn't have any tribal property or funds, and as had been established in 1949, individuals couldn't bring claims under the Indian Claims Commission Act. The Apaches on the Mescalero Reservation had valuable range and forest resources and tribal moneys, all of which they alleged had been mismanaged. Neither party wished to spend countless years in litigation, and the Weissbrodts and the government's attorneys used the few court decisions as very rough guidelines to predict the outcome. In 1980 they arrived at a figure of $2 million, a settlement accepted by the Mescalero tribe. This settlement concluded the claims of the Chiricahua Apaches. No court passed judgment on the propriety of the government's actions in managing their resources and funds, just as no court had evaluated the propriety of the government's actions in imprisoning the tribe for twenty-seven years.[47]

In a judicial context, settlement of these impossible-to-litigate cases was the only means of resolution that made sense. It meant that, as with the land claims, every tribe that had asserted accounting and misman-agement claims prior to August 13, 1951, recovered a moderate amount. Whether it was more or less than they would have recovered after years of litigation from courts making scores of simplifying and distorting as-sumptions is unknowable.

. . .

Negotiated resolutions of the accounting and mismanagement cases may have been prudent, but they came at a significant cost. The information gathered in litigating the cases could have greatly enhanced this coun-try's knowledge of the early twentieth-century federal Indian policies and their contribution to the deterioration of most tribes. To try the cases, each party would have engaged historians, accountants, and econ-omists to synthesize voluminous information about the reservation years, presented it in a series of reports, and cross-examined the other party's experts. Our collective knowledge about these crucial years would have increased enormously.

The knowledge would have been humbling. A series of policies, many undertaken with good intentions, had not worked to improve In-dians' affairs, regardless of the criteria used. An inspector for the Senate Subcommittee on Indian Affairs in the 1930s discussed some of the problems at Fort Belknap:

> My inspection . . . failed to reveal any real foundation for self-congratu-lation on the part of Indian Bureau officials. As a matter of fact, agricul-ture among the Fort Belknap Indians is retro-grading; the livestock industry has practically disappeared; their tribal fund has been almost completely dissipated without any tangible results; administrative mat-ters at the agency were in a chaotic condition . . . and the Indians themselves are . . . in a semidestitute condition which is showing itself in an abnormally high death rate.[48]

The plaintiffs' historical expert attempted to summarize the conditions at Fort Belknap in 1955, exactly one century after the government's management began. It was a bleak picture:

> Long after World War II, the Fort Belknap Indians owned little more than their grandparents had in 1887—the residue of the lands remaining after cessions to the United States. Now, these lands were covered with mortgages and most Indians were debt-ridden. . . . [I]t was a community which had an unpromising future, a future which had been mortgaged by the mistakes of the past.[49]

These descriptions were most unusual in Indian claims cases. Except in the cases brought by the Aleuts and the Belknap and Blackfeet tribes, the Commission—and perforce the Court of Claims—was almost never forced to consider the deplorable condition of the majority of Indians during the first half of the twentieth century, a condition for which governmental policies were largely to blame. The tribunals established to right the wrongs committed prior to 1946—like almost all white Americans to this day—knew almost nothing of the lives of Indians after they had been forced onto reservations.

This widely shared ignorance makes it easy for simplistic policy solutions to be advanced to address the intractable problems that the Indian Claims Commission Act did not resolve or even reduce.

TWELVE

DISTRIBUTION OF THE AWARDS

Money is like muck, not good except it be spread.
—Sir Francis Bacon

In all, the Indian Claims Commission awarded tribes $818 million over its thirty-one years of existence. Through the end of 1994, when fewer than ten cases remained undecided, the Court of Claims has awarded tribes an additional $400 to $500 million in Indian Claims Commission Act cases, bringing the total to about $1.3 billion.[1]

As of 1980 about 1.5 million Native Americans lived in the United States, so the awards have averaged less than $1,000 apiece. In the lawsuit-happy United States of the late twentieth century, $1,000 per person is a pittance. Under an act passed in 1988, citizens of Japanese ancestry who were interned during World War II became eligible to receive $20,000 apiece, as well as a formal apology from Congress.[2]

Once tribes procured these judgments, they had to decide how to spend the money. For the most part, they followed Sir Francis Bacon's advice: they spread the money widely among their members.

.   .   .

After the Commission or Court of Claims entered a judgment, the United States Treasury set aside sufficient funds to pay the award. Unfortunately for the tribes, the Treasury is not like a bank from which an account holder may easily withdraw its funds. An appropriate government official must authorize the removal of funds from the Treasury, and governmental approval of a plan of distribution was required before an official could authorize the withdrawal of Indian judgment funds.

The requirement of governmental approval created a situation unique in all of Anglo-American jurisprudence: a *defendant* determined how a successful *plaintiff* could use the funds awarded from the defendant. The incongruity was all the more striking for awards in accounting cases. The power to dictate how funds would be distributed arose out of the United States' continuing role as Indians' trustee, even though, in the accounting cases, the government paid money to compensate tribes for its shortcomings in that role.

The procedures by which the government devised, evaluated, and approved distribution plans changed over the years, as did the purposes that the plans were designed to achieve. During the 1950s, Congress enacted legislation after each award authorizing a plan for the distribution of the money. Although there were no set procedures, apparently officials of the Bureau of Indian Affairs generally consulted with some tribal members and drafted legislation for Congress. Little was needed in terms of procedures because there were few final awards and because there was little disagreement about how they should be distributed. Most of the acts provided for the distribution of the entire award, less attorneys' fees and expenses, equally among tribal members. Generally no money went to the tribal governments for use on tribal projects. Tribal members wanted the money, and these "per capita" distribution plans were consistent with the prevailing federal policy of terminating the special relationship between the United States and Indian tribes and ending the tribal way of life for Native Americans.[3]

But in 1961, the assistant secretary of the Interior Department enunciated a new strategy in a congressional hearing to consider a plan of distribution for the Omaha tribe of Nebraska: "We believe that a judgment recovered by an Indian tribe should ordinarily be regarded as a tribal asset, and that the individual members of the tribe have no right to a per capita distribution. The money should be programmed as other tribal funds. Exceptions will need to be made, of course, when the tribe that recovers the judgment does not have a cohesive membership or organization." The plan thus divided recipients of awards into two groups. For descendants of aboriginal groups most of whose members didn't live on or near a reservation, such as the Fort Sill Apaches or the Indians of California, awards would continue to be distributed primarily per capita. In much of the country outside the Southwest, more than half of many tribes' members live off reservations. Under those circumstances, if awards were spent by modern tribal organizations, the tribal members located far from the reservations would probably realize few benefits. But the Interior Department intended to push for a very different disposition of awards made to aboriginal tribes most of whose members lived on or near a reservation, such as the Mescalero, Chiricahua, and Lipan Apaches who were members of the Mescalero Tribe of the Mescalero Reservation, as well as awards to the modern tribe itself, such as for accounting claims. Those awards, the Interior Department maintained, should be devoted primarily, if not solely, to tribal projects.[4]

The Interior Department's new policy for the distribution of awards was part of the general shift away from termination and toward the strengthening of tribal institutions. The practice, however, fell short of the policy. Even for tribes whose members lived primarily on or near the reservation, generally only about 20 percent of the money was devoted to tribal programs. The balance of the awards was distributed per capita.[5]

In 1973, the procedures for deciding upon and approving distribution plans were revised. The Indian Claims Commission Act had been enacted largely to save Congress the time and effort consumed by considering special jurisdictional acts for each tribe. As the pace of adjudication in the Indian Claims Commission accelerated during the 1960s, Congress, and particularly the committees dealing with Indian affairs, could not keep up with the demand for distribution acts that followed each award. Long delays in getting funds to the tribal beneficiaries resulted, and consideration of more substantive Indian legislation was postponed. In the early 1970s about half the time of the House and Senate subcommittees dealing with Indian affairs was devoted to consideration of distribution acts. Despite all of that work, Congress in 1973 still had a backlog of over thirty tribes awaiting distribution acts.[6]

To eliminate this legislative overload, Congress in October 1973 enacted the Distribution of Judgment Funds Act, applicable to all tribes. This act, which was amended in 1983, requires the secretary of the interior to prepare and submit to Congress a plan for distribution of each award within a specified time after a judgment is entered (since 1983, this has been a year, with the possibility of a 180-day extension). Unless Congress disapproves the plan within 60 days, the plan becomes effective. Between 1973 and 1983 a resolution passed by either house of Congress was sufficient to express disapproval; since 1983 a joint resolution has been required.[7]

These procedures constitute a workable, albeit unconstitutional, compromise between no congressional involvement and the requirement that Congress enact a plan for distribution. In 1983, the Supreme Court ruled unconstitutional a provision in an immigration statute that, like the Distribution of Judgment Funds Act, allowed one house of Congress to block an administrative action by disapproving of it. The Court reasoned that when Congress "vetoed" an administrative action it effectively legislated, but the Constitution allows Congress to legislate only by passing an act and, if the president vetoes the act, by overriding the veto with a two-thirds majority. In response, Congress amended the immigration act, the Distribution of Judgment Funds Act, and other legislation to require disapproval by a resolution adopted by both houses of Congress. Like a one-house veto, however, a congressional resolution is not subject to presidential veto.[8]

·   ·   ·

Congress has not tried to use its veto power over a plan of distribution, in part because the procedures and criteria created in October 1973 reduce the bases for viable disputes over a distribution plan. The act requires the Department of the Interior to provide "legal, financial, and other expertise" to assist a tribe receiving an award to prepare a distribution plan. Moreover, the department must hold a public hearing after appropriate notice to obtain the testimony of tribal leaders and members concerning the use of the funds and to assure that the desires of any dissenting members of the tribe are fully considered. These provisions, if followed, vitiate any complaints from tribal members that they didn't have an opportunity to voice their opinions about distribution of an award.[9]

More important for this book, the Distribution of Judgment Funds Act also establishes guidelines for plans for distribution of funds. A "significant portion" of any judgment, but not less than 20 percent, must be devoted to "common tribal needs" or other tribal purposes unless the secretary of the interior determines that the particular circumstances of a tribe clearly warrant less. The 1983 amendments to the act didn't alter this requirement.[10]

During congressional hearings concerning the act, the Department of the Interior urged that the 20 percent figure be increased to 25 percent. Even 25 percent represented a huge retreat from the official 100 percent goal. Congress, however, knew that many tribes, not just those with members scattered off-reservation, wanted to distribute the entirety of awards per capita, and enshrined the 20 percent compromise.[11]

Despite the department's desire to allocate as much of the awards as possible to tribal programs, it continued to allow tribes with scattered members to distribute the entirety of awards per capita. The Fort Sill Apaches, for example, were able to convince the Department of the Interior that, with no reservation and members dispersed around the country, all of their share of the aboriginal land and trespass awards the Weissbrodts obtained during the 1970s should be distributed per capita.

Tribes generally opted to distribute as much money as permitted per capita primarily because individual tribal members wanted to decide themselves how their share of the money would be spent. Officials in the Bureau of Indian Affairs, with their lingering racist and paternalistic attitudes, objected to the per capita distributions because they believed that the individuals squandered their money at the invitation of merchants who extended easy credit terms.[12]

Most tribes may also have chosen per capita payments due to a well-placed mistrust of the federal government. The secretary of the interior openly informed Congress in 1971 that payment of Indian claims would not be a net loss because applying judgment funds to existing federal programs would reduce the need for further funding of those programs. Carried to its logical extreme, this also would mean that the Indians would realize no net benefits from the claims. If the government already were paying $10 million a year toward activities on a reservation and, after the tribe received a $4 million judgment, the government reduced its support to $6 million, the Indians' condition would not have been improved at all. At least if the money were spent quickly on items that the government had not previously been providing, tribal members would be assured of some benefit.[13]

Finally, Indians' decisions to distribute money per capita reflected a lack of faith in tribal governments and the political weakness of most tribal leaders. As has been shown, most tribes had no native institutions that were distinctly governmental; those institutions generally did not exist until the 1930s, when they were imposed in a constitutional form foreign to Indian cultures. Even when tribal governments began to expand their spheres of activity in the 1960s, the Bureau of Indian Affairs placed significant restraints on them. It is not surprising then that most tribal members preferred to have money under their personal control rather than that of the still-novel tribal governments of uncertain authority.[14]

More recently, Congress has shown less restraint in dictating how funds have been distributed. The Indian Gaming Regulatory Act of 1988 permits tribes to operate gambling enterprises under defined circumstances. For about two hundred tribes, gambling has brought significant income for the first time since they were placed on reservations, especially if a tribe's land is located within a few hours of a major metropolitan area. The Gaming Act, however, requires the tribes to spend gambling revenue on specified types of social, welfare, and economic-assistance programs, and many tribes, not just the Pequots as discussed in Chapter Nine, have used gambling revenues to improve the lives of tribal members significantly. In early 1996, only about 10 percent of the tribes operating gambling enterprises were distributing any of the profits per capita. The federal government has justified cutbacks in assistance programs to Indians by citing the gambling earnings applied to social, welfare, and economic programs, one of the benefits that government officials vainly had hoped to realize from the Indian Claims Commission Act.[15]

·   ·   ·

Possibly Indian Claims Commission Act awards would have improved Indians' lives more if they hadn't been distributed per capita, but the method of distribution was not the major problem. The size of the awards was. Gambling has had a more positive impact on the quality of life on reservations than did the Indian Claims Commission Act primarily because tribal income from it reached over $4 billion in 1994 alone, more than two and a half times the total amount of the awards under the Indian Claims Commission Act.[16]

The recent history of the Apaches on the Mescalero Reservation helps to demonstrate that the distribution of Commission awards played at most a minor role in determining their impact. The Weissbrodts obtained $36 million in judgments between 1966 and 1981. In 1990 the reservation had about 3,200 tribal members. Thus, the awards averaged about $11,000 per person, many times greater than the national average under the Indian Claims Commission Act. After deduction of 10 percent for attorneys' fees, over $32 million remained for use by the Apaches.[17]

Wendell Chino, as head of the tribe, has proven adept at obtaining money from the federal government and elsewhere. With these funds as well as significant percentages of the Indian Claims Commission awards, Chino has led the tribe during the last few decades on a series of ambitious projects, exploiting the reservation's three major natural resources: timber, range, and natural beauty. The tribe runs its own logging industry and maintains a herd of six thousand to seven thousand head of beef cattle. It has built and operates a four-hundred-room luxury resort hotel and casino, the Inn of the Mountain Gods, and a ski resort, Ski Apache. Other income has been devoted to a scholarship fund. The tribe has had money to try to improve the lives of its members.[18]

Yet the substantial amount of judgment funds and the enduring efforts of Chino and the tribal government have not lifted many of the people out of poverty. The tribal industries don't create enough jobs, and little private business has developed on the reservation. Almost 50 percent of the reservation population lived below the poverty level as of the early 1990s. Desperate to bring additional income and employment to the reservation, Chino even has obtained by referendum the tribe's approval to negotiate the use of a corner of the reservation as a short-term repository for nuclear waste. The very willingness to consider such a possibility shows the straits in which the Mescalero tribe, including the descendants of the Chiricahua Apaches who fought for so many years to live in their homeland, still finds itself.[19]

THIRTEEN

AN END TO WILD JUSTICE

Lawyers reason from precedent—and call that reasoning.
—Paul J. Bohannan

While it was greeted with enthusiasm at the outset, the Indian Claims Commission, when it finally dissolved, had become little more than an unimportant sideshow in Indian affairs. Although all but a few tribes were happy to receive an award under the act, other issues—some legal but most of them political—were drawing far more attention. Tribes were seeking to gain greater control over their affairs and to develop continuing sources of revenue.

It is tempting to blame these disappointing results on individuals. To begin with, presidents repeatedly appointed commissioners who, while enjoying strong congressional backing, had little understanding of Indian cultures or practices. By and large, the judges on the Court of Claims from 1946 until the mid-1960s, most notably Benjamin Littleton, outshone the commissioners in their understanding of the unique issues and their imaginative resolution of them. In the 1970s, the commissioners surpassed the judges of the Court of Claims in their understanding of the issues, but the court was able to block the Commission from altering the pattern of decisions significantly. Towering over the whole process sat Supreme Court justices who were by and large uninterested in Indian claims, and whose only significant contribution was to assure that Indians would be paid in late-twentieth-century dollars for nineteenth-century wrongs.

Blame also could be heaped on many of the tribal attorneys. Almost all of them failed to state claims outside the scope of familiar legal concepts, and for claims that were brought, the quality of representation varied greatly. Ultimately, it fell to a few individuals—notably the lawyers of Wilkinson, Cragun & Barker, Weissbrodt and Weissbrodt and Z. Simpson Cox—to explore the limits of the Indian Claims Commission's jurisdiction.

.   .   .

To blame the individuals involved, however, is to obscure the fundamental problems with the Indian Claims Commission Act. The act asked lawyers for both the government and the tribes *and* lawyers who sat on the Commission and the courts to do the impossible. The judicial system was incapable of handling the Indian claims. It is ironic that Felix Cohen, who insightfully compared Indians to miners' canaries, was one of the two primary authors of an act that effectively placed tribes in that role again. By prosecuting their claims under the Indian Claims Commission Act, tribes unknowingly and unwillingly exposed the limits of the American legal system.

Conceptual differences between the types of injuries the tribes suffered and the types of injuries that generally give rise to lawsuits between non-Indians caused many of the difficulties for the legal system. The focus of the American legal system is on the individual in relation to other individuals and to the government. Groups of people in a common endeavor, such as a corporation or a church congregation, are considered as a legal individual. A corporation, like an individual, may sue when its property is injured or taken without its consent or if its agreements are breached. But the role that corporations and other groups play in instilling values, identity, and culture in what has been called "civil society" receives almost no protection. No employer could sue a state government for sponsoring a lottery that offered the possibility of instant riches without labor, and thus interfered with the values of hard work and loyalty that the company was trying to instill in its employees. Similarly, although the First Amendment protects the rights of individuals to freedom of religion and against an establishment of religion, no legal document protects the rights of religious groups to impart their values and beliefs.

The Commission and courts were unable to transform legal theories based on the rights of individuals in order to recognize the fundamental injury that tribal groups had suffered: the destruction of their identity and culture. The few tribes that sought compensation for this injury—notably, the Pimas and Maricopas, the Joseph Band, and the Chiricahuas—were rebuffed without a trial.

The attorneys and judges lacked the intellectual tools for resolving such claims, even though the language of the act seemed to give the Commission the authority to hear them under the fair and honorable dealings clause. If the Commission had considered the merits of such claims, it first would have had to reach a working definition of a "culture." Anthropologists, whose job it is to study culture, still argue over what it means.

Even assuming that "culture" could be defined, and the culture of a particular tribe adequately proved (probably through the testimony of anthropologists), a court would have to determine whether a tribe had a right in that culture that should be compensated if it was destroyed. Can culture be owned? Currently, many tribes are angry that New Age folk are adopting their own versions of various Indian ceremonies, from sweat lodges to elaborate prayers with Indian-style pipes. Natives insist that their culture is being "stolen," in some form akin to property. They claim that such usage will "mutate" the real ceremonies, weakening their restorative powers and impeding their transmission to a new generation. American law extends protection to intellectual property, but extending protection to a culture, or even to a generic form of its expression such as kachina dolls or a tribe's traditional basketry designs, would require a huge leap for American legal philosophy, some kind of copyrighting of a largely undefinable essence.

If a tribe had a compensable right in its culture, what would constitute sufficient damage or destruction of the culture to give rise to liability? In white society, the government might condemn a church that is in the way of a public highway, but no one would claim that the culture of the congregation had been destroyed. To a believer in Christianity, Judaism, or Islam, God isn't reachable only from a particular edifice. But if a mountain, by Indian thinking, does not simply house God but *is* God, a serious question exists: If the mountain is strip-mined, has the culture (and the god) been maimed, or destroyed?

The mere fact that tribal cultures changed after contact with Anglos certainly couldn't be sufficient to give rise to a claim. Plains Indian culture was never the same after the arrival of the Spanish horse and the gun, and Navajo culture shifted direction after the tribe started raising sheep. The tribes adopted these changes voluntarily. On the other hand, the Chiricahuas' entire way of life was forcibly disrupted by the United States Army after they were subdued. The former seems like adaptation, the latter like destruction. However, the boundary between voluntary and involuntary changes, and between adaptation and destruction, often blurs. Was Black Elk's devout acceptance of Christianity destructively forced upon him, or did he willingly accept it once he found it present?

Closely linked to the issue of what constitutes cultural damage or destruction is when it occurs. Was a culture severely damaged or destroyed when it could no longer be transmitted? Transmitted in whole or in part? What is a culture's unique core, without which it no longer exists?

The gap between the concepts of American law and native cultures was illustrated poignantly in the late 1970s when thieves absconded with some wooden objects, immortal deities that the Hopi Indians considered irreplaceable. The most severe charge that a U.S. attorney could propose against the unknown thieves (assumed to be Hopis who had then sold the objects into the international art market) was embezzlement. It was later learned that the stolen gods had been destroyed. So what American law called embezzlement was, to the Hopis, deicide, a concept unknown to American law. Had such an incident come before the Commission and courts, the jurists would have been equally befuddled.

Aboriginal land claims seemed to fit into the fabric of American law. Tribes, like corporate landowners, could bring suits alleging loss of or damage to their land. To a jurist, tribes stood in the same shoes as an individual landowner. But in reality, aboriginal tribes were not mere landowners. For most if not all of them, the very distinction between land and culture, or land and tribe, made no sense. Native peoples did not divide their world into economic, religious, political, and educational compartments. Each tribe's homeland was the core of its way of life. Virtually every mountain, stream, or other significant geographic feature had spiritual, historical, and psychological significance. The land and its resources directly provided a large percentage of every tribe's subsistence, and children learned their roles in the tribe by helping as the tribe gathered and hunted the land's riches. When the United States took part or all of a tribe's aboriginal land, it didn't just take something of monetary value; rather, it took a crucial means for the tribe to maintain its identity. From the tribal viewpoint, an Anglo-American lawyer's distinction between a claim for land taken and a claim for destruction of a culture made no sense.

The very idea of a land's market value also made no sense. Most Americans, including lawyers, understand land to be a form of property, a commodity that can be privately owned, bought, and sold. The American idea of property was not foreign to the great majority of Indian tribes, many of which engaged in trade involving handiwork, livestock, and other forms of "property." But few if any tribes saw land as constituting such property. It was not bought and sold. In the words of Tecumseh, "Sell a country! Why not sell the air, the clouds and the great sea, as well as the earth? Did not the Great Spirit make them all for the use of his children?"

To deal with the land claims in terms of the tribes' loss, the Commission would have had to treat those claims as cultural destruction claims, and again, that was something the judges and lawyers couldn't do. The Anglo and Indian perspectives couldn't be reconciled; the Indian's gave way. By authorizing only monetary evaluation and compensation of lost lands, the Indian Claims Commission Act turned aboriginal land into something it had never been: property.

. . .

Evidentiary problems, like the differences between white and Indian concepts, made the courts incapable of resolving the claims in a judicial manner. The size and complexity of the Indian claims, the passage of scores of years between the time of the alleged wrongs and the trials, and the nature of the evidence—all required the courts and Commission to modify traditional notions of proof.

Aboriginal land claims presented one set of problems. No written records identified the lands used before the coming of Europeans. Oral traditions might identify geographical features within a tribe's aboriginal landholdings, but under judicial evidentiary rules such traditions consti-

tuted the rankest form of hearsay. Attorneys spent months poring
through old archives for contemporaneous records by non-Indians, but
no amount of documentation guaranteed accuracy. The authors' ignorance of Indian languages and societies made any of their observations
highly suspect. The lawyers balanced these evidentiary inadequacies by
relying on expert witnesses (primarily anthropologists and historians) to
an unprecedented extent during the 1950s and the 1960s, but their testimony was really no more dependable than the fragments of oral, written, and physical information available to them.

While these scholarly experts lent a veneer of plausibility to deter-
minations of the boundaries, nothing could do that for the Commission's valuations of the lands. Real estate appraisers could perform
painstaking research—and some gathered remarkable information about
economic conditions during the nineteenth century—but the bottom
line was that there was *no* market for such vast tracts of undeveloped
land on the outskirts of the country's frontier. The Commission could
pick almost any value between rival opinions with equal justification.

The accounting and mismanagement claims presented the paradox
of both too much and too little evidence. In typical trust-fund cases the
wisdom of even a hundred-dollar disbursement by a private trustee can
generate many pages of documentary evidence and argumentation. The
government made thousands of disbursements from the trust funds of
several of the larger tribes, and any attempt to analyze the claims at that
level would have overwhelmed the attorneys and the tribunal. Out of
necessity, they resorted to analysis based on broad categories. The result
was rough justice at best, but even that was hard to come by thanks to a
crucial paucity of information.

For the most part, the only explanation of payments or projects on
any reservation came from the government's supervisory agent in correspondence and reports to the commissioner of Indian affairs. Generally,
those documents trumpeted the wise and valiant efforts of his employees to make their native charges self-supporting. Perhaps the most accurate picture of reservation affairs came when agents turned over. The
successor frequently painted a highly critical picture of his predecessor's
efforts. On many reservations, however, such turnover was too infrequent to provide much illumination.

Resource mismanagement claims presented much the same story.
Few agents gave meaningful information about the specific conditions

they confronted, and there were too many management decisions, over too long a period, for a small number of lawyers, experts, and judges to analyze the wisdom of even a small percentage of them adequately.

. . .

The third fundamental problem with the Indian Claims Commission Act was its susceptibility to political manipulation. In one sense, this was unavoidable: virtually all legal doctrines further important policy objectives. Sometimes this is overt, as with environmental or worker protection legislation. More often, legal doctrines evolve through a series of judicial decisions issued over a long period of time, thus mirroring changing public policies. The multitude of courts inhibits the facile adoption of a single set of principles to govern a particular type of dispute.

The multiplicity of plaintiffs and defendants and the dialogue among judges from which legal doctrines generally evolve weren't present for the Indian claims. On one side stood the United States Treasury, and ultimately the tens of millions of taxpayers; on the other, about one million of the poorest, most isolated people in the country, asking not for present reforms, but for large damages for what had happened to their ancestors. With those contestants, the quality of the legal representation and the strength of the legal arguments had relatively little to do with the outcomes. The judiciary had to make sure the tribes recovered—otherwise the congressional purpose to rid itself of the claims would be frustrated—but not enough to hurt taxpayers seriously. By restricting the claims to a commission with a deadline on its life, and limiting the right of appeal to the specialized Court of Claims, Congress facilitated the development of doctrines consistent with these goals and ensured that they would be applied to all tribes. When the Supreme Court or the Court of Claims adopted a principle that blocked recovery under a novel theory, no other tribe could seek another, perhaps friendlier, forum.

Finally, the Indian Claims Commission Act restricted the Commission to awarding only monetary relief. The possibility of other types of relief, such as land restoration or improved educational facilities, would surely have increased the act's significance to the Indians and fanned tribal enthusiasm. The Yakimas and Taos Pueblos used interlocutory decisions from the Commission to help pry land restorations from the political branches (Chapter Nine). The Sioux and the Western Shoshone, by contrast, tried too late to reclaim land, and ended up with monetary awards that they neither wanted nor, to date, have collected.

.   .   .

Ironically underlying these four fundamental flaws was the same attitude that underlay many of the earlier wrongs that came before the Commission. As with the General Allotment Act sixty years earlier, Congress decided that a single program would serve as a panacea for all tribes, regardless of how distinct. The program would implement the white man's method of resolving disputes—which is to say, adjudication—rather than the widespread Indian approach of mediation. The lawyers who presented and decided the cases would be overwhelmingly white men, and the only remedy would be the white man's favorite—money.

Congressional proponents of the Indian Claims Commission Act during the 1940s argued that its work would permit the budget of the Bureau of Indian Affairs to be drastically reduced, because the awards would help tribes or individual Indians to become self-supporting. The appropriation for the Bureau for the fiscal year ending June 30, 1947, was about $40 million; for the fiscal year ending September 30, 1995, it has skyrocketed to over $1.7 billion. Even allowing for inflation, clearly the act did not have the desired effect. The BIA's budget has mushroomed despite the work of the Indian Claims Commission, while the Indians have remained at the bottom of the socioeconomic heap.

Essentially, Congress hoped to solve an intractable social problem by having the judicial system make restitution for some of the government's actions. Unable to adjudicate the claims cases satisfactorily with established judicial doctrines, the Commission was reduced first to collecting historical and anthropological information and then to dispensing moderate sums to the tribes. The agency's unlamented demise illustrates how badly the courts function as money dispensers when they are asked to adjudicate disputes that are beyond the limitations of the judicial process.

LOCATIONS OF
UNPUBLISHED MATERIALS

The unpublished materials cited in this book can be found in several locations. Most are located at the National Archives in Washington, D.C. The archives contain not only the records of the military and civil authorities who dealt with American Indians during the nineteenth and twentieth centuries, but also records of Indian claims proceedings before the Indian Claims Commission and the Court of Claims. Unpublished documents at the National Archives have no special designation in the footnotes below.

We reviewed documents designated WF (for "Weissbrodt file") in over twenty boxes located in the attic of the offices of I. S. Weissbrodt in Washington, D.C. Many of the documents in that file can be found at the National Archives in Washington, D.C. The files have been microfilmed under a grant from the National Historical Publications and Records Commission. Weissbrodt has one set of the microfilmed copies, and according to the Commission's records, other sets were given to the Oklahoma Historical Society and the Fort Sill Apache Tribe.

We also relied on documents located at four presidential libraries. Documents designated HST, DDE, LBJ, and RMN were obtained from the presidential libraries of Harry S. Truman, Dwight D. Eisenhower, Lyndon B. Johnson, and Richard M. Nixon, respectively.

Copies of nineteenth-century newspapers and most of the secondary sources cited in the footnotes can be found at the Library of Congress.

NOTES

ONE: Wild Justice

1. A. Riding, *Distant Neighbors: A Portrait of the Mexicans* (New York: Alfred A. Knopf, 1985), 26–29.
2. E. Spicer, *Cycles of Conquest: The Impact of Spain, Mexico, and the United States on the Indians of the Southwest, 1533–1960* (Tucson: University of Arizona Press, 1962), 152–69.
3. Riding, *Distant Neighbors,* 30; Spicer, *Cycles of Conquest,* 16, 152, 229–31; R. Brown, *Historical Geography of the United States* (New York: Harcourt, Brace & Co., 1948), 68–86.
4. Gordon Baldwin, *The Warrior Apaches* (Tucson: Dale King, 1965), 21; Spicer, *Cycles of Conquest,* 161–62, 166, 236–39.
5. Garrick and Roberta Bailey, *A History of the Navajos: The Reservation Years* (Seattle: University of Washington Press, 1986), 11–13; Baldwin, *The Warrior Apaches,* 14–15.
6. Baldwin, *The Warrior Apaches,* 15–16.
7. Morris Opler, *An Apache Life Way: The Economic, Social and Religious Institutions of the Chiricahua Indians* (Chicago: University of Chicago Press, 1941), 18–19, 24–25, 462–71.
8. Baldwin, *The Warrior Apaches,* 16–17; Transcript of trial before Indian Claims Commission in Dockets 30 and 48 concerning taking of aboriginal lands (December 11, 1962) (testimony of Morris Opler), and 309 (December 13, 1962) (testimony of Alfred Thomas).
9. Opler, *Apache Life Way,* 332–34 (quoting informant).
10. Baldwin, *The Warrior Apaches,* 24–26; Spicer, *Cycles of Conquest,* 229.
11. David Roberts, *Once They Moved Like the Wind: Cochise, Geronimo and the Apache Wars* (New York: Touchstone, 1984), 48.
12. Baldwin, *The Warrior Apaches,* 25–26; Spicer, *Cycles of Conquest,* 238–39.
13. Baldwin, *The Warrior Apaches,* 24–27; Spicer, *Cycles of Conquest,* 236–41.
14. K. Jack Bauer, *The Mexican War 1846–1848* (New York: Macmillan, 1974).
15. Robert F. Berkhofer, *The White Man's Indian* (New York: Knopf, 1978), 165–66;

S. Tyler, *A History of Indian Policy* (Washington, D.C.: U.S. Department of the Interior, 1973), 35–36.

16. Report from Governor Lane to Commissioner of Indian Affairs Manypenny dated May 21, 1853 (WF); Annual Report of Agent Steck to Commissioner of Indian Affairs Denver dated August 7, 1857 (WF).

17. *The Arizona Miner,* May 25, 1864, p. 2, col. 3; Report from Lieutenant Mowry to Commissioner of Indian Affairs Denver dated November 10, 1857 (WF); Report of the Commissioner of Indian Affairs dated November 1, 1872, 3–4 (WF).

18. Elliott Arnold, "Cochise: Greatest of the Apaches," *Arizona Quarterly* 7 (1951), 5; Report of Major Steen to Captain McLaws dated March 24, 1850 (WF); Report of Commissioner of Indian Affairs Bartlett to Secretary of the Interior Stuart dated July 5, 1851 (WF); *The Arizona Citizen,* May 22, 1875, p. 1, col. 2.

19. Baldwin, *The Warrior Apaches,* 27, 29.

20. Treaty of July 1, 1852, ratified March 23, 1853, 10 Stat. 979; Compact between Governor Lane and Mimbres and Gila Apaches dated April 7, 1853 (WF); Letter from Commissioner of Indian Affairs Manypenny to Governor Lane dated April 9, 1853 (WF); Letter from Captain Gordon to Lieutenant Wilkins dated July 28, 1859 (WF).

21. Baldwin, *The Warrior Apaches,* 29–30; Dee Brown, *Bury My Heart at Wounded Knee: An Indian History of the American West* (New York: Holt, Rinehart & Winston, 1970), 211.

22. Virtually every book about the Chiricahua wars has a version of this story, each differing slightly depending on the sources on which each author relies. Among them are Baldwin, *The Warrior Apaches,* 30–31; Brown, *Bury My Heart,* 193–94; O. Faulk, *The Geronimo Campaign* (New York: Oxford University Press, 1969), 9–11; and Arnold, "Cochise," 6–7.

23. Brown, *Bury My Heart,* 190–95; Arnold, "Cochise," 7–10.

24. Faulk, *The Geronimo Campaign,* 57 (quoting J. Bourke, *On the Border with Crook* (New York: Charles Scribner's Sons, 1891).

25. J. Ross Browne, *Adventures in the Apache Country* (New York: Harper & Bros., 1869), 144.

26. Bailey & Bailey, *History of the Navajos,* 9–11.

27. Brown, *Bury My Heart,* 193–94.

28. Ibid., 194–95; Annual Report of Superintendent Norton to Commissioner of Indian Affairs dated August 24, 1867 (WF); Letter from General Carleton to Superintendent Steck dated March 16, 1865 (WF); Undated Letter from Superintendent Steck to Commissioner of Indian Affairs, presumably from late March 1865 (WF).

29. Indian Claims Commission transcript, 129 (testimony of Morris Opler) (N.A.)

30. Report of the Commissioner of Indian Affairs dated November 1, 1872, 3–6 (WF); Letter from Agent Drew to Superintendent Clinton dated September 29, 1869 (WF); Letter from Agent Drew to Superintendent Clinton dated February 28, 1870 (WF); Report from Agent Hennisee to Superintendent Clinton dated June 30, 1870 (WF); Annual Report from Agent Hennisee to Commissioner of Indian Affairs dated August 31, 1870 (WF).

31. Brown, *Bury My Heart,* 195–206; Arnold, "Cochise," 10–11; *The Arizona Citizen,* October 26, 1872, p. 2, col. 2.

32. Brown, *Bury My Heart,* 205–6; Report of Agent Jeffords to Commissioner of Indian Affairs dated August 31, 1873 (WF). A historian testifying before the Indian Claims

Commission estimated that at mid-century the Chiricahuas probably numbered about three thousand. Transcript, 309 (testimony of Alfred Thomas). If each band had one-third, each would have had about one thousand members. Corroboration comes from estimates that Cochise had about three hundred braves, Brown, 194; normally, warriors numbered about one quarter of a tribe's population. During 1873, after the Chiricahua Reservation had been established, up to 1,150 Chiricahuas, drawn from both the Central and Southern bands, received rations there. Report of Agent Jeffords to Commissioner of Indian Affairs dated August 31, 1873 (WF).

33. *The Arizona Citizen,* December 7, 1872, p. 1, col. 3; Brown, *Bury My Heart,* 206–7; Executive Order of December 14, 1872.

34. Report from General Crook to Assistant Adjutant General, December 13, 1872 (WF); *The Arizona Citizen,* December 13, 1873, p. 2, col. 2.

35. *The Arizona Citizen,* August 8, 1874, p. 2, col. 2; March 6, 1875, p. 1, col. 4; May 22, 1875, p. 1, cols. 2–3; Report from Agent Jeffords to Commissioner of Indian Affairs dated August 31, 1873 (WF).

36. Roberts, *Once They Moved,* 141–42; Alexander B. Adams, *Geronimo* (New York: Putnam, 1971), 195.

37. Faulk, *The Geronimo Campaign,* 14–16; Telegram from John L. Harris and Governor Safford to Commissioner of Indian Affairs Smith dated April 17, 1876 (WF); Letter from Commissioner of Indian Affairs Smith to Secretary of the Interior dated April 20, 1876 (WF); Special Report on Chiricahua Agency from Former Agent Jeffords to Commissioner of Indian Affairs dated October 3, 1876 (WF).

38. Faulk, *The Geronimo Campaign,* 14; J. Harte, *The San Carlos Indian Reservation, 1872–1886: An Administrative History,* vol. I, 314–18 (unpublished Ph.D. dissertation, 1972); *Arizona Citizen,* March 6, 1875, p. 1, col. 4; February 28, 1874, p. 2, col. 1; Shenon and Full, *An Appraisal of the Mineral Resources in the Lands of the Chiricahua Apache Tribe as Decided on June 28, 1968 Before the Indian Claims Commission* (unpublished expert report, December 1, 1969), 50–51 (WF).

39. Britton Davis, *The Truth About Geronimo* (New Haven: Yale University Press, 1929), 47–49; Faulk, *The Geronimo Campaign,* 16; Harte, *San Carlos Reservation,* 189–296, 324–32.

40. Report of Agent Hennisee to Superintendent of Indian Affairs Clinton dated August 31, 1870 (WF); Report of Agent Piper to Superintendent of Indian Affairs Pope dated August 31, 1872 (WF); Report of Agent Thomas to Commissioner of Indian Affairs dated August 31, 1874 (WF); Report of Agent Shaw to Commissioner of Indian Affairs dated September 1, 1875 (WF); Report of Agent Shaw to Commissioner of Indian Affairs dated September 1, 1876 (WF); Report of Agent Davis to Commissioner of Indian Affairs dated August 10, 1877 (WF).

41. Report of Agent Shaw to Commissioner of Indian Affairs dated September 1, 1875.

42. Faulk, *The Geronimo Campaign,* 17–18; Harte, *San Carlos Indian Reservation,* 354–70; Affidavit of Sam Hoazons dated December 16, 1950 (WF); Memorandum from Commissioner of Indian Affairs Smith to Secretary of the Interior dated July 22, 1876 (WF); Letter from Secretary of the Interior Chandler to Commissioner of Indian Affairs dated July 24, 1876 (WF).

43. Annual Report of the Commissioner of Indian Affairs to the Secretary of the Interior for the year 1876, vii; Annual Report of the Commissioner of Indian Affairs to the Secretary of the Interior for the year 1877 (WF), 20–21; Report from Late

Agent Clum to Commissioner of Indian Affairs dated September 18, 1877; Bourke, *On the Border with Crook,* 438–40; Brown, *Bury My Heart,* 377–78; Faulk, *The Geronimo Campaign,* 42–45.

44. Affidavit of James Kaywaykla dated January 12, 1951, 1–2 (WF); Brown, *Bury My Heart,* 375.

45. Brown, *Bury My Heart,* 376; Faulk, *The Geronimo Campaign,* 22–24.

46. Baldwin, *The Warrior Apaches,* 42–44; Affidavit of Alfred Chato dated July 19, 1928 (WF).

47. Faulk, *The Geronimo Campaign,* 145 (quoting General Miles).

48. Baldwin, *The Warrior Apaches,* 38–39; Brown, *Bury My Heart,* 376–77; Haozons [Haozous] Affidavit, 2; Affidavit of Talbot Gooday dated December 2, 1961, as recorded by Benedict Jozhe (WF).

49. Baldwin, *The Warrior Apaches,* 39–42; Brown, *Bury My Heart,* 377–81; Faulk, *The Geronimo Campaign,* 31–36.

50. Baldwin, *The Warrior Apaches,* 42–45; Brown, *Bury My Heart,* 379–81; Faulk, *The Geronimo Campaign,* 36.

51. Faulk, *The Geronimo Campaign,* 47–56; Kaywaykla Affidavit, 2 (WF); *Fort Sill Apache Tribe v. United States,* 25 Ind. Cl. Comm. 352, 366–69 (1971).

52. Faulk, *The Geronimo Campaign,* 57–85; Roberts, *Once They Moved,* 283; Haozons [Haozous] Affidavit, 3; Affidavit of Duncan Balatchu, Leonard Kaneswah, and Samuel E. Kenoi dated August 13, 1928 (WF).

53. Faulk, *The Geronimo Campaign,* 69–70, 77–80, 107–9; Affidavit of Stephen Kyzha, Arnold Kinzhonna, Joe Baheda, and Zozonnie dated August 15, 1928 (WF); Affidavit of Waldo Sunderman, Jim Miller, William Coonie, and Paul Gondelcon, Sr., dated August 11, 1928 (WF).

54. Faulk, *The Geronimo Campaign,* 85–91; Report from General Crook to General Sheridan dated March 27, 1886 (WF).

55. Faulk, *The Geronimo Campaign,* 91–94, 96; Telegram from General Sheridan to General Crook dated March 30, 1886 (WF); Letter from General Crook to General Sheridan dated March 30, 1886 (WF).

56. Faulk, *The Geronimo Campaign,* 94–96; Letter from General Crook to General Sheridan dated March 31, 1886 (WF).

57. Faulk, *The Geronimo Campaign,* 96–119; Letter from General Miles to Assistant Adjutant General dated July 17, 1886 (WF).

58. Letter from Governor Ross to Secretary of the Interior Lamar dated July 16, 1886 (WF).

59. Letter from Captain Dorst to the Adjutant General dated February 28, 1890 (WF).

60. Faulk, *The Geronimo Campaign,* 117–31.

61. Ibid., 133–50.

62. *Scott v. United States,* 33 Ct. Cl. 486, 488 (1898).

63. Faulk, *The Geronimo Campaign,* 161–62; Affidavit of Duncan Balatchu, Leonard Kaneswah, and Samuel E. Kenoi dated August 13, 1928 (WF).

64. Faulk, *The Geronimo Campaign,* 162–65.

65. Ibid., 166–74; Dispatch from President Cleveland, quoted in Orders from Acting Secretary of War Drum to General Miles dated August 25, 1886 (WF).

TWO: Imprisonment

1. W. Skinner, *The Apache Rock Crumbles* (Pensacola, FL: Skinner Publications, 1987), 114–21, 217.

2. Letter from Acting Secretary of War R. C. Drum to Lieutenant General of War, August 24, 1886 (WF); Letter from Colonel Loomis Langdon to Adjutant General, August 24, 1886 (WF).

3. Skinner, *The Apache Rock Crumbles,* 75–80, 100–107.

4. Letter from Dr. Horace Caruthers to Mr. Jesup, January 20, 1887 (WF); Report from Langdon to Assistant Adjutant General, October 1, 1886, reproduced in S. Ex. Doc. 73, 49th Cong., 2d Sess.; Indian Rights Association, *The Apache Prisoners in Fort Marion, St. Augustine* (1887) (WF).

5. F. Hoxie, *A Final Promise: The Campaign to Assimilate the Indians, 1880–1920* (Cambridge: Cambridge University Press, 1984), 54–63; Skinner, *The Apache Rock Crumbles,* 161–62.

6. Hoxie, *A Final Promise,* 54–63.

7. Skinner, *The Apache Rock Crumbles,* 137–38; Jason Betzinez, *I Fought with Geronimo* (New York: Bonanza, 1959), 149; Report of Langdon to Assistant Adjutant General, August 23, 1886, in S. Ex. Doc. 73, 49th Cong., 2d Sess.

8. Skinner, *The Apache Rock Crumbles,* 110, 113; Letter from Dr. Horace Caruthers to Mr. Jesup, January 20, 1887 (WF).

9. Memorandum entitled "Apache Prisoners of War" dated December 18, 1894, provided by the War Department to the Chairman of the House Committee on Military Affairs (WF).

10. Skinner, *The Apache Rock Crumbles,* 103–7, 121.

11. Report of Langdon to Assistant Attorney General, June 28, 1887 (WF); Skinner, *The Apache Rock Crumbles,* 148, 150.

12. O. Faulk, *The Geronimo Campaign* (New York: Oxford University Press, 1969), 207; Report from Langdon to Assistant Adjutant General, March 24, 1887 (WF).

13. D. Goodman, *Apaches as Prisoners of War, 1886–1894* (Ph.D. dissertation, 1969), 84–104.

14. Ibid., 104–8; Report from Colonel R. B. Ayres to Assistant Adjutant General, April 27, 1887 (WF); Special Order 92 of Major General Schofield, May 10, 1888 (WF).

15. Skinner, *The Apache Rock Crumbles,* 164–68; Letter from Secretary of War Proctor to Commissioner of Indian Affairs Morgan, August 15, 1889; H. Ex. Doc. 41, 51st Cong., 2d Sess. (1890); Proceedings of conference, September 21, 1911 (WF).

16. Skinner, *The Apache Rock Crumbles,* 176–77, 217; Report from Pratt to Commissioner of Indian Affairs, May 24, 1889 (WF).

17. Report from Lieutenant Wotherspoon to Secretary of War, March 24, 1894 (WF); S. Ex. Doc. 35, 51st Cong., 1st Sess. (1890), reprinting report of Lieutenant Guy Howard, December 23, 1889.

18. Senate Ex. Doc. 35, 51st Cong., 1st Sess. (1890).

19. Ibid.; see generally Goodman, *Apaches as Prisoners of War,* 118–93.

20. Undated historical sketch prepared by Adjutant General's office (WF); Skinner, *The Apache Rock Crumbles,* 282–89; Goodman, *Apaches as Prisoners of War,* 156–85.

21. Report of the Secretary of War for 1894, Vol. I, 26–27; Goodman, *Apaches as Prisoners of War,* 222; 26 *Cong. Rec.* 7367 (July 12, 1894).

22. E. McReynolds, *Oklahoma: A History of the Sooner State* (Norman, OK: University of Oklahoma Press, 1954), 109–40.

23. Ibid., 87–108, 140–65, 229–43.

24. S. Tyler, *A History of Indian Policy* (Washington, D.C.: U.S. Department of the Interior, 1973), 95–124.

25. McReynolds, *Oklahoma,* 278–307.

26. Skinner, *The Apache Rock Crumbles,* 396–97; Proceedings of conference, September 21, 1911 (WF).

27. Hugh Scott, *Some Memories of a Soldier* (New York: Century, 1928), 187–88.

28. Betzinez, *I Fought with Geronimo,* 166–67; Skinner, *The Apache Rock Crumbles,* 397–98; Report from Scott to Adjutant General, October 31, 1896 (WF).

29. Agreement of February 17, 1897 (WF).

30. Report from Scott to Adjutant General, October 31, 1896 (WF); Report of Captain Farrand Sayre to Adjutant General, June 30, 1902 (WF); Letter from Colonel Scott to Commissioner of Indian Affairs, January 11, 1912 (WF); Skinner, *The Apache Rock Crumbles,* 398.

31. Report of Special Agent Frank Armstrong to the Secretary of the Interior, December 17, 1901 (WF); Report of Inspector Randlett to Commissioner of Indian Affairs, June 2, 1903 (WF).

32. Letter from the Secretary of the Interior to the Honorable Moses Clapp, Chairman of the Senate Committee on Indian Affairs, included in S. Rep. No. 379, 61st Cong., 2d Sess. (1910).

33. Memorandum for the Annual Report of the Adjutant General for 1900 (WF); Memorandum of Major General J. F. Bell to Captain W. M. Wright, July 9, 1907 (WF); Proceedings of conference held September 21, 1911 (WF); Skinner, *The Apache Rock Crumbles,* 447.

34. Report of Captain Farrand Sayre, July 2, 1902 (WF); H. Rep. No. 489, 62d Cong., 2d Sess. (1912); Census of the Apache Prisoners of War, Fort Sill, Oklahoma, December 1, 1912 (WF).

35. McReynolds, *Oklahoma,* 304–7; Report of Special Agent Frank Armstrong to the Secretary of the Interior, December 17, 1901 (WF); Report of Captain Sayre, June 30, 1902 (WF); Report of Colonel Crowder, December 29, 1903 (WF); Letter from Colonel Scott to Commissioner of Indian Affairs, January 11, 1912 (WF).

36. Faulk, *The Geronimo Campaign* 209–14; Skinner, *The Apache Rock Crumbles,* 423–33; Betzinez, *I Fought with Geronimo,* 198.

37. Report from Colonel Scott to Adjutant General, August 30, 1902 (WF); Report from Colonel Scott to Secretary of War, November 3, 1911 (WF).

38. Letter from George Grinnel to Secretary of War, November 12, 1903 (WF); Memorandum from Secretary of War to Secretary of the Interior, December 20, 1903 (WF); Report of Colonel E. H. Crowder, December 29, 1903 (WF); Report from Captain Sayre to Adjutant General, February 17, 1904 (WF); Letter from George Grinnel to Secretary of War, February 24, 1904 (WF).

39. Letter from Representative Ferris to Carmi Thompson, Second Assistant Secretary of the Interior, January 6, 1912 (WF).

40. Proceedings of conference, September 21, 1911 (Betzinez) (WF).

41. Report from Major Goode to Colonel Scott, October 17, 1911 (WF); Letter from Colonel Scott to Commissioner of Indian Affairs, January 11, 1912 (WF).

42. Proceedings of conference, September 21, 1911 (Daklugie) (WF).

43. Letter from the Secretary of the Interior to the Honorable Moses Clapp, Chairman of the Senate Committee on Indian Affairs, included in S. Rep. No. 379, 61st Cong., 2d Sess. (1910); Letter from the Secretary of the Interior to John Stephens, Chairman of the House Committee on Indian Affairs, May 9, 1912 (WF).

44. Proceedings of conference, September 21, 1911; Betzinez, *I Fought with Geronimo,* 147.

45. Minutes of conference between James McLaughlin and Mescalero Apaches held June 26, 1909 (WF); Letter from Secretary of War to Representative Scott Ferris, January 23, 1911 (WF); Betzinez, *I Fought with Geronimo,* 195.

46. Undated Memorandum of Board of Indian Commissioners prepared on or after November 1, 1911; Letter from the Secretary of War to the Secretary of the Interior, January 23, 1911 (WF); Memorandum from Colonel Scott to Chief of Staff, November 6, 1911 (WF); Letter from Representative Ferris to the Secretary of the Interior, April 28, 1912 (WF).

47. S. 6776 and H.R. 24326, 62d Cong., 2d Sess. (1912).

48. Letter from Senator Catron to the Secretary of War and the Secretary of the Interior, December 30, 1912 (WF).

49. 48 *Cong. Rec.* 11336-37 (August 19, 1912); *The Philadelphia Record,* March 10, 1912, 3.

50. Act of August 24, 1912, ch. 388, 37 Stat. 518, 534, § 18 (1934); Report of Colonel Scott and Lieutenant Stecker to Adjutant General, October 16, 1912 (WF); Letter from S. M. Brosius of Indian Rights Association to Commissioner of Indian Affairs, October 17, 1912 (WF).

51. Report from Colonel Scott, H. C. Phillips, and C. L. Ellis to the Secretary of War and the Secretary of the Interior, December 2, 1912 (WF); Census of the Apache Prisoners of War, Fort Sill, Oklahoma, April 1, 1913 (WF).

THREE: A Tribunal for Indian Claims

1. William Lewis, "Is the American Indian Entitled to His Day in Court?" (pamphlet) (1926), 11.

2. Eve Ball, *Indeh: An Apache Odyssey* (Provo, UT: Brigham Young University Press, 1980), 135, 144.

3. W. Skinner, *The Apache Rock Crumbles* (Pensacola, FL: Skinner Publications, 1987), 470.

4. Shenon and Full, *An Appraisal of the Mineral Resources in the Lands of the Chiricahua Apache Tribe* (unpublished expert report for trial in Docket Nos. 30-A and 48-A, November 1969), 51, 86–87 (WF).

5. W. Cowen, P. Nichols, and M. Bennett, *The United States Court of Claims: A History—Part II: Origin—Development—Jurisdiction 1855–1978* (Washington, D.C.: Committee on the Bicentennial, 1978), 1–11.

6. Ibid., 12–15; W. Cowen, *A Symposium—Part I: The United States Court of Claims,* 55 Geo. L.J. 393, 393 (1966).

7. Cowen, Nichols, and Bennett, *Court of Claims,* 17–25; Cowen, *Symposium,* 393–94.

8. G. Wilkinson, *Indian Tribal Claims Before the Court of Claims,* 55 Geo. L.J. 511, 511–12 (1966).

9. Act of March 3, 1881, 21 Stat. 504.

10. E. Lazarus, *Black Hills, White Justice: The Sioux Nation Versus the United States 1775 to the Present* (New York: HarperCollins, 1991), 127–82.

11. *Confederated Bands of Ute Indians v. United States,* Affidavit of Ernest L. Wilkinson Respecting Attorneys' Services Rendered in the Above Captioned Cases executed October 26, 1950 (Ct. Cl. Nos. 45585, 46640, 47564, 47566), 2–3, 17–18, 29–31.

12. Hearings Before the Senate Committee on Indian Affairs on S. 2731, 74th Cong., 1st Sess. (testimony of Rufus Poole, Assistant Solicitor for Department of the Interior, June 10, 1935), 9–10.

13. Ibid.; *Ute Indians v. U.S.,* Affidavit of Ernest L. Wilkinson, 31, 57–58 n.12, 104; Hearings before the House Committee on Indian Affairs on H.R. 1198 and 1341, 79th Cong., 1st Sess. (statement of former senator Thomas Gore on March 3, 1945), 45.

14. *Ute Indians v. U.S.,* Affidavit of Ernest L. Wilkinson, Appendix 3; table compiled from data appended to letter from Commissioner of Indian Affairs William A. Brophy to Representative Henry M. Jackson dated October 2, 1945, reprinted in Hearings before the House Committee on Indian Affairs on H.R. 1198 and 1341, 79th Cong., 1st Sess., 163–75.

15. Senate Committee, S. 2731 hearings (testimony of Rufus Poole), 11–12.

16. Memorandum from Attorney George Stormont to Assistant Attorney General Blair dated March 3, 1934; 81 *Cong. Rec.* 6252 (June 23, 1937) (Representative Nichols of Oklahoma); 50 Stat. 650 (August 16, 1937).

17. Hearings before a Subcommittee of the Senate Committee on the Judiciary on S. 3083, 76th Cong., 3d Sess. (testimony of Ernest L. Wilkinson, February 14, 1940), 59–65.

18. Felix Cohen, *Handbook of Federal Indian Law* (Washington, D.C.: U.S. Department of the Interior, 1941), 373–78.

19. House Committee, hearings on H.R. 1198 and 1341 (testimony of attorney Paul Niebell), 31.

20. S. Tyler, *A History of Indian Policy* (Washington, D.C.: U.S. Department of the Interior, 1973), 125–39; J. Wise and V. Deloria, *The Red Man in the New World Drama: A Politico-Legal Study with a Pageantry of American Indian History* (New York: Macmillan, 1971), 357–60.

21. Letter from the Secretary of the Interior to Senator Elmer Thomas dated March 27, 1935; Senate Committee, hearings on S. 2731 (testimony of Rufus Poole), 15.

22. H.R. 7963, 71st Cong., 2d Sess. (introduced January 6, 1930); S. 3444, 73d Cong., 2d Sess. (introduced April 17, 1934); S. 1465, 74th Cong., 1st Sess. (introduced January 21, 1935).

23. The bills included: H.R. 6655, 74th Cong., 1st Sess. (1935); H.R. 7837, 74th Cong., 1st Sess. (1935); S. 2731, 74th Cong., 1st Sess. (1935); S. 1902, 75th Cong., 1st Sess. (1937); H.R. 5817, 75th Cong., 1st Sess. (1937); and S. 4206, 76th Cong., 3d Sess. (1940). S. 2731 passed the Senate July 29, 1935, 79 *Cong. Rec.* 11976. A companion bill, H.R. 7837, was reported favorably by the House Indian Affairs Committee, H. Rep. No. 1268, 74th Cong., 1st Sess. (1935), but no action was taken by the full House. S. Rep. No. 230, 75th Cong., 1st Sess. (March 23, 1937), 1. S. 1902 passed the Senate April 22, 1937, 81 *Cong. Rec.* 3717, but was defeated by the House June 23, 1937. 81 *Cong. Rec.* 6267. The quotations are found at 81 *Cong. Rec.* 6058 (June 21, 1937) and 81 *Cong. Rec.* 6243 (June 23, 1937).

24. *Ute Indians* v. *U.S.,* Affidavit of Ernest L. Wilkinson, 101; House Committee, hearings on H.R. 1198 and 1341, 81; Letter from Franklin Roosevelt to Secretary of the Interior Ickes dated August 18, 1941.

25. H.R. 1198, 79th Cong., 1st Sess. (1945); H.R. 1341, 79th Cong., 1st Sess. (1945); H.R. 4497, 79th Cong., 1st Sess. (1945); H. Rep. No. 1466, 79th Cong., 1st Sess. (1945).

26. Indian Claims Commission, Final Report 4 (September 30, 1978).

27. D. Fixico, *Termination and Relocation: Federal Indian Policy 1945–1960* (Albuquerque: University of New Mexico Press, 1986), 3–8; H. Rep. No. 1466, 79th Cong., 1st Sess. (1945), 2; 92 *Cong. Rec.* 5320 (May 20, 1946).

28. Fixico, *Termination and Relocation,* 15–20, 22–23, 28; H. Rep. No. 1466, 79th Cong., 1st Sess. (1945), 8; 92 *Cong. Rec.* 5314–15 (Representative Jackson), 5318 (Representative Stigler).

29. "Felix S. Cohen: July 3, 1907–October 19, 1953," *Rutgers L. Rev.* 9 (1954), 345, 346–48.

30. Feldman, "Felix S. Cohen and His Jurisprudence: Reflections on Federal Indian Law," *Buffalo L. Rev.* 35 (1986), 479, 497–503, 512–14.

31. *Ute Indians* v. *U.S.,* Affidavit of Ernest L. Wilkinson, 17–18; Hearings before a Subcommittee of the Senate Committee on the Judiciary on S. 3083, 76th Cong., 3d Sess. (statements of Senators Wiley and King on February 13, 1940), 62; Hearings before the House Committee on Indian Affairs on H.R. 1198 and 1341, 79th Cong., 1st Sess. (Wilkinson testimony on June 11, 1945), 79.

32. House Committee, hearings on H.R. 1198 and 1341, 112, 133, 140–50; *Ute Indians* v. *U.S.,* Affidavit of Ernest L. Wilkinson, 92 *Cong. Rec.* 5323 (October 26, 1950), 105–6.

33. Hearings before the Senate Committee on Indian Affairs on the Indian Claims Commission Act, 79th Cong., 2d Sess. (July 13, 1946), 47–82; 92 *Cong. Rec.* 9219 (July 17, 1946).

34. *Ute Indians* v. *U.S.,* Affidavit of Ernest L. Wilkinson, 110–18; Letter from Cohen to Commissioner Brophy dated July 22, 1946; Note from the Secretary of the Interior to Cohen dated July 25, 1946; 92 *Cong. Rec.* 10403.

35. *Ute Indians* v. *U.S.,* Affidavit of Ernest L. Wilkinson, 119; Letter from the Secretary of the Interior to the President dated August 1, 1946; Signing Statement, August 13, 1946.

36. 92 *Cong. Rec.* 10403 (July 29, 1946) (Representatives Stigler, Mundt, and Robertson).

37. Indian Claims Commission Act §§ 2, 24 (formerly codified at 25 U.S.C. §§ 70a, 1505).

38. Ibid., §§ 12, 23 (formerly codified at 25 U.S.C. §§ 70k, 70v).

39. Indian Claims Commission, Final Report 12, 20 (September 30, 1978).

40. 28 U.S.C. § 2501; H. Rep. No. 1466, 79th Cong., 1st Sess. (1945), 5; Indian Claims Commission Act § 2 (formerly codified at 25 U.S.C. § 70a).

41. Indian Claims Commission Act § 2.

42. Ibid.; House Committee, hearings on H.R. 1198 and 1341, 86 (Representative Stigler); H. Rep. No. 1466, 79th Cong., 1st Sess. (1945), 12; 92 *Cong. Rec.* 5313 (Representative Jackson).

43. Signing Statement, August 13, 1946.

44. Indian Claims Commission Act § 2; H. Rep. No. 2693, 79th Cong., 2d Sess. (1946), 6–7.

FOUR: Promised Lands

1. R. Boyer and N. Gayton, *Apache Mothers and Daughters: Four Generations of a Family* (Norman: University of Oklahoma Press, 1992), 176.

2. Letter from Superintendent O. M. Boggess to Commissioner of Indian Affairs dated October 2, 1928; Letter from Superintendent O. M. Boggess to Commissioner of Indian Affairs dated May 9, 1927.

3. Letter from Superintendent O. M. Boggess to Commissioner of Indian Affairs dated July 30, 1929; Letter from William Madison to Honorable Walter Newton dated February 11, 1932; Letter from William Madison to Homer Yanoyhe dated February 24, 1932.

4. H. Stockel, *Women of the Apache Nation: Voices of Truth* (Reno: University of Nevada Press, 1991), 56–57; Letter from Brigadier General Greble to Commissioner of Indian Affairs dated July 13, 1917; Letter from Superintendent William Light to Commissioner of Indian Affairs dated May 23, 1919; Letter from Superintendent Ernest Stecker to Commissioner of Indian Affairs dated July 19, 1919.

5. Letter from Brigadier General Greble to Commissioner of Indian Affairs dated July 13, 1917; Letter from Asa Daklugie, Duncan Balatchu, and Eugene Chihuahua to Commissioner of Indian Affairs dated April 15, 1918; Letter from Asa Daklugie, Duncan Balatchu, and Eugene Chihuahua to Commissioner of Indian Affairs dated August 1, 1918; Letter from Superintendent Ernest Stecker to Commissioner of Indian Affairs dated July 19, 1919.

6. Letter from Asa Daklugie, Duncan Balatchu, and Eugene Chihuahua to Commissioner of Indian Affairs dated April 15, 1918; Letter from Asa Daklugie, Duncan Balatchu, and Eugene Chihuahua to Commissioner of Indian Affairs dated August 1, 1918; Letter from Superintendent Ernest Stecker to Commissioner of Indian Affairs dated July 19, 1919.

7. Boyer and Gayton, *Apache Mothers and Daughters,* 266–69, 279, 307–8.

8. Letter from the Warm Springs Apaches to Commissioner of Indian Affairs dated November 12, 1914; Letter from Duncan Balatchu, David Kazhe, and Charles Istee to Commissioner of Indian Affairs received November 30, 1915; Letter from Superintendent William Light to Commissioner of Indian Affairs dated August 6, 1918.

9. Boyer and Gayton, *Apache Mothers and Daughters,* 250; Letter from Superintendent O. M. Boggess to Commissioner of Indian Affairs dated July 30, 1929.

10. Peter Iverson, *The Navajo Nation* (Albuquerque: University of New Mexico Press, 1983), 19–22.

11. 25 U.S.C. § 476; S. Tyler, *A History of Indian Policy* (Washington, D.C.: U.S. Department of the Interior, 1973), 127–33.

12. Letter from Superintendent O. M. Boggess to Commissioner of Indian Affairs dated July 30, 1929; Letter from Superintendent P. W. Danielson to Commissioner of Indian Affairs dated March 8, 1932, with enclosures; Act of March 3, 1871 (codified at 25 U.S.C. § 81); S. 4903, 72d Cong., 1st Sess. (1932).

13. Letter from Secretary of the Interior Wilbur to Senator Frazier, enclosing Memorandum of Assistant Commissioner Scattergood dated July 16, 1932; Petition from Kenoi and others to Commissioner of Indian Affairs received February 11, 1933;

Letter from Kenoi as Secretary of the Chiricahua Apache Indian Business Committee to Commissioner of Indian Affairs dated May 15, 1933; Letter from Kenoi as Secretary of the Chiricahua Indian Business Committee to Commissioner of Indian Affairs dated September 7, 1933.

14. Letter from Kenoi to Commissioner of Indian Affairs dated July 26, 1938; Letter from Superintendent Newman to Commissioner of Indian Affairs dated January 11, 1939; S. 2238, 76th Cong., 1st Sess.; Letter from Secretary of the Interior Ickes to Senator Thomas dated July 14, 1939.

15. Letter from Acting Commissioner Meritt to Jason Betzinez, James Kawaykla, and Talbot Gooday dated January 22, 1921; Letter from Superintendent Stecker to Commissioner of Indian Affairs dated December 14, 1914; Letter from Superintendent Stecker and others to Commissioner of Indian Affairs dated May 11, 1914; Letter from Commissioner Cato Sells to George Vaux, Jr., dated December 9, 1913.

16. Letter from Acting Secretary of the Interior E. C. Finney to the Honorable Selden Spencer dated March 15, 1922; Letter from Acting Commissioner E. B. Meritt to Superintendent Buntin dated February 19, 1923; Letter from former congressman to Commissioner Charles Burke dated May 25, 1923.

17. Report of Hugh Scott of the Board of Indian Commissioners dated June 12, 1920.

18. Tyler, *A History of Indian Policy*, 97, 124.

19. Report of Malcolm McDowell of the Board of Indian Commissioners dated December 10, 1922.

20. Report of Hugh Scott of Board of Indian Commissioners dated December 25, 1927; Stockel, *Women of the Apache Nation*, 149–50.

21. J. Betzinez, *I Fought with Geronimo* (Harrisburg, PA: Stackpole Co., 1959), 199; Undated Memorandum of Morris E. Opler, Assistant Anthropologist.

22. B. Perlman, *Allan Houser* (Boston: D. R. Godine, 1987), 101.

23. Betzinez, *I Fought with Geronimo,* Foreword, 26, 200–205.

24. Undated Memorandum of Morris E. Opler, Assistant Anthropologist.

25. Perlman, *Allan Houser,* 61–62, 64–66, 75–81.

26. Ibid., 81, 94–96; Stockel, *Women of the Apache Nation,* 132, 142.

27. Perlman, *Allan Houser,* 95–96, 101.

28. *Washington Post,* January 5, 1953, p. 10, col. 6; Hearings before the Senate Subcommittee on the Judiciary on S. 3083, February 14, 1940, 130 (testimony of Grady Lewis); Transcript of meeting of Kiowas, Comanches, and Kiowa Apaches held September 21, 1938, 7.

29. Attorney's Contract between Sam Haozous, Talbot Gooday, and Benedict Jozhe, Jr., on behalf of the Fort Sill Apache Tribe and Grady Lewis dated December 1, 1939.

FIVE: The Commission Becomes a Court

1. Indian Claims Commission Act § 3 (formerly codified at 25 U.S.C. § 70b(a)); Supreme Court Rule 5.

2. H. Rep. No. 1466, 79th Cong., 1st Sess. (1945), 10.

3. Memorandum from Assistant Solicitor of the Interior Department Bruce Wright to the Undersecretary of the Interior dated August 21, 1946 (HST); Undated Summary of Recommendations Made to the President for Appointments to the Indian Claims Commission (HST); United States Indian Claims Commission Final Report, 17 (1978).

4. Letter from Acting Secretary of the Interior Chapman to President Truman dated August 22, 1946 (HST); Letter from Senator James Mead to President Truman dated August 28, 1946 (HST); Undated Summary of Recommendations Made to the President for Appointments to the Indian Claims Commission (HST).

5. Hearings before a Subcommittee of the House Appropriations Committee on the Supplemental Appropriation Bill for 1948 held June 12, 1947, 494–95.

6. Undated Summary of Recommendations Made to the President for Appointments to the Indian Claims Commission (HST).

7. T. Connally, *My Name Is Tom Connally* (New York: Crowell, 1954), 17, 181; Letters from Senator Connally to President Truman dated June 12, 1946, August 1, 1946, August 7, 1946, November 19, 1946 (HST); Letter from Speaker Rayburn to President Truman dated August 6, 1946 (HST); Memorandum from RB to Mr. Connally dated November 27, 1946 (HST); Memorandum from aje to Miss Barrows dated December 6, 1946 (HST); Letter from J. Edgar Hoover to George Schoeneman dated January 10, 1947, enclosing FBI report of same date (HST).

8. Memorandum of George Schoeneman concerning recommendation of Holt dated December 30, 1946 (HST); Letter from J. Edgar Hoover to George Schoeneman dated January 3, 1947, attaching FBI report (HST); Letter from Senator Butler to President Truman dated March 3, 1947 (HST).

9. Letter from Senator O'Mahoney to Undersecretary of the Interior Oscar Chapman dated October 19, 1947 (HST); Memorandum from MJC to the President dated October 19, 1947 (HST); Memorandum from MJC to the President dated January 17, 1947 (HST); Letter from Senator O'Mahoney to the President dated March 3, 1947 (HST); Memorandum from George Schoeneman to the President dated March 6, 1947 (HST); Letter from Charles Brannan to the President dated March 11, 1947 (HST); Handwritten note at bottom of letter from Gael Sullivan to George Schoeneman dated March 4, 1947 (HST).

10. Handwritten note on Memorandum from George Schoeneman to the President dated March 6, 1947 (HST); Memorandum from George Schoeneman to Mr. Connally dated April 10, 1947 (HST).

11. Independent Offices Appropriations for 1955, Hearings before the Subcommittee of the House Committee on Appropriations on H.R. 8583, H1434-1-A, 91, 98; Letters from Foster to Witt dated September 23, 1955.

12. Indian Claims Commission Act § 13.

13. P. Shattuck and J. Norgren, *Partial Justice: Federal Indian Law in a Liberal Constitutional System* (New York: St. Martin's Press, 1991), 146–48; Letter from Chief Commissioner Arthur Watkins to Representative James Haley dated June 11, 1965.

14. Attachment to Memorandum from Felix Cohen to Commissioner of Indian Affairs dated April 22, 1946; *Pawnee Indians* v. *United States,* 124 Ct. Cl. 324 (1953).

15. Indian Claims Commission Final Report, 5.

16. Ibid., 6, 8.

17. Kobler, "These Indians Struck it Rich," *Saturday Evening Post* (September 6, 1952), 134.

18. Ibid.

19. 102 *Cong. Rec.* 5779.

20. Conversations with Abe W. Weissbrodt of March 10, 1993, and May 18, 1993; Conversation with I. S. Weissbrodt of May 18, 1993; H. D. Rosenthal, *Their Day in Court: A History of the Indian Claims Commission* (New York: Garland, 1990), 122.

21. P. Drucker, "The Bombardment and Burning of Angoon, Alaska in 1882" (unpublished manuscript, Pl. Ex. 25 in Indians Claims Commission Docket No. 278-B).

22. Ibid.; Narrative by Esther Billman dated June 5, 1973 (Def. Ex. S-21 in Docket No. 278-B).

23. Ibid.; Drucker, "The Bombardment and Burning of Angoon."

24. Conversation with Abe W. Weissbrodt of December 18, 1992; "Indians Are Paid for Attack by Navy—Yes, the Navy," *National Observer,* November 17, 1973.

25. Kootznoowoo Heritage Foundation, *In Commemoration,* p. 9 (WF).

SIX: The Fall and Rise of the Imprisonment Claim

1. Attorney's Contract between Fort Sill Apache Indians of the State of Oklahoma and Grady Lewis dated January 29, 1947; *Choctaw Nation* v. *United States,* 1 Ind. Cl. Comm. 291 (1950); Interview with Paul Niebell.

2. Brief of Choctaw Nation dated June 13, 1949, 6, 14–15, 19.

3. D. Hoover, *The Red and the Black* (Chicago: Rand McNally, 1976), 274–79.

4. *Choctaw Nation* v. *United States,* 332.

5. Letter Agreement between Lewis and Shenkin dated November 19, 1947.

6. H. Viola, *The National Archives of the United States* (New York: H. N. Abrams, 1984), 52.

7. Letter from Shenkin to Lewis dated September 5, 1947 (WF); Letter from Haozous to Lewis dated October 14, 1947 (WF); Undated Letter from Lewis to Shenkin (WF); *Fort Sill Apaches* v. *United States,* Docket No. 30, Petition filed May 26, 1948.

8. Letter from Lewis to Acting Commissioner of Indian Affairs Zimmerman dated March 1, 1949 (WF); Undated draft of Petition (WF).

9. *Fort Sill Apaches* v. *United States.*

10. Ibid.

11. Conversations with I. S. Weissbrodt, January 26, 1992, and May 20, 1993.

12. Ibid.; "Truman Accepts Wyatt Resignation," *Washington Post,* December 5, 1946, 8B:1.

13. Interview with I. S. Weissbrodt, January 26, 1992.

14. Ibid.

15. Letter from David Cobb to Grady Lewis dated October 11, 1948 (WF).

16. *Fort Sill Apaches* v. *United States,* 1 Ind. Cl. Comm. 137, 144–48 (1949).

17. Indian Claims Commission Act § 2 (formerly codified at 25 U.S.C. § 70a); Hearings before the House Committee on Expenditures in the Executive Depts., 74th Cong., 1st Sess. (testimony of Assistant Attorney General Blair, March 8, 1935), 9.

18. *Blackfeather* v. *United States,* 190 U.S. 368 (1903).

19. *Fort Sill Apaches* v. *United States,* 139–43.

20. Ibid.; *Baltimore and Potomac Railroad Co.* v. *Fifth Baptist Church,* 108 U.S. 317 (1883).

21. Letter from Grady Lewis to Acting Commissioner William Zimmerman dated March 1, 1949 (WF).

22. Interview with I. S. Weissbrodt, January 26, 1992.

23. Ibid.; United States Senate, *Attorney Contracts with Indian Tribes,* Rep. No. 8, 83d Cong., 1st Sess. (1953), 5–9; Central Council of Tlingit and Haida Indian Tribes of Alaska, *Curry-Weissbrodt Papers of the Tlingit and Haida Indian Tribes of Alaska: An Inventory* (January 1983), 10.

24. Senate Report No. 8, 9–11; Interview with I. S. Weissbrodt, January 26, 1992.

25. Letter from I. S. Weissbrodt to Grady Lewis dated July 7, 1949 (WF); Agreement among Curry, Hoag and Lindquist, and Cobb and Weissbrodt dated April 2, 1950 (WF); Letter from I. S. Weissbrodt to Commissioner Dillon Myer dated January 22, 1952 (WF); Interview with I. S. Weissbrodt.

26. Interview with I. S. Weissbrodt, January 26, 1992.

27. Petition in Docket No. 182 filed July 24, 1951; First Amended Petition in Docket No. 30 filed July 30, 1951.

28. Petition in Docket No. 49 filed October 3, 1949.

29. Motion for Summary Judgment and to Extend Time to Answer or Otherwise Plead, dated December 12, 1949; Petitioners' Statement of Points and Authorities in Opposition to Respondent's Motion for Summary Judgment, dated January 30, 1950.

30. Transcript of Oral Argument conducted November 14, 1950, 5–6, 14–15.

31. Order Overruling Motion for Summary Judgment Without Prejudice, dated December 29, 1950.

32. See Motion dated February 27, 1951, 16; *Gila River Pima-Maricopa Tribe* v. *United States,* 29 Ind. Cl. Comm. 144, 149–50 (1972); *Absentee Shawnee Tribe* v. *United States,* 12 Ind. Cl. Comm. 174, 177 (1963), aff'd, 165 Ct. Cl. 510 (1964); *Creek (Freedmen)* v. *United States,* 1 Ind. Cl. Comm. 156 (1949).

33. Letter from Superintendent John Crow to Commissioner of Indian Affairs dated July 27, 1948 (WF); Resolution of Chiricahua Claims Committee dated March 5, 1948 (WF); Contract between Roy Mobley and Claims Committee dated March 5, 1948, and approved January 7, 1949 (WF).

34. Unsigned Letter from Claims Committee to James Curry dated June 9, 1947 (WF); Letter from Superintendent John Crow to Commissioner of Indian Affairs dated July 27, 1948 (WF); Petition filed August 15, 1949, by the Chiricahua and Warm Springs Tribes of Apache Indians and assigned to Docket No. 48; Letter from Mobley to Martin dated September 21, 1949 (WF); Letter from Martin to Mobley dated October 4, 1949 (WF).

SEVEN: Land Claims: Fiction with a Purpose

1. William Lewis, "Is the American Indian Entitled to His Day in Court?" (pamphlet) (1926), 11.

2. H. Rep. No. 1466, 79th Cong., 1st Sess. (1945), 8–9.

3. House Subcommittee of the Committee on Appropriations, Hearings on Appropriations for Interior Department and Related Agencies for 1956, 84th Cong., 1st Sess. (1955), 573–80 (emphasis added).

4. Paul J. Bohannan, personal communication.

5. 180 U.S. 261, 265–66 (1901).

6. *Yuchi Tribe* v. *United States,* 3 Ind. Cl. Comm. 515, 517 (1955).

7. A. L. Kroeber, "Nature of the Landholding Group," *Ethnohistory* 2:4 (1955), 304.

8. S. Rep. No. 1055, 70th Cong., 1st Sess. (1928).

9. Ibid.; *Thompson* v. *United States,* 8 Ind. Cl. Comm. 1, 17, 31 (1959).

10. Testimony of Robert Barker, Docket No. 31 et al., February 8, 1966, 30.

11. E. Wilkinson and W. Skousen, *Brigham Young University: A School of Destiny* (Provo, UT: Brigham Young University Press, 1976), 432, 463, 735; Second Supplemental Appropriation Bill, 1956, Hearings before the Senate Committee on Appropriations on H.R. 10004, S1162-1, 461.

12. *Thompson* v. *United States,* 1 Ind. Cl. Comm. 366 (1950), rev'd, 122 Ct. Cl. 348 (1952).

13. *Thompson* v. *United States,* 122 Ct. Cl. 348 (1952).

14. Brief for the Appellant, the United States, in Appeals Docket No. 2-61, dated June 1, 1961, 189.

15. *Thompson* v. *United States,* 8 Ind. Cl. Comm. 31–32; Reply Brief of the Indians of California dated August 31, 1962, 36 n.27.

16. *Wichita Indians* v. *United States,* 89 Ct. Cl. 378 (1939); *Assiniboine Indian Tribe* v. *United States,* 77 Ct. Cl. 347 (1933); *Choctaw Nation* v. *United States,* 34 Ct. Cl. 17 (1899).

17. *Pawnee Indian Tribe* v. *United States,* 1 Ind. Cl. Comm. 230 (1950); *Snake or Piute Indians* v. *United States,* 1 Ind. Cl. Comm. 422 (1950); *Quapaw Tribe* v. *United States,* 1 Ind. Cl. Comm. 474 (1951); *Red Lake, Pembina and White Earth Bands* v. *United States,* 1 Ind. Cl. Comm. 584 (1951); *McCauley* v. *United States,* 1 Ind. Cl. Comm. 617 (1951).

18. *Pawnee Indian Tribe* v. *United States,* 124 Ct. Cl. 324 (1953); *Snake or Piute Indians* v. *United States,* 125 Ct. Cl. 241 (1953); *Red Lake, Pembina and White Earth Bands* v. *United States,* unnumbered opinion dated March 13, 1953.

19. *Pawnee Indian Tribe* v. *United States,* 8 Ind. Cl. Comm. 648 (1960); *Snake or Piute Indians* v. *United States,* 7 Ind. Cl. Comm. 555 (1959); *Red Lake, Pembina and White Earth Bands* v. *United States,* 6 Ind. Cl. Comm. 305 (1958); United States Indian Claims Commission, Final Report, 36, 67, 99.

20. D. Wishart, "The Pawnee Claims Case, 1947–64," in I. Sutton (ed.), *Irredeemable America: The Indians' Estate and Land Claims* (Albuquerque: University of New Mexico Press, 1985), 157–62; Transcript of Hearing of April 8, 1948, 129 (testimony of Dr. Waldo Wedel).

21. Wishart, "Pawnee Claims Case," 163–69, 183–84.

22. Transcript of trial of January 29, 1948, 13–92 (testimony of Indians); Transcript of trial of April 8, 1948, 121–22 (testimony of Dr. Wedel).

23. Transcript of trial of April 8, 1948, 132, 135–37; Transcript of trial of November 8, 1948, 286–89.

24. *Pawnee Indian Tribe* v. *United States,* 1 Ind. Cl. Comm. 262–65.

25. *Pawnee Indian Tribe* v. *United States,* 124 Ct. Cl. 324 (1953), aff'g in part & rev'g in part, 1 Ind. Cl. Comm. 230 (1950); conversation with Margaret Pierce of October 28, 1993.

26. Stipulation with Otoe and Missouria Tribes dated August 28, 1953; Stipulation with Sioux Tribe dated September 1, 1953; Stipulation with Osage Nation dated September 1, 1953; Stipulation between Pawnees and Cheyenne-Arapaho Tribes dated September 23, 1953; Stipulation with Kansas or Kaw Tribe dated December 2, 1953; Stipulation with Ponca Tribe filed December 22, 1953. For the impact of those stipulations, compare Claimants' Exhibit 39 (map showing claims during first trial) with Claimants' Exhibit 144 (map showing claims during second trial).

27. *Pawnee Indian Tribe* v. *United States,* 5 Ind. Cl. Comm. 224 (1957).

28. Interior Department and Related Agencies Appropriations for 1956, Hearings before the Subcommittee of the House Committee on Appropriations on H.R. 5085, H1484-3, 576 (testimony of Commissioner Witt on February 9, 1956).

29. *Johnson* v. *McIntosh,* 8 Wheat. 543 (1823); *Cherokee Nation* v. *Georgia,* 5 Pet. 1 (1831); *Worcester* v. *Georgia,* 6 Pet. 515 (1832).

30. *Johnson* v. *McIntosh,* 8 Wheat. 572–74, 591–92; *Worcester* v. *Georgia,* 6 Pet. 544–45.

31. J. Wise and V. Deloria, Jr., *The Red Man in the New World Drama: A Politico-Legal Study with a Pageantry of American Indian History* (New York: Macmillan, 1971), 220.

32. *Lone Wolf* v. *Hitchcock,* 187 U.S. 553, 554–60 (1903).

33. Ibid., 564–66; J. Wunder, *The Kiowa* (New York: Chelsea House, 1989), 73–75; M. Mayhall, *The Kiowas* (Norman: University of Oklahoma Press, 1962), 256.

34. *United States* v. *Creek Nation,* 295 U.S. 103 (1935); *Shoshone Tribe* v. *United States,* 299 U.S. 476 (1937); *United States* v. *Klamath and Moadoc Tribes,* 304 U.S. 119 (1938).

35. *United States* v. *Alcea Band of Tillamooks,* 329 U.S. 40, 41–44 (1946); *United States* v. *Alcea Band of Tillamooks,* 103 Ct. Cl. 494, 501–40 (1945); Brief for the Respondents before the Supreme Court in the second *Alcea* case, filed February 19, 1951, 31.

36. *United States v. Alcea Band of Tillamooks,* 329 U.S. 45–53.

37. Ibid., 54–55 (Black, J., concurring); ibid. 55, 64 (Reed, J., with Rutledge and Burton, JJ., dissenting).

38. *United States* v. *Alcea Band of Tillamooks,* 341 U.S. 48 (1951); *Tee-Hit-Ton Indians* v. *United States,* 348 U.S. 272, 283, n.17 (1955).

39. *Tee-Hit-Ton Indians* v. *United States,* 348 U.S. 272 (1955); *Assiniboine Indian Tribe* v. *United States,* 2 Ind. Cl. Comm. 272 (1952), aff'd, 128 Ct. Cl. 617 (1954).

40. *Tee-Hit-Ton Indians* v. *United States,* 348 U.S. 272 (1955).

41. Brief for the United States before the Supreme Court in second *Alcea* case, filed February 6, 1951, 19–20; *World Almanac and Book of Facts* (New York: World Almanac, 1990), 75.

42. Brief for Respondents before the Supreme Court in second *Alcea* case, filed February 19, 1951, 25–29; Brief for the United States, second *Alcea* case, Appendices A–C.

43. *Tee-Hit-Ton Indians* v. *United States,* 348 U.S. 290–91.

44. Interior Department and Related Agencies Appropriations for 1956, Hearings before a Subcommittee of the Senate Committee on Appropriation on H.R. 5085, S1120-2, 718 (testimony of Commissioner Witt on April 11, 1955).

45. *Otoe and Missouria Tribe* v. *United States,* 2 Ind. Cl. Comm. 355, 360–65 (1953).

46. Ibid.

47. *Otoe and Missouria Tribe* v. *United States,* 131 Ct. Cl. 593 (1955); Departments of State and Justice, the Judiciary, and Related Agencies Appropriations for 1957, Hearings before the Subcommittee of the House Committee on Appropriations, H1529-1-B, 103 (testimony of Assistant Attorney General Perry Morton on January 31, 1956); Edward Lazarus, *Black Hills, White Justice: The Sioux Nation Versus the United States 1775 to the Present* (New York: HarperCollins, 1991), 227.

48. *Otoe and Missouria Tribe* v. *United States,* 131 Ct. Cl. 598–624.

49. *United States* v. *Otoe and Missouria Tribe,* Petition for a Writ of Certiorari to the United States Court of Claims, 11–13; *United States* v. *Otoe and Missouria Tribe,* Brief for the Otoe and Missouria Tribe in Opposition, 18–22; *United States* v. *Otoe and Missouria Tribe,* 350 U.S. 848 (1955).

50. Second Supplemental Appropriation Bill, 1956, Hearings before the Senate Committee on Appropriations on H. R. 10004, S1162-1, 476–78.

51. Departments of State and Justice, the Judiciary, and Related Agencies Appropriations for 1957, Hearings before the Subcommittee of the House Committee on Appropriations, H1529-1-B, 101–3 (Morton testimony on January 31, 1956); Second Supplemental Appropriation Bill, Hearings before Subcommittees of the House Committee on Appropriations, H1526-5, 117–18 (Morton testimony on February

27, 1956); Second Supplemental Appropriation Bill, 1956, Hearings before the Senate Committee on Appropriations on H.R. 10004, S1162-1, 453–74 (Morton testimony); S. Representative No. 1727, 84th Cong., 2d Sess. (1956), 2–3; 102 *Cong. Rec.* 5776 (March 28, 1956) (Representative Metcalf); ibid., 5777, 5788 (Representative Edmondson); ibid., 5778 (Representative Fernandez); ibid., 5779–80 (Representative Udall); ibid., 11932-33 (July 6, 1956) (Senator O'Mahoney).

52. 102 *Cong. Rec.* 11937 (July 6, 1956).

53. 102 *Cong. Rec.* 11933 (July 6, 1956); Nomination of Arthur V. Watkins, Hearing before the Senate Committee on Interior and Insular Affairs, 86th Cong., 1st Sess. (August 11, 1959), 1, 3, 7.

54. *United States* v. *Shoshone Tribe,* 304 U.S. 111 (1938).

55. *Otoe and Missouria Tribe* v. *United States,* 131 Ct. Cl. 629–34.

56. Ibid.

57. *Tlingit and Haida Indians* v. *United States,* 182 Ct. Cl. 130, 154 (1968) (Nichols, J., dissenting).

58. Interior Department and Related Agencies Appropriations for 1957, Hearings before the Subcommittee of the House Committee on Appropriations on H.R. 9390, H1522-1, 633 (testimony of Commissioner Witt on January 18, 1956).

59. *Sac and Fox Tribe* v. *United States,* 17 Ind. Cl. Comm. 544, 552 (1967).

60. Reply Brief of the Indians of California dated August 31, 1962, 32.

EIGHT: An Eleven-Million-Dollar Mistake

1. *Washington Post,* December 12, 1962, p. 1, col. 8; Transcript of Hearing of December 11, 1962, 13, 75.

2. *New York Times,* March 4, 1934, § 3, p. 1, col. 8; Interview with Abe Weissbrodt, April 13, 1993.

3. Interview with Abe Weissbrodt, April 13, 1993.

4. Ibid.

5. *Washington Post,* January 5, 1953, p. 10, col. 6; Letter from I. S. Weissbrodt to Sam Haozous, Benedict Jozhe, and Robert Gooday dated February 11, 1953 (WF); Letter from I. S. Weissbrodt to Benedict Jozhe dated June 10, 1953 (WF); Attorney Contract dated June 25, 1953 (WF).

6. Letter from I. S. Weissbrodt to Benedict Jozhe dated February 11, 1953 (WF); Letter from I. S. Weissbrodt to Benedict Jozhe dated June 10, 1953 (WF); Letter from I. S. Weissbrodt to Benedict Jozhe dated November 23, 1953 (WF); Letter from I. S. Weissbrodt to Benedict Jozhe dated March 5, 1954 (WF).

7. 70 Stat. 624 (July 24, 1956).

8. D. Fixico, *Termination and Relocation: Federal Indian Policy, 1945–60* (Albuquerque: University of New Mexico Press, 1986), 59–77.

9. 67 Stat. B132 (1953).

10. Act of June 17, 1954, 68 Stat. 250 (formerly codified at 25 U.S.C. §§ 891–902) (Menominees); Act of August 13, 1954, 68 Stat. 718 (codified at 25 U.S.C. § 564 *et seq.*) (Klamaths); Act of August 13, 1954, 68 Stat. 724 (codified at 25 U.S.C. §§ 691–708) (western Oregon tribes); Act of August 23, 1954, 68 Stat. 769 (codified at 25 U.S.C. §§ 721–28) (Alabamas and Coushattas); Act of August 27, 1954, 68 Stat. 868 (codified at 25 U.S.C. § 677 *et seq.*) (mixed-blood Utes); Act of September 1, 1954, 68 Stat. 1099 (codified at 25 U.S.C. §§ 741–60 (Utah Paiutes).

11. F. Prucha (ed.), *Documents of United States Indian Policy* (Lincoln: University of Nebraska Press, 1990), 238–39 (reproducing Senator Watkins's article originally appearing in *Annals of the American Academy of Political and Social Science* [May 1957], 311).

12. Herman J. Viola, *After Columbus: The Smithsonian Chronicle of the North American Indians* (Washington, D.C.: Smithsonian Books, 1990), 238–39, 243.

13. Charles F. Wilkinson, *American Indians, Time, and the Law* (New Haven: Yale University Press, 1987), 14–19.

14. Letter from Mrs. Sadie Rhodes Tyner to President Eisenhower dated October 28, 1957.

15. *Oklahoma Indian Newsletter* 1:2 (August 1958); V. Deloria and C. Lytle, *American Indians, American Justice* (Austin: University of Texas Press, 1983), 194; Draft of Unsent Letter from Commissioner Glenn Emmons to Will J. Pitner, the Anadarko Area Director, filed under May 6, 1958.

16. Fixico, *Termination and Relocation,* 208; Letter from Benedict Jozhe to I. S. Weissbrodt dated September 12, 1957 (WF); Memorandum of Presley LaBreche to Chief, Branch of Tribal Programs dated November 6, 1957 (WF).

17. Letter from I. S. Weissbrodt to Benedict Jozhe dated September 24, 1957 (WF); Letter from Benedict Jozhe to I. S. Weissbrodt dated January 31, 1958 (WF); Resolution of Fort Sill Apaches dated February 22, 1958 (WF); Letter from Benedict Jozhe to Counsel, Association on American Indian Affairs dated February 25, 1958 (WF); Field Trip Report from Presley T. LaBreche to Homer B. Jenkins dated February 26, 1958; *Oklahoma Indian Newsletter,* 1:2 (August 1958); Telephone conversation with Abe Weissbrodt, May 18, 1993.

18. Letter from Area Director Pitner to Commissioner of Indian Affairs dated September 10, 1958; Seaton's speech reproduced at 105 *Cong. Rec.* 3105 and in Prucha, *Documents of United States Indian Policy,* 240; Letter from Commissioner of Indian Affairs Emmons to Pitner dated October 29, 1958.

19. Viola, *After Columbus,* 255–56.

20. Ibid., 255; Charles L. Sonnichsen, *The Mescalero Apaches,* 2d ed. (Norman, OK: University of Oklahoma Press, 1972), 297; Henry F. Dobyns, *The Mescalero Apache People* (Phoenix: Indian Tribal Series, 1973), 84–89.

21. Dobyns, *Mescalero Apache People,* 87–88; Interview with Abe Weissbrodt, May 18, 1993.

22. 358 U.S. 217 (1959).

23. Stipulation and Agreement dated March 1961 (WF); Letter from James Kunen to William Briggs dated October 10, 1960 (WF); *Confederated Tribes of the Colville Reservation* v. *United States,* 8 Ind. Cl. Comm. 429 (1960); *Omaha Tribe* v. *United States,* 8 Ind. Cl. Comm. 407 (1960); *Williams* v. *United States,* Docket 180-A (Ind. Cl. Comm. July 5, 1960); *Northern Paiute Nation* v. *United States,* 7 Ind. Cl. Comm. 381 (1959); *Skokomish Tribe* v. *United States,* 6 Ind. Cl. Comm. 152 (1958).

24. David Cobb is now deceased, and the authors have elected not to present only Lefty Weissbrodt's version of the events leading to the partnership breakup.

25. Report on Chiricahua Apache Land Claims dated May 31, 1961, by I. S. Weissbrodt (WF); Telephone conversation with Abe Weissbrodt, May 18, 1993.

26. Memorandum entitled "Powers of the President: Indian Claims Commission," received in the White House Central Files April 27, 1960 (DDE); Unsigned Confidential Memorandum dated February 28, 1958, concerning meeting of writer with Elmer Bennett of the Interior Department and Robert Gray of the White

House to discuss the appointment of T. Harold Scott to Indian Claims Commission (DDE).

27. Fixico, *Termination and Relocation,* 107–8, 186; "Powers of the President,"

28. Interior Department and Related Agencies Appropriations for 1957, Hearings before a Subcommittee of the Senate Committee on Appropriations on H.R. 9390, S1169-1, 555, 557 (testimony of Commissioner Witt on March 9, 1956).

29. Attachment to "Powers of the President."

30. Memorandum from Robert Gray, Special Assistant, to Deputy Attorney General William P. Rogers dated August 15, 1956 (DDE); Memorandum from Acting Assistant Attorney General Frederick W. Ford to Robert Gray dated October 2, 1956 (DDE); Memorandum from Robert Gray to Harris Ellsworth, Chairman of the Civil Service Commission, dated September 12, 1957 (DDE); Letter from Chief Commissioner Witt to Robert Hampton dated May 25, 1959 (DDE); Memorandum from Attorney General William P. Rogers for Associate Special Counsel to the President Henry Roemer McPhee dated August 24, 1959.

31. Harvey Rosenthal, *Their Day in Court: A History of the Indian Claims Commission* (New York: Garland, 1990), 175–91; Senate Committee on Interior and Insular Affairs, *Hearings on the Nomination of Arthur V. Watkins to Be Associate Commissioner of the Indian Claims Commission,* 86th Cong., 1st Sess. (August 11, 1959), 4; *Washington Post* A20:1 (September 13, 1967), A20:1; Arthur Watkins, *Enough Rope: The Inside Story of the Censure of Senator Joe McCarthy by His Colleagues* (Englewood Cliffs, NJ: Prentice-Hall, 1969), 178.

32. D. Lythgoe, *Let 'em Holler: A Political Biography of J. Bracken Lee* (Salt Lake City: Utah State Historical Society, 1982), 210; Fixico, *Termination and Relocation,* 92–93; Nancy Lurie, "Epilogue," in Imre Sutton (ed.), *Irredeemable America: The Indians' Estate and Land Claims* (Albuquerque: University of New Mexico Press, 1985), 363; Memorandum to Senate Subcommittee on Indian Affairs from Chief Commissioner Watkins re Proposed Amendments to S. 3068 dated August 16, 1966.

33. Letter from Senators Millikin and Allott to Sherman Adams dated November 14, 1956 (DDE); Letter from T. Harold Scott to Robert Gray dated December 21, 1956, with enclosure (DDE); Unsigned confidential memorandum dated February 28, 1958, concerning meeting of writer with Elmer Bennett of the Interior Department and Robert Gray of the White House to discuss the appointment of T. Harold Scott to Indian Claims Commission (DDE); Letter from Senator Gordon Allott to President Dwight D. Eisenhower dated March 5, 1958 (DDE); Letter from Senator Gordon Allott to the President dated November 3, 1959 (DDE); Letter from Senator Harry F. Byrd to the President dated January 28, 1960 (DDE); Letter from four Colorado congressmen to the President dated February 1, 1960 (DDE); Letter from Senator Spessard L. Holland to the President dated February 2, 1960 (DDE); Letter from Senator Francis Case to Robert Hampton dated March 1, 1960 (DDE).

34. Telephone conversation with Abe Weissbrodt, May 18, 1993; Memorandum from John W. Macy, Jr., to the President dated July 18, 1967 (DDE). These counts exclude decisions approving of agreements between the parties and decisions dealing with issues in which the United States did not have a direct interest, such as decisions awarding attorneys' fees after the conclusion of a case.

35. *Pueblo of Taos v. United States,* 15 Ind. Cl. Comm. 688, 694–95 (1965).

36. Biographical Summary: Morris Edward Opler, submitted as Pl. Ex. 436; Tr. 79–85 (December 11, 1962).

37. Professional Background of Albert H. Schroeder, submitted as Def. Ex. S-436; Publications of Albert H. Schroeder, submitted as Def. Ex. S-437; Tr. 474–86 (December 14, 1962).

38. Tr. 98–99 (December 11, 1962) (Opler testimony); ibid., 424 (December 14, 1962) (Opler testimony).

39. Tr. 469–70 (December 14, 1962) (government's opening statement); ibid., 503 (December 14, 1962) (Schroeder testimony); ibid., 689 (December 18, 1962) (Schroeder testimony).

40. Petitioners' Proposed Findings of Fact on Issues of Title and Liability and Accompanying Brief dated January 17, 1964; Defendant's Proposed Findings of Fact, Objections to Petitioners' Proposed Findings of Fact, and Brief, dated May 28, 1964; Petitioners' Reply to Defendant's Proposed Findings of Fact, Objections and Brief, dated April 30, 1965; Memorandum to files by Abe Weissbrodt dated May 23, 1966 (WF).

41. *Fort Sill Apache Tribe* v. *United States,* 19 Ind. Cl. Comm. 212, 217, 253–56 (1968); Tr. 239–40 (December 12, 1962); Telephone interview with Abe Weissbrodt, April 26, 1993.

42. Tr. 894–910 (December 19, 1962) (Schroeder testimony); Letter from Abe Weissbrodt to Morris Opler dated December 28, 1962 (WF); *Fort Sill Apache Tribe* v. *United States,* 19 Ind. Cl. Comm. 241 (1968); *Fort Sill Apache Tribe* v. *United States,* 22 Ind. Cl. Comm. 527 (1970).

43. 19 Stat. 176, 195 (1876).

44. Petitioners' Proposed Findings of Fact on Issues of Title and Liability and Accompanying Brief, 94–99; Letter from Roy P. Full to I. S. Weissbrodt dated June 10, 1963 (WF).

45. Tr. 222–32 (December 12, 1962) (Campbell cross-examination of Opler); Tr. 469–70 (opening statement of DeNunzio); Defendant's Proposed Findings of Fact, Objections to Petitioners' Proposed Findings of Fact, and Brief, 132.

46. Tr. 223, 224.

47. *Fort Sill Apache Tribe* v. *United States,* 19 Ind. Cl. Comm. 263 (1968).

48. Abe Weissbrodt's Notes for Meeting with Campbell and Barney on Compromise Settlement on Wed., March 5, 1969 (WF); Abe Weissbrodt's Notes for Meetings with Barney on July 7, 1969 (WF); *Fort Sill Apache Tribe* v. *United States,* 25 Ind. Cl. Comm. 352, 361–62 (1971).

49. *Fort Sill Apache Tribe* v. *United States,* 34 Ind. Cl. Comm. 81, 96 (1974); Shenon and Full, "An Appraisal of the Mineral Resources in the Lands of the Chiricahua Apache Tribe" (November 1969), 85; Roy P. Full, "An Analysis of the Mineral Production Prior to September 4, 1886 in the Lands of the Chiricahua Apache Tribe" (October 1971), 8, 16–24, 29–30, 54–57; Ernest Oberbillig, "Production and Royalty Value Fort Sill Apache Tract" (February 1972), 7–8.

50. *Fort Sill Apache Tribe* v. *United States,* 25 Ind. Cl. Comm. 366–67 (1971).

51. Government's Motion to Reschedule Trial dated May 25, 1970; *Fort Sill Apache Tribe* v. *United States,* 25 Ind. Cl. Comm. 336 (1971).

52. *Tlingit and Haida Indians* v. *United States,* 182 Ct. Cl. 130, 323–27, 333–34, 335 (1968); *Washoe Tribe* v. *United States,* 21 Ind. Cl. Comm. 447, 454–63 (1969).

53. *Fort Sill Apache Tribe* v. *United States,* 25 Ind. Cl. Comm. 382 (1971); *Fort Sill Apache Tribe* v. *United States,* 23 Ind. Cl. Comm. 417 (1970); *Fort Sill Apache Tribe* v. *United States,* 533 F.2d 531, 533 (Ct. Cl. 1976).

54. *Fort Sill Apache Tribe* v. *United States,* 26 Ind. Cl. Comm. 193, 197, 198 (1971).

55. Memorandum for the Files from Abe W. Weissbrodt dated August 25, 1971 (WF); Letter from I. S. and Abe W. Weissbrodt to Benedict Jozhe and Wendell Chino dated September 3, 1971 (WF); Letter from I. S. Weissbrodt to Ralph Barney dated November 1, 1971 (WF); Letter from I. S. and Abe W. Weissbrodt to Solicitor General Erwin Griswold dated December 6, 1971 (WF).

56. Judge Marion T. Bennett, *The United States Court of Claims: A History, Part I: The Judges 1855–1976* (Washington, D.C.: Committee on the Bicentennial, 1976), 216–17.

57. *Fort Sill Apache Tribe* v. *United States,* 480 F.2d 819, 823–25, 826–28 (1973).

58. *Fort Sill Apache Tribe* v. *United States,* 34 Ind. Cl. Comm. 81, 104 (1974); Full, "Analysis of Mineral Production"; Oberbillig, "Production and Royalty Value."

59. *Western Shoshone Identifiable Group* v. *United States,* 29 Ind. Cl. Comm. 5, 50–57 (1972).

60. *United States* v. *Fort Sill Apache Tribe,* 533 F.2d 531, 532 (Ct. Cl. 1976).

61. Bennett, *United States Court of Claims,* 201–3.

62. *United States* v. *Fort Sill Apache Tribe,* 533 F.2d 536.

63. Report by Claims Attorneys on Proposed Settlement of Tribal Claims in Docket No. 182 (Appeal No. 3-78) and Docket No. 182-A before the Court of Claims, dated February 1979 (WF); Letter from I. S. Weissbrodt to Assistant Attorney General James Moorman dated June 12, 1978 (WF).

64. Court of Claims Order dated April 6, 1979.

65. *United States* v. *Sioux Nation,* 448 U.S. 371, 390, 424 (1980); Leonard Carlson, "What Was It Worth? Economic and Historical Aspects of Determining Awards in Indian Land Claims Cases," in Sutton, *Irredeemable America,* 97–102.

NINE: The Return of the Natives

1. Nell Newton, "Indian Claims in the Courts of the Conqueror," *American University Law Review* 41 (1982), 753, 818; Harvey Rosenthal, *Their Day in Court: A History of the Indian Claims Commission* (New York: Garland, 1990), 65; H. Rep. No. 1466, 79th Cong., 1st Sess. (1945), 4.

2. *United States* v. *Santa Fe Pacific Railroad Co.,* 314 U.S. 339 (1941).

3. Herman Viola, *After Columbus: The Smithsonian Chronicle of the North American Indians* (Washington, D.C.: Smithsonian Books, 1990), 86, 110; *Oneida Indian Nation* v. *County of Oneida,* 414 U.S. 661 (1974).

4. Treaty of Fort Stanwix, October 22, 1784, 7 Stat. 15, art. II; Treaty at Fort Harmar, January 9, 1789, 7 Stat. 33, art. III; Treaty of Canandaigua, November 11, 1794, 7 Stat. 44, art. II; Nonintercourse Act, 1 Stat. 137 (1790); *County of Oneida* v. *Oneida Indian Nation,* 470 U.S. 226 (1985); George Shattuck, *The Oneida Land Claims: A Legal History* (Syracuse: Syracuse University Press, 1991), 50–52.

5. *Oneida Nation of New York* v. *United States,* Docket No. 301, Petition filed August 10, 1951.

6. *Oneida Nation of New York* v. *United States,* 20 Ind. Cl. Comm. 337 (1969); 26 Ind. Cl. Comm. 138 (1971); 26 Ind. Cl. Comm. 583 (1971).

7. George Shattuck, *The Oneida Land Claims,* 3–19.

8. Ibid., 20–26.

9. Ibid., 27–38; *Oneida Indian Nation* v. *County of Oneida,* 414 U.S. 661 (1974).

10. *Oneida Indian Nation* v. *County of Oneida,* 414 U.S. 670.

11. Bob Woodward and Scott Armstrong, *The Brethren: Inside the Supreme Court* (New York: Simon and Schuster, 1979), 57–58, 359–60.

12. David Lamb, "A Tribe That Means Business," *Los Angeles Times* (December 1992) A1:1; Francis O'Toole and Thomas Tureen, "State Power and the Passamaquoddy Tribe: 'A Gross National Hypocrisy?'," *Maine Law Review* 23 (1971): 1, 6–9; *Joint Tribal Council of the Passamaquoddy Tribe* v. *Morton,* 528 F.2d 370, 373–74 (1st Cir. 1975).

13. Paul Brodeur, *Restitution: The Land Claims of the Mashpee, Passamaquoddy, and Penobscot Indians of New England* (Boston: Northeastern University Press, 1985), 83–84; Interview with I. S. Weissbrodt.

14. Brodeur, *Restitution,* 81–87; *Joint Tribal Council of Passamaquoddy Tribe* v. *Morton,* 528 F.2d 370, 373–75 (1st Cir. 1975).

15. Brodeur, *Restitution,* 87–98; *Joint Tribal Council of the Passamaquoddy Tribe* v. *Morton,* 528 F.2d 370, 373–74 (1st Cir. 1975).

16. H. Rep. No. 96-1353 (September 19, 1980), 13–14, reprinted in *U.S. Code Congressional & Administrative News* 4 (1980), 3789.

17. Brodeur, *Restitution,* 97.

18. Ibid., 98–131; Maine Indian Claims Settlement Act of 1980, P.L. 96-420, 94 Stat. 1785 (1980).

19. Brodeur, *Restitution,* 84.

20. Lamb, "A Tribe That Means Business," A1:1.

21. Laurence Hauptman and James Wherry, Preface to *The Pequots in Southern New England: The Fall and Rise of an American Indian Nation* (Norman: University of Oklahoma Press, 1990), xv; William Starna, "The Pequots in the Early Seventeenth Century," in ibid., 33–34, 45–46; Laurence Hauptman, "The Pequot War and Its Legacies," in ibid., 71–77.

22. Jack Campisi, "The Emergence of the Mashantucket Pequot Tribe, 1637–1975," in ibid., 117–40.

23. Ibid., 140; Josh Getlin, "Against All Odds," *Los Angeles Times* (February 21, 1992), E1:2.

24. Mashantucket Pequot Indian Claims Settlement Act, P.L. 98–134, 97 Stat. 851 (October 18, 1983).

25. "Casinos Deal Indians a Winning Hand," *Washington Post* (March 5, 1996), A8; "Towns Weigh Pequots' Proposal," *The Day* (July 31, 1993), A1; Getlin, "Against All Odds," E1:2; Ken Ringle, "The Casino on Sacred Ground," *Washington Post* (February 15, 1992), C1:2; Paul Lieberman, "Lady Luck Turns on Indians," *Los Angeles Times* (October 6, 1991), A1:1.

26. *United States* v. *Santa Fe Pacific Railroad Co.,* 314 U.S., 347, 355–56.

27. *Shoshone Tribe* v. *United States,* 11 Ind. Cl. Comm. 408–9; Treaty of Ruby Valley dated October 1, 1863, 18 Stat. 689 (1869).

28. *Shoshone Tribe of Indians* v. *United States,* 11 Ind. Cl. Comm. 387, 390, 408–12 (1962).

29. *United States* v. *Dann,* 572 F.2d 222, 224 (9th Cir. 1978); Richard Clemmer and Omer Stewart, "Treaties, Reservations and Claims," in Warren D'Azevedo (ed.), *Great Basin* (Vol. 11 in Smithsonian Institution's *Handbook of North American Indians* series) (Washington, D.C.: Smithsonian Institute, 1986), 535–36.

30. Clemmer and Stewart, "Treaties, Reservations and Claims," 547–49.

31. Clemmer and Stewart, ibid., 547–49, 554–55; Transcript of Oral Argument on November 14, 1974, in Docket No. 326-K, 3.

32. Caroline Orlando, "Aboriginal Title Claims in the Indian Claims Commission: *United States* v. *Dann* and its Due Process Implications," *Boston College Environmental Affairs Law Review* (1986): 241, 266 and n.224; Transcript of Oral Argument on July 18, 1977, in Docket No. 326-K, 37, 44–47, 64; Transcript of Oral Argument on November 14, 1974, in Docket No. 326-K, 21.

33. *Shoshone Tribe* v. *United States,* 11 Ind. Cl. Comm. 387, 416 (1962); Petitioners' Proposed Findings of Fact and Brief in Docket No. 326 filed February 16, 1961, 145–52; Defendant's Requested Findings of Fact, Defendant's Objections to Petitioners' Proposed Findings of Fact, and Defendant's Brief filed July 28, 1961, 41–42; Transcript of Oral Argument on November 14, 1974, in Docket No. 326-K, 4.

34. *Western Shoshone Identifiable Group* v. *United States,* 652 F.2d 41, 43–45 (Ct. Cl. 1981); *Western Shoshone Legal Defense and Education Ass'n* v. *United States,* 531 F.2d 495, 496–97 (Ct. Cl. 1976).

35. *Western Shoshone Identifiable Group* v. *United States,* 35 Ind. Cl. Comm. 457 (1975); *Western Shoshone Identifiable Group* v. *United States,* 209 Ct. Cl. 43 (1976).

36. *Western Shoshone Identifiable Group* v. *United States,* 652 F.2d 41, 45–46 (Ct. Cl. 1981); *TeMoak Band of Western Shoshone Indians* v. *United States,* 593 F.2d 994, 996 (Ct. Cl. 1979); Transcript of Oral Argument on July 18, 1977, in Docket No. 326-K, 38–41.

37. Jennifer Warren, "U.S.-Indian Land Feud Heats Up," *Los Angeles Times* (September 24, 1991), A3:3.

38. *United States* v. *Dann,* 470 U.S. 39 (1985).

39. R. C. Gordon-McCutchan, *The Taos Indians and the Battle for Blue Lake* (Santa Fe: Red Crane Books, 1991), 4–9.

40. Ibid., 9–39.

41. Ibid., 42–84.

42. P.L. No. 91-550, 84 Stat. 1437 (1970).

43. Act of July 30, 1946, P.L. 79-566, 60 Stat. 715; Indian Claims Commission Act § 11; *Confederated Salish and Kootenai Tribes* v. *United States,* 8 Ind. Cl. Comm. 60 (1959).

44. *Confederated Salish and Kootenai Tribes* v. *United States,* 173 Ct. Cl. 398 (1965).

45. *Confederated Bands of Ute Indians* v. *United States,* Affidavit of Ernest L. Wilkinson executed October 26, 1950, 18; Interview with I. S. Weissbrodt; *Confederated Salish and Kootenai Tribes* v. *United States,* 401 F.2d 785 (Ct. Cl. 1968).

46. Imre Sutton, "Incident or Event? Land Restoration in the Claims Process," in Sutton, *Irredeemable America: The Indians' Estate and Land Claims* (Albuquerque: University of New Mexico Press, 1985), 215; *Yakima Tribe* v. *United States,* 2 Ind. Cl. Comm. 443 (1953).

47. Interview with Paul Niebell, November 7, 1991.

48. *Yakima Tribe* v. *United States,* 16 Ind. Cl. Comm. 553, 560–64 (1966); 18 Ind. Cl. Comm. 426 (1967); 20 Ind. Cl. Comm. 76 (1968); Letter from Executive Assistant Bradley Patterson to Leo Vocu, Executive Director of NCAI, dated November 11, 1971, Nixon Presidential Materials, WHCF Subject Files, Gen IN 101/71-12/31/71 (RMN); Executive Order No. 11670, 37 Fed. Reg. 10431.

49. *Puyallup Tribe* v. *United States,* 17 Ind. Cl. Comm. 16 (1966); *Settlement of Land Claims of Puyallup Tribe of Indians in the State of Washington,* Hearing before the Senate Select Committee on Indian Affairs on S. 402, 101st Cong., 1st Sess. (February 24, 1989), 31–33 (testimony of attorney Harry Sachse).

50. Leslie Brown, "Land Dispute Ends for Puyallups after a 100-Year Battle," *Morning*

News Tribune (Tacoma) (March 25, 1990), § 1, 1:1; *Settlement of Land Claims of Puyallup Tribe of Indians in the State of Washington,* Hearing before the Senate Select Committee on Indian Affairs on S. 402, 101st Cong., 1st Sess. (February 24, 1989), 31–33 (testimony of attorney Harry Sachse); ibid., 50 (testimony of tribal council member Gabriel Landry).

51. Petition filed August 5, 1951; Letter from Executive Director David Bigelow to David Getches of NARF dated December 8, 1970; Letter from Associate Commissioner of Indian Affairs James E. Officer to Arthur Watkins dated August 17, 1964; *Puyallup Tribe v. United States,* 17 Ind. Cl. Comm. 16 (1966).

52. Order Resetting Case for Trial dated January 28, 1970; Opinion of Plaintiff's Motion to Dismiss Petition, March 19, 1979 (Wood, T. J.).

53. Memo from Harry E. Webb, Chief Counsel, to Ms. Oswald dated November 3, 1972; Undated draft, Additional Findings of Fact.

54. *Puyallup Tribe of Indians v. Port of Tacoma,* 525 F. Supp. 65 (W.D. Wash. 1981); *Puyallup Indian Tribe v. Port of Tacoma,* 717 F.2d 1251 (9th Cir. 1983).

55. *Settlement of Land Claims of Puyallup Tribe of Indians in the State of Washington,* Hearing before the Senate Select Committee on Indian Affairs on S. 402, 101st Cong., 1st Sess., (February 24, 1989), 34–35, 62, 65–68 (testimony of attorney Harry Sachse, John McCarthy, Vice-President of the Port Commissioners of the Port of Tacoma, Cory McFarland, and Karl Anderson).

56. Timothy Egan, "Indian Tribe Agrees to Drop Claim to Tacoma Land for $162 Million," *New York Times* (August 29, 1988), I,1:1; Leslie Brown, "Puyallups OK Land Settlement," *Sunday News Tribune* (Tacoma), (August 28, 1988), A1:1; Leslie Brown, "Land Dispute Ends for Puyallups after a 100-Year Battle," *Morning News Tribune* (Tacoma) (March 25, 1990), § 1, 1:1.

57. Felix Cohen, *Handbook of Federal Indian Law,* xi (1941).

TEN: The Death of Fairness and Honor

1. Harvey Rosenthal, *Their Day in Court: A History of the Indian Claims Commission* (New York: Garland, 1990), 183–98.

2. Memorandum for the President from John Macy dated July 18, 1967, WHCF FG 250/A (LBJ); Letter from Commissioner Watkins to President Johnson dated September 9, 1967, WHCF FG 250/A (LBJ); Note from LBJ dated September 21, 1967, concerning letter to Watkins, WHCF FG 250/A (LBJ).

3. Memorandum from John Macy to the President dated July 18, 1967, John Macy office file labeled "John T. Vance" (LBJ); Biographical Sketch of John Thomas Vance, John Macy office file "John T. Vance" (LBJ); Memorandum from John Macy to the President dated August 30, 1967, John Macy office file "John T. Vance" (LBJ); Press Release dated March 19, 1968, John Macy office file "John T. Vance" (LBJ).

4. Memorandum from Marvin [Watson] to the President dated December 1, 1967, WHCF Name File, Box 279 (Jerome Kuykendall) (LBJ); Memorandum from John Macy to the President dated November 22, 1967, John Macy office file, Box 322 (Jerome K. Kuykendall) (LBJ); Memorandum from Charles R. Pogue to Bob Cox dated November 13, 1967, John Macy office file, Box 322 (Jerome K. Kuykendall) (LBJ); Memorandum from John Macy to the President dated November 10, 1967, John Macy office file, Box 322 (Jerome K. Kuykendall) (LBJ); Evaluation of Jerome

J. Kuykendall by Charles R. Pogue dated November 1, 1967, John Macy office file, Box 322 (Jerome K. Kuykendall) (LBJ); Letter from Senator Everett Dirksen to John Macy dated October 26, 1967, John Macy office file, Box 322 (Jerome K. Kuykendall) (LBJ).

5. Memorandum from Mildred Stegall to Cartha D. DeLoach dated May 29, 1967, John Macy office files, Box 660 (Richard W. Yarborough) (LBJ); page 3 of minutes from undated meeting on which item 14 is Richard Yarborough, John Macy office files, Box 660 (Richard W. Yarborough) (LBJ); Memorandum from John Macy to the President dated August 30, 1967, John Macy office files, Box 660 (Richard W. Yarborough) (LBJ); White House Press Release dated December 4, 1967, John Macy office files, Box 660 (Richard W. Yarborough) (LBJ); Interview with Margaret Pierce of November 1, 1993.

6. Memorandum from William Hopkins to [John] Macy dated October 8, 1968, John Macy office files, Box 457 (Pierce, Margaret H.) (LBJ); Memorandum from the President for John Macy dated October 3, 1968, John Macy office files, Box 457 (Pierce, Margaret H.) (LBJ); Memorandum from the President for John Macy dated September 30, 1968, John Macy office files, Box 457 (Pierce, Margaret H.) (LBJ); Letter to the President from Margaret Pierce dated October 16, 1967, John Macy office files, Box 457 (Pierce, Margaret H.) (LBJ); Elizabeth Shelton, "She'll Delve into History to Settle Indian Claims," *Washington Post* (October 29, 1968); Interview with Margaret Pierce, November 1, 1993.

7. Press Release dated November 14, 1968, WHCF, FG 250 (LBJ); Undated memorandum from Jon Rose to Mr. Robert Ellsworth, Assistant to the President, Nixon Presidential Materials, WHCF Subject Files, Indian Claims Commission (oversize materials) (RMN).

8. Hearing Before the Senate Committee on Interior and Insular Affairs on the Nomination of Brantley Blue, 91st Cong., 1st Sess. (April 24, 1969); Statement by Richard M. Nixon dated September 27, 1968, Nixon Presidential Materials, WHCF Subject Files, FG 142 Indian Claims Commission (oversize materials) (RMN); Interview with Margaret Pierce of November 1, 1993.

9. Edward Spicer, *Cycles of Conquest: The Impact of Spain, Mexico, and the United States on the Indians of the Southwest, 1533–1960* (Tucson: University of Arizona Press, 1962), 13, 118–34, 146–48; *Gila River Pima-Maricopa Indian Community v. United States,* 24 Ind. Cl. Comm. 301, 316–30 (1970); *Gila River Pima-Maricopa Indian Community v. United States,* 684 F.2d 852, 854–56 (Ct. Cl. 1982).

10. *Gila River Pima-Maricopa Indian Community v. United States,* 684 F.2d 856–60 (Ct. Cl. 1982).

11. Ibid., 860 n.7; Spicer, *Cycles of Conquest,* 149–50, 408–9, 437–39; Anna Shaw, *A Pima Past* (Tucson: University of Arizona Press, 1974), 5–8.

12. *I Martindale-Hubbell Law Directory* A224P (1996).

13. Government's Motion for Summary Judgment filed August 12, 1968; Petitioner's Memorandum Opposing Defendant's Motion to Dismiss filed October 16, 1968; Transcript of Oral Argument of October 18, 1968, 19.

14. *Gila River Pima-Maricopa Indian Community v. United States,* 20 Ind. Cl. Comm. 131 (1968).

15. *Gila River Pima-Maricopa Indian Community v. United States,* 427 F.2d 1194, 1197 (Ct. Cl. 1970).

16. Ibid., 1197–1200.

17. Ibid., 1200–1201.

18. Ibid., 1201.

19. Ibid., 1196–97.

20. *Nez Perce Tribe* v. *United States,* 18 Ind. Cl. Comm. 1, 87–118 (1967).

21. *Confederated Tribes of the Colville Reservation* v. *United States,* 25 Ind. Cl. Comm. 128, 132 (1971); *Nez Perce Tribe of Indians* v. *United States,* 8 Ind. Cl. Comm. 220, 221–29, 232 (1959); *Nez Perce Tribe of Indians* v. *United States,* 3 Ind. Cl. Comm. 571, 572–78 (1955); Charles Royce, *Indian Land Cessions in the United States* (Washington, D.C.: Government Printing Office, 1900), 806, 826, and plates 16, 51, 60.

22. *Confederated Tribes of the Colville Reservation* v. *United States,* 25 Ind. Cl. Comm. 130–40; Robert A. Scott, *Chief Joseph and the Nez Perces* (New York: Facts on File, 1993), 37.

23. Scott, *Chief Joseph,* 60–71.

24. Ibid., 72–95; Dee Brown, *Bury My Heart at Wounded Knee: An Indian History of the American West* (New York: Holt, Rinehart & Winston, 1970), 322–29.

25. Scott, *Chief Joseph,* 96–120; *Confederated Tribes of the Colville Reservation* v. *United States,* Plaintiffs' Proposed Findings of Fact on Issues of Liability filed March 30, 1970, 44–49.

26. Agreement and Assignment of Interest in Attorney Contract executed by Grady Lewis and I. S. Weissbrodt dated February 27, 1950 (WF).

27. *Confederated Tribes of the Colville Reservation* v. *United States,* Transcript of hearing conducted January 28, 1970, and filed February 2, 1970, 28, Plaintiffs' Proposed Findings of Fact on Issues of Liability filed March 30, 1970, and Defendant's Requested Findings of Fact, Objections to Petitioners' Proposed Findings of Fact, and Brief on Question of Liability filed June 1970, 13, 19–20.

28. *Confederated Tribes of the Colville Reservation* v. *United States,* 25 Ind. Cl. Comm. 99, 104–8 (Yarborough), 116–17 (Blue), 124 (Kuykendall) (1971).

29. Ibid., 126.

30. Letter from I. S. Weissbrodt to Benedict Jozhe and Wendell Chino dated May 8, 1970, 2–3 (WF).

31. Motion to Dismiss filed May 17, 1971.

32. Treaty concluded July 1, 1852, by representatives of the United States and the Apache Nation of Indians, ratified March 23, 1853, 10 Stat. 979; Plaintiffs' Points and Authorities in Opposition to Defendant's Motion to Dismiss filed July 23, 1971, 6–7.

33. *Fort Sill Apache Tribe* v. *United States,* 26 Ind. Cl. Comm. 281, 290–91 (Pierce and Kuykendall), 294–95 (Yarborough, concurring), 298–99 (Blue and Vance, dissenting) (1971); Interview with Margaret Pierce of November 1, 1993.

34. Brief for Appellants in Appeals Docket No. 2-72, 43–46.

35. *Fort Sill Apache Tribe* v. *United States,* 477 F.2d 1360, 1361 (Bennett, J., w/ Cowen, C. J., and Skelton, J.), 1377 (Nichols, J., w/ Durfee and Kunzig, JJ., dissenting) (Ct. Cl. 1973).

36. Ibid., 1368–77.

37. Ibid., 1365 (Bennett, J.), 1368 (Davis, J.).

38. Petition for a Writ of Certiorari to the United States Court of Claims, Docket No. 73-1220, filed February 8, 1974, 12–13.

39. Brief of Amicus Curiae Native American Rights Fund in Docket No. 73-1220;

Brief of Association on American Indian Affairs, Inc., as Amicus Curiae in Support of Petitioner in Docket No. 73-1220; 416 U.S. 993 (1974).

40. *Aleut Community* v. *United States,* 42 Ind. Cl. Comm. 1, 45–52 (1978).

41. *Aleut Community* v. *United States,* 42 Ind. Cl. Comm. 61–104; United States Department of the Interior, Fish and Wildlife Service, Wildlife Leaflet 323: "Old Man of the Pribilofs" (July 1949).

42. Ibid., 40, 53, 58–61; Dorothy Jones, *A Century of Servitude: Pribilof Aleuts Under United States Rule* (Lanham, MD.: University Press of America, 1980), 39.

43. *Aleut Community* v. *United States,* 42 Ind. Cl. Comm. 150.

44. *Aleut Community* v. *United States,* 27 Ind. Cl. Comm. 177, 184 (1972).

45. *Aleut Community* v. *United States,* 480 F.2d 831, 838–42 (Ct. Cl. 1973).

46. *Aleut Tribe* v. *United States,* 42 Ind. Cl. Comm., 39–41.

47. Memorandum Report for Judgment filed June 21, 1979; Transcript of Videotape Presentation to the Communities of St. Paul and St. George Islands (taped on February 8, 1979), 4, accompanying Stipulation filed June 18, 1979.

ELEVEN: Accounting for Reservation Management

1. United States Department of the Interior, *General Data Concerning Indian Reservations* (October 15, 1929).

2. See generally Edward Lazarus, *Black Hills, White Justice: The Sioux Nation Versus the United States 1775 to the Present* (New York: HarperCollins, 1991).

3. *Sioux Tribe of Indians* v. *United States,* 64 F. Supp. 312, 105 Ct. Cl. 725, cert. denied, 329 U.S. 684 (1946).

4. 105 Ct. Cl. 780–97.

5. Ibid., 800–802, 812–15.

6. *Menominee Tribe of Indians* v. *United States,* 95 Ct. Cl. 232, 234–36 (1941); Patricia Ourada, *The Menominee Indians: A History* (Norman: University of Oklahoma Press, 1979), xi, 4–10, 71, 79.

7. *Menominee Tribe* v. *United States,* 101 Ct. Cl. 22 (1944).

8. Ibid., 40–41; *Menominee Tribe* v. *United States,* 118 Ct. Cl. 290, 327 (1951).

9. *Menominee Tribe* v. *United States,* 91 F. Supp. 917, 920, 931, 932 (Ct. Cl. 1950); *Menominee Tribe* v. *United States,* 121 Ct. Cl. 492, 493 (1952).

10. Act of March 3, 1883, 22 Stat. 582, 590; Act of March 2, 1887, 24 Stat. 449, 463.

11. *Te-Moak Bands of Western Shoshone Indians* v. *United States,* 31 Ind. Cl. Comm. 427, 428–29 (1973).

12. Act of September 11, 1841, 5 Stat. 465.

13. *Te-Moak Bands of Western Shoshone Indians* v. *United States,* 31 Ind. Cl. Comm. 430–77.

14. Ibid., 539 (majority), 554–55 (Yarborough and Kuykendall); *United States* v. *Mescalero Apache Tribe,* 518 F.2d 1309, 1341 (Ct. Cl. 1975) (Davis, J., dissenting).

15. *Blackfeet and Gros Ventre Tribes* v. *United States,* 18 Ind. Cl. Comm. 241, 242 (1967); William Farr, *The Reservation Blackfeet, 1882–1945: A Photographic History of Cultural Survival* (Seattle: University of Washington Press, 1984), 4–5; Bob Scriver, *No More Buffalo* (Kansas City, MO.: Lowell Press, 1982), 3–22; John Ewers, "Ethnological Report on the Blackfeet and Gros Ventre Tribes of Indians" for Docket No. 279-A.

16. Farr, *Reservation Blackfeet,* 5–6; Edward Barry, "Historical Report of the Fort Bel-

knap Reservation in Montana: 1878–1946," prepared for Docket Nos. 250-A and 279-C; *Blackfeet Nation* v. *United States,* 81 Ct. Cl. 101, 105–8 (1935).

17. Farr, *Reservation Blackfeet,* 7–8; Scriver, *No More Buffalo,* 22.

18. *Blackfeet and Gros Ventre Tribes* v. *United States,* 2 Ind. Cl. Comm. 302, 317 (1952); Plaintiffs' Requested Findings of Fact and Brief in Docket Nos. 279-C and 250-A, filed October 20, 1976, Finding F-86, 116; H. Rep. No. 2505, 82d Cong., 2d Sess. (1952), 1188–98.

19. Motion for Attorneys' Fees in Docket Nos. 279-C and 250-A, filed January 13, 1981, 15. For comparison see, e.g., *Mescalero Apache Tribe* v. *United States,* 23 Ind. Cl. Comm. 181 (1970); *Te-Moak Bands of Western Shoshone Indians* v. *United States,* 23 Ind. Cl. Comm. 70 (1970); *Fort Peck Indians* v. *United States,* 28 Ind. Cl. Comm. 171 (1972).

20. *Blackfeet and Gros Ventre Tribes* v. *United States,* 32 Ind. Cl. Comm. 65, 142 (1973).

21. Ibid., 77–78.

22. *United States* v. *Mescalero Apache Tribe,* 518 F.2d 1309 (Ct. Cl. 1975).

23. Ibid., 1324 (emphasis in original); Marion Bennett, *The United States Court of Claims, A History: Part I, the Judges 1855–1976* (Washington, D.C.: Committee on the Bicentennial, 1976), 198–99.

24. *United States* v. *Mescalero Apache Tribe,* 518 F.2d 1324–26.

25. Ibid., 1340.

26. *Gila River Pima-Maricopa Tribe* v. *United States,* 218 Ct. Cl. 74, 85–86 (1978); *Pueblo of San Ildefonso* v. *United States,* 39 Ind. Cl. Comm. 34, 36 (1976).

27. *Gila River Pima-Maricopa Indian Community* v. *United States,* 25 Ind. Cl. Comm. 250, 250–53 (1971).

28. Ibid., 262, 272, 274–75.

29. Ibid., 256–57; *Gila River Pima-Maricopa Indian Community* v. *United States,* 467 F.2d 1351, 1357 (Ct. Cl. 1972).

30. *White Mountain Apache Tribe* v. *United States,* 10 Cl. Ct. 115, 117–18 (1986).

31. Plaintiffs' Requested Findings of Fact and Brief in Docket Nos. 279-C and 250-A, filed November 2, 1976, Finding I-11, 16.

32. Plaintiffs' Findings and Brief, Finding F-67, 94.

33. Ibid., Findings F-120, F-123, 159, 165.

34. Barry, "Historical Report of the Fort Belknap Reservation," 71, 84–86 (quoting Letter from Charles McNichols to the Commissioner of Indian Affairs, dated July 7, 1902, and Affidavit of M. L. Bridgeman in *United States* v. *Bridgeman*); Plaintiffs' Requested Finding of Fact F-97.

35. Plaintiffs' Findings and Brief, Finding F-113, 149–51; Defendant's Objections and Brief, Finding F-110, 618.

36. Barry, "Historical Report of the Fort Belknap Reservation," 62, 80 (quoting Report of W. J. McConnell to the Secretary of the Interior dated August 9, 1897), 82.

37. Ibid., 92–94, 105.

38. Ibid., 120–22 (quoting Annual Report for 1915, 13, and Report of Inspector C. R. Trowbridge to the Secretary of the Interior, dated October 4, 1920), 130, 145; Plaintiffs' Finding of Fact F-150.

39. Defendant's Objections to Plaintiffs' Proposed Findings and Brief, filed August 18, 1977, Finding F-87, 565.

40. Plaintiffs' Findings and Brief, Finding F-87, F-134, 117, 177; Barry, "Historical Report of the Fort Belknap Reservation," 184.

41. Defendant's Objections and Brief, Finding F-101, 586; ibid., 868.

42. Michael F. Foley, "An Historical Analysis of the Administration of the Fort Belknap Indian Reservation by the United States 1855–1950s," 42, 55, 58, 68, 71.

43. Ibid., 383–84, 404, 408–9, 412.

44. Transcript of Hearing in *Fort Belknap Indian Community* v. *United States,* Docket No. 250, 203.

45. *Fort Belknap Indian Community* v. *United States,* Docket No. 250-A, Reference to Trial Judge (November 7, 1978).

46. Motion for Attorneys' Fees, 23; Interview with Abe Weissbrodt; *Blackfeet and Gros Ventre Tribes* v. *United States,* 226 Ct. Cl. 724 (1981); *Blackfeet Tribe of Indians* v. *United States,* 228 Ct. Cl. 924 (1981).

47. *Mescalero Apache Tribe* v. *United States,* 226 Ct. Cl. 724 (1981).

48. Foley, "Historical Analysis," 405.

49. Ibid., 439–40.

TWELVE: Distribution of the Awards

1. Reports of the Proceedings of the Judicial Conference of the United States for 1993, Table G-2a; Indian Claims Commission, Final Report, 125. The total awards in Indian Claims Commission cases in which the Court of Claims issued final judgments between 1978 and 1982 were about $313 million. Over two-thirds of the transferred cases were resolved during those years. It is thus reasonable to estimate that the total awards since 1978 fall between $400 and $500 million.

2. *The World Almanac and Book of Facts 1990* (New York: World Almanac, 1989), 431; Restitution for World War II Internment of Japanese-Americans and Aleuts, 50 U.S.C. § 1989b.

3. Examples include P.L. 85-395, 72 Stat. 105 (1958) (Otoe and Missouria), P.L. 86-97, 73 Stat. 221 (1959) (Quapaw), and P.L. 86-246, 73 Stat. 477 (1959) (Siletz).

4. H. Rep. No. 1004 (1961).

5. For examples of acts providing for 100 percent per capita distributions, see P.L. 87-775, 76 Stat. 776 (1962) (Cherokees) and P.L. 88-464, 78 Stat. 563 (1964) (Snake or Paiute Indians). The acts of P.L. 88-412, 78 Stat. 387 (1964) (Lower Pend D'Oreille or Kalispel Indians) and P.L. 88-457, 78 Stat. 555 (1964) are examples of acts authorizing the distribution of funds in accordance with tribal plans approved by the government. An act providing greater specificity concerning the distribution of money was P.L. 90-117, 81 Stat. 337 (1967) (Cheyenne-Arapaho Tribes) ($500,000 for education and scholarships for tribal members).

6. Hearing Before the Senate Subcommittee on Indian Affairs on the Indian Judgment Funds Distribution Act of 1973 (April 13, 1973), 1; H. Rep. No. 93-377, 93d Cong., 1st Sess. (1973); Indian Claims Commission, Final Report 125.

7. 25 U.S.C. §§ 1402, 1405.

8. 25 U.S.C. §§ 1401 et. seq.; *Immigration and Naturalization Service* v. *Chadha,* 462 U.S. 919 (1983).

9. 25 U.S.C. § 1403.

10. 25 U.S.C. § 1403(b)(5); distribution plans after 1983.

11. H. Rep. No. 93-377, 93d Cong., 1st Sess. (1973); Hearing, Senate Subcommittee, Indian Judgment Funds Distribution Act, 20.

12. D. Fixico, *Termination and Relocation: Federal Indian Policy, 1945–1960* (Albuquerque:

University of New Mexico Press, 1986), 41; Nancy Lurie, "Epilogue," In Imre Sutton (ed.) *Irredeemable America: The Indians' Estate and Land Claims* (Albuquerque: University of New Mexico Press, 1985), 364–65.

13. Russel Barsh and James Henderson, *The Road: Indian Tribes and Political Liberty* (Berkeley: University of California Press, 1980), 95 n.40; Lurie, "Epilogue," 367.

14. E. Cahn (ed.), *Our Brother's Keeper: The Indian in White America* (Washington, D.C.: New Community Press, 1969), 112–23.

15. 25 U.S.C. § 2710; Dennis McAuliffe, Jr., "Casinos Deal Indians a Winning Hand," *Washington Post* (March 5, 1996), A8.

16. Ibid.

17. *Mescalero Apache Tribe* v. *United States,* 18 Ind. Cl. Comm. 378 (1967) ($8,500,000); *Lipan Apache Tribe* v. *United States,* 37 Ind. Cl. Comm. 239 (1976) ($10,000,000); *Mescalero Apache Tribe* v. *United States,* 226 Ct. Cl. 724 (1981) ($2,000,000); *Fort Sill Apache Tribe* v. *United States,* 26 Ind. Cl. Comm. 198 (1971) (70 percent of $16,500,000, or $11,500,000); *Fort Sill Apache Tribe* v. *United States,* Ct. Cl. 182 (April 6, 1979) (70 percent of $6,000,000, or $4,200,000); T. Lippman, "Tribe Considers Nuclear Dump," *Washington Post* (October 21, 1991), A17:4.

18. R. Abramson, "New Mexico Apaches Have a Hot Idea: Providing Nuclear Waste Storage," *Los Angeles Times* (May 28, 1994), A22:1; G. Johnson, "Nuclear Waste Dump Gets Tribe's Approval in Re-vote," *New York Times* (March 11, 1995), A6:5.

19. United States Bureau of the Census, *1990 Census of Population, Social and Economic Characteristics, American Indians and Alaska Natives,* Table 5, 88; Johnson, "Nuclear Waste Dump Gets Tribe's Approval"; Lippman, "Tribe Considers Nuclear Dump."

INDEX

MICHAEL LIEDER has been a lawyer since graduating from Georgetown University Law Center in 1984. He now works in Washington, D.C., and has taught at the University of Toledo College of Law and published several articles in legal journals, including *Analyses of American Indian Law.*

JAKE PAGE, a former editor of *Smithsonian* magazine, is a science writer and novelist whose fictional work includes *The Stolen Gods,* a Southwestern mystery concerning the theft of Indian religious artifacts. Called by *The Denver Post* "one of the Southwest's most distinguished authors," he has written numerous magazine articles on Indian affairs. With his wife, photographer Susanne Page, he wrote *Hopi* and *Navajo,* and is producing a forthcoming volume of American Indian mythology.

ABOUT THE TYPE

This book was set in Bembo, a typeface based on an old-style Roman face that was used for Cardinal Bembo's tract *De Aetna* in 1495. Bembo was cut by Francisco Griffo in the early sixteenth century. The Lanston Monotype Machine Company of Philadelphia brought the well-proportioned letter forms of Bembo to the United States in the 1930s.

DATE DUE

GAYLORD			PRINTED IN U.S.A.